YOUTH JUSTICE IN AMERICA

MARYAM AHRANJANI

American University
Washington College of Law

ANDREW G. FERGUSON

Attorney, Washington, D.C.

JAMIN B. RASKIN

American University
Washington College of Law

CQ PRESS

A DIVISION OF CONGRESSIONAL QUARTERLY INC.
WASHINGTON, D.C.

CQ Press
1255 22nd Street, NW, Suite 400
Washington, DC 20037

Phone, 202-729-1900; toll-free, 1-866-427-7737 (1-866-4CQ-PRESS)

Web: www.cqpress.com

Text credits can be found on page 345.

Cover design: Auburn Associates, Inc.

♾ The paper used in this publication exceeds the requirements of the American National Standard for Information Sciences—Permanence of Paper for Printed Library Materials, ANSI Z39.48-1992.

Printed and bound in the United States of America

09   08   07   06   05   1   2   3   4   5

Library of Congress Cataloging-in-Publication Data

Ahranjani, Maryam.
    Youth justice in America / Maryam Ahranjani, Andrew G. Ferguson, Jamin B. Raskin.
        p.   cm.
    Summary: "Explores important issues related to juvenile justice and presents key cases, accompanied by expert commentary, involving the Fourth, Fifth, Sixth, and Eighth Amendments. Examines the constitutional rights and responsibilities of youths in America. Includes glossary, suggestions for further reading, and class exercises"—Provided by publisher.
Includes bibliographical references and index.
    ISBN 1-56802-986-1 (hardback : alk. paper) — ISBN 1-56802-987-X (pbk. : alk. paper)
    1. Juvenile justice, Administration of—United States—Popular works. 2. Juvenile courts—United States—Popular works. 3. Juvenile delinquents—Legal status, laws, etc.—United States—Popular works. I. Ferguson, Andrew G. II. Raskin, Jamin B. III. Title.

    KF9780.A37 2005
    345.73′08—dc22   2005006450

Contents

Foreword

At some point in your life, you probably will be stopped by the police. Are you prepared? After you read this book, you will be. Think of it as an instruction manual for the real world.

Most people have no idea what their rights are. Your locker gets searched, or a cop pats you down. Maybe you are angry, you feel like your privacy was invaded, but you don't know what to do. What if you get locked up? Should you talk to the police? You heard on TV that you have a right to a lawyer, but is that really true? At this point you are probably clueless, and that is a dangerous thing. If you don't know your rights, it is more likely that your rights will be abused. Knowledge is power.

I needed a book like this when I was a teenager. As a kid, I didn't trust the police much, and some of them seemed to feel the same way around me. When I was thirteen I rode my bike to a mainly white neighborhood. I stuck out maybe, a black kid riding his bike anywhere he pleased through the segregated neighborhoods of Chicago. That, however, was the last thing on my mind. It was a beautiful day. I felt free in a way that you feel only when you are thirteen and it is spring and you are on a bike. I felt like the whole world was mine. Until a police car pulled up next to me and the window rolled down and a cop asked, "Is that your bike?"

Now what was I supposed to say? Of course it was my bike. Why was he asking? I was angry but my mother had taught me to always be polite to police officers. I mumbled something and sped off. I did not like feeling accused and scared when I had not done anything wrong.

Fast forward to the future. I am grown now and live in a neighborhood with a lot of crime. Once I came back to my house, and something didn't feel right. A window was open that I didn't remember opening. No way was I going in that house alone. Who did I call? The police, of course.

When they came, "they" turned out to be one guy. I explained the situation to him, and he said he would go in and look around. He went inside, looked around, and said everything looked fine. I said "What about the closets?" We went back inside, and he looked in every closet. Nothing was amiss, so the officer left to respond to another call. I was totally freaked out, but it was just another day on the job for him.

It reminded me of a public service commercial from years ago. It showed the classic dark and stormy night, and you saw this haunted-looking house. There was a roll of thunder and something made the door of the house creak open. Then you heard the announcer say, "You wouldn't go in that house for a million dollars. A cop does it for a lot less than that." It's true. I don't always like cops, but sometimes I need them.

The people who wrote the Bill of Rights had some of the same conflicting feelings that I have about police power. They wanted to be safe. They wanted to be free. So they made some strong rules. This book is about those rules.

The rules, as you will see, are kind of radical. The Constitution is very suspicious of authority. It gives citizens all kinds of freedom, and it greatly limits the power of government. Maybe you will agree with the way the Supreme Court has interpreted these principles, maybe you will not agree. In any case, I hope that you finish this book with a new respect for the awesome privileges that you have as a person who lives in the United States of America.

You have important responsibilities also. It's up to you to make sure that the country lives up to its highest ideals. You have to agitate when you feel as if it's not doing so. The Beastie Boys have a song in which they say, "You gotta fight for your right to party." Really, though, you have to fight to keep all of your rights.

Even today, in one of the greatest, most free nations there ever was, there are too many people who are locked up. There are still some police officers who don't follow the rules. If you see the police do something that you think is wrong, you should be respectful and polite, for your own safety. But pay close attention and, at the appropriate time, you should report your concerns. Vigilance is one of the obligations of being a good citizen. Another responsibility, obviously, is to obey the law. My hope is that you will learn about the juvenile justice system from this book, and not from personal experience!

Each year, thousands of young people find themselves accused of crime. The Constitution belongs to them, as much as it belongs to anyone else. As you read this book, think about ways to make our justice system more fair. Our society is far from perfect, but young people have the imagination and the power to make it better. Read this important book, and then decide what your role shall be.

Paul Butler
Professor of Law
George Washington University

Paul Butler is professor of criminal law, civil rights, and jurisprudence at the George Washington University Law School. A graduate of Harvard Law School, Butler formerly served as a federal prosecutor with the U.S. Department of Justice, where his specialty was public corruption.

Preface

The authors of this book have been involved in an educational experiment since 1999. We work with dozens of law students who teach a course every year in "constitutional literacy" to hundreds of high school students in Washington, D.C., and Maryland. This experiment, the Marshall-Brennan Constitutional Literacy Project, has been launched in high schools and law schools across America, from Camden, New Jersey, to Tempe, Arizona. Thousands of young people, including the residents of one juvenile correctional facility in Maryland, are reading and using the Constitution as a tool for understanding and changing their lives and communities.

The text that we currently use, *We the Students*, analyzes a collection of cases involving issues that affect students at school: censorship of school newspapers, prayer in schools, segregation, affirmative action, sexual harassment, and so on. Many high school students, however, have pressed us to go further. They want to learn more about the criminal justice process—the police, prosecutors and defense lawyers, judges, the process of investigation, and a young person's rights and responsibilities in the system.

Many students are curious about the intrinsically fascinating aspects of the criminal justice process. However, many teenagers are drawn to the subject because they have been participants in the process—through direct and repeated encounters with police, prosecutors, and judges. Others are interested because they have friends and family who are participants—willing or unwilling—in the process.

In *Youth Justice in America* we resume our conversation about the Constitution, focusing on crime and punishment in America. *Youth Justice* provides a broad overview of constitutional rights in the criminal justice process as well as detailed studies of particular cases, most of them involving young Americans who have gotten into serious trouble. The book portrays a part of America that we do not always want to see but certainly cannot afford to ignore.

Teachers and law students who use our text, *We the Students*, in classrooms across the country have shared with us effective and road-tested tools for teaching students about juvenile justice and provoking them to think critically about the subject. We are convinced that students learn and understand law by reading actual cases, not watered-down paraphrases; in *Youth Justice* we present carefully edited cases related to searches and seizures, right to counsel, privilege against self-incrimination, execution of juveniles, and more. The case law is enhanced with stunning photographs, teaching hypotheticals, and recurring features, including "Your Thoughts," "Points to Ponder," and "Additional Sources." "Your Thoughts" poses hard questions to elicit students' opinions on topics raised in subsequent sections. "Points to Ponder" offers follow-up reflections on tricky issues. "Additional Sources" directs students to further reading on the subject. The text is accompanied by helpful appendix features, including a class exercise, the U.S. Constitution, a glossary of legal terms, and a bibliography.

We hope that everything you learn in these pages will help you to "increase the peace," strengthen democracy, and advance justice in your communities.

Acknowledgments

Maryam Ahranjani

Without keen insights and support from my friends and colleagues Sheila Bedi, Stephanie Joseph, professors Angela Davis and Victor Streib, Mark Soler, and Michelle Carhart, my participation in this book would not have been possible. Trisha Hubacher, Jazzy Wright, Martin Ryan, Christine Murphy, and Brian Middlebrook provided invaluable research assistance. Young law students Martin Ryan, Ed Hertwig, Rebecca Freedman, Rebecca Goldfrank, Bill Kamens, Cindy Hamra, Jacob Rahavi, Danielle Metzer, Kaleb Kasperson, Claire Rajan, Theresa Barbadoro, Kelly Barrett, Dan McNamee, and Mike Glover served as pioneers, bravely agreeing to teach the material without a textbook. On a personal note, thank you to my parents, who moved to this country with dreams of equality and equity; my two dear sisters; and my brilliant and patient husband. Thank you also to my coauthors, who inspire and motivate me in countless ways.

Andrew G. Ferguson

Thanks to James Forman Jr., David Rudovsky, Sandra Simpkins, John Copacino, Abbe Smith, Zack Rosenburg, Giovanna Shay, my parents, and, of course, my wife, Alissa, for your inspiration, support, and belief in this project.

Jamin B. Raskin

Thanks to my wonderful coauthors, the indispensable Angela Davis, Cynthia Jones, Dean Claudio Grossman, Mary Beth Tinker, Paul Butler, Christine Murphy, and Qiana Parker. My wife, Sarah, and my children, Hannah, Tommy, and Tabitha, give me hope and joy every day. All power to the Marshall-Brennan Fellows and to the young people who learn from them.

The three authors express gratitude and indebtedness to their committed CQ Press editors—Joan Gossett, Doug Goldenberg-Hart, and David Arthur—who thoroughly believed in the project and did everything possible to ensure its success!

About the Authors

Maryam Ahranjani is a lawyer, teacher, and lecturer and is the associate director of the Program on Law and Government at American University Washington College of Law. As a coordinator of the Marshall-Brennan Constitutional Literacy Project, she has taught the "We the Students" constitutional literacy course in Washington, D.C., public schools for the past five years.

Andrew G. Ferguson is a practicing public defender in Washington, D.C., representing juvenile, adult, and appellate clients. Before working as a public defender, he was awarded an E. Barrett Prettyman Fellowship at the Georgetown Criminal Justice Clinic and clerked for a federal judge on the United States Court of Appeals for the Fifth Circuit.

Jamin B. Raskin is a professor of constitutional law and the First Amendment at American University Washington College of Law and founder of the Marshall-Brennan Fellows program, in which law students teach constitutional literacy courses in public high schools across America. A former state assistant attorney general, Raskin is an active public interest lawyer who defends the rights of political expression and participation for youths and adults. He is the author of *We the Students: Supreme Court Cases for and about Students,* 2nd edition (CQ Press, 2003) and *Overruling Democracy* (2003), a *Washington Post* best seller. Raskin and his wife, Sarah, have three children, Hannah, Tommy, and Tabitha.

AMERICAN SOCIETY, CRIME, AND THE CONSTITUTION

1

"In America the law is king."   THOMAS PAINE, *COMMON SENSE*

If you want to see where the get-tough juvenile offender policies adopted during the late twentieth century are taking the country in the twenty-first, you could do worse than spend some time in the Sunshine State. Florida has a lot of poverty, a lot of crime, and a lot of punishment. It also has one of the nation's highest youth incarceration rates.

Florida took the lead in prosecuting minors as adults by giving prosecutors—instead of judges—the crucial power to make the decision to charge juveniles as adults. After a youth crime wave in the early 1990s, Florida passed the Juvenile Justice Reform Act of 1994, which gave state prosecutors the power to try children defendants as adult criminals if they already have committed other crimes. In 1995, according to the *Palm Beach Post,* seven thousand juveniles in Florida were brought up on criminal charges as adults. In the other forty-nine states combined, only twenty-seven hundred children were tried as adults. Florida quickly became the nation's top jurisdiction for prosecuting children as adults and sending them to adult prisons. No other state even comes close.

Most of the children in Florida's criminal justice system are African American and Hispanic. Although racial and ethnic minorities make up one-fourth of the state's population between the ages of ten and seventeen, they are three-fourths of the people in that age group incarcerated in the state's prisons. This means that a teen or preteen in Florida who is African American or Hispanic is three times more likely to be behind bars than a white youngster in the same age group.

These young people get little or no education behind bars. They also do not obtain the right to vote when they turn eighteen in prison. Even when they are released from prison many years later, they are disenfranchised for life under Florida state law—that is, unless they receive a special pardon from the governor granting them the right to vote. As of 2005, more than 400,000 people in Florida have done their time but remain disenfranchised.

It costs about $43,000 a year to keep a juvenile prisoner behind bars.

Following are profiles of some young incarcerated Floridians based on coverage of their cases in the *Palm Beach Post* between 2000 and 2002.

Name: Jessica Robinson
Date of birth: August 1, 1983
Hometown: Miami
Prison: Dade Correctional
Institution
Offense: Robbery, burglary,
kidnapping
Sentence: Nine years
Release date: June 9, 2006

Jessica Robinson

Source: Jean Hart Howard

On August 1, 2004, Jessica Robinson turned twenty-one at the Dade Correctional Institution in Florida. Locked up since age thirteen, Jessica has become something of a prison celebrity in Florida. An alternately bubbly and depressed blonde who participated in the robbery of her own grandmother, Jessica was, for a long while, the youngest girl incarcerated in Florida's adult prisons. The subject of long profiles in the *Palm Beach Post* and the *New York Times Magazine,* Jessica has spent her entire adolescence behind bars, building a complete family system out of her fellow female inmates.

Although Jessica differs in gender and race from most other juvenile prisoners, her life story is typical of the broken family lives that most of her peers in prison have experienced and have had so much time to dwell upon.

When Jessica was three years old, her mother brought her and her older sister to Miami, fleeing from Jessica's violent, cocaine-using father. In Florida, Jessica's mother worked as a waitress at night and frequently took her anger out on Jessica and her other daughter. The household was violent and abusive. Education was never a priority, and Jessica did poorly in school. At thirteen, she threw a plate that broke her sister's nose, and things spiraled downward from there: detention center, relationship with a drug dealer who was much older, more domestic violence.

Jessica was sent to live with her grandparents, with whom she also had a stormy relationship. According to Paolo Annino, a clinical law professor at Florida State University who has prepared Jessica's clemency petitions to the governor, Jessica's grandmother had always favored Jessica over her obese and emotionally ruined sister. She would frequently promise Jessica that she was going to leave her all of her money and jewelry, but then she would abruptly revoke the promise. Although she once doted on Jessica, her grandmother soon lost patience for the rebellious adolescent who knew no boundaries and no emotional stability. After Jessica caused another fight, her grandmother called the police and she was taken back to the detention center. There, fatefully, Jessica met up with Barbara Abad, a juvenile with a real criminal record.

When Jessica got out, she and Barbara and a sixteen-year-old boy returned to Jessica's grandparents' house. The kids rang the doorbell and, when Jessica's grandfather came to the door, they forced an entry. Jessica and Barbara searched the house for money and jewelry while the boy used a knife to slash furniture—and Jessica's grandfather's hand. Jessica's grandmother was terrified, though unhurt.

Jessica was fourteen when the crime occurred. She had no weapon and did not participate in the violence, but the public was horrified by a girl who could rob her own grandparents. The state prosecutors charged her as an adult. She pleaded guilty to robbery, burglary, and kidnapping. When Dade County circuit judge Barbara Levenson asked Jessica to apologize to her grandparents, she stood there and did nothing. "Animals don't treat their families the way you treated your family," Judge Levenson said to Jessica at her sentencing.

Judge Levenson sentenced Jessica to nine years in prison as an adult. The boy who brought and used a knife was given an eight-year sentence.

Two weeks after being sent to the Jefferson Correctional Institution in Monticello, Jessica attempted suicide. The prison then took her clothes and placed her in solitary confinement for two days. Since that time, her mental health has been on a roller coaster ride, but the *Palm Beach Post* has reported that she has now taken on a complete prison family made up of fellow women prisoners, including not only a girlfriend who she calls "Wohdie," but also a twenty-five-year-old second-degree murderer who she calls "Dad," a "grandfather," a "mother," and a host of "sisters."

Jessica's real mother—who now lives in Kansas with her new husband, who is in the army—visited Jessica only once during her first five years of incarceration. Still, in the harsh and brutish confines of prison, Jessica seems to have found the protective family structure that she never had at home. Although Jessica is not now in school and has not learned a trade, Marshall Fenster, a clinical psychologist who examined Jessica for her clemency petition, says that she "has excellent potential to become a productive member of society." Although her requests for clemency have been rejected thus far, her clemency was brought before the governor in November 2004, and the board is still considering her case. Annino and his students continue to work on her case.

Michael Clarkson   *Source: Jean Hart Howard*

Name: Michael Clarkson
Date of birth: April 1, 1983
Hometown: St. Petersburg
Prison: Sumter Correctional
Institution
Offense: First-degree murder,
robbery
Sentence: Thirty-five years
Release date: January 7, 2032

Michael's mother, Lorraine, said that Michael went to a special school and was a slow learner. Constantly teased as a boy for being stupid, Michael was diagnosed as mildly retarded. He followed an older person, a mental patient, to an International House of Pancakes restaurant in St. Petersburg where they rounded up all the diners and robbed them at gunpoint. One of the patrons died during the robbery, making Michael guilty of felony murder.

Name: Tobias Thomas
Date of birth: January 31, 1985
Hometown: Fort Pierce
Prison: Indian River Correctional Institute
Offense: Home invasion, assault and battery of a person over sixty-five
Sentence: Six years
Release date: March 3, 2004

Tobias Thomas   *Source: Jean Hart Howard*

Before going to jail, Tobias dreamed of becoming a fireman and always loved doing math. His mother, Glenda, who is the ninth of ten children from a poor family in Alabama, was a housecleaner before she was hit by a car in front of her house. Glenda was anxious about Tobias not learning anything while he was in prison and so went to lobby the school board to provide him classes there, which they did. Glenda visited her son every Saturday for six hours and bought him food out of the prison's vending machines.

Name: James Conley
Date of birth: January 23, 1983
Hometown: Perry
Prison: Brevard Correctional Institution
Offense: Second-degree murder
Sentence: Fourteen years
Release date: January 20, 2009

James was a slight twelve-year-old, weighing eighty-five pounds, who loved sports. But he was enough of a troublemaker to be in a dropout prevention program. One day he was shooting baskets in his backyard when two older and bigger boys (each over 165 pounds) dropped by and took him to visit a homeless veteran

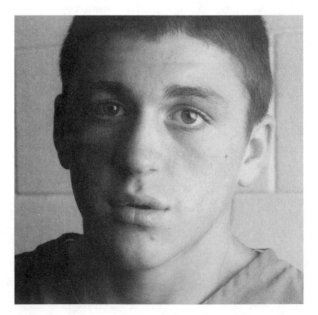

James Conley   *Source: Jean Hart Howard*

who lived behind a grocery store in their town. A disagreement ensued, and the man grabbed James by the neck. The three boys proceeded to beat up the homeless man and kick him while on the ground. He died three days later. Although James was the smallest of the three assailants and wore tennis shoes at the time, he was convicted of second-degree murder. He had been in jail for eighteen months before he was convicted and sentenced to prison for fourteen years as an adult.

The Constitution and Crime

Who wants to waste his life in the criminal justice system? No one does. On the list of things to look forward to in life—for example, falling in love, reading great books, seeing funny movies, getting your first job, collecting your first paycheck, making friends, going to college, getting married, having a family—who would add getting arrested, standing trial, or going to jail? No one would.

If four- or five-year-olds are asked what they want to be when they grow up, they might say "president," "football player," "firefighter," "ballet dancer," "police officer," "writer," "movie star," "rapper," "pilot," or another occupation, but rarely will they respond "criminal," "defendant," "prisoner," or "burglar." People commit crimes for a number of reasons—for example, bad judgment, greed, immaturity, desperation, poverty, cruelty, boredom, depression, alcohol and drug abuse, peer pressure, the influence of television and popular culture, and mental illness. Few would say that committing crimes represents their highest aspirations or dreams. Yet many people drift toward crime or come close enough to it to make serious trouble for themselves. Every year millions in the United States are arrested, prosecuted, convicted, incarcerated, or serve time on probation or parole. In 2003 there were 6.9 million Americans in the criminal justice system. And hundreds of thousands of them were young people.

The drafters of the Constitution accepted that crime would be a persistent problem and tried to work around this reality. They were optimistic about Americans' ability to govern themselves, but they were realistic about the flaws and vices of human nature. A society that believes crime can be stamped out would not give criminal defendants the legal protections provided in the Constitution: due process, right to a fair trial by an **impartial** jury, right to counsel, right against **double jeopardy**, right ordinarily not to have one's home or privacy invaded by the government without a search warrant based upon **probable cause**, right against **self-incrimination**, and right against cruel and unusual punishment. In **authoritarian** societies, such protections do not always exist. In some countries, punishment can be swift and harsh from an American perspective. For example, someone in Saudi Arabia found guilty of shoplifting would have his hand amputated. While such a punishment could be an effective **deterrent** against further crime, it contradicts the basic belief in the United States that even criminals should be treated fairly and decently and their punishments meted out proportionate to their crimes.

The U.S. constitutional system was created to address the problem of not only street criminals but also people in government who abuse their power. The founders understood, as historian Lord John Acton would declare, that "power corrupts, and absolute power corrupts absolutely." They felt it just as important to prevent government officials from violating the basic boundaries of civilization and destroying respect for the people

The Bill of Rights consists of the first ten amendments to the U.S. Constitution, which were ratified on December 15, 1791.

Amendment I

Congress shall make no law respecting an establishment of religion, or prohibiting the free exercise thereof; or abridging the freedom of speech, or of the press; or the right of the people peaceably to assemble, and to petition the government for a redress of grievances.

Amendment II

A well regulated militia, being necessary to the security of a free state, the right of the people to keep and bear arms, shall not be infringed.

Amendment III

No soldier shall, in time of peace be quartered in any house, without the consent of the owner, nor in time of war, but in a manner to be prescribed by law.

Amendment IV

The right of the people to be secure in their persons, houses, papers, and effects, against unreasonable searches and seizures, shall not be violated, and no warrants shall issue, but upon probable cause, supported by oath or affirmation, and particularly describing the place to be searched, and the persons or things to be seized.

Amendment V

No person shall be held to answer for a capital, or otherwise infamous crime, unless on a presentment or indictment of a grand jury, except in cases arising in the land or naval forces, or in the militia, when in actual service in time of war or public danger; nor shall any person be subject for the same offense to be twice put in jeopardy of life or limb; nor shall be compelled in any criminal case to be a witness against himself, nor be deprived of life, liberty, or property, without due process of law; nor shall private property be taken for public use, without just compensation.

Amendment VI

In all criminal prosecutions, the accused shall enjoy the right to a speedy and public trial, by an impartial jury of the state and district wherein the crime shall have been committed, which district shall have been previously ascertained by law, and to be informed of the nature and cause of the accusation; to be confronted with the witnesses against him; to have compulsory process for obtaining witnesses in his favor, and to have the assistance of counsel for his defense.

Amendment VII

In suits at common law, where the value in controversy shall exceed twenty dollars, the right of trial by jury shall be preserved, and no fact tried by a jury, shall be otherwise reexamined in any court of the United States, than according to the rules of the common law.

Amendment VIII

Excessive bail shall not be required, nor excessive fines imposed, nor cruel and unusual punishments inflicted.

Amendment IX

The enumeration in the Constitution, of certain rights, shall not be construed to deny or disparage others retained by the people.

Amendment X

The powers not delegated to the United States by the Constitution, nor prohibited by it to the states, are reserved to the states respectively, or to the people.

as to deter individual citizens from committing crimes. A majority of the rights contained in the Bill of Rights protect the rights of the people against police, prosecutors, and lack of fairness in the trial process.

"We the People" and the War on Drugs: Politicians and Their Families, Athletes, Entertainers

In the ongoing war on drugs, Americans have been arrested and incarcerated under tough laws, for example, those embodied in the federal sentencing guidelines and requiring mandatory minimum sentences. Millions across the country are living behind bars for dealing drugs or possessing them. At the same time, politicians at the highest levels of government have admitted using illegal drugs in the past, including former president Bill Clinton and former Speaker of the House of Representatives Newt Gingrich, both of whom confessed to having experimented with marijuana. (Clinton famously stated that he smoked marijuana but did not inhale it.) President George W. Bush, an admitted former problem drinker, is widely rumored to have used drugs before addressing his substance abuse problems. In 2005, a tape surfaced in which Bush said he would not discuss his past marijuana use during the 2000 campaign because he didn't want to send the wrong message to kids. Marion Barry was serving as the mayor of Washington, D.C., when police caught him on tape smoking crack cocaine. After a criminal conviction and jail time in a federal prison on charges stemming from this incident, Barry returned to politics and subsequently won reelection as mayor. In November 2004, he won a seat on Washington's city council.

Every profession and social group has been affected by drug abuse. Everyone is vulnerable: professional football, baseball, tennis, and basketball players; Hollywood actors, rock stars, and musicians; doctors, lawyers, and businesspeople; police officers, teachers, military personnel, and many others. Numerous famous personalities have run into trouble with the legal system. For example, at the age of fourteen, Jennifer Capriati was a tennis star and the youngest player ever to reach the semifinals of the French Open and win a match at Wimbledon. She was in 1990 to tennis what Freddy Adu is today to soccer. The media noted her every mistake and success, including her gold medal at the 1992 Barcelona Olympics. A year later, reeling from the stress of the professional tennis tour, Capriati decided to leave the tour and focus on her studies. Her entire career seemed in jeopardy at the age of seventeen, when police arrested her for shoplifting and illegal drug possession. Capriati eventually rebounded from the events of her troubled youth and after rejoining the tour in 1996 again became one of the top tennis players in the world.

Actress Drew Barrymore is another celebrity who got involved with drugs after early success. At the age of seven, she became a Hollywood star with her role in *E.T.*, one of the biggest blockbusters of all time. A daughter of two movie actors with struggling careers, Barrymore began attending nightclubs with her mother and took up drinking at the age of nine. At ten, she started smoking marijuana; at twelve, she was using cocaine. It soon became an open secret that Barrymore had a drug and alcohol problem, which ruined her opportunities to work for major movie companies. Barrymore ultimately got herself together and reemerged as a major actress during her twenties, formed a production company, and began producing her own movies.

Actor and singer Mark Wahlberg grew up in a rough neighborhood in South Boston, Massachusetts. His brother, Donnie, became a star as a part of the musical group New Kids on the Block. While Mark was one of its original members, he dropped out as the boy band rose in popularity. After returning to school, Mark began committing minor crimes such as shoplifting. At sixteen he got arrested and spent forty-five days in jail for beating up two men from whom he had stolen beer. Mark subsequently got help from Donny and formed the band Marky Mark and the Funky Bunch, known best for a remake of "Good Vibrations." Since then, Mark was a model for Calvin Klein and more recently acted in major films, winning acclaim for his roles in, for example, *Boogie Nights* and *Three Kings*.

Before he became the rapper Snoop Dogg, Calvin Broadus was better known for his basketball skills. Because of legal troubles, however, Broadus was unable to pursue a basketball career. After graduating from high school, he served time for possession of cocaine and spent the next several years in and out of prison. He would become one of the most famous (and notorious) rappers in the early 1990s, after his friend Warren G. introduced his music to Dr. Dre, who helped promote him. Broadus's legal problems followed him into his adulthood, as he faced trial in 1995 and 1996 for a 1993 murder charge. He subsequently was **acquitted**, but rumors persisted of more recent wrongdoings, particularly drug possession. Despite his acquittal, many blame Snoop Dogg for promoting gangster rap, which, they say, glorifies violence. Broadus has publicly stated that he no longer uses drugs or alcohol to be more of a role model to his children.

Presidential family members have also had drug- and alcohol-related missteps with the law. Twice, at the age of seventeen, President George W. Bush's daughter Jenna faced **misdemeanor** citations for underage drinking in Texas. Her cousin Noelle, daughter of Florida governor Jeb Bush, was convicted of

Executive producer Mark Wahlberg and director Leslie Neale attend the March 2004 screening of their documentary, *Juvies,* a riveting study of juveniles serving long sentences. Wahlberg, also an actor, former model, and rapper, served jail time as a juvenile offender. The photograph behind Wahlberg and Neale is of Duc Ta, a participant in the Juvies project serving time as an adult for gang-related attempted murder. For more information on *Juvies,* visit www.juvies.net. *Sources: Hugh Williams; photo of Duc Ta by Ara Oshagan.*

Snoop Dogg, a former juvenile offender, went on to become a successful rap artist. Here he gestures from his courtside seat before the start of Game 4 of the 2002 NBA finals in East Rutherford, New Jersey. *Source: Mike Blake/Reuters/Landov*

drug possession (crack cocaine) and was sentenced to ten days in county jail for criminal **contempt** of court. A sitting U.S. representative from South Dakota, William J. Janklow, spent one hundred days in jail upon being convicted of speeding, running a stop sign, reckless driving, and committing second-degree **manslaughter** after he struck a motorcyclist in 2003.

In the worlds of rock and roll, heavy metal, hip-hop, and rhythm and blues (R&B) music, the criminal drug abuse problem and other legal problems are pervasive. For example, R&B and soul artist R. Kelly was arrested for child pornography, rap and hip-hop musician Jay-Z and R&B and soul artist Keke Wyatt were involved in stabbings, rap and hip-hop musician Sean "Puffy" Combs was charged with illegal gun possession, and rap and hip-hop artist 50 Cent was once a drug dealer before succeeding in the music industry. From Janis Joplin to Sid Vicious to the Rolling Stones to Guns N' Roses, the stories of criminal drug abuse are legion, and the number of careers ruined and lives wasted is extraordinary. However, this criminal behavior and drug abuse, while affecting all sorts of people, need not define them or prevent them from rehabilitating themselves.

Criminal Justice: Not the End of the Story

Besides Russia, the United States has the highest rate of criminal incarceration of all countries on Earth. In fact, most industrial democracies imprison their citizens at a rate one-sixth to one-tenth of America.[1] The millions of people, hailing from different backgrounds, who become involved in the criminal justice system represent a sweeping national problem. But those who have experienced criminal arrest, prosecution, and jail time can still turn their lives around if they struggle hard enough to develop their talents and gifts.

The *Autobiography of Malcolm X* tells the story of an African American man's rise from the depths of despair, ignorance, crime, and racism to become a political activist and one of the great popular leaders of the twentieth century. While serving time on a burglary charge, Malcolm Little was introduced to the Nation of Islam and through its teachings gained a spiritual perspective and a strong political consciousness. Upon release from prison, as Malcolm X, he became the national spokesman for the Nation of Islam, recruiting hundreds of thousands of new members. After breaking with the group, he reevaluated his beliefs and adopted a more inclusive perspective. He remains a towering role model for convicted criminals seeking to reform themselves.

Many people who have been convicted of criminal offenses and are in jail become embittered and hardened by their experience. Surrounded by other criminals, they become committed to an outlaw lifestyle. Some criminologists (people who study crime) say

Malcolm X made an extraordinary journey from gifted student to petty criminal to prison inmate to member of the Nation of Islam to independent political leader. He recorded his journey in the widely read *Autobiography of Malcolm X*. He was assassinated at the age of 39.
Source: Library of Congress

that prisons and juvenile reformatories too often can become places for young people who may be in trouble for lesser offenses, such as theft or drug possession, to learn about how to commit more serious offenses, such as armed robbery or murder.

Some prisoners, however, such as Malcolm X, manage to use their time locked up to develop their intellects, acquire new skills, and analyze what choices, events, and influences brought them to incarceration.

Jean-Jacques Rousseau, an eighteenth-century French philosopher, wrote in his autobiographical work, *Confessions,* about a terrible boss (or master) who humiliated him and caused him to develop various vices he never would have had: "My master's tyranny ended by making unbearable to me work that I would have loved, and by giving me vices that I would have hated, such as lying, laziness, theft. . . . Covetousness [wanting what someone else has] and powerlessness lead to this. That is why all lackeys are knaves. . . . It is almost always good feelings badly directed that make children take the first step toward evil."

Rousseau took responsibility for his stealing, but he stressed that young people develop criminal habits within a social context. Children are not born bad but can develop bad behaviors when they live in situations that exploit, damage, humiliate, and degrade them. If people figure out why they fall into a criminal lifestyle, they can climb out of it. Although never walking down the road of crime in the first place is preferable, a way back to lawfulness can almost always be found.

The American System of Juvenile Justice

The U.S. Supreme Court stated in its *In Re Gault* decision: "Under our Constitution, the condition of being a boy does not justify a kangaroo court. The traditional ideas of Juvenile Court procedure, indeed, contemplated that the time would be available and care would be used to establish precisely what the juvenile did and why he did it." [2]

What Is the Juvenile Justice System?

The juvenile justice system is designed to address crimes allegedly committed by young people under the age of eighteen. A juvenile found guilty of breaking the law is usually called a juvenile **delinquent**. In every state and the District of Columbia, special laws have been designed to address what happens when someone under eighteen breaks the law.

Ever since 1899, when the first juvenile court in America was created, similar questions have been asked about whether juveniles should be treated differently from adults in the criminal process and how juveniles should be held accountable for their criminal actions. Society has treated young people who commit crimes in different ways at different times in U.S. history.

But two general trends have emerged. First, young people who commit crimes are not let off the hook entirely. Juvenile delinquents must be held accountable for their actions. Second, young people usually are treated differently from adults. In terms of the responsibilities of citizenship, children under eighteen are not sufficiently mature to vote, smoke, drink, sign contracts, serve in the military, or marry.[3] Similarly, juvenile delinquents generally face a different kind of criminal justice process. Sometimes it has been harsher than the adult process; more often it is more gentle and humane. For more than a century, it has purported to offer more attention to the personal welfare of the young people involved. Sometimes the accountability takes the form of punishment, sometimes rehabilitation, but generally a mixture of both. Throughout the history of juvenile justice, debate ensued over the best means to sanction, punish, control, and improve the lives of young people who have violated the law.

YOUR THOUGHTS

Why establish a separate juvenile justice system? Why treat people who are under eighteen differently than those over eighteen? Is eighteen an arbitrary cutoff? What, if anything, should be different about punishment focused on people under eighteen years old?

EXERCISE 1.1. Hip-hop artist and actor Mos Def said: "You do not arrive at justice by punishing a child as a man. In the same way you do not arrive at justice by punishing a man as a child. This type of policy in law does nothing to deter youth from crime, rather it criminalizes youth. I can't imagine what type of adults that this hostile, bitter, angry climate hopes to produce. For the sake of our young people in this country and across the world I beg you to help this child. Sending him to reach adulthood in prison is of no benefit to anyone and is a poor testament to our level of commitment and compassion to our youth. If this generation is lost, it is because we have let go of their hands." Do you agree or disagree that children should never be punished as adults?

Why a Separate System for Juveniles?

Why should people of different ages be treated differently for committing the same crimes? Consider the following story about shoplifting involving the Bugs brothers.

The day of the town's big Fourth of July barbeque, everyone cooks outside. The three Bugs brothers, Oliver (age twenty-six), Mickey (age sixteen), and Yogi (age six) go to the grocery store. Oliver explains to Yogi that they are going to play a game of hide-and-seek with food items. Oliver takes several steaks from the meat counter and slips them under his jacket. Yogi, who wants to play, too, hides some hamburger buns under his shirt. Mickey stares at his two brothers and then looks to the meat counter. After waiting for a while, and then being glared at by Oliver, Mickey reluctantly stuffs some chicken inside his jacket. Oliver tries to lead his brothers out of the store, but all are stopped by store security and arrested by the police for shoplifting.

What happens next? Should Oliver, who is twenty-six, and Yogi, who is six, be treated the same way in court? If they are convicted, should they be punished the same way? What about Mickey? Where does he fit in as a sixteen-year-old?

In most states, each brother will face a different kind of justice process. At twenty-six, Oliver will face adult criminal charges in adult criminal court. As a sane and mentally competent adult, he is presumed to be fully aware of what is right and wrong. Like other grown-ups, he is also legally presumed to know what is against the law and can never assert ignorance of the law's requirements as an excuse. Because he is an adult, he will be tried in a court of law with all the protections available in his state's legal system. If convicted, he will be sentenced as an adult and have an adult criminal record.

At six, Yogi will likely avoid any criminal sanction. Unless the crime is severe (such as murder), courts and legislatures have decided that young people under a certain age—historically, seven or below—can never have the legal **intent** required to commit a crime and therefore cannot be tried in the criminal justice system. The reasoning here is that, at such a young age, kids cannot necessarily tell the difference between right and wrong. Yogi may have thought he was playing a game, thus not committing a crime. He may not even know what a crime is or be able to appreciate it. He is not presumed to know what laws, his constitutional rights, or the role of the police, judges, or prosecutors are. Society has determined that some children are just too young to be tried for their criminal actions.

At sixteen, Mickey is in-between. He is presumed to be old enough to know the difference between right and wrong, but he is not considered by society to be a fully mature person with adult judgment. Thus, he will be charged and processed through the juvenile justice system, which will try to balance all the different considerations.

On the one hand, Mickey knew that what he was doing was wrong. On the other hand, he was reluctant to shoplift and was acting under pressure from his older brother. Should he be required to stand trial? Likely he will. Does he have the same rights as adults to a lawyer and to due process protections? Yes, he does. Will he be given a criminal conviction that will affect his chances of going to college, getting into the military, being a politician or lawyer, or becoming a law enforcement officer? Depending on his state of residence and his offense, he will have a criminal record until he reaches age eighteen, but it may be expunged afterward. Should he go to a juvenile detention center or should he be provided services to rehabilitate him so that he does not break the law in the future? Should Mickey be treated less harshly than an adult would be? Why?

YOUR THOUGHTS

Could Mickey fully understand the consequences of his actions? Do you think he weighed the legal sanctions that a criminal conviction could have on his record? Do you think he understands the constitutional protections that are available to him in a court of law? Do you think he would be able to help his lawyer as much as an adult would? Should he have to stand trial the same as an adult?

Are Juveniles Different? American Society's View

Generally, American society has assumed that people younger than eighteen have several traits in common that make them somewhat less responsible than adults. These differences make it necessary to have a separate juvenile justice system. Do you think the following list of traits of juveniles is accurate?[4]

- Juveniles are more likely to act impulsively in committing an offense.
- Juveniles are more likely to act under the pressure of peer influence.
- Juveniles are less likely to understand the legal consequences of their actions.
- Juveniles are less likely to weigh the risks and long-term consequences of their actions.
- Juveniles are less familiar with the legal system.
- Juveniles are less able to consult with their lawyers about the case. This may be because of a lack of understanding legal terms, cultural or age barriers, or general ignorance of the law.
- Juveniles may have an inadequate understanding of the case against them.

- What if a young person is, in fact, familiar with the legal system and understands everything going on? Should he be treated as an adult?
- Do you know young people who withstand peer pressure, who correctly weigh risks and long-term consequences? Do you know adults who incorrectly weigh risks and act for the short term?
- Aren't there many adults who are unfamiliar with the legal system, do not know their rights, are unable to help their lawyers, and make bad decisions? What is the difference between these immature adults and juveniles?
- How would you characterize the differences between adult and juvenile offenders?
- What are the goals of a legal system set up for young people? For example, is the purpose to inculcate societal values of right and wrong? To punish and provide accountability? To protect the community? To rehabilitate? How should the goals be met?

Are Juveniles Different? The Court's View

Consider some of the statements made by U.S. Supreme Court justices about juvenile offenders.

[A]dolescents, particularly in the early and middle teen years, are more vulnerable, more impulsive, and less self-disciplined than adults. Crimes committed by youths may be just as harmful to victims as those committed by older persons, but they deserve less punishment because adolescents may have less capacity to control their conduct and to think in long-range terms as adults.—*Eddings v. Oklahoma*[5]

[T]he reasons why juveniles are not trusted with the privileges and responsibilities of an adult also explain why their irresponsible conduct is not as morally reprehensible as that of an adult.—*Thompson v. Oklahoma*[6]

Our society recognizes that juveniles in general are in the earlier stages of their emotional growth, that their intellectual development is incomplete, that they have had only limited practical experience, and that their value systems have not yet been clearly identified or firmly adopted.—*Schall v. Abrams*, quoting from *Wayburn v. Schupf*[7]

The Child—essentially good, as [the reformer] saw it—was to be made "to feel that he was the object of [the state's] care and solicitude," not that he was under arrest or under trial. . . . The idea of crime and punishment was to be abandoned. The child was to be treated and rehabilitated and the procedures, from apprehension through institutionalization, were to be "clinical" rather than **punitive**.—*In Re Gault*[8]

- Do you agree with the justices' statements?
- Do you think children are necessarily more impressionable? More vulnerable? More impulsive? Less controlled?
- Do you think that the primary purpose of the juvenile justice system should be treatment and rehabilitation—to make the young person a better person and prepare him for adulthood? Or should it be punishment and deterrence of future crime—making the delinquent pay and suffer for his crimes? Write a one-page essay about this and explain your thinking.

A Brief History of Juvenile Justice

The news media reflect and reinforce Americans' fear of juvenile offenders. Newspaper headlines announce teenage school massacres in Columbine, Colorado, and Jonesboro, Arkansas. Television reports cover the murder trials of youthful killers. Magazines discuss the rise of the "superpredator"—a mythical young person who is violent, remorseless, uncontrollable, and fundamentally different from young people in the past. Over the last several decades, politicians, police, and the media have publicized the sensational—and senseless—crimes of disturbed young people. In the current era, "tough on crime" means "tough on juveniles."

This tough-on-crime rhetoric was heard even though juvenile crime declined. Since 1994, when juvenile crime peaked, the crime rate for juveniles has been coming down. More generally, the incidents of violent crime have also declined.[9] To understand the current state of the juvenile justice system, the three stages of its history need to be reviewed.

The Creation of the Juvenile Justice Court and the Ideals of Rehabilitation and Protection. The juvenile justice system was created because of the hopeful belief that all children could be rehabilitated into law-abiding, productive citizens. Before 1899, juveniles and adults were treated largely the same in courts of law. Thus, if a child com-

Judge Julian Mack, one of the first judges on the newly created juvenile court stated: "Why is it not just and proper to treat these juvenile offenders, as we deal with the neglected children, as a wise and merciful father handles his own children whose errors are not discovered by the authorities? Why is it not the duty of the state, instead of asking merely whether a boy or girl has committed a specific offense, to find out what he is physically, mentally, morally, and then if it learns that he is treading the path that leads to criminality, to take him in charge, not so much to punish as to reform, not to degrade but to uplift, not to crush but to develop, not to make him a criminal but a worthy citizen."

—Julian W. Mack, "The Juvenile Court," *Harvard Law Review* 23 (1907): 104, 106

Every state has a separate system of juvenile courts for the prosecution of offenses allegedly committed by minors.
Source: Photography Collections, University of Maryland, Baltimore County

mitted an adult offense, he faced adult punishment. However, starting at the end of the nineteenth century, a movement of progressive child-centered activists began thinking about the need for special, child-centered courts that could save young children who primarily came from impoverished, immigrant backgrounds. The idea was that the government could be the guardian of these children. As guardians, the courts would give them individualized treatment to remove their negative influences and keep them from turning into adult criminals. Courts focused on what was in the best interests of the child instead of concerning themselves solely with issues of criminal guilt or punishment. The underlying principle was that children were different and could be rehabilitated if given a second chance. Because of these beliefs, the juvenile court system was created.

The 1960s and 1970s: Protecting the Constitutional Rights of Juveniles. While the juvenile justice system was created to protect the best interests of the child, it always remained a system of justice. It punished youthful offenders, sometimes severely. Juvenile court judges thus had tremendous power to affect the lives of young people. Because the system was informal (to allow judges to consider the individual needs of children), judges sometimes did not properly focus on the question of whether a child was guilty ("delinquent") of a crime. Sometimes the power of the court overshadowed the child's own interests in personal liberty. Sometimes, in the name of rehabilitating or punishing young people, judges forgot about a young person's rights or simply ran over them.

In the 1960s and 1970s this indifference to the rights of the juvenile began to change, and courts focused on juvenile rights in the system. A series of cases resulted in more legal and constitutional protections for juveniles. Specifically, the Supreme Court found that juveniles have a right to a lawyer, a right to a court hearing, a right to notice of the charges against them, a right to cross-examine witnesses, and a right to be proved guilty based on

In Arizona, Gerald Gault was accused of making prank phone calls. This is not harmless fun; it is a real offense. But, as crimes go, it is minor. Had Gerald been an adult, he would have been fined not more than $50 and incarcerated for not more than two months. However, because he was a juvenile, he was sent to a youth detention facility for a period of six years. The judge sentenced him to confinement without ever appointing a lawyer for him and without conducting a formal hearing.

The U.S. Supreme Court decided that Gerald's constitutional rights had been violated because the legal process used was fundamentally unfair and reversed the whole rationale for having a juvenile system. Justice Abe Fortas explained that juveniles should certainly not have fewer rights than adults.

[W]e confront the reality of that portion of the Juvenile Court process with which we deal in this case. A boy is charged with misconduct. The boy is committed to an institution where he may be restrained of liberty for years.

In view of this, it would be extraordinary if our Constitution did not require the procedural regularity and the exercise of care implied in the phrase 'due process.' Under our Constitution, the condition of being a boy does not justify a kangaroo court.

. . . If Gerald had been over 18, he would not have been subject to Juvenile Court proceedings. For the particular offense immediately involved, the maximum punishment would have been a fine of $5 to $50, or imprisonment in jail for not more than two months. Instead, he was committed to custody for a maximum of six years. If he had been over 18 and had committed an offense to which such a sentence might apply, he would have been entitled to substantial rights under the Constitution of the United States as well as under Arizona's laws and constitution.

an adult standard of proof. In essence, just as in adult court, certain rules had to be followed to protect the liberty and due process rights of young people. The most important decision in this movement was the Supreme Court's ruling in the case of Gerald Gault in 1967.

"Get Tough" Reform Movement. More recently, the shift has been to be tougher on juvenile offenders. Legislators have passed laws eliminating juvenile court **jurisdiction** for some types of serious crimes, meaning that young people can be tried in adult court. In addition, legislators have weakened some of the confidentiality rules that have historically protected young people in later life from their mistakes.[10] At the same time, legislators have increased the length and harshness of sentences available to juvenile judges to impose. Prosecutors have begun charging juveniles as adults on a more frequent basis. Calls have been made to equalize the sentences for adults and juveniles charged with the same offense. The age when a juvenile can be considered an adult has been lowered in some states. In addition, the age when a juvenile can be transferred ("waived") to adult court has been lowered in most states. In general, the move has been away from rehabilitation and the idea that "juveniles are different" toward increased punishment and confinement and a blurring of the adult and juvenile systems.[11]

- In which of the periods of juvenile criminal justice would it have been better to be a juvenile offender: when juveniles were treated like adults, when they were treated more informally and gently but without the rights grown-ups have, when they had the same rights as adults but judges were concerned with their rehabilitation, or today when many jurisdictions are moving to treat young people like adults again? Which of the periods of reform would you prefer if you lived in a neighborhood filled with juvenile offenders? Under which system would you want to raise children?
- Federal and state legislators have sought to increase the punishment available to juveniles on the theory that some children have done such terrible crimes that they forfeit the rehabilitative emphasis of the juvenile court. For example, Utah senator Orrin G. Hatch, Republican member of the Senate Judiciary Committee, has stated: "When a juvenile commits an act as heinous as the worst adult crime, he or she is not a kid anymore." [12] What do you think of Hatch's statement?
- Compare Senator Hatch's comment to the following statement by a clinical professor and criminal defense lawyer:

> Kids who commit crime are kids. The mere fact that an eleven-year-old—or even a seventeen-year-old commits a crime does not suddenly transform the child into an adult. It doesn't matter what the crime is. There are too many circumstances under which teenagers and children end up committing crimes—even violent crimes to allow the event of lawbreaking to trigger adulthood for purposes of criminal punishment.—Abbe Smith[13]

What Happens in Juvenile Court?

Each state has different rules in place to control what happens to juveniles accused of a crime, but the process is similar everywhere. To see what happens, review the Bugs brothers incident and look at the situation Mickey found himself in after stealing food with his brothers for the barbeque.

Arrest. The police arrest the Bugs brothers on suspicion of shoplifting. For Mickey, this means going down to the police station and being processed by the police. Assuming this is Mickey's first time in trouble, the police will want to know his name, address, school, parents' names, and whether or not he has been in trouble with the law before. They will probably take his picture and his fingerprints. All this information will be recorded, and the police will decide what to do next.

Referral to Juvenile Court. The arresting police officer initially gets to decide what happens to Mickey.[14] In essence, the police officer has three options. He could decide not to go forward with the charges against Mickey. Usually this is done if the evidence is weak or the offense trivial. Second, he could informally resolve the matter. This might mean calling up Mickey's mother and having her come down for a conference and then take him home to be punished. Third, he could begin the process of a **formal intervention**, which means that the officer would begin prosecuting Mickey in juvenile court for the crime of shoplifting. To begin the formal process, a petition (a written document) is filed to charge Mickey as delinquent.

Prosecution in Juvenile Court. If a petition is filed, a criminal case begins against Mickey. The government will attempt to prove that Mickey shoplifted the chicken from the store. A trial will take place. Mickey will have a lawyer appointed to defend him (assuming the family does not hire one). The government prosecutor will put on evidence against Mickey. A judge will hear the evidence and decide whether or not the government has made its case and proven Mickey guilty. In later chapters, we will discuss the details of what happens in a criminal trial. For purposes here, you should simply know that there is not much difference between a juvenile trial and an adult trial except for the potential sentence (**disposition**) and the fact that juveniles do not have jury trials unless they are tried as adults.

Disposition. If a juvenile charged with a crime is found guilty, he is adjudicated "delinquent." Now the juvenile court has the power to punish or rehabilitate the child as the judge sees fit. In terms of punishment, juveniles can be required to do community service, be put on probation (meaning that they have to check in with a probation officer at regular intervals), or be placed in a group home, residential setting, or secure detention center similar to a jail. In terms of rehabilitation, the court can order services covering educational, mental health, medical, drug and alcohol rehabilitation, and social needs. Job training, schooling, and drug or alcohol counseling are often required through probation. Many times a combination of punishment and treatment is ordered. The stated goal of the juvenile justice system is to provide care and rehabilitation to the youthful offender.

Arrest ──────▶ Referral to Juvenile Court ──────▶ Prosecution in Juvenile Court ──────▶ Disposition

Copping a Plea

Ninety-five percent of all **felony** convictions in the United States result from plea agreements. What if you just want to admit that you did it? You were caught red-handed breaking the law. While you have rights and you know the government has the burden to prove your guilt beyond a reasonable doubt, you just want to fess up. You want to admit you were wrong, you messed up, you screwed up, you just done wrong. You can enter a guilty plea or, in slang, you can "cop a plea."

A guilty plea is an agreement to admit your guilt thus doing away with the need for a trial. In legal terms you **waive** your right to a trial and all of the protections that come with trial. A plea bargain is a deal between you and the prosecutor, usually to arrange for a lighter sentence in return for an admission of guilt.

Why would you want to enter into a guilty plea and give up your right to trial? The answer is that sometimes it makes sense to get your legal problems behind you. Sometimes you can arrange a deal to get a lesser charge or better sentence. Sometimes the government's evidence is overwhelming. Or sometimes you just want to take responsibility and acknowledge you did something wrong.

Why would the government want you to plea? Plea bargains save time and money for overworked prosecutors. Trials are long and expensive undertakings, and too many cases come through the system. Thus, many times prosecutors offer pleas to clear up their caseloads, or to make the system move along. Pleas are efficient, quick, and easy.

Consider the case of Jimmy Lowdown. Jimmy Lowdown is a seventeen-year-old first-time offender caught possessing a dime bag of marijuana. When Jimmy saw the police coming for him, he ran away. When Jimmy was caught, a scuffle ensued, and he kicked the police officer trying to handcuff him. He is charged with misdemeanor possession of marijuana and felony assault on a police officer. The government offers to drop the more serious felony charge if Jimmy pleas guilty to drug possession.

In deciding whether to take the plea, Jimmy has to think through its consequences. What are the factors he should consider?

- Charge. The government is offering to drop the serious charge if he pleads guilty to the other charge. That reduces the number of charges from two to one.
- Sentence. With a lesser charge and one fewer charge, he is facing less punishment. He can bargain with less risk of punishment. For example, the prosecutor could say that if Jimmy goes to trial and is found guilty of the felony, he faces a term of incarceration. However, if he pleads guilty, he would be offered probation. This choice would be even starker if mandatory enhanced penalties are attached to the charge or you live in a three-strikes state. As you can see, sentencing considerations can determine whether you get sent to jail or go home.
- Legal case. What if Jimmy had a good case against the drug possession charge? What if he was innocent of drug possession, and he would not plead guilty to something he did not do. Jimmy must evaluate the strength of his case and the weaknesses of the government's case. Going to trial and beating all the charges is better than pleading guilty to any of them. Innocent people sometime lose at trial, however. The risk of going to trial thus means that you are penalized for invoking your legal rights. Does this seem fair?
- Facts before the judge. In addition to the strength of Jimmy's case, he needs to think about what facts the judge will hear. Does he want the judge to know that he kicked a police officer who was just doing his job? Wouldn't he rather just have the judge think he had been in possession of drugs and not add the fact of violence to the case? In a plea agreement, Jimmy can also negotiate the facts that will be read to the judge who imposes the sentence. For example, if Jimmy pleads guilty to drug possession and not assault on a police officer, the judge will not hear the facts underlying the kicking incident. This might affect his sentence.
- Judge. Knowing the judge sometimes matters. Some judges, especially juvenile judges, want offenders to admit their guilt, take responsibility, and understand what they did was wrong. Judges consider this part of the growing-up process. In addition, judges are human beings; some are known to give light sentences and some to give harsh sentences.

If you were Jimmy's attorney, what would you advise Jimmy to do? Keep in mind, however, that no matter your advice, Jimmy and only Jimmy must decide whether or not to take a plea.

Waiving the Right to Trial. To waive your right to trial and take a guilty plea, a judge must make sure that your waiver is knowing and voluntary. Why? Because you are giving up serious and important constitutional rights such as the right to trial, **appeal**, and the ability to make the government meet its burden of proof.

Before you plead guilty, a judge must review those rights with you. This is called a plea colloquy and is simply a conversation between you and the judge. The judge will determine whether you know that

- you could face the maximum sentence provided by law.
- the judge decides the ultimate sentence and is not bound by the plea agreement with the government (unless you have entered into a binding plea).
- you are giving up the right to trial by judge or jury.
- this means giving up the right to have the government prove its case to the highest standard known to law.
- you are giving up the right to confront and cross-examine your accusers.
- you have the right to counsel.
- you are giving up your right to appeal.
- the conviction could result in immigration consequences if you are not a U.S. citizen.
- you are giving up these rights knowingly and willingly, and no one has pressured you to take the plea.
- you are pleading guilty freely and voluntarily.
- you are factually guilty of the crime charged.
- you are sure that you want to waive your right to trial.

Then the judge will ask: "How do you wish to plead, guilty or not guilty?" If you say guilty, the judge will accept your plea and your right to trial will be gone. All that is left is sentencing.

Problems with Pleas. What if the plea agreement goes forward, and you do not know your rights? What if you are without a lawyer, and no one explains what should happen? Consider the following case.

D.L., A CHILD, APPELLANT,
V.
STATE OF FLORIDA, APPELLEE

District Court of Appeal of Florida,
Fifth District
No. 97-3455.
Sept. 11, 1998.
Rehearing Denied Oct. 19, 1998.

ORFINGER, M., Senior Judge.

D.L. appeals from an **adjudication** of **delinquency** and from an order denying his **motion** [a written legal argument] to withdraw his guilty plea, which, motion asserted, among other grounds, that the plea was uncounseled. We reverse.

At **arraignment**, the court addressed all those assembled, and as part of the colloquy, advised that:

There are two forms of plea that are acceptable here. There's a plea of guilty and a plea of not guilty. If you enter a plea of guilty, that tells me that you admit the charge that the State has filed against you, and that you wish to resolve the matter here this morning. If you enter a plea of not guilty, that tells me you deny the charge and that you wish to have a trial on the matter.

You have the right to have a lawyer represent you in defending you against this charge. And if you cannot afford a lawyer, you have the right to request that the Court consider the appointment of a Public Defender. If you are thinking of pleading not guilty here this morning and requesting the appointment of a Public Defender, you, your parent or guardian should have received from the court deputy before I came out, a financial **affidavit**. You should have filled it out, and when your case is called, hand that financial affidavit to me, I'll review it, and determine whether or not you qualify for the appointment of a Public Defender.

If you are thinking about pleading guilty here this morning, you need to be aware that in entering the plea of guilty, you are telling me certain things, and I will outline for you what it is that you will be telling me if you enter the plea of guilty. If you enter the plea of guilty, you will be telling me that you understand the charge. You'll be telling me that you admit the charge. You'll be telling me that you wish to give up your right to have a trial. That you wish to give up your right to have a lawyer represent you here today. That you wish to give up your right to appeal the facts of this case unless you've specifically reserved your right to appeal a pretrial matter. That you are entering this plea freely and voluntarily. That no one has forced you, coerced you, or made you any promises in order to get you to enter this plea. That you are entering the plea in order to resolve this matter here this morning.

When appellant's case was called, he entered pleas of guilty to two counts and not guilty to a third. He also acknowledged that he had violated an earlier community control order by committing the offenses to which he had pled guilty. Thereupon, the following colloquy took place:

THE CLERK: . . . In the Interest of D . . . L . . .
THE COURT: Good morning.

THE CHILD: Good morning.

THE COURT: Tell me your name.

THE CHILD: D . . . L . . .

THE COURT: All right. D . . . you're here for arraignment in two cases. . . . In this case, State has filed a Petition for Delinquency against you. They allege that you've committed the following offenses in three counts; first count, aggravated assault with a deadly weapon, third-degree felony. How do you wish to plead to that charge, guilty or not guilty?

THE CHILD: Guilty.

THE COURT: Second count, **battery**, domestic violence, a first-degree misdemeanor. How do you wish to plead to that charge, guilty or not guilty?

THE CHILD: Not guilty.

THE COURT: Okay. Did you hear the arraignment speech I gave when I first came out?

THE CHILD: Yes, sir.

THE COURT: Did you hear and do you understand the constitutional rights you're giving up or waiving by entering this plea?

THE CHILD: Yes, sir.

THE COURT: And do you also understand you're at some disadvantage this morning because you're without a lawyer? That if you wanted a lawyer, I would consider appointing one for you.

THE CHILD: Yes, sir.

THE COURT: Do you wish to give up that right?

THE CHILD: Yes, sir.

THE COURT: Okay. Are you entering this plea freely and voluntarily?

THE CHILD: Yes, sir.

THE COURT: Has anybody forced you, coerced you, made you any promises in order to get you to enter this plea?

THE CHILD: No, sir.

THE COURT: Are you presently under the influence of any drugs or alcohol?

THE CHILD: No, sir.

THE COURT: Do you have any mental or emotional disabilities?

THE CHILD: No, sir.

THE COURT: The Court finds you're alert and intelligent. You've entered this plea freely and voluntarily. There is a factual basis for the Court's acceptance of your plea found in the sworn affidavit of the law enforcement officer . . . and in Petition for Revocation of Community Control. . . . The Court does accept your pleas of guilty to Counts I and III, and your admission of the violation of community control in 96-9744.

. . . Florida Rules of Juvenile Procedure states that a child shall not be deemed to have waived assistance of counsel until the ". . . entire process of offering counsel has been completed and a thorough inquiry into the child's comprehension of that offer and capacity to make that choice intelligently and understandingly has been made. . . ."

There was a letter in the file from the child's mother to the trial judge complaining that she had not been notified of the arraignment and was thus not present. At the hearing on the motion to withdraw the plea, there was **testimony** from the mother and medical testimony that the child was suffering from mental health and emotional disorders and had been on medication for these problems. A case worker from the Department of Juvenile Justice, who was familiar with appellant, and who interviewed appellant after the arraignment (but who himself was not present at arraignment), testified that he was aware of the child's disabilities, that the child attended a special school, Devereux, a "behavioral school," was on medication for his emotional problems, and that he, the case worker, did not believe that the child could understand the nature of his plea. The child's mother also testified that from her discussions with her son she was certain that he did not understand the nature of his plea.

It is clear from the transcript of the hearing on the motion to withdraw the plea that there should have been at least some doubt as to this 14 year old's clear understanding of the nature of the charges against him and of his ability to intelligently and understandingly waive his right to counsel. The motion to withdraw his plea should have been granted.

REVERSED AND REMANDED.

POINTS TO PONDER

- Do you agree with the appellate court's decision? Why did it reverse the case? What would a lawyer have done differently? What would you have wanted the judge to do differently? Didn't he cover most of the plea colloquy?
- Why do you think so many people take pleas? In a country known for trials by jury, isn't the 95 percent figure high?
- What do you think of the trade-offs in the plea process? Is it fair for an innocent person to risk additional jail time, just because he wants to invoke his constitutional rights? Why should the prosecutor have this power?
- Do you think that any plea can really be voluntary, knowing this pressure?
- What should a defense lawyer do in a situation in which his client is innocent but is given a great plea deal? When should someone plead guilty to a crime he did not do, just to avoid serious punishment?

Juvenile Detention

The juvenile justice system is no joke. Many delinquents are detained in secure detention facilities with severe restrictions on liberty of movement and expression similar to an adult jail. They are guarded by corrections officers in a highly disciplined environment, with few pleasures or freedoms. Many juvenile facilities are underfunded, poorly staffed, and dangerous. The American Bar Association (ABA) has studied juvenile detention facilities and reported on their deficiencies. In a report called *America's Children at Risk,* the ABA stated that "75 percent of confined juveniles live in facilities that violate at least one critical physical design standard (e.g. capacity, sleeping areas, size of living unit)" and that "one-third of all confined juveniles sleep in windowless rooms." [15] According to Congress, in some states, juvenile detention centers have become warehouses for mentally ill youth, including many who have not committed any crimes.[16] The youths are sent to the detention centers because they are unable to get mental health services in their communities. In addition, juvenile detention facilities can be dangerous places where physical and even sexual assaults are a constant peril.[17]

The following are two views of juvenile detention from the inside.

By Peter M., 17, Central Juvenile Hall, California

I open my eyes from a restless night's sleep and stare at the nightlight on the ceiling of my dirt-saturated room. I try not to touch the yellow stains running alongside my bed, because I have no clue as to where they came from. I nestle up to get in a couple of extra zzz's but to no avail. Soon I hear the jingle of keys, and the door unlocks while the detention services officer yells at me to get dressed and wash up. This has been my morning routine for the past 18 months.

Being a 17-year-old facing prison time is not easy—especially when I'm looking at 12 years. I'm locked up in Central Juvenile Hall on charges of a home invasion robbery with possession of a firearm. I face a maximum sentence of 30 years in state prison. I'll take a deal for the minimum amount of time I can serve for my crime—12 years with one strike. If I run a good program, hopefully I'll be out by 2010.

I got arrested a month after I turned 16 and it was a big joke to me. When they read my charges and how much time I was facing, I laughed in the courtroom and thought it was the dumbest thing I'd ever heard. Now it's not so dumb. It's reality. I still haven't come to truly grasp it, but my mind is starting to perceive it. It's just hard to believe that a first-time offender, especially a juvenile, can receive such a harsh punishment. But they did it to me without thinking twice.

Now I'm in the dark with no hope of starting a family, going to the beach with my friends or even relaxing at home with my family in the near future. What makes it even harder is knowing that when I get out, my dad might not be there to hold me in his arms.

My dad was diagnosed with terminal intestinal cancer in early 1999 and has since undergone four operations. His left kidney is failing and a tumor has saturated into the bone. If the doctors cut it out, he risks the loss of movement in his leg. In a few months, he will be operated on again to remove the damaged kidney. It's pretty much downhill from there.

I can't think of a more severe pain than knowing that one of your loved ones will not make it with you through your times of distress.

Times Weren't Always So Bad

I had a better childhood than most people could wish for. My parents were there for me though thick and thin, never letting me down. I've played classical music on the piano for nine years and was a child prodigy. The only reason I stopped was because I got locked up. I have awards, certificates and ribbons that can fill up a wall and had a scholarship to go along with them all.

If you knew me on the outside, you'd need a minute for the surprise to pass before you could believe that I was arrested. I never had a criminal past, and all of my family and relatives refer to me as a well-mannered, polite, smart kid who always had a hand out to help. That hand is what got me in here. I got into trouble.

I grew up as the kid who made friends with everyone and made everybody laugh. I never hung around the gangs or the junkies. I hung around with a crowd that had the resources to do anything.

When I take my 12-year deal, I will have a felony on my record and a strike that will stick with me for the rest of my life. I'll have to live with being discriminated against and looked upon as a criminal for the rest of my life, because of a stupid mistake that was made in the past.

Life in juvenile hall has been uncomfortable because I'm always being told what to do. They tell me when I have to wake up, when to eat and drink, when I can use the restroom, when I can talk and when to go to sleep. I'm in my room all the time and the four dirty white walls are confining. I get mad when they send the group down early, because that's more time spent in my 8- by 11-foot closet.

I Try to Stay Positive

Believe it or not, juvenile hall has its upside also. The school system is one of the best in Los Angeles County, and they offer you a slew of programs that keep you occupied and educate you at the same time. The facility I'm in right now is one of the oldest and offers an array of programs that often overlap each other on certain days. I participate in all of them because I would go insane if I ran a regular program.

I'm in an art class, a GED [general equivalency diploma] class, photography and film class, a college class and my most preferred, the writing class. It's called Inside OUT Writers. My teacher, . . . is a staff writer for the Los Angeles Times. He is also my mentor. Through his wisdom and knowledge, I learned to unlock my writing skills, to express my heart and emotions through essays and poetry.

But all this is a front to hide the real problem of the halls: prejudice, discrimination, corruption, hatred, anger, violence and scandalous politics. There are at least two fights a day, one riot a month and racial tension is always present. Some staff who are supposed to be here to protect you only care about the money they make and consider you a nuisance that someone else should handle. I've seen 16-year-olds get life and smile the next day like nothing happened.

But at night we all cry. The mask comes off and you don't have to hide anymore.

Part of My Life Is Gone

Life in the halls is not all fun and games like some people assume. It's where you wait to be sent to places like county jail, youth authority and state prison. You have to grow up and mature real fast, because if you don't your life could very well be over.

The most important part of my life is gone. I would give anything to get it back. So far, I've spent my 17th birthday in here, two Easters, two Christmases and will spend every holiday incarcerated until sometime in 2010.

I get lonely in here because I only get to talk to my parents on the phone for 10 minutes a week and only see them one hour on Sundays.

Every day since I heard about my sentence, I ask myself only one question: Will I be able to hold my family in my arms if I make it out of prison?

It's hard on my soul, but they gave me no choice and left me without any options.

By Sheala, incarcerated youth

> **Young & Changing**
> I came to jail at a young age.
> My mind filled with trouble, my heart filled with rage.
> So much confusion and hate in the air.
> No one to love you or show you that they care.
> Trying to grow up and learn on ya own.
> If you're not in the game you feel all alone.
> No one to help you or ease your mind.

The only thing you think of is all that time.
Experiencing things like never before.
Getting older and expected to be more mature.
But I'm surrounded by children, I don't know how to act.
Then they look at repeat offenders and wonder how
    they come back.
Simple answer:
It's a place of corruption and confusion, not
    correction.[18]

POINTS TO PONDER

- What is the message of Peter's article? How does he view the juvenile justice system?
- Do you think the system is rehabilitating him? Punishing him?
- What are the costs to Peter of his incarceration?
- What is the lesson of Sheala's poem? Who should be teaching children in juvenile detention facilities? How can she find a role model if she is surrounded by other children in trouble? Do you agree with her "simple answer"? Are the rehabilitation efforts in the juvenile justice system working?
- What about the serious cost of crime? Shouldn't someone have to give up freedom as a price of his harmful and illegal actions?
- The average cost of incarcerating a juvenile for one year is $35,000–$64,000.[19] The cost of sending a child to a prestigious college for one year is $25,000–$35,000. Which is a better investment?

Juvenile Delinquency and Guilt

Most of the same legal and constitutional standards apply in juvenile as in adult criminal cases. Because of the juvenile rights reform movement, courts now protect the rights of juveniles largely to the same extent as adults. As a juvenile, you are presumed innocent of the charges against you. The government must prove the charges "beyond a reasonable doubt." The government must prove your guilt with evidence that demonstrates that you did in fact commit the offense and that you had the required mental state (intent) when you did the act. In addition, you have the right to a lawyer and to due process protections every step along the way.

Maybe you have heard about some of these legal protections from television, books, or personal experience. Many of these concepts will be addressed in greater detail in other chapters, but first focus on a recurring problem in juvenile court: whether the young person had the required intent for the crime alleged. (Intent means what is going on in your mind—whether you purposely did the wrongful act.)

In the Bugs brothers case, the youngest brother, Yogi, did not know he was stealing the hamburger buns. He thought he was playing a game with his oldest brother, Oliver. If Yogi was playing a game and honestly was not intending to steal someone else's property, he would not be guilty of the shoplifting charge. Why? Because most criminal offenses require a level of criminal intent. Without intent, there is no real wrongdoing.

This is the same type of problem—the level of criminal intent—that the Louisiana Supreme Court faced in the case of thirteen-year-old Jeffery Glassberg.

IN THE INTEREST OF JEFFERY GLASSBERG

Supreme Court of Louisiana
No. 42871.
June 11, 1956.

HAMITER, Justice.

Jeffery Glassberg (age 13) was charged in the Juvenile Court for the Parish of Orleans . . . with being a juvenile delinquent in that he committed aggravated battery on one Barbara Ann Caire (age 14) by shooting her in the face with a dangerous weapon, to-wit: An 8 MM Mauser rifle. In accordance with the petition he was adjudged delinquent; and he was placed on probation, in the custody of his parents, for a period of three years. From the judgment he has appealed.

The record discloses that during the afternoon of November 21, 1955 appellant went into the yard of a neighbor to play with other children who were there, he taking the rifle with him and initially placing it on a 'shoot-the-shoot' (a slide). In the chamber of the gun was a cartridge containing paper wadding. As to whether he was responsible for the loading is a question on which the testimony is conflicting and unsatisfactory. Nevertheless, on his regaining possession of and holding the gun later in the afternoon it discharged and inflicted the injury to Miss Caire. Filing of the instant charge followed. . . .

* * *

To warrant a conclusion in the instant case that criminal intent was present, and hence that aggravated battery was committed, a showing that appellant intended to injure Barbara Ann Caire was not essential; only necessary was a proving that he voluntarily committed the act which resulted in her injury. For example, the existence of general criminal intent could be concluded if proof were made that appellant had voluntarily pulled the trigger of the gun to discharge it, for then he would have intentionally committed an act which under the circumstances might reasonably be expected to result in criminal consequences—a battery on one of the children with whom he was playing at the time.

However, according to our appreciation of the record appellant's pointing of the gun in the general direction of Miss Caire and the discharging of it with the resulting injury were wholly accidental acts. He emphatically denied having intentionally aimed at anyone or pulled the trigger, steadfastly maintaining that the gun fired accidentally as he arose from the ground with his dog. And the testimony of other children who were present tends to support his version, particularly that of the wounded child.

The latter testified as follows:

Q. Did he point the gun at you?

A. I don't believe at me, just in the general direction.

* * *

Q. You and Jeffery have known each other since you were tiny children?
A. Four years old.
Q. Have you always been very good friends?
A. Yes.
Q. As a matter of fact, you usually exchange Christmas gifts or cards, do you not?
A. Yes.
Q. Has there ever been any serious disagreements between you, or fights or arguments?
A. No.

* * *

Q. Now, you and he had no argument on the day of this explosion or shooting, did you? You were still friendly on that day, were you not?
A. Yes.

* * *

Q. Now, Barbara, Jeffery had his dog there in the yard with him that day, didn't he? Do you know Jeffery's dog when you see it?
A. I believe the dog was there.
Q. Now, think back. Do you recall Jeffery stooping down on the ground, holding the dog by the collar, with the gun in one hand and the dog in the other?
A. I know he was sitting on the ground for a little while.

* * *

Q. Tell the Judge the incidents that happened at that time, the game, and the interval after that.
A. Well, after he chased me around the yard, then he stopped and I was playing with the children, and we were talking about school, or something. We often talked about school. I don't think it made him angry, or anything like that. Because I think that anything to do with the shooting was purely accidental. He could have been playing with the gun and it went off.

By The Court:
Q. You think the shooting was accidental?
A. Yes, I thought that since it happened.

Accordingly, we hold that appellant was not guilty of the crime of aggravated battery.

- To prove that someone committed a crime, the government must show that he did the act (**actus reus**) with an intentional state of mind (**mens rea**). Courts often do find that children have the mental intent necessary to establish a crime. Children have been found responsible for murder, rape, arson, armed robbery, and shoplifting, among other things. The court in Jeffery's case simply found that the government had not shown beyond a reasonable doubt that he had the intent to commit an aggravated battery on the victim. Do you agree with the judge that Jeffery did not have intent to hurt Barbara Ann Caire? What facts support your thinking?

- Do you think the same discussion of intent would have been relevant if Jeffrey had been an adult? Adults are presumed to understand how dangerous guns are, and, if they act recklessly with guns, this will ordinarily be enough to establish intent in a case such as Jeffery's. But what about adults who are mentally retarded? Do they have the capacity to form legal intent?

When a Child Is Treated as an Adult: Waiver to Adult Court

Juveniles, for purposes of the juvenile justice system, are generally defined by their age. However, in certain circumstances with certain serious crimes or serial offenders, cases can be transferred to adult court. This transfer process is called "waiver" because the juvenile court is waiving its jurisdiction and control over the juvenile.

When, if ever, should a juvenile be charged as an adult and forced to face adult prosecution and punishment? Should it depend on the crime? Should it depend on the criminal record of the juvenile? Should an age cutoff be set so that some children would always be too young to be tried as an adult? Will rehabilitation not work for some kinds of juveniles?

Generally, a juvenile can be waived into adult court to be tried as an adult via a **statutory waiver**, a **judicial waiver**, or a **prosecutorial waiver**.

Statutory Waiver. Some states provide in their statutes (their laws) that certain serious crimes automatically trigger an adult prosecution. Usually these crimes are the most serious ones: murder, arson, rape, and certain aggravated assault.

Judicial Waiver. Some states allow judges to decide whether or not a juvenile will be tried as an adult. Usually, these states have statutory provisions that allow for trial of juveniles as adults but designate the judge to make a final determination based on the particular individual circumstances of the case and the child.

Prosecutorial Waiver. Some states have allowed prosecutors to decide whether to bring the case in juvenile or adult court. With a prosecutorial waiver, individual prosecutors can decide whether or not a juvenile can be tried as an adult in adult court.

Consider the real-life case of Nathaniel Abraham, an eleven-year-old charged with first-degree murder and waived into adult court.[20] At age eleven, Nathaniel Abraham shot and killed Ronnie Green outside a Michigan liquor store. It was a random act of violence. According to official reports prepared for trial, Nathaniel functioned at the level of a six-year-old, both intellectually and emotionally. At the time of the murder, he was enrolled in special education classes. When arrested he was brought to the police station in his Halloween costume and even during his trial asked his lawyer when he would get to go home.

However, according to prosecutors he had told classmates that he planned to shoot someone and practiced shooting at targets before he shot and killed Ronnie Green. Even though he was only eleven, Nathaniel had already had between ten and twenty previous run-ins with local law enforcement, an extraordinary number. His mother had repeatedly but unsuccessfully sought help from officials for her son before the murder.

Michigan law allows for the transfer of any juvenile charged with murder to adult court. The local prosecutors' office requested a transfer and charged Nathaniel with first-degree murder in adult court. Thus, at age thirteen, Nathaniel went to trial facing life in prison without parole for the murder. At the time of his trial, Nathaniel was the youngest child in the United States to be tried for murder.

Did the prosecutors make the right decision charging Nathaniel as an adult? Who should make that determination? What information would you want to know about the child before making such a decision?

FACTORS THAT MAY BE CONSIDERED IN DETERMINING WAIVER TO ADULT COURT

- How serious is the offense?
- Is the offense so serious that waiver is necessary to protect the community?
- How was the offense committed? Was it violent? Premeditated?
- Was anyone injured or killed?
- Is the government's case strong, or is it a weak or politically motivated case?
- How mature is the juvenile?
- Is there anything about the juvenile's background, family, or living situation that would give reason to be concerned about him committing more crime in the future?
- What is the juvenile's criminal record? How many times has he been in trouble with the law?

- Using the above description of the situation, if you were the prosecutor, what would your decision be about transferring Nathaniel? Does your answer change if you are a judge? What would you say to argue that Nathaniel should be tried as a juvenile? How about as an adult?
- Do you think that statutory waiver (automatic waiver to adult court for certain serious crimes) is a good or necessary thing? Are certain crimes—such as murder—not appropriate for juvenile courts?
- What values are protected by having such automatic waiver?
- Should there ever be an age that is just too young for waiver? Is six years old too young?
- What about the principle of individualized justice, meaning that the justice system is supposed to look at the person as an individual?
- What about rehabilitation? Are there some juveniles, because of the crimes they commit, who simply cannot be rehabilitated?
- What happens after a juvenile is waived to adult court?
- Do you think it is right to have juveniles spend time in adult jail? Do you think it is safe for them? Do you think they might be taken advantage of? Abused? Do you think they will come out of jail as productive citizens? Should young people tried as adults still get separate prisons?
- What are the consequences of putting juveniles in prison with adults? Which of the following do you think are true statements about the consequences of doing adult time?[21]
  a. Adult prisons are schools for crime.
  b. Prison provides social networking for the criminal underworld.
  c. Prison creates defiance, bitterness, and frustration—traits that are counterproductive when you get to the outside.
  d. An adult conviction means it is hard to get a job out of prison.
  e. The older prisoners will teach the young ones to get off the criminal path.
  f. Young prisoners will be so terrified by the adult prison that they will be "scared straight."
- A Florida study on juvenile waiver showed that transferring juveniles to adult courts only increased the likelihood that the juveniles would re-offend. Two researchers followed three thousand juveniles who were transferred to adult criminal court in 1987 and another group of control juveniles who remained in the juvenile system. The young people were compared for the crimes they committed, their age, sex, and race. The researchers then went back and looked at the two groups one year later and six years later. At both periods, the young people who went to adult prison were more likely to commit other crimes and to return to the system.[22] What do you think about the success of juvenile waiver into adult court?

Judicial Review of Waiver to Adult Court

Even in states that favor statutory or prosecutorial waiver, usually judges make the final decision as to whether or not a juvenile should be tried as an adult. That can be a difficult decision for the judge, as well as the most important decision for the young person. As a result, judges should follow strict procedures before waiving a juvenile to adult court. However, this has not always been the practice in lower courts.

In *Kent v. United States,* the Supreme Court addressed one such example of a particularly sloppy waiver of a young defendant.[23] Morris Kent first came in contact with the juvenile justice system at age fourteen. He was convicted of some housebreakings and a purse snatching and put on juvenile probation. His probation officers kept a social service file on him, which detailed information about his upbringing, social problems, and criminal history. At age sixteen, he was arrested for robbery and rape. He was taken into custody by police and asked questions about the crimes for two days. His mother did not find out where he went until late on the second day. Morris was held in a juvenile home for more than a week. Morris's lawyer sought to have him evaluated by psychiatrists to see whether he had any mental problems. Two psychiatrists and a psychologist interviewed him and recommended that he be hospitalized for psychiatric observation. Morris's lawyer also filed a legal motion with the juvenile court judge requesting that the juvenile court keep jurisdiction over Morris and not waive him into adult court. The lawyer also requested access to the social services file on Morris because the lawyer knew that the judge would use the information in the file to make a determination about Morris's suitability to be tried in adult court.

The juvenile court judge ignored the motions. The judge did not hold a hearing about waiver. He did not consult with Morris, his mother, or Morris's lawyer. He simply decided to waive Morris to adult court. He entered a court order stating that "after full investigation, I do hereby waive jurisdiction of [Morris]." He made no findings of fact that stated why he was waiving jurisdiction and sending Morris to be tried as an adult. He did not give any reason.

Because Morris and his lawyer thought this result unfair, they appealed to the Supreme Court. The Court agreed with Morris.

MORRIS A. KENT, JR., PETITIONER, V. UNITED STATES

Supreme Court of the United States
No. 104.
Argued January 19, 1966.
Decided March 21, 1966.

Mr. Justice FORTAS delivered the opinion of the Court.

. . . The facts and the contentions of counsel raise a number of disturbing questions concerning the administration by the police and the Juvenile Court authorities of the District of Columbia laws relating to juveniles. . . .

Petitioner attacks the waiver of jurisdiction on a number of statutory and constitutional grounds. He contends that the waiver is defective because no hearing was held; because no findings were made by the Juvenile Court; because the Juvenile Court stated no reasons for waiver; and because counsel was denied access to the Social Service file which presumably was considered by the Juvenile Court in determining to waive jurisdiction.

We agree that the order of the Juvenile Court waiving its jurisdiction and transferring petitioner for trial in the United States District Court for the District of Columbia was invalid. . . .

The statute gives the Juvenile Court a substantial degree of discretion as to the factual considerations to be evaluated, the weight to be given them and the conclusion to be reached. It does not confer upon the Juvenile Court a license for arbitrary procedure. The statute does not permit the Juvenile Court to determine in isolation and without the participation or any representation of the child the 'critically important' question whether a child will be deprived of the special protections and provisions of the Juvenile Court Act. . . . It does not authorize the Juvenile Court, in total disregard of a motion for hearing filed by counsel, and without any hearing or statement or reasons, to decide—as in this case—that the child will be taken from the Receiving Home for Children and transferred to jail along with adults, and that he will be exposed to the possibility of a death sentence instead of treatment for a maximum, in Kent's case, of five years, until he is 21. . . .

The theory of the District's Juvenile Court Act, like that of other jurisdictions, is rooted in social welfare philosophy rather than in the corpus juris. Its proceedings are designated as civil rather than criminal. The Juvenile Court is theoretically engaged in determining the needs of the child and of society rather than adjudicating criminal conduct. The objectives are to provide measures of guidance and rehabilitation for the child and protection for society, not to fix criminal responsibility, guilt and punishment. The State is **parens patriae** rather than prosecuting attorney and judge. But the admonition to function in a 'parental' relationship is not an invitation to procedural arbitrariness. . . .

While there can be no doubt of the original laudable purpose of juvenile courts, studies and critiques in recent years raise serious questions as to whether actual performance measures well enough against theoretical purpose to make tolerable the immunity of the process from the reach of constitutional guaranties applicable to adults. There is much evidence that some juvenile courts, including that of the District of Columbia, lack the personnel, facilities and techniques to perform adequately as representatives of the State in a parens patriae capacity, at least with respect to children charged with law violation. There is evidence, in fact, that there may be grounds for concern that the child receives the worst of both worlds: that he gets neither the protections accorded to adults nor the solicitous care and regenerative treatment postulated for children. . . .

It is clear beyond dispute that the waiver of jurisdiction is a 'critically important' action determining vitally important statutory rights of the juvenile. . . .

Meaningful review requires that the reviewing court should review. It should not be remitted to assumptions. It must have before it a statement of the reasons motivating the waiver including, of course, a statement of the relevant facts. It may not 'assume' that there are adequate reasons, nor may it merely assume that 'full investigation' has been made. Accordingly, we hold that it is incumbent upon the Juvenile Court to accompany its waiver order with a statement of the reasons or considerations therefor. . . .

Correspondingly, we conclude that an opportunity for a hearing which may be informal, must be given the child prior to entry of a waiver order. . . . [T]he child is entitled to counsel in connection with a waiver proceeding, and . . . counsel is entitled to see the child's social records. These rights are meaningless—an illusion, a mockery—unless counsel is given an opportunity to function.

The right to representation by counsel is not a formality. It is not a grudging gesture to a ritualistic requirement. It is of the essence of justice. Appointment of counsel without affording an opportunity for hearing on a 'critically important' decision is tantamount to denial of counsel. . . .

Reversed and remanded.

POINTS TO PONDER

- Do you agree that the lower court should have done more before deciding that Morris should be tried as an adult? What should a court do? How much information should a court have?
- What should "meaningful review" mean?
- What is the purpose of a court hearing? What should happen at a hearing? Why would it be necessary to have a lawyer there?
- Justice Abe Fortas wrote this decision in 1966 when the juvenile rights movement was gathering strength. How have the ideals articulated in the decision been realized or frustrated over the past forty years? Do you think that our attitudes and policies toward crime move in cycles?
- Justice Fortas thought that young people were getting neither the rights accorded to adults nor the care and attention that the juvenile system theoretically promised. What is the danger he saw that young people would have the worst of both worlds in the criminal justice system? How might they be given the best of both worlds? Should an effort be made to do that?

Notes

1. Elliott Currie, *Crime and Punishment in America* (New York: Henry Holt and Company, 1998).
2. *In Re Gault,* 387 U.S. 1, 28 (1967).
3. Paul Wake, "Helping Children through the Juvenile Justice System: A Guide for Utah Defense Attorneys," *Brigham Young University Journal of Public Law* 15 (2000): 31, 32.
4. Lisette Blumhardt, "In the Best Interests of the Child: Juvenile Justice or Adult Retribution?" *University of Hawaii Law Review* 23 (2000): 341, 350–354.
5. *Eddings v. Oklahoma,* 455 U.S. 104, 116, n. 11 (1982).
6. *Thompson v. Oklahoma,* 487 U.S. 815, 835 (1988).
7. *Schall v. Abrams,* 467 U.S. 253, 267 (1984); *Wayburn v. Schupf,* 350 N.E.2d 906, 908–909 (N.Y. 1976).
8. *In Re Gault,* 387 U.S. 1, 15–16 (1967). See also Lawrence L. Koontz Jr., "Reassessment Should Not Lead to Wholesale Rejection of the Juvenile Justice System," *University of Richmond Law Review* 31 (1997): 179.
9. Sacha M. Coupet, "What to Do with the Sheep in Wolf's Clothing: The Role of Rhetoric and Reality about Youth Offenders in the Constructive Dismantling of the Juvenile Justice System," *University of Pennsylvania Law Review* 148 (2000): 1303, 1331; Christine Chamberlin, "Not Kids Anymore: A Need for Punishment and Deterrence in the Juvenile Justice System," *Boston College Law Review* 42 (2001): 391, 392.
10. Koontz, "Reassessment Should Not Lead to Wholesale Rejection of the Juvenile Justice System."
11. Christina Dejong and Even Schwitzer Merrill, "Getting 'Tough' on Crime: Juvenile Waiver and the Criminal Court," *Ohio Northern University Law Review* 27 (2001): 175, 175–176, 182–184; Chamberlin, "Not Kids Anymore," 391, 399–401; Coupet, "What to Do with the Sheep in Wolf's Clothing"; Barry Feld, "The Transformation of the Juvenile Court," *Minnesota Law Review* 75 (1991): 691.

12. U.S. Congress, Senate, *Congressional Record,* daily ed., 106th Cong., 1st sess., May 11, 1999, S4981, S4984, reprinted in Coupet, "What to Do with the Sheep in Wolf's Clothing," 1303, 1327, n. 131.

13. Abbe Smith, "They Dream of Growing Older: On Kids and Crime," *Boston College Law Review* 36 (1995): 953.

14. E. Poe-Yamagata and M. Jones, *And Justice for Some: Differential Treatment of Minority Youth in the Juvenile Justice System,* prepared by the National Council on Crime and Delinquency (Washington, D.C.: Building Blocks for Youth, April 2000).

15. American Bar Association, *America's Children at Risk: A Report of the American Bar Association Presidential Working Group on the Unmet Legal Needs of Children and their Families* (Chicago, Ill.: American Bar Association, July 1993), reprinted in Stacy Gurian-Sherman, "Back to the Future: Returning Treatment to Juvenile Justice," *15-SPG Criminal Justice* (2000): 30, 31–32.

16. Pamela Brogan, "Report: Juvenile Jails Being Substituted for Mental Hospitals," *USA Today,* July 7, 2004, available at http://www.usatoday.com/news/nation/2004-07-07-jailed-kids_x.htm.

17. See *Schall v. Abrams,* 467 U.S. 253, 291 (1984) (Marshall, J. dissenting).

18. *Ya Heard Me,* special edition (Juvenile Justice Project of Louisiana, December 2002).

19. American Civil Liberties Union, "ACLU Fact Sheet on the Juvenile Justice System," July 5, 1996, available at http://www.aclu.org.

20. Deanna M. Maher, "Michigan Juveniles Are Denied Equal Defenses before the Law: The State of Michigan's Reaction to Juvenile Delinquents," *University of Detroit Mercy Law Review* 78 (2001): 259; Dejong and Merrill, "Getting 'Tough' on Crime," 175, 175–176, 185; Chamberlin, "Not Kids Anymore," 391.

21. John Braithwaite, "A Future Where Punishment Is Marginalized: Realistic or Utopian," *UCLA Law Review* 46 (1999): 1727, 1738–1739.

22. Howard N. Snyder and Melissa Sickmund, *U.S. Department of Justice, Juvenile Offenders, and Victims: 1999 National Report* (Washington, D.C.: Government Printing Office, 1999), p. 103, available at http://www.ncjrs.org/html/ojjdp/nationalreport99/toc.html, cited in Blumhardt, "In the Best Interests of the Child," *University of Hawaii Law Review* 23 (2000): 341, 355.

23. *Kent v. United States,* 383 U.S. 541 (1966).

WHAT IS CRIME?

2

In repressive societies, government leaders continually invent new variations on what are considered crimes and never fail to find ways to punish "enemies of the state." People living in such societies have to assume that if something is not specifically authorized by government, it is forbidden and criminal. The criminal law creates a regime of fear.

In free societies, the reverse is true: If something is not specifically outlawed by government, then the people can assume that it is allowed. No action is a crime except if it is defined that way explicitly by law, and no one is punished unless he has committed a crime. This is the theory of crime and punishment in a liberal state.

So, who defines crime in America? Theoretically we all do—through our elected legislators, state legislators, and county and local officeholders.

Does this mean anything can be made into a crime and then be punished in the courts? No. Criminal laws cannot be valid if they fail to meet constitutional standards. Even if a law is properly enacted, it will be struck down if it violates a constitutional rule or principle. This is why the Constitution needs to be studied.

Constitutional Limits on Government's Power to Make Crimes

Throughout U.S. history, the states and federal government tried to turn many things into crimes: spitting on the sidewalk, swearing in public, **loitering** (hanging around in public), **vagrancy**, avoiding the military draft, trespassing, refusing to give up your seat on a bus for a white person, marrying someone of another race, having sex with someone of the same gender, entering the country illegally, paying someone below the minimum wage, **perjury** (lying in court or on an official document), **assault**, shoplifting, prostitution, **embezzlement**, drug possession, drug distribution, armed **robbery**, **rape**, **murder**, and **conspiracy**.

But several of these actions described as criminal by legislators were found to be innocent and constitutionally protected by the courts. For example, laws making it a crime to refuse to give up one's seat on a bus for a white person and to marry someone of another race were struck down as **unconstitutional** by the courts. Like segregation laws, they violate the Equal Protection clause. Similarly, the U.S. Supreme Court has ruled that states cannot make it a crime for people to have sex with someone of the same gender.

Two general constitutional principles control and limit the ability to create new crimes. One is the principle of notice, and the other is the principle of harm.

Luis Gutierrez, pictured here at twenty-five years old, was one of thousands of young people arrested under Chicago's extremely broad anti-loitering ordinance, which was struck down by the Supreme Court in *City of Chicago v. Morales* (1999). *Source: Pablo Martinez Monsivais/AP Wide World Photos*

The Principle of Notice

The principle of notice requires that people be held criminally accountable only for violating laws that are specific and definite and that describe precisely what conduct is forbidden. If a state law is too vague, too general, or too foggy to give reasonable people a real sense of what they can and cannot legitimately do, then such a law is "void for vagueness" and violates the Fourteenth Amendment **Due Process Clause**.

In *Chicago v. Morales*, the Supreme Court considered a Chicago anti-gang ordinance that gave police the power to arrest people who looked like gang members for loitering. More than forty-two thousand people were arrested for violating this ordinance before it was challenged for being vague. The Court's majority agreed that the ordinance failed to give people "notice" and struck it down as void for vagueness. What are the dangers of a vague law such as this in the eyes of the Court? What dangers do you see? What is "loitering" anyway?

CITY OF CHICAGO
V.
MORALES

Supreme Court of the United States
No. 97-1121.
Argued December 9, 1998.
Decided June 10, 1999.

Justice STEVENS announced the judgment of the Court and delivered the opinion of the Court with respect to Parts I, II, and V, and an opinion with respect to Parts III, IV, and VI, in which Justice SOUTER and Justice GINSBURG join.

In 1992, the Chicago City Council enacted the Gang Congregation Ordinance, which prohibits "criminal street gang members" from "loitering" with one another or with other persons in any public place. The question presented is whether the Supreme Court of Illinois correctly held that the ordinance violates the Due Process Clause of the Fourteenth Amendment to the Federal Constitution.

I

Before the ordinance was adopted, the city council's Committee on Police and Fire conducted hearings to explore the problems created by the city's street gangs, and more particularly, the consequences of public loitering by gang members. . . .

The council found that a continuing increase in criminal street gang activity was largely responsible for the city's rising murder rate, as well as an escalation of violent and drug related crimes. It noted that in many neighborhoods throughout the city, "the burgeoning presence of street gang members in public places has intimidated many law abiding citizens." Furthermore, the council stated that gang members "establish control over identifiable areas . . . by loitering in those areas and intimidating others from entering those areas; and . . . [m]embers of criminal street gangs avoid arrest by committing no offense punishable under existing laws when they know the police are present. . . ." It further found that "loitering in public places by criminal street gang members creates a justifiable fear for the safety of persons and property in the area" and that "[a]ggressive action is necessary to preserve the city's streets and other public places so that the public may use such places without fear." Moreover, the council concluded that the city "has an interest in discouraging all persons from loitering in public places with criminal gang members."

The ordinance creates a criminal offense punishable by a fine of up to $500, imprisonment for not more than six months, and a requirement to perform up to 120 hours of community service. Commission of the offense involves four predicates. First, the police officer must reasonably believe that at least one of the two or more persons present in a "public place" is a "criminal street gang membe[r]." Second, the persons must be "loitering," which the ordinance defines as "remain[ing] in any one place with no apparent purpose." Third, the officer must then order "all" of the persons to disperse and remove themselves "from the area." Fourth, a person must disobey the officer's order. If any person, whether a gang member or not, disobeys the officer's order, that person is guilty of violating the ordinance.

Two months after the ordinance was adopted, the Chicago Police Department promulgated General Order 92-4 to provide guidelines to govern its enforcement. That order purported to establish limitations on the enforcement discretion of police officers "to ensure that the anti-gang loitering ordinance is not enforced in an arbitrary or discriminatory way." The limitations confine the authority to arrest gang members who violate the ordinance to sworn "members of the Gang Crime Section" and certain other designated officers, and establish detailed criteria for defining street gangs and membership in such gangs. In addition, the order directs district commanders to "designate areas in which the presence of gang members has a demonstrable effect on the activities of law abiding persons in the surrounding community," and provides that the ordinance "will be enforced only within the designated areas."

II

During the three years of its enforcement, the police issued over 89,000 dispersal orders and arrested over 42,000 people for violating the ordinance. . . .

This ordinance, for reasons that are not explained in the findings of the city council, requires no harmful purpose and applies to nongang members as well as suspected gang members. It applies to everyone in the city who may remain in one place with one suspected gang member as long as their purpose is not apparent to an officer observing them. Friends, relatives, teachers, counselors, or even total strangers might unwittingly engage in forbidden loitering if they happen to engage in idle conversation with a gang member.

Ironically, the definition of loitering in the Chicago ordinance not only extends its scope to encompass harmless conduct, but also has the perverse consequence of excluding from its coverage much of the intimidating conduct that motivated its enactment. As the city council's findings demonstrate, the most harmful gang loitering is motivated either by an apparent purpose to publicize the gang's dominance of certain territory, thereby intimidating nonmembers, or by an equally apparent purpose to conceal ongoing commerce in illegal drugs. . . . [W]e assume that the ordinance means what it says and that it has no application to loiterers whose purpose is apparent. The relative importance of its application to harmless loitering is magnified by its inapplicability to loitering that has an obviously threatening or illicit purpose. . . .

VI

. . . [T]he ordinance does not provide sufficiently specific limits on the enforcement discretion of the police "to meet constitutional standards for definiteness and clarity." We recognize the serious and difficult problems testified to by the citizens of Chicago that led to the enactment of this ordinance. "We are mindful that the preservation of liberty depends in part on the maintenance of social order." However, in this instance the city has enacted an ordinance that affords too much discretion to the police and too little notice to citizens who wish to use the public streets.

Accordingly, the judgment of the Supreme Court of Illinois is

Affirmed. . . .

Justice THOMAS, with whom THE CHIEF JUSTICE and Justice SCALIA join, dissenting.

The duly elected members of the Chicago City Council enacted the ordinance at issue as part of a larger effort to prevent gangs from establishing dominion over the public streets. By invalidating Chicago's ordinance, I fear that the Court has unnecessarily sentenced law-abiding citizens to lives of terror and misery. The ordinance is not vague. . . . Nor does it violate the Due Process Clause. The asserted "freedom to loiter for innocent purposes," is in no way "deeply rooted in this Nation's history and tradition." I dissent. . . .

At the outset, it is important to note that the ordinance does not criminalize loitering *per se*. Rather, it penalizes loiterers' failure to obey a police officer's order to move along. A majority of the Court believes that this scheme vests too much discretion in police officers. Nothing could be further from the truth. Far from according officers too much discretion, the ordinance merely enables police officers to fulfill one of their traditional functions. Police officers are not, and have never been, simply enforcers of the criminal law. They wear other hats—importantly, they have long been vested with the responsibility for preserving the public peace. Nor is the idea that the police are also *peace officers* simply a quaint anachronism. In most American jurisdictions, police officers continue to be obligated, by law, to maintain the public peace. . . .

In order to perform their peacekeeping responsibilities satisfactorily, the police inevitably must exercise discretion. Indeed, by empowering them to act as peace officers, the law assumes that the police will exercise that discretion responsibly and with sound judgment. That is not to say that the law should not provide objective guidelines for the police, but simply that it cannot rigidly constrain their every action. By directing a police officer not to issue a dispersal order unless he "observes a person whom he reasonably believes to be a criminal street gang member loitering in any public place," Chicago's ordinance strikes an appropriate balance between those two extremes. Just as we trust officers to rely on their experience and expertise in order to make spur-of-the-moment determinations about amorphous legal standards such as "probable cause" and "reasonable suspicion," so we must trust them to determine whether a group of loiterers contains individuals (in this case members of criminal street gangs) whom the city has determined threaten the public peace. . . .

In concluding that the ordinance adequately channels police discretion, I do not suggest that a police officer enforcing the Gang Congregation Ordinance will never make a mistake. Nor do I overlook the *possibility* that a police officer, acting in bad faith, might enforce the ordinance in an arbitrary or discriminatory way. But our decisions should not turn on the proposition that such an event will be anything but rare. Instances of arbitrary or discriminatory enforcement of the ordinance, like any other law, are best addressed when (and if) they arise, rather than prophylactically through the disfavored mechanism of a facial challenge on vagueness grounds. . . .

The plurality's conclusion that the ordinance "fails to give the ordinary citizen adequate notice of what is forbidden and what is permitted," is similarly untenable. There is nothing "vague" about an order to disperse. While "we can never expect mathematical certainty from our language," it is safe to assume that the vast majority of people who are ordered by the police to "disperse and remove themselves from the area" will have little difficulty understanding how to comply. . . .

Today, the Court focuses extensively on the "rights" of gang members and their companions. It can safely do so—the people who will have to live with the consequences of today's opinion do not live in our neighborhoods. Rather, the people who will suffer from our lofty pronouncements are people like Ms. Susan Mary Jackson; people who have seen their neighborhoods literally destroyed by gangs and violence and drugs. They are good, decent people who must struggle to overcome their desperate situation, against all odds, in order to raise their families, earn a living, and remain good citizens. As one resident described: "There is only about maybe one or two percent of the people in the city causing these problems maybe, but it's keeping 98 percent of us in our houses and off the streets and afraid to shop." By focusing exclusively on the imagined "rights" of the two percent, the Court today has denied our most vulnerable citizens the very thing that Justice STEVENS elevates above all else—the "freedom of movement." And that is a shame. I respectfully dissent.

EXERCISE 2.1. Vague laws violate due process because they fail to give people proper notice of what is criminal and what is lawful, and they invite arbitrary and discriminatory enforcement by police and prosecutors. Which of the following rules or criminal prohibitions seem overly vague and therefore unconstitutional to you?

1. No taking advantage of other people's inexperience.
2. No driving over sixty-five miles per hour.
3. No driving at unreasonable speeds.
4. No taking more than your fair share of food samples from a supermarket food display.
5. No boisterous conduct on the school bus.
6. No talking to the school bus driver while the bus is moving, except in an emergency.
7. No one under eighteen permitted to hunt with a firearm.
8. No immature children allowed to carry a firearm without a parent's permission.

POINTS TO PONDER

- How is No. 2 different from No. 3? No. 2 is a "rule" because it is more precise; No. 3 is a "standard" because it is more general and vague. The more standard-like a law is, the more likely it will be "void for vagueness." Write some laws that appear to be rules and some that appear to be standards.

Another criminal prosecution fought by criminal defendants on constitutional grounds related to a Florida anti-vagrancy statute. The statute there made various people criminals simply for being "common gamblers," "common drunkards," "disorderly persons," and so on.

Although the terms of this statute were not vague but very specific, they criminalized entirely innocent behavior. In *Papachristou v. City of Jacksonville* (1972), the Supreme Court declared the statute unconstitutional.

PAPACHRISTOU V. CITY OF JACKSONVILLE

Supreme Court of the United States
No. 70-530.
Argued December 8, 1971.
Decided February 24, 1972.

MR. JUSTICE DOUGLAS delivered the opinion of the Court.

This case involves eight defendants who were convicted in a Florida municipal court of violating a Jacksonville, Florida, vagrancy ordinance.[1]

Their convictions [entailing fines and jail sentences] were affirmed by the Florida Circuit Court .... For reasons which will appear, we reverse.[2]

... Margaret Papachristou, Betty Calloway, Eugene Eddie Melton, and Leonard Johnson were all arrested early on a Sunday morning, and charged with vagrancy—"prowling by auto."

Jimmy Lee Smith and Milton Henry were charged with vagrancy—"vagabonds."

Henry Edward Heath and a co-defendant were arrested for vagrancy—"loitering" and "common thief."

Thomas Owen Campbell was charged with vagrancy—"common thief."

Hugh Brown was charged with vagrancy—"disorderly loitering on street" and "disorderly conduct-resisting arrest with violence."

Papachristou and Calloway are white females. Melton and Johnson are black males. Papachristou was enrolled in a job-training program sponsored by the State Employment Service at Florida Junior College in Jacksonville. Calloway was a typing and shorthand teacher at a state mental institution located near Jacksonville. She was the owner of the automobile in which the four defendants were arrested. Melton was a Vietnam war veteran who had been released from the Navy after nine months in a veterans' hospital. On the date of his arrest he was a part-time computer helper while attending college as a full-time student in Jacksonville. Johnson was a tow-motor operator in a grocery chain warehouse and was a lifelong resident of Jacksonville.

At the time of their arrest the four of them were riding in Calloway's car on the main thoroughfare in Jacksonville. They had left a restaurant owned by Johnson's uncle where they had eaten and were on their way to a night club. ...

The arresting officers denied that the racial mixture in the car played any part in the decision to make the arrest. The arrest, they said, was made because the defendants had stopped near a used-

---

1. Jacksonville Ordinance Code § 26-57 provided at the time of these arrests and convictions as follows:

    Rogues and vagabonds, or dissolute persons who go about begging, common gamblers, persons who use juggling or unlawful games or plays, common drunkards, common night walkers, thieves, pilferers or pickpockets, traders in stolen property, lewd, wanton and lascivious persons, keepers of gambling places, common railers and brawlers, persons wandering or strolling around from place to place without any lawful purpose or object, habitual loafers, disorderly persons, persons neglecting all lawful business and habitually spending their time by frequenting houses of ill fame, gaming houses, or places where alcoholic beverages are sold or served, persons able to work but habitually living upon the earnings of their wives or minor children shall be deemed vagrants and, upon conviction in the Municipal Court shall be punished [ninety days imprisonment, $500 fine, or both].

2. Florida also has a vagrancy statute ... which reads quite closely on the Jacksonville ordinance.

car lot which had been broken into several times. There was, however, no evidence of any breaking and entering on the night in question.

Of these four charged with "prowling by auto" none had been previously arrested except Papachristou who had once been convicted of a municipal offense.

Jimmy Lee Smith and Milton Henry were arrested between 9 and 10 a.m. on a weekday in downtown Jacksonville, while waiting for a friend who was to lend them a car so they could apply for a job at a produce company. Smith was a part-time produce worker and part-time organizer for a Negro political group. He had a common-law wife and three children supported by him and his wife. He had been arrested several times but convicted only once. Smith's companion, Henry, was an 18-year-old high school student with no previous record of arrest.

This morning it was cold, and Smith had no jacket, so they went briefly into a dry cleaning shop to wait, but left when requested to do so. They thereafter walked back and forth two or three times over a two-block stretch looking for their friend. The store owners, who apparently were wary of Smith and his companion, summoned two police officers who searched the men and found neither had a weapon. But they were arrested because the officers said they had no identification and because the officers did not believe their story.

Heath and a codefendant were arrested for "loitering" and for "common thief." Both were residents of Jacksonville, Heath having lived there all his life and being employed at an automobile body shop. Heath had previously been arrested but his codefendant had no arrest record. Heath and his companion were arrested when they drove up to a residence shared by Heath's girlfriend and some other girls. Some police officers were already there in the process of arresting another man. When Heath and his companion started backing out of the driveway, the officers signaled to them to stop and asked them to get out of the car, which they did. Thereupon they and the automobile were searched. Although no contraband or incriminating evidence was found, they were both arrested, Heath being charged with being a "common thief" because he was reputed to be a thief. The codefendant was charged with "loitering" because he was standing in the driveway, an act which the officers admitted was done only at their command.

Campbell was arrested as he reached his home very early one morning and was charged with "common thief." He was stopped by officers because he was traveling at a high rate of speed, yet no speeding charge was placed against him.

Brown was arrested when he was observed leaving a downtown Jacksonville hotel by a police officer seated in a cruiser. The police testified he was reputed to be a thief, narcotics pusher, and generally opprobrious character. The officer called Brown over to the car, intending at that time to arrest him unless he had a good explanation for being on the street. Brown walked over to the police cruiser, as commanded, and the officer began to search him, apparently preparatory to placing him in the car. In the process of the search he came on two small packets which were later found to contain heroin. When the officer touched the pocket where the packets were, Brown began to resist. He was charged with "disorderly loitering on the street" and "disorderly conduct-resisting arrest with violence." While he was also charged with a narcotics violation, that charge was [dropped]. . . .

This ordinance is void-for-vagueness, both in the sense that it "fails to give a person of ordinary intelligence fair notice that his contemplated conduct is forbidden by the statute," . . . and because it encourages arbitrary and erratic arrests and convictions. . . .

Living under a rule of law entails various suppositions, one of which is that "All [persons] are entitled to be informed as to what the State commands or forbids." *Lanzetta v. New Jersey* . . . is one of a well-recognized group of cases insisting that the law give fair notice of the offending conduct. . . .

The poor among us, the minorities, the average householder are not in business and not alerted to the regulatory schemes of vagrancy laws; and we assume they would have no understanding of their meaning and impact if they read them. Nor are they protected from being caught in the vagrancy net by the necessity of having a specific intent to commit an unlawful act. . . .

The Jacksonville ordinance makes criminal activities which by modern standards are normally innocent. "Nightwalking" is one. Florida construes the ordinance not to make criminal one night's wandering, . . . only the "habitual" wanderer or as the ordinance describes it "common night walkers." We know, however, from experience that sleepless people often walk at night, perhaps hopeful that sleep-inducing relaxation will result.

Luis Munoz-Marin, former Governor of Puerto Rico, commented once that "loafing" was a national virtue in his Commonwealth and that it should be encouraged. It is, however, a crime in Jacksonville.

"Persons able to work but habitually living on the earnings of their wives or minor children"—like habitually living "without visible means of support"—might implicate unemployed pillars of the community who have married rich wives.

"Persons able to work but habitually living on the earnings of their wives or minor children" may also embrace unemployed people out of the labor market, by reason of a recession or disemployed by reason of technological or so-called structural displacements.

Persons "wandering or strolling" from place to place have been extolled by Walt Whitman and Vachel Lindsay. The qualification "without any lawful purpose or object" may be a trap for innocent acts. Persons "neglecting all lawful business and habitually spending their time by frequenting . . . places where alcoholic beverages are sold or served" would literally embrace many members of golf clubs and city clubs.

Walkers and strollers and wanderers may be going to or coming from a **burglary**. Loafers or loiterers may be "casing" a place for a holdup. Letting one's wife support him is an intra-family matter, and normally of no concern to the police. Yet it may, of course, be the setting for numerous crimes.

The difficulty is that these activities are historically part of the amenities of life as we have known them. They are not mentioned in the Constitution or in the Bill of Rights. These unwritten amenities have been in part responsible for giving our people the feeling of independence and self-confidence, the feeling of creativity. These amenities have dignified the right of dissent and have honored the right to be nonconformists and the right to defy submissiveness. They have encouraged lives of high spirits rather than hushed, suffocating silence.

They are embedded in Walt Whitman's writings especially in his Song of the Open Road. They are reflected too, in the spirit of Vachel Lindsay's I Want to go Wandering and by Henry D. Thoreau.

This aspect of the vagrancy ordinance before us is suggested by what this Court said in 1876 about a broad criminal statute enacted by Congress: "It would certainly be dangerous if the legislature could set a net large enough to catch all possible offenders, and leave it to the courts to step inside and say who could be rightfully detained, and who should be set at large." . . .

While that was a federal case, the due process implications are equally applicable to the States and to this vagrancy ordinance. Here the net cast is large, not to give the courts the power to pick and choose but to increase the arsenal of the police. . . .

Where the list of crimes is so all-inclusive and generalized as the one in this ordinance, those convicted may be punished for no more than . . . affronts to police authority: . . .

Another aspect of the ordinance's vagueness appears when we focus, not on the lack of notice given a potential offender, but on the effect of the unfettered discretion it places in the hands of the Jacksonville police. Caleb Foote, an early student of this subject, has called the vagrancy-type law as offering "punishment by analogy." Such crimes, though long common in Russia, are not compatible with our constitutional system. We allow our police to make arrests only on "probable cause," a Fourth and Fourteenth Amendment standard applicable to the States as well as to the Federal Government. Arresting a person on suspicion, like arresting a person for investigation, is foreign to our system, even when the arrest is for past criminality. Future criminality, however, is the common justification for the presence of vagrancy statutes. . . . Florida has indeed construed her vagrancy statute "as necessary regulations," *inter alia,* "to deter vagabondage and prevent crimes." . . .

A direction by a legislature to the police to arrest all "suspicious" persons would not pass constitutional muster. A vagrancy prosecution may be merely the cloak for a conviction which could not be obtained on the real but undisclosed grounds for the arrest. . . .

Those generally implicated by the imprecise terms of the ordinance—poor people, nonconformists, dissenters, idlers—may be required to comport themselves according to the lifestyle deemed appropriate by the Jacksonville police and the courts. Where, as here, there are no standards governing the exercise of the discretion granted by the ordinance, the scheme permits and encourages an arbitrary and discriminatory enforcement of the law. It furnishes a convenient tool for "harsh and discriminatory enforcement by local prosecuting officials, against particular groups deemed to merit their displeasure." . . . It results in a regime in which the poor and the unpopular are permitted to "stand on a public sidewalk . . . only at the whim of any police officer." . . .

A presumption that people who might walk or loaf or loiter or stroll or frequent houses where liquor is sold, or who are supported by their wives or who look suspicious to the police are to become future criminals is too precarious for a rule of law. The implicit presumption in these generalized vagrancy standards—that crime is being nipped in the bud—is too extravagant to deserve extended treatment. Of course, vagrancy statutes are useful to the police. Of course they are nets making easy the round-up of so-called undesirables. But the rule of law implies equality and justice in its application. Vagrancy laws of the Jacksonville type teach that the scales of justice are so tipped that even-handed administration of the law is not possible. . . .

EXERCISE 2.2. The anti-loitering ordinance in *Morales* failed because it was vague, while the anti-vagrancy statute in *Papachristou* failed because it penalized people for doing innocent and even desirable things, such as walking around outside and juggling. Is there an inescapable problem with laws that try to criminalize loitering or vagrancy? Is there a definable and harmful crime in hanging out? Form a small group of students and try to write a law that would make it a crime to do one of these things. Can you make it specific enough to avoid vagueness problems? Can you identify real harms?

The Principle of Harm

The Supreme Court has clearly stated in various ways that government cannot criminalize harmless behavior. Real crimes involve real harms. This principle sometimes emerges when the Court strikes down laws that violate the Eighth Amendment ban on cruel and unusual punishment. It also surfaces when the Court finds that government has

In *Lawrence v. Texas* (2003), the Supreme Court struck down anti-sodomy laws that made it a crime for adults of the same sex to engage in sex in their homes. The Court ruled that people have a right to sexual privacy and liberty. Supporters of the anti-sodomy laws prayed in front of the Court in June 2003. *Source: Evan Vucci/Reuters/ Landov*

unconstitutionally criminalized private consensual sexual behavior between adults that hurts no one. In *Lawrence v. Texas,* the Supreme Court struck down a Texas law making it a crime to commit **sodomy** in the state. The Court found that such a law violates the due process liberty interests that people have to define and pursue their own intimate relationships, even if those relationships involve two people of the same sex.

—·—

JOHN GEDDES LAWRENCE AND TYRON GARNER, PETITIONERS,
V.
TEXAS

Supreme Court of the United States
No. 02-102.
Argued March 26, 2003.
Decided June 26, 2003.

Justice KENNEDY delivered the opinion of the Court.

Liberty protects the person from unwarranted government intrusions into a dwelling or other private places. In our tradition the State is not omnipresent in the home. And there are other spheres of our lives and existence, outside the home, where the State should not be a dominant presence. Freedom extends beyond spatial bounds. Liberty presumes an autonomy of self that includes freedom of thought, belief, expression, and certain intimate conduct. The instant case involves liberty of the person both in its spatial and more transcendent dimensions.

I

The question before the Court is the validity of a Texas statute making it a crime for two persons of the same sex to engage in certain intimate sexual conduct.

In Houston, Texas, officers of the Harris County Police Department were dispatched to a private residence in response to a reported weapons disturbance. They entered an apartment where one of the petitioners, John Geddes Lawrence, resided. The right of the police to enter does not seem to have been questioned. The officers observed Lawrence and another man, Tyron Garner, engaging in a sexual act. The two petitioners were arrested, held in custody over night, and charged and convicted before a Justice of the Peace.

The complaints described their crime as "deviate sexual intercourse, namely anal sex, with a member of the same sex (man)." The applicable state law . . . provides: "A person commits an offense if he engages in deviate sexual intercourse with another individual of the same sex." . . .

The petitioners . . . challenged the statute as a violation of the Equal Protection Clause of the Fourteenth Amendment and of a like provision of the Texas Constitution. . . . The petitioners were adults at the time of the alleged offense. Their conduct was in private and consensual.

II

We conclude the case should be resolved by determining whether the petitioners were free as adults to engage in the private conduct in the exercise of their liberty under the Due Process Clause of the Fourteenth Amendment to the Constitution. For this inquiry we deem it necessary to reconsider the Court's holding in *Bowers [v. Harwick]*.

. . . The facts in *Bowers* had some similarities to the instant case. A police officer . . . observed Hardwick, in his own bedroom, engaging in intimate sexual conduct with another adult male. The conduct was in violation of a Georgia statute making it a criminal offense to engage in sodomy. One difference between the two cases is that the Georgia statute prohibited the conduct whether or not the participants were of the same sex, while the Texas statute, as we have seen, applies only to participants of the same sex. Hardwick was not prosecuted, but he brought an action in federal court to declare the state statute invalid. He alleged he was a practicing homosexual and that the criminal prohibition violated rights guaranteed to him by the Constitution. The Court, in an opinion by Justice White, sustained the Georgia law. . . . Four Justices dissented.

The Court began its substantive discussion in *Bowers* as follows: "The issue presented is whether the Federal Constitution confers a fundamental right upon homosexuals to engage in sodomy and hence invalidates the laws of the many States that still make such conduct illegal and have done so for a very long time." That statement, we now conclude, discloses the Court's own failure to appreciate the extent of the liberty at stake. To say that the issue in *Bowers* was simply the right to engage in certain sexual conduct demeans the claim the individual put forward, just as it would demean a married couple were it to be said marriage is simply about the right to have sexual intercourse. The laws involved in *Bowers* and here are, to be sure, statutes that purport to do no more than prohibit a particular sexual act. Their penalties and purposes, though, have more far-reaching consequences, touching upon the most private human conduct, sexual behavior, and in the most private of places, the home. The statutes do seek to control a personal relationship that, whether or not entitled to formal recognition in the law, is within the liberty of persons to choose without being punished as criminals.

. . . When sexuality finds overt expression in intimate conduct with another person, the conduct can be but one element in a personal bond that is more enduring. The liberty protected by the Constitution allows homosexual persons the right to make this choice.

Having misapprehended the claim of liberty there presented to it, and thus stating the claim to be whether there is a fundamental right to engage in consensual sodomy, the *Bowers* Court said: "Proscriptions against that conduct have ancient roots." . . .

It was not until the 1970's that any State singled out same-sex relations for criminal prosecution, and only nine States have done so. Post-*Bowers* even some of these States did not adhere to the policy of suppressing homosexual conduct. Over the course of the last decades, States with same-sex prohibitions have moved toward abolishing them.

In summary, the historical grounds relied upon in *Bowers* are . . . not without doubt and, at the very least, are overstated.

It must be acknowledged, of course, that the Court in *Bowers* was making the broader point that for centuries there have been powerful voices to condemn homosexual conduct as immoral. . . . Chief Justice Burger joined the opinion for the Court in *Bowers* and further explained his views as follows: "Decisions of individuals relating to homosexual conduct have been subject to state intervention throughout the history of Western civilization. Condemnation of those practices is firmly rooted in Judeao-Christian moral and ethical standards." As with Justice White's assumptions about history, scholarship casts some doubt on the sweeping nature of the statement by Chief Justice Burger as it pertains to private homosexual conduct between consenting adults. In all events we think that our laws and traditions in the past half century are of most relevance here. These references show an emerging awareness that liberty gives substantial protection to adult persons in deciding how to conduct their private lives in matters pertaining to sex. "[H]istory and tradition are the starting point but not in all cases the ending point of the substantive due process inquiry."

. . . *Bowers* was not correct when it was decided, and it is not correct today. It ought not to remain binding precedent. *Bowers v. Hardwick* should be and now is overruled.

The present case does not involve minors. It does not involve persons who might be injured or coerced or who are situated in relationships where **consent** might not easily be refused. It does not involve public conduct or prostitution. It does not involve whether the government must give formal recognition to any relationship that homosexual persons seek to enter. The case does involve two adults who, with full and mutual consent from each other, engaged in sexual practices common to a homosexual lifestyle. The petitioners are entitled to respect for their private lives. The State cannot demean their existence or control their destiny by making their private sexual conduct a crime. Their right to liberty under the Due Process Clause gives them the full right to engage in their conduct without intervention of the government. "It is a promise of the Constitution that there is a realm of personal liberty which the government may not enter." The Texas statute furthers no legitimate state interest which can justify its intrusion into the personal and private life of the individual. . . .

It is so ordered.

EXERCISE 2.3. Justice Antonin Scalia, who dissented in *Lawrence,* has repeatedly suggested that if the Due Process Clause protects the right of straight and gay people to engage in sodomy, then it must also protect the rights of people to be prostitutes, to practice incest, to engage in bestiality (sex with animals), or to practice polygamy (marriage to more than one person at a time). Is he right? Are these also harmless activities that people, by analogy, will also have the liberty to pursue?

The Structure of Criminal Laws

Assume that a criminal law sufficiently specifies truly harmful conduct and does not violate another part of the Constitution, such as the First Amendment. Such a valid law would require the state to demonstrate that the alleged criminal actor committed a voluntary bad act (the actus reus) caused by a culpable intent (the mens rea). Think of these as the physical and the mental elements of crime. A prosecutor—whether a district attorney, state's attorney, or U.S. attorney—would have to prove beyond a reasonable doubt both the physical conduct and the mental state that are the elements of the crime. "Beyond a reasonable doubt" is the standard of proof that the government must reach as to each and every element of a crime for a jury to **convict**.

A felony is a crime punishable by imprisonment for one year or longer (or by death). In most jurisdictions, burglary, **arson**, robbery, rape, **larceny**, murder, and manslaughter are felonies. A misdemeanor is a crime punishable by imprisonment for only up to one year or by a criminal fine. Simple assault and battery are typically considered misdemeanors.

Although crimes and punishments vary by jurisdiction, the following inventory rounds up the major offenses and defenses recognized by most jurisdictions as defined at common law.

Theft Offenses

The theft offenses are larceny, embezzlement, **false pretenses**, and robbery.

Larceny. The crime of larceny involves a trespassory taking and carrying away of the personal property of another with intent to steal. Pickpocketing is a good example of larceny.

Embezzlement. Embezzlement consists of a fraudulent conversion of the property of another by one who is already in lawful possession of it. Conversion means depriving the owner of a significant part of the property's usefulness for a significant period of time. For example, a banker who lawfully holds the money of bank depositors but then steals it by transferring it to his own account is guilty of embezzlement.

False Pretenses. False pretenses is a deliberate false representation that causes a victim to pass ownership of his property to the trickster. For example, a criminal who pretends to be a charitable solicitor for a hospital and then convinces an old lady to sign over a check for $10,000 and some stock certificates is guilty of false pretenses.

Robbery. A robbery is a larceny in which the taking of property from someone is accomplished by using force or putting the owner in fear. For example, if you are stopped on the street by a tall man wearing a trench coat who says, "Give me your wallet or I'll kill you," and you give the man your wallet, you have been robbed. The man has committed a larceny (the taking and carrying away of someone else's property with the intent to permanently deprive him of it) and has done so by taking the property from you and putting you in fear of what might happen if you resist.

Offenses against Property

Offenses against the habitation are burglary and arson.

Burglary. Burglary is the breaking and entering of the dwelling place of another person at night with intent to commit a felony inside. Each element must be satisfied for burglary to exist. For example, under common law if the owner of a house leaves his window open, no burglary can take place because the "breaking" requirement is not met. Under modern statutory law, the act would certainly be burglary.

Arson. Arson is the burning of the dwelling of another person. But the burning cannot be an accident or the result of mere negligence; it must be intentional or reckless. The dwelling does not have to be substantially or totally damaged for arson to apply.

EXERCISE 2.4. Sally, known to have set small fires in her backyard and at school, sets her mattress on fire one afternoon when she is home alone. The fire spreads quickly and before the fire engines arrive, the house is severely damaged. Assuming she is tried as an adult, can Sally be found guilty of arson?

Answer: Yes, because some of the property is that of her parents (assuming she does not live alone). If she lived by herself and only burned her own belongings, she might not be guilty.

Offenses against the Person

Other crimes against the person are battery, assault, **homicide** (murder and manslaughter), **kidnapping**, and rape.

Battery. Battery exists when someone either causes bodily injury or touches another in an offensive manner. For example, imagine you are standing in a parking spot in a crowded lot, trying to save the parking space for your friend. An aggressive driver tells you that you cannot save the spot and proceeds to drive very slowly into it, repeatedly hitting you because you will not get out of the way. Battery has occurred.

Assault. Assault occurs when someone attempts to commit a battery and fails or someone places another person in fear of imminent (or immediate) injury.

Homicide. There are different kinds of homicide, which means generally any unlawful taking of a human life. The two main kinds are murder and manslaughter.

In many jurisdictions, murder is divided into first-degree and second-degree murder. Generally, first-degree murder consists of killings committed "with premeditation and deliberation," which means some kind of planning or consideration ahead of time, and those killings committed during the course of felonies. Second-degree murder is a killing without the elements of premeditation and deliberation.

EXERCISE 2.5. Jenny found out that her boyfriend, Arnie, was cheating on her with a classmate, Francine. Devastated by his betrayal, Jenny plotted her revenge. After school, Jenny stole her father's gun and went to Arnie's house to kill him. She broke into the house waiting for him to return. As she waited, she started having second thoughts about her plan. Eventually, she decided to leave. As she was walking down the driveway, she saw Francine. Francine was wearing Arnie's varsity jacket and admiring a locket with Arnie's picture in it. Without thinking, Jenny shot Francine. Of what type of murder is Jenny likely guilty?

Answer: Probably second-degree murder. Although Jenny had the premeditated and deliberate intent to kill Arnie, she did not have the same intent toward Francine. Of course, she will likely be punished very harshly for her crime.

There are two kinds of manslaughter: voluntary and involuntary. **Voluntary manslaughter** in most cases involves an intentional killing committed in the heat of passion, when a person is enraged or emotionally agitated. **Involuntary manslaughter** usually consists of an unintentional killing committed recklessly, grossly negligently, or during the commission of a misdemeanor.

EXERCISE 2.6. Chen and his fiancé, Karen, get into a huge fight while on a road trip. Karen slaps Chen and calls him terrible names. Enraged and shouting, Chen swerves to a screeching halt on the shoulder of the road, pulls out a knife he stores in the glove compartment, and repeatedly stabs Karen. A few days later, Karen dies from the stab wounds. Of what type of homicide is Chen probably guilty?

Answer: Chen will most likely be found guilty of voluntary manslaughter because he committed the crime in the heat of passion. If Chen had waited until they arrived at their destination and then stabbed Karen, he would probably be found guilty of murder because of his premeditation of the crime.

Some states have created additional forms of homicide, such as vehicular homicide, which is an unintentional death caused by the driver of a car.

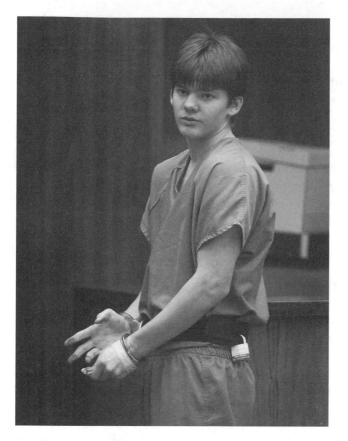

James Watson looks to his mother and brother after being sentenced for manslaughter and fingerprinted in March 2003. A court found him delinquent in the 2002 death of Shane Farrell in New Smyrna Beach, Florida. Watson received nine to twelve months in a high-risk juvenile facility.
Source: Kelly Jordan/AP Wide World Photos

Kidnapping. Kidnapping is usually defined as the unlawful confinement of another person, along with either a moving of the victim or an effort to hide him.

Rape. Rape is generally defined as unlawful, forcible sexual intercourse with a female without her consent.

EXERCISE 2.7. Brad, who is twenty-two years old, meets Emily and her friends in a bar. Emily is nineteen. Brad asks Emily out, and they begin dating and having sex. After two months, Emily is tired of Brad's bad jokes and constant put-downs. At her apartment, she tells Brad that she is breaking up with him. He says she cannot do that, but she tells him that it is over and he should leave. Brad forces himself upon Emily and says he wants to have sex one last time. She yells no and tries to fight him off, but he overpowers her. Before leaving, he says, "All right, let's be friends, OK?" Is Brad guilty of rape?

Answer: Yes. His prior relationship with Emily does not give him any right to have sex with her. She denied consent, and he used force.

Inchoate Crimes

Inchoate crimes (crimes that are partial or unfinished) include, for example, **solicitation**, attempt, and conspiracy.

Solicitation. Solicitation occurs when one person asks or encourages another to perform a criminal act, regardless of whether the other person ultimately agrees.

EXERCISE 2.8. Juan and Phillip are two high school students eating lunch in the school cafeteria. They are chatting but stop talking when Bronco, known around the school as a bully, begins taunting a student at the next table about her clothes. Phillip says to Juan, "That guy is a jerk and should really be given a taste of his own medicine." A few days later, Juan slashes Bronco's tires. Is Phillip guilty of solicitation?

Answer: No, because Phillip did not intend for Juan to slash Bronco's tires. A fine line exists between casual conversation and true solicitation to commit a crime. If Phillip had said to Juan, "You should show that guy what he deserves and I'll pay you to slash his tires in the parking lot," then there would be a strong case for solicitation.

Attempt. In general, all states punish certain unsuccessful attempts to commit crimes. Generally, the defendant must have had a mental state that would have been enough to satisfy the mens rea requirement—purposely or knowingly committing the crime. Also, the defendant must have conducted some overt act in furtherance of his plan. For example, if an angry movie star tries to punch a paparazzo but misses in throwing the punch, he has attempted to assault him. He had the intent to hit him, and his swing constitutes the act necessary for the attempted assault or attempted battery charge.

Conspiracy. Conspiracy is an agreement between two or more people to do either an unlawful act or a lawful act by unlawful means and engage in at least one overt act to make it happen. An example is when two people agree to rob a bank, and one perpetrator waits in the getaway car while the other goes in to hold up the bank.

Defenses

A successful defense negates some element or elements of a crime. An alibi defense says in effect, "I didn't commit the crime." Affirmative defenses say, in effect, "I committed the crime but [I was insane at the time], [it was self-defense], [I had no choice]. . . ."

Self-Defense. People have the right to defend themselves against the use of unlawful force. But five requirements must be met for self-defense to be found an effective defense. First, the defendant must have been resisting present or imminent unlawful force. Second, the defendant must have used only the amount of force that was reasonably necessary to defend himself. In other words, the defendant cannot use excessive force. Third, the defendant may not have used deadly force unless the danger the defendant faced was also deadly force. Fourth, the defendant must not have been the original aggressor. Fifth, in some states, the defendant must not have been in a position where he could have safely retreated unless the attack took place in the defendant's dwelling or the defendant used only nondeadly force.

Defense of Others. Generally, a person may use force to defend another person in similar circumstances that would justify using force to defend himself. For this defense to work, the defendant must reasonably believe that the other person is in imminent danger of unlawful bodily harm. The defendant may use only the degree of force necessary to prevent the harm. Finally, the defendant must believe that the person he is helping would have the right to use in his own defense the force that the defendant proposes to use in assistance.

Defense of Property. A person has the right to use limited force to defend his property. For this defense to be valid, the force must be reasonable under the circumstances.

EXERCISE 2.9. One afternoon, Harry decides to steal his classmate Gerald's brand-new Knicks lined jacket. He hatches a plan to break into Gerald's locker at school and take the jacket. Gerald happens to be walking down the hall when he sees Harry grabbing the jacket. Gerald yells, "What are you doing, man? Drop my jacket!" Harry slams the locker and runs down the hall with the jacket. Gerald pulls a small pistol out of his pants and shoots Harry in the back. Harry dies. Can Gerald successfully defend against a murder charge by claiming he was defending his property?

Answer: No. Deadly force is never justified in the defense of an item of property, especially not something such as a jacket. Deadly force can be used only to repel deadly force or, in some states, in defense of one's home.

Duress. A defendant can claim duress if he commits a criminal act because of the threat of the use of force against him. The force in this case influences the defendant's mind, not his body. For example, John tells Lee that if he does not shoot whomever John instructs him to shoot, he will kill him. In a subsequent murder prosecution, Lee can raise the defense of duress. For him, he would argue, it was kill or be killed. In duress, the harm the defendant seeks to avoid does not have to be serious bodily harm. It can be nonserious bodily harm or even property damage.

Necessity. Generally, a defendant can raise the defense of **necessity** when he has been forced to commit a criminal act—not by another person but by nonhuman events. The theory behind this defense is that the defendant made the best choice under the circumstances by choosing the lesser of two evils. Four requirements must be met for a necessity defense to be successful. First, the harm sought to be avoided must be greater than the harm committed. Second, no other alternative must have been available. Third, the danger must have been imminent or immediate. Fourth, the situation was not caused by the defendant.

Prevention of Crime. Law enforcement officials may raise this defense, which allows them to violate the law if they do so reasonably. For example, a police officer may speed through a stoplight to chase after a fleeing convict if it is reasonable under the circumstances.

Entrapment. **Entrapment** may be asserted as a defense when a law enforcement official or someone cooperating with him has induced the defendant to commit the crime. Most courts use the "predisposition" test to determine whether entrapment occurred. The "predisposition" test requires the defendant to show that the government initiated the crime and induced the defendant to participate and that the defendant is an innocent person not predisposed to the crime. For example, an undercover narcotics officer at Middlebrook High School offers to sell heroin to Frank after school one day. Frank says no but the officer keeps hounding him until he agrees. If the officer originated the whole deal and Frank has never before used or bought heroin, then Frank would have a good chance of getting his prosecution thrown out on the grounds that he was never predisposed to use heroin and was entrapped by the officer.

Robert Tulloch, 17, is escorted into an Indiana court in 2001 before his extradition to New Hampshire, where he was accused of the murders of Dartmouth College professors Half and Susanne Zantop. Tulloch initially pleaded not guilty by reason of insanity—in a court motion, his public defenders stated their concerns that he suffered from "serious mental illness." Tulloch later dropped that defense and pleaded guilty to murder conspiracy.
Source: Chuck Robinson/AP Wide World Photos

Intoxication. If you decide to get drunk or high, your voluntary intoxication does not generally excuse any criminal conduct that follows. Intoxication can become a good defense only if it is involuntarily achieved.

EXERCISE 2.10. To celebrate the end of the school year, Michael hosts a big party at his parents' house. When Brandi arrives, Michael hugs her and offers her some punch. Assuming there was probably alcohol in the punch, Brandi declines the offer because of her religious beliefs. Michael insists that he made the punch himself and put no alcohol in it. Brandi then accepts a glass. Unfortunately, unbeknownst to both Michael and Brandi, Michael's football buddy Derrell has spiked the punch with a strong tequila. Brandi does not taste the tequila in the punch and quickly becomes drunk and violent. She picks up a lamp and throws it at Michael. Michael is hit in the head and ends up dying because of the blow. When Brandi is charged with murder, can she successfully assert a defense of involuntary intoxication?

Answer: Yes, Brandi can assert a defense of involuntary intoxication, which is a valid defense. Because she did not know the punch was spiked and because the crime did not rise to the level of recklessness, she would probably be found not guilty by reason of involuntary intoxication.

Insanity. If a defendant can prove he was suffering from a mental disease or illness such that he could not tell the difference between right and wrong at the time he committed a criminal act, he may be entitled to a verdict of "not guilty by reason of insanity." In almost all states, a defendant using the **insanity defense** who is exonerated cannot just walk out of the courtroom. Such a defendant likely will be committed to a mental institution.

Diminished Capacity. The **diminished capacity defense** can be used when a defendant who is not insane argues that he suffers a mental impairment that makes him unable to formulate the required intent for a particular offense. Judges most often allow this defense in homicide cases, usually when the defendant is charged with first-degree murder but seeks to reduce the charge to second-degree murder.

These are the standard criminal offenses and defenses. There are hundreds of crimes in the states and localities, and Congress has created hundreds more at the federal level, such as mail fraud, wire fraud, assaulting a federal officer, aiding terrorism, and obstructing access to abortion clinics. Because of the complexity of the criminal law, it really does take lawyers to negotiate the twists and turns of the legal system.

3 FOURTH AMENDMENT: PROTECTION FROM UNREASONABLE SEARCHES AND SEIZURES

Imagine you are in your bedroom making an entry in your journal about how much you hate your older sister, who has turned cold and snobby to you. On those tear-stained pages are words of anger and frustration that you would never say, threats that you would never actually make or carry out. But it sure feels good to get out your feelings. As you lie in bed, police break down your front door, come into your bedroom, and grab the journal. They read through it. On several pages the statement "I am going to kill her!" is written in the margins. The police find these passages and arrest you. You are charged with the crime of felony threats.

On your way to the police station, you ask the police officer why he came into your home, into your bedroom? How did he know that you had written anything? The police officer answers that he did not know but finds his job easier if he goes into everyone's house and looks for potential crimes, instead of having to wait to investigate after they happen. This way the police can protect against future crime, threats, or even terrorist attacks. The police officer says that reading people's journals, diaries, and e-mails is especially helpful to know what people are thinking. In his view, he prevented you from following through on the threat you wrote about in the journal. Thus, he feels justified in coming into your home.

A person's desire to be left alone as pitted against the police's desire for information about a potential crime reflects the tension in the Fourth Amendment. In this case, we will see, the officer crossed over to the wrong side of the law.

The Right to Be Left Alone

The right of the people to be secure in their persons, houses, papers and effects, against unreasonable searches and seizures, shall not be violated, and no Warrants shall issue but upon probable cause, supported by Oath or affirmation, and particularly describing the place to be searched, and the persons or things to be seized. —U.S. Constitution, Amendment IV

The Fourth Amendment protects the right of all Americans to be left alone from unreasonable government **intrusion**. It is the reason that police cannot simply walk into your house, read your mail, or stop and search you on the street. It is the reason that they cannot read your journal or diary without legal justification. The amendment safeguards your privacy interests by preventing law enforcement from interfering with personal freedoms or private property without just cause. Privacy interests might attach to your conversations, what you choose to read or write, or what you keep hidden in your closet. Personal freedoms might be what you choose to do in the privacy of your home or whom you choose to hang out with or how you choose to express your opinions. Private property is the stuff in your home, apartment, car, or backpack. As U.S. Supreme Court justice Louis Brandeis wrote in *Olmstead v. United States:*

> The makers of our Constitution . . . sought to protect Americans in their beliefs, their thoughts, their emotions and their sensations. They **conferred**, as against the Government, the right to be let alone—the most comprehensive of rights and the right most valued by civilized men. To protect that right, every unjustifiable intrusion by the Government upon the privacy of the individual, whatever the means employed, must be deemed a violation of the Fourth Amendment.[1]

The Fourth Amendment has two parts. First, it protects people from unreasonable searches and seizures of their persons, houses, papers, effects. Second, it requires search or arrest warrants be supported by particular facts and enough evidence to constitute probable cause.

What is meant by "unreasonable searches and seizures"? The principle underlying the Fourth Amendment is that all people should be able to live their lives free from unreasonable interference, **surveillance**, or oversight. Friction arises when police and other law enforcement personnel need to investigate crimes and prevent unlawful behavior in society. So, on one hand, people want to have the liberty to do what they want, and, on the other hand, they want to live in a safe society without criminal behavior. To resolve this tension, courts have interpreted the Fourth Amendment to protect you against some searches and seizures but not others. The test is one of reasonableness. Reasonableness often requires the police to have a search warrant, though not always. There are times when the character of the situation renders a search reasonable even without a warrant.

The Exclusionary Rule

Suppose you are prosecuted for the crime of threats for the comments in your journal. You now know that the Fourth Amendment gives you the right to be left alone in ordinary circumstances. Given the lack of a warrant and unacceptable invasion of your room, you understand that the government has violated your rights. If the journal is the sole piece of evidence against you, how can the government be punished for violating your Fourth Amendment rights? How about if the tainted piece of evidence is excluded in your trial? What if the prosecutor cannot use the journal as evidence against you? Is that an effective strategy to deter police misconduct?

Or consider another example of the interaction of the Fourth Amendment and the expectation of privacy.

You are hanging out in front of your house with your sister. You are sitting on the steps not doing anything wrong. A school friend stops by and asks if you want to buy a new DVD of a summer movie blockbuster. He hands you two brand-new DVDs. As you are admiring them, police cars drive into the block. Lights flashing, they stop outside your house. The police officers see you with the DVDs. You run inside, close the door behind you, and hide the DVDs in your sweatshirt. Meanwhile, your friend runs away. The police yell at you to open up, but you do not. The police then break down the front door and walk into your house. They find you hiding behind your closed bedroom door. The police search you, by going through all of the pockets in your clothes. They find one DVD because it is sticking out of a corner of your sweatshirt pocket. They search the room. They ask if they can look in your closet and drawers. They find the second DVD in your sock drawer. They take the DVDs into their possession. They arrest you and bring you down to the station. Later, you find out that both DVDs were stolen property. The police had been following your friend from the store where the movies had been stolen. You are charged with receiving stolen property. Your friend is never arrested.

How does the Fourth Amendment work in this case? The issue to consider is your privacy rights, not whether you did anything wrong or criminal. The relevant question is whether the police violated your constitutional rights, not whether you violated the law.

You were searched. Your house was searched. Property in your possession—the DVDs—were seized. You were seized. You might think that the police stopping you, breaking down your door, searching you and your room was unreasonable. However, the police were following up on a stolen DVD. They saw that you had the DVD. In fact, you were found to be in possession of two stolen DVDs. They entered your house because they had reason to believe you had stolen property. The only property they seized from you was the DVDs. The government, thus, would argue that the search and **seizure** were reasonable and represented good police work.

When the actions of the police come into conflict with a person's liberty, we use the Fourth Amendment to resolve the issue. Usually, these conflicts arise in the course of a criminal case. As a result, government violation of the Fourth Amendment in the form of an unreasonable search or seizure is corrected in the criminal context.

YOUR THOUGHTS

How should Fourth Amendment constitutional rights be enforced? If rights are violated, what options for recourse are available? What should happen?

- Can the police officer be fired?
- Should the evidence be suppressed?
- Can the case be dismissed?
- Can someone be sued?

Generally, if the police acted unreasonably in searching or seizing you, the evidence they get cannot be used in trial. The evidence is **suppressed** and excluded from trial. "Suppressed" means that the unconstitutionally obtained evidence is kept out of the case. This is called the **exclusionary rule**. It is "exclusionary" because evidence obtained in violation of the Fourth Amendment is excluded from trial. However, if the police acted reasonably, the evidence can be used.

Thus, in reference to the threats in your journal, if the government cannot use the journal against you (because it has been excluded), you likely will not be prosecuted. It would be hard to convict you of making threats without the only written proof of them.

In the DVD case, if a court determines that your Fourth Amendment rights were violated, the evidence found (the DVDs) would be suppressed and excluded at trial. For example, if a court found that the police unconstitutionally broke down your front door, went into your room, and searched you or your sock drawer, then a Fourth Amendment violation occurred and the DVDs could not be used in trial. Again, if the government could not use the stolen DVDs in its case, you likely would not be prosecuted for having received the stolen DVDs. After all, if the government cannot prove that there was stolen property, it could not prove you ever had the property. Thus, because the police violated your rights, the case would be dismissed. That is, when evidence is suppressed, the court has found a constitutional violation.

At the end of the second Fourth Amendment chapter, we will come back to this problem and analyze it. At that time, we will also evaluate the costs and benefits of the exclusionary rule. It is enough for now to understand that the consequence of a Fourth Amendment violation (in a criminal case) is that the evidence obtained will be excluded at trial.

Reasonable Expectation of Privacy

The Fourth Amendment protects your privacy interests against the intrusion of the government. But how much privacy should be expected from the government? When should the government be allowed to read your journal or listen into your phone conversations? What is a reasonable expectation of privacy?

Whether you have a reasonable expectation of privacy in an area such as your home or bedroom or in your belongings kept in your locker depends on a two-part analysis. First, do you actually expect privacy? That is, do you have a sense that what you are doing or what you own is rightly kept from other people? Second, is this expectation of privacy a reasonable one? That is, does society agree with you and validate your expectation of privacy in certain places or things? The Fourth Amendment only protects against searches that violate our reasonable expectations of privacy.

Has a reasonable expectation of privacy been interfered with and a search occurred

- if a police officer goes into your house and looks in your bedroom closet?
- if he just looks through the open window into your bedroom?
- if he uses binoculars to look through an open window?
- if he searches in your pocket?
- if he listens into your cell phone conversations?
- if he looks through your trash on the sidewalk?

For example, you talk to your friends and family all the time. You use your home phone, cell phone, e-mail, and occasionally letters. Should what you say be considered private? Don't you assume that what you say on the phone is private and is not being heard by the police? Isn't that a reasonable assumption? If the police suspected you of selling stolen DVDs or threatening people, would your reasonable expectation of privacy be any different?

Where does the idea of a "reasonable expectation of privacy" come from? The Supreme Court first addressed the issue in *Katz v. United States*.[2] The Court was asked to decide whether a man had a reasonable expectation of privacy in the conversation he had in a public phone booth.

Charles Katz was involved in an illegal gambling operation. The Federal Bureau of Investigation (FBI) had been watching him, knowing that he regularly conducted business out of a particular public phone booth. The phone booth was big, old-fashioned, and made of glass. A caller was required to pay money to engage the telephone. The FBI used an electronic device to bug the phone booth, allowing the government to listen to and record the phone calls Katz made of an illegal nature. The FBI heard information that confirmed its suspicions that he was involved in illegal gambling. Katz was arrested, and at his trial he challenged the use of the recorded phone calls because he claimed that they violated his Fourth Amendment rights. Katz claimed that he had an expectation of

Many young people have their cell phones with them twenty-four hours a day. In *Katz v. United States* (1967), the Supreme Court ruled that people have a reasonable expectation of privacy in their telephone conversations, meaning that police ordinarily need search warrants to tap phones. Should people such as this woman—speaking on a cell phone in public—have the same expectation of privacy? *Source: Daniel Acker/Bloomberg News/ Landov*

You arc standing in a public phone booth talking on the phone with the door open. Do you have a reason to expect that your phone call will be private so that the police cannot listen in from a nearby table? Does it matter how loud you are talking? Or how many people are around? Or whether the police are using an electronic device to pick up your voice?

privacy to talk on the phone without the government listening in—whether or not his phone call was to his bookie or his grandmother.

Do you agree with Katz's argument?

The Supreme Court agreed with Katz, holding that he had a reasonable expectation of privacy in his private phone calls, and thus his Fourth Amendment rights had been violated. In a famous opinion, Justice John Harlan set out the current test for an expectation of privacy under the Fourth Amendment. It has two parts: (1) the person must think that his actions deserve a level of privacy free from police interferences, and (2) society must agree that this type of action deserves privacy protection.

———

CHARLES KATZ, PETITIONER
V.
UNITED STATES

Supreme Court of the United States
No. 35.
Argued October 17, 1967.
Decided December 18. 1967.

Mr. Justice HARLAN, concurring.

'[T]he Fourth Amendment protects people, not places.' . . . My understanding of the rule that has emerged from prior decisions is that there is a twofold requirement, first that a person have exhibited an actual (subjective) expectation of privacy and, second, that the expectation be one that society is prepared to recognize as 'reasonable.' Thus a man's home is, for most purposes, a place where he expects privacy, but objects, activities, or statements that he exposes to the 'plain view' of outsiders are not 'protected' because no intention to keep them to himself has been exhibited. On the other hand, conversations in the open would not be protected against being overheard, for the expectation of privacy under the circumstances would be unreasonable. . . .

The critical fact in this case is that '(o)ne who occupies it, (a telephone booth) shuts the door behind him, and pays the toll that permits him to place a call is surely entitled to assume' that his conversation is not being intercepted. . . . The point is not that the booth is 'accessible to the public' at other times, . . . but that it is a temporarily private place whose momentary occupants' expectations of freedom from intrusion are recognized as reasonable. . . .

The facts in *Katz* involved a conversation in a phone booth, but the test can be applied to any factual situation. To determine whether the Fourth Amendment has been violated, you will first have to decide whether the reasonable expectation of privacy has been violated.

REASONABLE EXPECTATION OF PRIVACY TEST

1. Do you expect your activities to remain private?
2. Does society agree that you deserve privacy in this activity?

If the answer to both questions is yes, then a reasonable expectation of privacy exists, and the Fourth Amendment protects you.

In evaluating a reasonable expectation of privacy, courts look at

- the kind of property at issue (home, car, purse, pocket, and so on).
- what a person has done to make the area or item private.
- the way in which the government interfered with property.
- social attitudes and values respecting such expectations.

POINTS TO PONDER

- In *Katz,* the Court distinguishes a home where one would expect conversations to be private from an open field where one would not expect such privacy. What is different about having a conversation in a home as opposed to a field? If you were having a conversation at home, why would you expect your conversation to be private? What is it about a home that supports your argument? What is different about a field?
- What if a person is yelling in his home and whispering in an open field? Does the Court's reasoning still make sense?
- Do you agree with the Supreme Court that the enclosed phone booth in *Katz* is more like a home than an open field? The phone booth at issue was partially glass, and the door might not have stopped someone from getting close and listening in. Does it matter what kind of phone booth is at issue? Would that change the expectation of privacy? What about a cell phone? What about a cell phone conversation in a phone booth?
- What are the benefits of privacy? Discuss the issues of security, individuality, autonomy, intimacy, freedom of belief, freedom of economic interests, and freedom of thought.[3]
- What are the costs of privacy? Discuss the costs to law enforcement of not being able to observe all of its citizens' actions. What were the costs to the police in *Katz*?
- How does the concept of reasonable expectation of privacy change over time? The technology exists to listen into most conversations (through wiretaps, cell phone intercepts, e-mail). People know this, but do they still have the expectation of privacy? Is this a reasonable expectation?

- According to the U.S. Census Bureau, 139 million Americans in 2003 owned cell phones. If Katz had been using a cell phone, how would that change the analysis of reasonable expectation of privacy? Do cell phones seem more or less private than enclosed public phone booths?
- Think about the second part of the test. How would you determine if other people would think your expectation of privacy is reasonable? For example, how do you tell if other people will respect your right to private conversations in a house? Does that depend on your family or your culture? Does it depend on the kind of house?
- How is a reasonable expectation of privacy determined? Should it be left to courts? Should it be written into laws?

Fourth Amendment Search

If you have flown on a plane, gone to a ballgame, or entered a secure building, you understand the basic concept of a search. Your body, clothing, and bags are examined. The security personnel go through your pockets, frisk you, or see if you have any weapons or contraband. Searches can also be of your papers (such as your journal), of your conversations, or of your house. The Fourth Amendment covers "people, houses, papers, and effects."

Beyond its explicit language, the Fourth Amendment has been broadened to cover areas closely associated with persons, houses, papers, and things. Generally courts have decided that the Fourth Amendment protects against searches of people (including clothes and body), houses (including apartments, offices, and mobile homes), papers (including letters, diaries, business documents), and effects (almost anything else people own).

But the amendment does not protect against all such searches. As the *Katz* case shows, the Fourth Amendment protects people only when they have a reasonable expectation of privacy in the area or item searched. Thus, the first question that courts ask in any Fourth Amendment case is whether the person had a reasonable expectation of privacy in the area or item searched. If he did, a Fourth Amendment violation might have occurred. If he did not, no Fourth Amendment violation is possible because no constitutionally protected area of privacy was interfered with. For example, if police walk by a car and look in its windows to see a machine gun sitting on the front seat, this is no

---

YOUR THOUGHTS

Beyond its language, should the Fourth Amendment protect

- people: body, clothes, purse, pockets, luggage, DNA?
- houses: apartment, business office, mobile home, hotel room, tool shed?
- papers: letters, diaries, school papers, business records, e-mail?
- effects: car, trash, money, clothes, CD collection?

---

search because we do not have a reasonable expectation of privacy in the things we leave open to public view in our cars. However, whether or not there has been a violation is not always clear.

Constitutional Garbage

A person's trash reveals much about him. Think about everything you throw away in a week. Think about what could be sitting in your family's garbage can right now—tax returns, bills, magazines, love letters, medical prescriptions, photographs, report cards. What is revealed if your classmates get to root through your trash to find out information about you? What if the government does?

In 1988 the Supreme Court was asked to evaluate how much of an invasion of privacy there was when police went through Billy Greenwood's garbage.

In *Greenwood v. California,* police suspected Billy Greenwood of selling drugs from his home.[4] As most people do, Greenwood put his trash out to be collected and taken to the dump by city trash haulers. On a regular basis Greenwood placed his trash right outside his door in dark trash bags. In an effort to look for clues, police investigators convinced

In 1995 FBI agents bagged evidence from trashcans at the home of Terry Nichols, who was suspected of involvement in the bombing of the Alfred P. Murrah Federal Building in Oklahoma City that year. In *California v. Greenwood* (1988), the Supreme Court found that citizens leaving trash at the curb retain no reasonable expectation of privacy regarding that garbage.
Source: Orlin Wagner/AP Wide World Photos

the trash haulers to give them Greenwood's trash. The police searched the trash and found evidence that supported their suspicion that Greenwood was involved in illegal activities. The information allowed the police to obtain a search warrant. Greenwood's house was searched, and Greenwood was arrested. At trial, Greenwood challenged the search of the trash bags he left outside his house. He claimed that the search violated the reasonable expectation of privacy he had in the garbage.

The Supreme Court thus had to decide whether people have a reasonable expectation of privacy in trash bags left outside their house to be picked up by trash collectors. The Supreme Court eventually decided that no reasonable expectation of privacy exists in trash. However, several justices disagreed with the result.

CALIFORNIA, PETITIONER
V.
BILLY GREENWOOD AND DYANNE VAN HOUTEN

Supreme Court of the United States
No. 86-684.
Argued January 11, 1988.
Decided May 16, 1988.

Justice WHITE delivered the opinion of the Court.

The issue here is whether the Fourth Amendment prohibits the warrantless search and seizure of garbage left for collection outside the curtilage of a home [the area right outside a home]. We conclude, in accordance with the vast majority of lower courts that have addressed the issue, that it does not. . . .

II

The warrantless search and seizure of the garbage bags left at the curb outside the Greenwood house would violate the Fourth Amendment only if respondents [Greenwood and friend] manifested a subjective expectation of privacy in their garbage that society accepts as objectively reasonable. . . . Respondents do not disagree with this standard.

They assert, however, that they had, and exhibited, an expectation of privacy with respect to the trash that was searched by the police: The trash, which was placed on the street for collection at a fixed time, was contained in opaque [non-see-through] plastic bags, which the garbage collector was expected to pick up, mingle with the trash of others, and deposit at the garbage dump. The trash was only temporarily on the street, and there was little likelihood that it would be inspected by anyone.

It may well be that respondents did not expect that the contents of their garbage bags would become known to the police or other members of the public. An expectation of privacy does not give rise to Fourth Amendment protection, however, unless society is prepared to accept that expectation as objectively reasonable.

Here, we conclude that respondents exposed their garbage to the public sufficiently to defeat their claim to Fourth Amendment protection. It is common knowledge that plastic garbage bags left on or at the side of a public street are readily accessible to animals, children, scavengers, snoops, and other members of the public. . . . Moreover, respondents placed their refuse at the curb for the express purpose of conveying it to a third party, the trash collector, who might himself have sorted through respondents' trash or permitted others, such as the police, to do so. Accordingly, having deposited their garbage "in an area particularly suited for public inspection and, in a manner of speaking, public consumption, for the express purpose of having strangers take it," . . . respondents could have had no reasonable expectation of privacy in the **inculpatory** items that they discarded. . . .

Justice BRENNAN, with whom Justice MARSHALL joins, dissenting.

Every week for two months, and at least once more a month later, the Laguna Beach police clawed through the trash that respondent Greenwood left in opaque, sealed bags on the curb outside his home. . . . Complete strangers minutely scrutinized their bounty, undoubtedly dredging up intimate details of Greenwood's private life and habits. . . .

Scrutiny of another's trash is contrary to commonly accepted notions of civilized behavior. I suspect, therefore, that members of our society will be shocked to learn that the Court, the ultimate guarantor of liberty, deems unreasonable our expectation that the aspects of our private lives that are concealed safely in a trash bag will not become public.

I

"A container which can support a reasonable expectation of privacy may not be searched, even on probable cause, without a warrant." . . . Thus, as the Court observes, if Greenwood had a reasonable expectation that the contents of the bags that he placed on the curb would remain private, the warrantless search of those bags violated the Fourth Amendment.

The Framers of the Fourth Amendment understood that "unreasonable searches" of "paper[s] and effects"—no less than "unreasonable searches" of "person[s] and houses"—infringe privacy. . . . Our precedent . . . leaves no room to doubt that had respondents been carrying their personal effects in opaque, sealed plastic bags—identical to the ones they placed on the curb—their privacy would have been protected from warrantless police intrusion. . . .

II

Respondents deserve no less protection just because Greenwood used the bags to discard rather than to transport his personal effects. Their contents are not inherently any less private, and Greenwood's decision to discard them, at least in the manner in which he did, does not diminish his expectation of privacy.

A trash bag . . . "is a common repository for one's personal effects" and, even more than many of them, is "therefore . . . inevitably associated with the expectation of privacy. . . . "[A]lmost every human activity ultimately manifests itself in waste products. . . ." A single bag of trash testifies eloquently to the eating, reading, and recreational habits of the person who produced it. A search of trash, like a search of the bedroom, can relate intimate details about sexual practices, health, and personal hygiene. Like rifling through desk drawers or intercepting phone calls, rummaging through trash can divulge the target's financial and professional status, political affiliations and inclinations, private thoughts, personal relationships, and romantic interests. It cannot be doubted that a sealed trash bag harbors telling evidence of the "intimate activity associated with the 'sanctity of a man's home and the privacies of life,' " which the Fourth Amendment is designed to protect. . . .

Beyond a generalized expectation of privacy, many **municipalities**, whether for reasons of privacy, sanitation, or both, reinforce confidence in the integrity of sealed trash containers by "prohibit[ing] anyone, except authorized employees of the Town . . . to rummage into, pick up, collect, move or otherwise interfere with articles or materials placed on . . . any public street for collection." . . . In fact, the California Constitution, as interpreted by the State's highest court, guarantees a right of privacy in trash vis-à-vis government officials. . . .

That is not to deny that isolated intrusions into opaque, sealed trash containers occur. When, acting on their own, "animals, children, scavengers, snoops, [or] other members of the public," . . . *actually* rummage through a bag of trash and expose its contents to plain view, "police cannot reasonably be expected to avert their eyes from evidence of criminal activity that could have been observed by any member of the public. . . ."

Had Greenwood flaunted his intimate activity by strewing his trash all over the curb for all to see, or had some nongovernmental intruder invaded his privacy and done the same, I could accept the Court's conclusion that an expectation of privacy would have been unreasonable. Similarly, had police searching the city dump run across incriminating evidence that, despite commingling with the trash of others, still retained its identity as Greenwood's, we would have a different case. But all that Greenwood "exposed . . . to the public," were the exteriors of several opaque, sealed containers. . . .

The mere *possibility* that unwelcome meddlers *might* open and rummage through the containers does not negate the expectation of privacy in their contents any more than the possibility of a burglary negates an expectation of privacy in the home; or the possibility of a private intrusion negates an expectation of privacy in an unopened package; or the possibility that an operator will listen in on a telephone conversation negates an expectation of privacy in the words spoken on the telephone. "What a person . . . seeks to preserve as private, *even in an area accessible to the public,* may be constitutionally protected." . . .

III

In holding that the warrantless search of Greenwood's trash was consistent with the Fourth Amendment, the Court paints a grim picture of our society. It depicts a society in which local authorities may command their citizens to dispose of their personal effects in the manner least protective of the "sanctity of [the] home and the privacies of life," . . . and then monitor them arbitrarily and without judicial oversight—a society that is not prepared to recognize as reasonable an individual's expectation of privacy in the most private of personal effects sealed in an opaque container and disposed of in a manner designed to commingle it imminently and inextricably with the trash of others. . . . The American society with which I am familiar "chooses to dwell in reasonable security and freedom from surveillance" . . . and is more dedicated to individual liberty and more sensitive to intrusions on the sanctity of the home than the Court is willing to acknowledge. . . . I dissent.

- What do you think about the Court's decision in *Greenwood*? Do you agree with the majority or the dissent? The majority opinion says that trash bags are open to the public and therefore not deserving of an expectation of privacy. The dissent disagrees. Think about the trash in your house.
- The majority bases its opinion in part on the fact that the trash bags were given over to the garbage collectors. Should you have an expectation of privacy in property you have abandoned or given to a stranger?
- The dissent bases its argument on the fact that the bags used were not clear (that is, they were opaque). What if the bags were clear transparent plastic? Would that change your thinking about the case? What if the bags were kept in a secure trash can? What if the trash can were locked?
- Why should trash bags be the type of effect that the framers of the Constitution would have cared about?
- What do you think about the dissent's view of the value of privacy in a single trash bag? Is that overstating the case? What about a trash bag from a police station, or even the Supreme Court? Should some people have a higher expectation of privacy in their trash than others?
- Does it change your decision on the correctness of this case to know that there was a law requiring all citizens, including Greenwood, to remove their trash each week from their home? Does it matter that Greenwood had to use the city's trash service to get rid of his trash?

Constitutional Baggage

Whether a gym bag or an overfilled family vacation suitcase, all people travel with stuff, and sometimes very personal stuff. Think about what an overnight bag says about you: It reveals your clothing style, reading choices, medical needs, and so on. When traveling, how much privacy should people expect when it comes to their bags? What if the plane, train, or bus has security requirements necessitating that the bags be searched? What if a person is carrying something he does not want others to see?

Consider another case in which the Supreme Court had to decide the limits of a constitutional search. In *Bond v. United States,* the Court was faced with a common situation in which police officers looking for drugs or weapons boarded a bus and physically

Do you have a reasonable expectation of privacy in your suitcase, or can police officers physically touch or poke the bag in an effort to search it? What is it about a suitcase that would suggest a reason to expect privacy? What interests would police have in searching bags?

searched (by touching or poking) the carry-on bags brought on by passengers.[5] The question for the Court was whether people had a reasonable expectation of privacy in the luggage they brought on board the bus.

STEVEN DEWAYNE BOND, PETITIONER,
V.
UNITED STATES

Supreme Court of the United States
No. 98-9349.
Argued February 29, 2000.
Decided April 17, 2000.

Chief Justice REHNQUIST delivered the opinion of the Court.

This case presents the question whether a law enforcement officer's physical manipulation of a bus passenger's carry-on luggage violated the Fourth Amendment's proscription against unreasonable searches. We hold that it did.

Petitioner Steven Dewayne Bond was a passenger on a Greyhound bus that left California bound for Little Rock, Arkansas. The bus stopped, as it was required to do, at the permanent Border Patrol checkpoint in Sierra Blanca, Texas. Border Patrol Agent Cesar Cantu boarded the bus to check the immigration status of its passengers. After reaching the back of the bus, having satisfied himself that the passengers were lawfully in the United States, Agent Cantu began walking toward the front. Along the way, he squeezed the soft luggage, which passengers had placed in the overhead storage space above the seats.

Petitioner was seated four or five rows from the back of the bus. As Agent Cantu inspected the luggage in the compartment above petitioner's seat, he squeezed a green canvas bag and noticed that it contained a "brick-like" object. Petitioner admitted that the bag was his and agreed to allow Agent Cantu to open it. Upon opening the bag, Agent Cantu discovered a "brick" of methamphetamine. The brick had been wrapped in duct tape until it was oval-shaped and then rolled in a pair of pants.

Petitioner was indicted for conspiracy to possess, and possession with intent to distribute, methamphetamine. . . . He moved to suppress the drugs, arguing that Agent Cantu conducted an illegal search of his bag. . . .

The Fourth Amendment provides that "[t]he right of the people to be secure in their persons, houses, papers, and effects, against unreasonable searches and seizures, shall not be violated. . . ." A traveler's personal luggage is clearly an "effect" protected by the Amendment. . . . Indeed, it is undisputed here that petitioner possessed a privacy interest in his bag.

But the Government asserts that by exposing his bag to the public, petitioner lost a reasonable expectation that his bag would not be physically manipulated. . . .

Here, petitioner concedes that, by placing his bag in the overhead compartment, he could expect that it would be exposed to certain kinds of touching and handling. But petitioner argues that Agent Cantu's physical manipulation of his luggage "far exceeded the casual contact [petitioner] could have expected from other passengers." . . . The Government counters that it did not.

Our Fourth Amendment analysis embraces two questions. First, we ask whether the individual, by his conduct, has exhibited an actual expectation of privacy; that is, whether he has shown that "he [sought] to preserve [something] as private." . . . Here, petitioner sought to preserve privacy by using an opaque bag and placing that bag directly above his seat. Second, we inquire whether the individual's expectation of privacy is "one that society is prepared to recognize as reasonable." . . . When a bus passenger places a bag in an overhead bin, he expects that other passengers or bus employees may move it for one reason or another. Thus, a bus passenger clearly expects that his bag may be handled. He does not expect that other passengers or bus employees will, as a matter of course, feel the bag in an exploratory manner. But this is exactly what the agent did here. We therefore hold that the agent's physical manipulation of petitioner's bag violated the Fourth Amendment.

POINTS TO PONDER

- Based on Chief Justice William H. Rehnquist's opinion, because Bond sought to preserve his privacy using an opaque bag (a non-see-through suitcase), he retained an expectation of privacy that society would deem reasonable. Why is this case any different from the *Greenwood* trash case? Is it because Greenwood put his trash outside the house and Bond kept his bag in sight? What if Bond checked his bags on the bus trip, and the officer had squeezed the bag? Would that be a search? Would Bond still have a reasonable expectation of privacy?
- In *Bond,* the Court held that manipulating the bags to look for drugs was a search. Why was this poking or prodding considered a search?
- What if the bags were checked by highly trained drug-sniffing dogs? Would that be a search for Fourth Amendment purposes? You might find the answer in the Court's decision in *Place*, below. Imagine you are traveling to visit your grandfather, who lives in a retirement community in Los Angeles. Like much of California, the retirement community is smoke-free. However, your grandfather enjoys cigars, and not just any cigars—Cuban cigars. He asks you, as his favorite grandson, to bring him a box of illegal Cuban cigars. You stick them in your backpack, carefully concealed. As you arrive at the Los Angeles International Airport, a drug-sniffing dog becomes alerted and police officials stop you. The dog wildly barks around your bag. Have you been searched under the Fourth Amendment?

In *United States v. Place,* the Supreme Court was confronted with a similar question.[6] A drug-sniffing dog was stationed in a major airport. It sniffed all of the incoming baggage. When Place's luggage came past the dog, the dog responded, as it was trained to do, when it smelled drugs. The bags were seized and later searched, and drugs were found. At trial, Place moved to suppress the evidence, arguing that his Fourth Amendment rights were violated by this search of his bag. The Supreme Court disagreed, holding that this type of sniff check was not a search for Fourth Amendment purposes. The Court decided that the luggage was in a public place when sniffed and was not opened and searched. As a result, no privacy right was violated. Do you agree with this analysis?

In the wake of school shootings and the events of September 11, 2001, local and federal officials greatly increased security measures in public buildings and airports, as at National Airport in Washington, D.C. Most courts have found that allowing dogs to sniff for substances are not "searches" within the context of the Fourth Amendment and thus do not require probable cause or search warrants to be carried out.
Source: Kevin Lamarque/Reuters/Landov

Why should there be a constitutional difference between a sniff and a squeeze? Does it depend on where the bag is when the check occurs? What if a dog were on the bus with Bond?

Other Expectations of Privacy

Whether there is a reasonable expectation of privacy and thus a legitimate Fourth Amendment search is determined case by case. If you are confused by the uncertain nature of the determination, you are not alone. A reasonable expection of privacy is a difficult and ever-changing concept. That is why it is important to have educated citizens such as yourselves learn and think about these concepts. You will help decide what is "reasonable" in the future.

To help you think through these concepts, consider two types of court cases concerning technological developments that aid police officers in searching private property and invading personal liberty. The first type involves "enhanced sight" through the use of airplanes or helicopters to search areas of property that otherwise could not be searched. The second type involves "heightened senses" using advanced electronic devices, such as satellite cameras and thermal imaging devices, to see things that otherwise could not be seen.

Plane View

Jeff Green, age seventeen, had a green thumb. Unfortunately, he tended a garden of marijuana plants, which are illegal, at his parents' house. He built a wall about eight to ten feet high around the house so no one could see inside. He grew his plants just tall enough so that the fence would block anyone snooping around. Suspecting that Jeff might be in the drug business, the police began investigating him. Unable to see over the garden fence, the police used a plane to fly over the backyard. From one thousand feet, two police officers were able to observe the marijuana plants growing. When Jeff was arrested, he argued that the visual search of his backyard was unconstitutional because it invaded his reasonable expectation of privacy. Was this a search for the purposes of the Fourth Amendment? Did Jeff have a reasonable expectation of privacy in his backyard?

Copped Out

Jeff Green served his time in juvenile hall for growing marijuana and leaves detention not having learned the lessons of responsibility and lawful behavior. Kicked out of his home, Jeff moves in with his brother. The brothers build a greenhouse about ten feet behind the mobile home. Two sides of the greenhouse were enclosed. The other two sides were blocked from sight by trees, shrubs, and the mobile home. The greenhouse had a covered roof, with only about 10 percent of the roof not covered. A wire fence surrounded the entire property and sported a big "Do Not Enter" sign. Again, suspecting Jeff was up to no good, police used a helicopter to fly over the greenhouse. Hovering from a close distance of four hundred feet, they saw marijuana growing. Was this a search for the purposes of the Fourth Amendment? Was a reasonable expectation of privacy violated?

Non-Company Business

Jeff Green completed a second stint in juvenile hall and, upon release, promised to do better. He moved out of his brother's place and got a job at the local chemical company. Run by Wow Chemical Company, Jeff secured a landscaping job at the two-thousand-acre industrial plant. The area consisted of numerous enclosed buildings. The company maintained elaborate security around the perimeter of the complex and barred ground-level or other public viewing of the facility. Jeff was given free access to wander the grounds. He discovered a wonderful spot to plant green things, and letting his inner demons take over, he decided to plant marijuana. Meanwhile, the Environmental Protection Agency (EPA), a government agency entrusted with enforcing environmental laws, attempted to conduct an on-site inspection of the facility. Asserting a right to privacy, Wow prevented the EPA from inspecting the facility. Undeterred, the EPA hired a commercial air photographer to take pictures of the facility from a height of twelve thousand to thirteen thousand feet. The photos were taken with a sophisticated high-tech camera. Discovered in the photographs were Jeff's plantings. Police arrested Jeff. Both

Wow and Jeff challenged the use of the photographs as a search, because it violated the reasonable expectation of privacy. Was this a Fourth Amendment search?

City Heat

Jeff Green left juvenile hall for the third and last time, ready for a fresh start. He headed to New York City for an urban environment without tempting fields of green. He moved into a small apartment in a large brownstone. With high food prices and low job prospects, temptation arose again. Jeff started growing marijuana in his closet. With high-intensity grow lights, he developed a little forest of narcotics. Federal agent William Elliot suspected that Jeff was doing something illegal. Knowing that people who grow marijuana indoors need strong lights to make the plants grow, Agent Elliot tried to figure out if an abnormal amount of heat came from the apartment. Agent Elliot used a device called an "Agema Thermovision 210 thermal imager" to scan the brownstone. This type of thermal device detects infrared radiation and converts the radiation into images based on relative warmth—black is cool, white is hot, shades of gray show relative differences. In essence, it is somewhat like a video camera showing heat images. Agent Elliot performed the scan sitting in his car, and the entire process took only a few minutes. The thermal scan confirmed Agent Elliot's suspicions, and a search warrant was issued for the apartment. Jeff moved to suppress the evidence claiming that the use of the thermal imager was a search for Fourth Amendment purposes. Was this a search? Did he have a reasonable expectation of privacy to be free from thermal imaging?

Expectation of Privacy or Not? Search or Not?

Considering each case, do you think Jeff had a reasonable expectation of privacy? Was it one society should accept as valid? Was a search conducted? Was the Fourth Amendment violated? See how the Supreme Court resolved cases similar to Jeff's.

New technology providing law enforcement with enhanced sight and heightened senses has introduced new Fourth Amendment issues. In 1998 the sheriff of Maricopa County in Arizona purchased a $1.25 million helicopter that can locate suspects with a heat-sensitive tracking system and spotlight. *Source: Rick D'Elia/AP Wide World Photos*

Plane View. In *California v. Ciraolo,* the Supreme Court ruled that while a homeowner clearly intended to keep his backyard private when he build a fence around it, a reasonable expectation of privacy was not created because people could still see into the yard.[7] The Court held that because the police viewed the backyard and could see illegally growing plants from the air, so could other people and thus the owner had lost his expectation of privacy. The Court was unconcerned with the fact that most people do not have planes from which to see over fences and into backyards. Thus, the police lawfully gathered evidence by flying over his backyard at one thousand feet.

- The Court agrees that a fence gives a person a reason to expect privacy. However, because others could see over the fence, no objective expectation of privacy existed. Do you agree?
- How many people have planes that could see what the police saw? Even if they had a plane, how many people would use planes to look into this particular yard?
- How common was it for people to look into the yard?
- What else could the owner have done to create a reasonable expectation of privacy in the yard?

Copped Out. In *Florida v. Riley,* four Supreme Court justices found, as in *Ciraolo,* that because it was lawful for a helicopter to be flying four hundred feet above a greenhouse (and thus other people might be able to see into the greenhouse), no expectation of privacy existed.[8] A fifth justice, Sandra Day O'Connor, agreed but grounded her opinion in the fact that the defendant had not provided any evidence to the Court that this type of flying and spying was unusual. Presumably, if it were shown that such flying was unusual, then Justice O'Connor would have decided differently. Four justices disagreed with the majority, arguing that such aerial spying was a violation of Riley's expectation of privacy and that people should not have to expect police helicopters to be looking in at them.

- Do you agree with the decision? Does this seem more or less intrusive than the planes flying overhead in *Ciraolo*?
- How high would the fence have to be to provide privacy the Court would respect? If only 10 percent of the roof was open, that means 90 percent of the roof was covered.
- What more could Riley have done to gain an expectation of privacy? What if just a window was open? Could the police have looked into the window?
- How many people have access to helicopters that the Court assumes could fly overhead? Is that a realistic assumption? Why should Riley have to prove that it was unusual for helicopters to fly overhead? Is it unusual in your opinion?

Non-Company Business. In *Dow Chemical Company v. United States,* the Supreme Court ruled that while photographs provided an enhanced view of an area, they were not so revealing of intimate details to raise a constitutional concern.[9] Because nothing intimate was being revealed, there was no expectation of privacy to violate. The Court did not answer the question of what would happen if technology advanced so much that the pictures would reveal intimate personal details.

- Do you agree with the decision?
- What if the photos had revealed something more intimate? What if they showed a Dow Company trade secret?
- What would happen if these types of pictures were taken of a person's property instead of a company's property? Do you think the Court would come to the same decision?

City Heat. In *Kyllo v. United States,* the Supreme Court said that Kyllo had a reasonable expectation of privacy to be free from thermal imaging.[10] The Court found that Kyllo had a reasonable expectation of privacy in his house. It held that because the thermal imaging device was not regularly used by the general public, and because the device could explore details of a home that would not otherwise have been obtained without physical intrusion into a constitutionally protected area, the use of the device did constitute a search. The Court put emphasis on the fact that the search occurred in a home and that private details could have been revealed by the device.

- What did the thermal imaging equipment reveal that deserved protection? Why should the temperature in your house determine whether you have Fourth Amendment protection? How else could the police have investigated this case?
- What does this case say about technology that would allow you to see through walls? Would the Fourth Amendment protect you from Superman's X-ray vision?
- Are you convinced that because most people do not own a thermal imaging device, the intrusion was greater? What about the fact that most people do not own planes or helicopters?

POINTS TO PONDER

- What lessons can be learned from these four Supreme Court cases? What do you think is the most protected area? What causes you to lose an expectation of privacy? What are the limits of technology in enhancing investigation? Do you feel satisfied by the distinctions drawn by the Court? If you were on the Court, how would you have decided each case?

What Is a Seizure?

In addition to protecting against unreasonable searches, the Fourth Amendment protects against unreasonable seizures. Seizures can be of your stuff or your person.

Bad Bust Stop

Imagine you are waiting for the bus to take you to school. It is 7:00 a.m., and no one else is around. You are standing, holding your lunch in a brown paper bag. A marked police

Have you been seized if

- a police officer grabs you off the street and brings you to the police station?
- police officers come up to you and surround you so you do not feel comfortable leaving?
- police officers order you to stop?
- police officers order you to stop and you ignore them?
- the police ask everyone over a loudspeaker at school to stand outside of the school for fifteen minutes after the final bell rings?

car with lights flashing pulls up in front of the bus stop. A uniformed police officer gets out of the car and walks toward you. He stands directly in front of you, looking you up and down. Another uniformed police officer gets out of the car with his hand on his gun. Without saying a word, the first officer grabs the paper bag from your hand. He then opens it and visually searches it. Seeing only your turkey sandwich, he apologizes to you. The officers then drive away.

Your lunch was seized for the purposes of the Fourth Amendment. A seizure of property means that a government official takes property from you. In almost all seizure of property cases, the question of whether the property was seized can be answered by looking at whether the law enforcement officer took control of an item. The legal test is whether a meaningful interference with an individual's possession of property occurred, as determined in *Arizona v. Hicks*.[11]

But what about the seizure of people? Should a different standard apply because people are not objects? Whether a person was seized for purposes of the Fourth Amendment involves a question of whether his freedom or liberty was impeded by government officials. The easy case is an arrest, when a person is handcuffed and led away to the police station. Clearly in that situation the person has been seized because his physical freedom and liberty were taken away. What about the situation at the bus stop when the police officers essentially cornered you? Was that a seizure? Was your liberty interfered with by the presence of the officers?

The question of whether you have been seized for Fourth Amendment purposes is difficult and depends on the specific facts of what happened to you.

The Free to Leave Standard

How would the Supreme Court go about looking at the issue of seizure? How would a court decide in a situation such as the one that took place at the bus stop? How would you know if the Fourth Amendment protected you and your turkey sandwich?

United States v. Mendenhall involves police questioning a woman at an airport.[12] Sylvia Mendenhall flew into Detroit International Airport. After getting off the plane, she

Have you been seized when two law enforcement officers approach you in an airport and inquire if they can ask you some questions? Does your answer change if they ask you to come with them to an office? How about if there are ten officers? How about if they order you to come with them? How about if they grab you?

walked into the airport terminal. Two Drug Enforcement Agency (DEA) special agents thought she looked suspicious because she was the last person to leave the plane, appeared nervous, scanned the area where agents were standing, left without claiming any baggage, and was scheduled on a different airline for her return flight. The agents approached her on the airport concourse, identified themselves as federal agents, and asked to see her identification and airline ticket. Mendenhall produced her drivers' license, which did not match the name on the airline ticket. The agents asked her where she had come from and how long she had been away. She became very nervous and had a hard time speaking. The agents then asked her if she would accompany them to the airport DEA office for further questions. She walked with the agents to the office. At the office, the agents asked permission to search her. She gave permission, and they found illegal drugs.

The question for the Supreme Court was whether Mendenhall had been seized for Fourth Amendment purposes when the agents stopped her and asked her to come back with them to the DEA office. Mendenhall argued that she was so seized, because she was not free to leave the presence of the two agents. The government argued that no seizure had occurred and that police should be allowed to ask questions of people without invoking the protections of the Fourth Amendment.

In this case, the Court created a test to determine when someone has been seized for Fourth Amendment purposes. In essence, the Court asked if a "reasonable person" would have felt free to leave.

UNITED STATES, PETITIONER
V.
SYLVIA L. MENDENHALL

Supreme Court of the United States
No. 78-1821.
Argued February 19, 1980.
Decided May 27, 1980.

Justice Stewart:

. . . The Fourth Amendment's requirement that searches and seizures be founded upon an objective justification, governs all seizures of the person, "including seizures that involve only a brief **detention** short of traditional arrest." . . . Accordingly, if the respondent [Mendenhall] was "seized" when the DEA agents approached her on the concourse and asked questions of her, the agents' conduct in doing so was constitutional only if they reasonably suspected the respondent of wrongdoing. . . .

We **adhere** to the view that a person is "seized" only when, by means of physical force or a show of authority, his freedom of movement is restrained. Only when such restraint is imposed is there any foundation whatever for invoking constitutional safeguards. The purpose of the Fourth Amendment is not to eliminate all contact between the police and the citizenry, but "to prevent arbitrary and oppressive interference by enforcement officials with the privacy and personal security of individuals." . . . As long as the person to whom questions are put remains free to disregard the questions and walk away, there has been no intrusion upon that person's liberty or privacy as would under the Constitution require some particularized and objective justification.

Moreover, characterizing every street encounter between a citizen and the police as a "seizure," while not enhancing any interest secured by the Fourth Amendment, would impose wholly unrealistic restrictions upon a wide variety of legitimate law enforcement practices. The Court has on other occasions referred to the acknowledged need for police questioning as a tool in the effective enforcement of the criminal laws. "Without such investigation, those who were innocent might be falsely accused, those who were guilty might wholly escape prosecution, and many crimes would go unsolved. In short, the security of all would be diminished." . . .

We conclude that a person has been "seized" within the meaning of the Fourth Amendment only if, in view of all of the circumstances surrounding the incident, a reasonable person would have believed that he was not free to leave. . . . Examples of circumstances that might indicate a seizure, even where the person did not attempt to leave, would be the threatening presence of several officers, the display of a weapon by an officer, some physical touching of the person of the citizen, or the use of language or tone of voice indicating that compliance with the officer's request might be compelled. . . . In the absence of some such evidence, otherwise inoffensive contact between a member of the public and the police cannot, as a matter of law, amount to a seizure of that person.

On the facts of this case, no "seizure" of the respondent occurred. The events took place in the public concourse. The agents wore no uniforms and displayed no weapons. They did not summon the respondent to their presence, but instead approached her and identified themselves as federal agents. They requested, but did not demand to see the respondent's identification and ticket. Such conduct without more, did not amount to an intrusion upon any constitutionally protected interest. The respondent was not seized simply by reason of the fact that the agents approached her, asked her if she would show them her ticket and identification, and posed to her a few questions. Nor was it enough to establish a seizure that the person asking the questions was a law enforcement official. . . . In short, nothing in the record suggests that the respondent had any objective reason to believe that she was not free to end the conversation in the concourse and proceed on her way, and for that reason we conclude that the agents' initial approach to her was not a seizure.

POINTS TO PONDER

- Do you think that if you were Sylvia Mendenhall you would have felt free to leave? Would you have felt free to disregard the officers' request? Did the Court give a realistic assessment of the situation?
- Does the meaning of the term "reasonable person" change with the type of person involved? For example, would Mendenhall and a traveling Supreme Court justice react to police in the same way? Does the passenger's age, gender, race, education level, or social class matter? What would the experience be of a sixteen-year-old girl traveling on a plane for the first time? An experienced criminal defense attorney who had attended the finest law school?
- Does the place or location of the seizure matter? What if police stopped you in a dark alley, at your home, in school?
- The Court equates seizure with "physical force" or a "show of authority." Are these the only reasons one might feel seized? What do you make of the other factors listed by the Court—namely, the presence of several officers, the display of weapons, physical touching, use of language?
- What about the situation in the airport hallway that makes it unlikely that someone would leave? What makes it less "free"? Would it depend on the tone of voice of the agents?
- What could make it more likely that someone would walk away without cooperating with police? Is there anything in the Court's decision that suggests that someone might walk away?

Seizure and Consent

Return to the scene of the bus stop: You are alone in the early morning. A police officer comes straight to you. He is in uniform and thus armed. He does not give you the option of leaving. Are you free to walk away? This time, he asks whether he can search your lunch bag. What do you say? You might say yes, because you have only a sandwich in there. But what if you have a stolen radio in the bag? What if you had something that would get you arrested? Would you still say yes? Could you realistically say no? The answer for Fourth Amendment purposes is asking what a reasonable person would do.

The "reasonable person" test represents the standard for a Fourth Amendment seizure. If a reasonable person would feel free to leave in the same situation, there is no constitutional seizure. This point becomes important because in many situations police come up and talk to people and ask them questions. This type of police-citizen encounter is considered a consensual encounter. The Fourth Amendment begins protecting you when the encounter turns from consensual to nonconsensual; that is, when you would not feel free to leave.

In the real world, this change becomes vitally important because as long as no seizure occurs police can ask all sorts of questions about, for example, searching your bag, your person, or your pockets without running afoul of the Fourth Amendment.

Consent to Search

The following description of another Supreme Court case, *Florida v. Bostick*, 501 U.S. 429 (1991), comes from David Cole's influential book on constitutional criminal law, *No Equal Justice: Race and Class in the American Criminal Justice System*.[13]

> Miami to Atlanta is 663 miles. If you had a choice, you'd fly. Those who can't afford air travel often make the trip by bus, a grueling nineteen-hour ride. On August 27, 1985, Terrance Bostick, a twenty-eight-year-old black man, was sleeping in the back seat of a Greyhound bus, on his way from Miami to Atlanta, when he awoke to find two police officers standing over him. They were wearing bright green "raid" jackets bearing the Broward County Sheriff's Office insignia and displaying their badges; one held a gun in a plastic gun pouch. The bus was stopped at a brief layover in Fort Lauderdale, and the officers were "working the bus," looking for persons who might be carrying drugs.
>
> Upon waking Bostick, the officers asked for his identification and ticket. He complied. They then asked to search his bag. Again, Bostick complied, somewhat inexplicable, because upon opening the bag, the officers found a pound of cocaine. The officers admitted that at no time prior to the search did they have any basis for suspecting Bostick of any criminal activity.[14]

Bostick challenged the search on Fourth Amendment grounds. He claimed he was seized for Fourth Amendment purposes by the actions of the sheriffs in cornering him and asking him questions without any justification. If he were seized without any justification, it would be unreasonable and a violation of the Fourth Amendment. The Supreme Court had to decide whether he had been seized or whether he had consented to the search.

YOUR THOUGHTS

You are sitting on a bus. Are you seized when two police officers come up and ask you whether they can search your bag? Why or why not?

FLORIDA, PETITIONER,
V.
TERRANCE BOSTICK

Supreme Court of the United States
No. 89-1717.
Argued February 26, 1991.
Decided June 20, 1991.

Justice O'CONNOR delivered the opinion of the Court.

We have held that the Fourth Amendment permits police officers to approach individuals at random in airport lobbies and other public places to ask them questions and to request consent to search their luggage, so long as a reasonable person would understand that he or she could refuse to cooperate. This case requires us to determine whether the same rule applies to police encounters that take place on a bus. . . .

II

The sole issue presented for our review is whether a police encounter on a bus of the type described above necessarily constitutes a "seizure" within the meaning of the Fourth Amendment. The State concedes, and we accept for purposes of this decision, that the officers lacked the reasonable suspicion required to justify a seizure and that, if a seizure took place, the drugs found in Bostick's suitcase must be suppressed as tainted fruit.

Our cases make it clear that a seizure does not occur simply because a police officer approaches an individual and asks a few questions. So long as a reasonable person would feel free "to disregard the police and go about his business," *California v. Hodari D.,* 499 U.S. 621, 628 (1991), the encounter is consensual and no reasonable suspicion is required. The encounter will not trigger Fourth Amendment scrutiny unless it loses its consensual nature. . . .

There is no doubt that if this same encounter had taken place before Bostick boarded the bus or in the lobby of the bus terminal, it would not rise to the level of a seizure. . . . We have stated that even when officers have no basis for suspecting a particular individual, they may generally ask questions of that individual, . . . ask to examine the individual's identification, . . . and request consent to search his or her luggage . . . as long as the police do not convey a message that compliance with their requests is required.

Bostick insists that this case is different because it took place in the cramped confines of a bus. A police encounter is much more intimidating in this setting, he argues, because police tower over a seated passenger and there is little room to move around. . . . Bostick maintains that a reasonable bus passenger would not have felt free to leave under the circumstances of this case because there is nowhere to go on a bus. Also, the bus was about to depart. Had Bostick disembarked, he would have risked being stranded and losing whatever baggage he had locked away in the luggage compartment. . . .

[However], the mere fact that Bostick did not feel free to leave the bus does not mean that the police seized him. Bostick was a passenger on a bus that was scheduled to depart. He would not have felt free to leave the bus even if the police had not been present. Bostick's movements were "confined" in a sense, but this was the natural result of his decision to take the bus; it says nothing about whether or not the police conduct at issue was coercive. . . .

Bostick's freedom of movement was restricted by a factor independent of police conduct—*i.e.*, by his being a passenger on a bus. Accordingly, the "free to leave" analysis on which Bostick relies is inapplicable. In such a situation, the appropriate inquiry is whether a reasonable person would feel free to decline the officers' requests or otherwise terminate the encounter. This formulation follows logically from prior cases and breaks no new ground. We have said before that the crucial test is whether, taking into account all of the circumstances surrounding the encounter, the police conduct would "have communicated to a reasonable person that he was not at liberty to ignore the police presence and go about his business." . . .

The facts of this case . . . leave some doubt whether a seizure occurred. Two officers walked up to Bostick on the bus, asked him a few questions, and asked if they could search his bags. As we have explained, no seizure occurs when police ask questions of an individual, ask to examine the individual's identification, and request consent to search his or her luggage—so long as the officers do not convey a message that compliance with their requests is required. Here, the facts recited by the Florida Supreme Court indicate that the officers did not point guns at Bostick or otherwise threaten him and that they specifically advised Bostick that he could refuse consent. . . .

We adhere to the rule that, in order to determine whether a particular encounter constitutes a seizure, a court must consider all the circumstances surrounding the encounter to determine whether the police conduct would have communicated to a reasonable person that the person was not free to decline the officers' requests or otherwise terminate the encounter. That rule applies to encounters that take place on a city street or in an airport lobby, and it applies equally to encounters on a bus. . . .

Justice MARSHALL, with whom Justice BLACKMUN and Justice STEVENS join, dissenting.

Our Nation, we are told, is engaged in a "war on drugs." No one disputes that it is the job of law-enforcement officials to devise effective weapons for fighting this war. But the effectiveness of a law-enforcement technique is not proof of its constitutionality. . . . In my view, the law-enforcement technique with which we are confronted in this case—the suspicionless police sweep of buses in intrastate or interstate travel—bears all of the indicia of coercion and unjustified intrusion associated with the general warrant. Because I believe that the bus sweep at issue in this case violates the core values of the Fourth Amendment, I dissent.

I

At issue in this case is a "new and increasingly common tactic in the war on drugs": the suspicionless police sweep of buses in interstate or intrastate travel. . . . Typically under this technique, a group of state or federal officers will board a bus while it is stopped at an intermediate point on its route. Often displaying badges, weapons or other indicia of authority, the officers identify themselves and announce their purpose to intercept drug traffickers. They proceed to approach individual passengers, requesting them to show identification, produce their tickets, and explain the purpose of their travels. Never do the officers advise the passengers that they are free not to speak with the officers. An "interview" of this type ordinarily culminates in a request for consent to search the passenger's luggage. . . .

These sweeps are conducted in "dragnet" style. The police admittedly act without an "articulable suspicion" in deciding which buses to board and which passengers to approach for interviewing. By proceeding systematically in this fashion, the police are able to engage in a tremendously high volume of searches. . . .

To put it mildly, these sweeps "are inconvenient, intrusive, and intimidating." . . . They occur within cramped confines, with officers typically placing themselves in between the passenger selected for an interview and the exit of the bus. . . . Because the bus is only temporarily stationed at a point short of its destination, the passengers are in no position to leave as a means of evading the officers' questioning. . . .

The question for this Court, then, is whether the suspicionless, dragnet-style sweep of buses in intrastate and interstate travel is consistent with the Fourth Amendment. The majority suggests that this latest tactic in the drug war is perfectly compatible with the Constitution. I disagree.

II

I have no objection to the manner in which the majority frames the test for determining whether a suspicionless bus sweep amounts to a Fourth Amendment "seizure." I agree that the appropriate question is whether a passenger who is approached during such a sweep "would feel free to decline the officers' requests or otherwise terminate the encounter." What I cannot understand is how the majority can possibly suggest an affirmative answer to this question.

. . . Two officers boarded the Greyhound bus on which respondent was a passenger while the bus, en route from Miami to Atlanta, was on a brief stop to pick up passengers in Fort Lauderdale. The officers made a visible display of their badges and wore bright green "raid" jackets bearing the insignia of the Broward County Sheriff's Department; one held a gun in a recognizable weapons pouch. . . . These facts alone constitute an intimidating "show of authority." . . . Once on board, the officers approached respondent, who was sitting in the back of the bus, identified themselves as narcotics officers and began to question him. . . . One officer stood in front of respondent's seat, partially blocking the narrow aisle through which respondent would have been required to pass to reach the exit of the bus.

. . . [The] issue is not whether a passenger in respondent's position would have felt free to deny consent to the search of his bag, but whether such a passenger—without being apprised of his rights—would have felt free to terminate the **antecedent** encounter with the police.

Unlike the majority, I have no doubt that the answer to this question is no. Apart from trying to accommodate the officers, respondent had only two options. First, he could have remained seated while obstinately refusing to respond to the officers' questioning. But in light of the intimidating show of authority that the officers made upon boarding the bus, respondent reasonably could have believed that such behavior would only arouse the officers' suspicions and intensify their interrogation. Indeed, officers who carry out bus sweeps like the one at issue here frequently admit that this is the effect of a passenger's refusal to cooperate. . . .

Second, respondent could have tried to escape the officers' presence by leaving the bus altogether. But because doing so would have required respondent to squeeze past the gun-wielding inquisitor who was blocking the aisle of the bus, this hardly seems like a course that respondent reasonably would have viewed as available to him. . . .

Even if respondent had perceived that the officers would *let* him leave the bus, moreover, he could not reasonably have been expected to resort to this means of evading their intrusive questioning. For so far as respondent knew, the bus's departure from the terminal was imminent. Unlike a person approached by the police on the street, . . . or at a bus or airport terminal after reaching his destination, . . . a passenger approached by the police at an intermediate point in a long bus journey cannot simply leave the scene and repair to a safe haven to avoid unwanted probing by law-enforcement officials. . . .

POINTS TO PONDER

- Which side do you agree with—the majority or dissent? Does it change your opinion to know that if Bostick had declined the officer's request he would have been stuck in the middle of rural Florida far away from Atlanta where he was heading?[15]
- Do you agree that there was a "show of authority" by the police? What contributes to that show of authority? Is it the close confines of a bus? Is it the close physical proximity of the police to Bostick? Is it the display of badges? Guns? Is it the tone of voice?
- Who is the "reasonable person" the Supreme Court is picturing? Even knowing that you have the right to say no to a search, would you feel free to terminate the encounter?
- Why do the dissenting justices discuss the war on drugs? Is that relevant to constitutional analysis? Why or why not?

Seizures on the Street

Standing at the bus stop, minding your own business, a police car pulls up. You see an officer and, before he gets out of the car, you take off running. Maybe you run because you are guilty. Maybe because you do not want to be hassled by police. Maybe you are running so you do not have to remember the rules of the Fourth Amendment. The question is: Have you been seized? What if the police officer never catches you? How could you be seized for purposes of the Fourth Amendment if you outrun the police?

In *California v. Hodari D.,* the Supreme Court was asked to decide if a young man named Hodari D. was seized when he fled from the sight of police.

YOUR THOUGHTS

Are you seized if an uniformed and armed police officer runs after you on a street ordering you to stop? How about if he tackles you to the ground? When does the seizure begin?

CALIFORNIA, PETITIONER

V.

HODARI D.

Supreme Court of the United States
No. 89-1632.
Argued January 14, 1991.
Decided April 23, 1991.

Justice SCALIA delivered the opinion of the Court.

Late one evening in April 1988, Officers Brian McColgin and Jerry Pertoso were on patrol in a high-crime area of Oakland, California. They were dressed in street clothes but wearing jackets with "Police" embossed on both front and back. Their unmarked car proceeded west on Foothill Boulevard, and turned south onto 63rd Avenue. As they rounded the corner, they saw four or five youths huddled around a small red car parked at the curb. When the youths saw the officers' car approaching they apparently panicked, and took flight. The respondent here, Hodari D., and one companion ran west through an alley; the others fled south. The red car also headed south, at a high rate of speed.

The officers were suspicious and gave chase. McColgin remained in the car and continued south on 63rd Avenue; Pertoso left the car, ran back north along 63rd, then west on Foothill Boulevard, and turned south on 62nd Avenue. Hodari, meanwhile, emerged from the alley onto 62nd and ran north. Looking behind as he ran, he did not turn and see Pertoso until the officer was almost upon him, whereupon he tossed away what appeared to be a small rock. A moment later, Pertoso tackled Hodari, handcuffed him, and radioed for assistance. Hodari was found to be carrying $130 in cash and a pager; and the rock he had discarded was found to be crack cocaine.

In the juvenile proceeding brought against him, Hodari moved to suppress the evidence relating to the cocaine. . . .

As this case comes to us, the only issue presented is whether, at the time he dropped the drugs, Hodari had been "seized" within the meaning of the Fourth Amendment. If so, respondent argues, the drugs were the fruit of that seizure and the evidence concerning them was properly excluded. If not, the drugs were abandoned by Hodari and lawfully recovered by the police, and the evidence should have been admitted. . . .

We have long understood that the Fourth Amendment's protection against "unreasonable . . . seizures" includes seizure of the person, *see Henry v. United States,* 361 U.S. 98, 100 (1959). From the time of the founding to the present, the word "seizure" has meant a "taking possession," 2 N. Webster, An American Dictionary of the English Language 67 (1828); 2 J. Bouvier, A Law Dictionary 510 (6th ed. 1856); Webster's Third New International Dictionary 2057 (1981). For most purposes at common law, the word connoted not merely grasping, or applying physical force to, the animate or inanimate object in question, but actually bringing it within physical control. . . . To constitute an arrest, however—the quintessential "seizure of the person" under our Fourth Amendment jurisprudence—the mere grasping or application of physical force with lawful authority, whether or not it succeeded in subduing the arrestee, was sufficient. . . .

The present case, however, is even one step further removed. It does not involve the application of any physical force; Hodari was untouched by Officer Pertoso at the time he discarded the cocaine. His defense relies instead upon the proposition that a seizure occurs "when the officer, by means of physical force *or show of authority,* has in some way restrained the liberty of a citizen." *Terry v. Ohio,* 392 U.S. 1, 19, n. 16, (1968) (emphasis added). Hodari contends (and we accept as true for purposes of this decision) that Pertoso's pursuit qualified as a "show of authority" calling upon Hodari to halt. The narrow question before us is whether, with respect to a show of authority as with respect to application of physical force, a seizure occurs even though the subject does not yield. We hold that it does not.

The language of the Fourth Amendment, of course, cannot sustain respondent's contention. The word "seizure" readily bears the meaning of a laying on of hands or application of physical force to restrain movement, even when it is ultimately unsuccessful. ("She seized the purse-snatcher, but he broke out of her grasp.") It does not remotely apply, however, to the prospect of a policeman yelling "Stop, in the name of the law!" at a fleeing form that continues to flee. That is no seizure. . . .

We do not think it desirable, even as a policy matter, to stretch the Fourth Amendment beyond its words and beyond the meaning of arrest, as respondent urges. Street pursuits always place the public at some risk, and compliance with police orders to stop should therefore be encouraged. Only a few of those orders, we must presume, will be without adequate basis, and since the addressee has no ready means of identifying the deficient ones it almost invariably is the responsible course to comply. Unlawful orders will not be deterred, moreover, by sanctioning through the exclusionary rule those of them that are *not* obeyed. Since policemen do not command "Stop!" expecting to be ignored, or give chase hoping to be outrun, it fully suffices to apply the deterrent to their genuine, successful seizures.

In sum, assuming that Pertoso's pursuit in the present case constituted a "show of authority" enjoining Hodari to halt, since Hodari did not comply with that injunction he was not seized until he was tackled. The cocaine abandoned while he was running was in this case not the fruit of a seizure, and his motion to exclude evidence of it was properly denied.

Justice STEVENS, with whom Justice MARSHALL joins, dissenting.

The Court's narrow construction of the word "seizure" represents a significant, and in my view, unfortunate, departure from prior case law construing the Fourth Amendment. . . . In particular, the Court now adopts a definition of "seizure" that is unfaithful to a long line of Fourth Amendment cases. Even if the Court were defining seizure for the first time, which it is not, the definition that it chooses today is profoundly unwise. In its decision, the Court assumes, without acknowledging, that a police officer may now fire his weapon at an innocent citizen and not **implicate** the Fourth Amendment—as long as he misses his target.

For the purposes of decision, the following propositions are not in dispute. First, when Officer Pertoso began his pursuit of respondent, the officer did not have a lawful basis for either stopping or arresting respondent. . . . Second, the officer's chase amounted to a "show of authority" as soon as respondent saw the officer nearly upon him. . . . Third, the act of discarding the rock of cocaine was the direct consequence of the show of authority. . . .

I

The Court today takes a narrow view of "seizure," which is at odds with the broader view adopted by this Court almost 25 years ago. In *Katz v. United States,* 389 U.S. 347 (1967), the Court considered whether electronic surveillance conducted "without any trespass and without the seizure of any material object fell outside the ambit of the Constitution." *Id.,* at 353. Over Justice Black's powerful dissent, we rejected that "narrow view" of the Fourth Amendment and held that electronic eavesdropping is a "search and seizure" within the meaning of the Amendment. *Id.,* at 353-354.

II

. . . The touchstone of a seizure is the restraint of an individual's personal liberty *"in some way."* . . .

In *United States v. Mendenhall,* 446 U.S. 544 (1980), the Court "adhere[d] to the view that a person is 'seized' only when, by means of physical force or a show of authority, his freedom of movement is restrained." *Id.,* at 553. The Court looked to whether the citizen who is questioned "remains free to disregard the questions and walk away," and if he or she is able to do so, then "there has been no intrusion upon that person's liberty or privacy" that would require some "particularized and objective justification" under the Constitution. *Id.,* at 554. The test for a "seizure," as formulated by the Court in *Mendenhall,* was whether, "in view of all of the circumstances surrounding the incident, a reasonable person would have believed that he was not free to leave." *Id.* Examples of seizures include "the threatening presence of several officers, the display of a weapon by an officer, some physical touching of the person of the citizen, or the use of language or tone of voice indicating that compliance with the officer's request might be compelled." *Id.* The Court's unwillingness today to adhere to the "reasonable person" standard, as formulated by Justice Stewart in *Mendenhall,* marks an unnecessary departure from Fourth Amendment case law. . . .

Even though momentary, a seizure occurs whenever an objective evaluation of a police officer's show of force conveys the message that the citizen is not entirely free to leave—in other words, that his or her liberty is being restrained in a significant way. . . .

III

. . . In this case the officer's show of force—taking the form of a head-on chase—adequately conveyed the message that respondent was not free to leave. Whereas in *Mendenhall,* there was "nothing in the record [to] sugges[t] that the respondent had any objective reason to believe that she was not free to end the conversation in the concourse and proceed on her way," 446 U.S., at 555, here, respondent attempted to end "the conversation" before it began and soon found himself literally "not free to leave" when confronted by an officer running toward him head-on who eventually tackled him to the ground. There was an interval of time between the moment that respondent saw the officer fast approaching and the moment when he was tackled, and thus brought under the control of the officer. The question is whether the Fourth Amendment was implicated at the earlier or the later moment. . . .

The deterrent purposes of the exclusionary rule focus on the conduct of law enforcement officers and on discouraging improper behavior on their part, and not on the reaction of the citizen to the show of force. In the present case, if Officer Pertoso had succeeded in tackling respondent before he dropped the rock of cocaine, the rock unquestionably would have been excluded as the fruit of the officer's unlawful seizure. Instead, under the Court's logic-chopping analysis, the exclusionary rule has no application because an attempt to make an unconstitutional seizure is beyond the coverage of the Fourth Amendment, no matter how outrageous or unreasonable the officer's conduct may be.

. . . It is too early to know the consequences of the Court's holding. If carried to its logical conclusion, it will encourage unlawful displays of force that will frighten countless innocent citizens into surrendering whatever privacy rights they may still have. . . .

I respectfully dissent.

- In *Hodari D.,* the seizure of the person turned on touch. Because Hodari had not been touched, he was not considered seized. Do you think this is the correct standard? Why is physical touching so important? Why was the "show of authority" not enough? Think back to the *Mendenhall* case. Would the result be different if Mendenhall had been lightly guided by the arm into the office by the agents?
- The dissenting justices were concerned with the time period right before Hodari was tackled to the ground. They viewed that time period, when he was being chased based on a show of authority, as a constitutional seizure. Do you agree?
- Do you think the case would have been different if it had involved an adult instead of a juvenile?
- What do you think of Justice Scalia's reference to the Fourth Amendment as a policy matter? How much of the case turns on the better law enforcement policy? Should the case be decided on policy grounds?
- What do you think about the dissent's warning about the consequences of the Court's decision? What do you think the justices were worried about?

Probable Cause and the Warrant Requirement

The Fourth Amendment has two parts. It protects you from unreasonable searches and seizures. But what about "reasonable" searches and seizures? What if the police have good reason to search you or seize your property? What if they know that you have done something wrong or that they should search your house?

Imagine the scenario of making threats against your sister in a journal, but in reverse. Your younger sister is a bit unstable. She has been arrested half a dozen times for assault. She has an uncontrollable rage and, when provoked, has been known to injure others. You just got her grounded for a month by ratting her out to your parents. She has been

> "No Warrants shall issue but upon probable cause, supported by Oath or affirmation, and particularly describing the place to be searched, and the persons or things to be seized."
>
> —U.S. Constitution, Amendment IV

uttering threats against you all night. You know she also makes these kinds of threats in her journal. She verbally threatens you again. She tells you that her boyfriend has a gun and she knows how to use it. You have had enough. You call a detective to have her investigated and tell him about the journal. The detective responds by saying that before he proceeds with the investigation, the police need to see the journal. The detective then tells you that to see the journal the police need to get a search warrant. Would getting a search warrant to see the journal be reasonable?

What does "reasonable" mean and who gets to decide? Courts have looked to the second part of the language of the Fourth Amendment for an answer.

Two important points come from this language.

Police officers need "probable cause" to search you or your property. The same is true with seizures of your property. A search based on a level of probable cause limits the power of police to stop, arrest, and search people on the streets or in their homes. Basically, it says police need to have sufficient truthful information about crime or criminal evidence to interfere with a person's expectation of privacy.

A **warrant** is a document containing a sworn statement by a police officer that is then looked over and signed by an independent judicial officer (usually a low-level judge). The sworn information must include specific facts about the officer's suspicions of wrongdoing—suspicions that must rise to the level of probable cause. The purpose of a warrant is to have a neutral judicial observer evaluate whether the police have enough information to search or seize you. A warrant supported by probable cause, therefore, limits the power of the police. Only after this official document is signed does the search or seizure become "reasonable." A lawful warrant gives the police the power to go into your house to arrest you or search your belongings.

Probable Cause

What level of information does a police officer need to invade your reasonable expectation of privacy? How specific or accurate does the information have to be? For example, in the journal case, what information should the detective know before invading the bedroom and inner thoughts of a person? For the lunch bag scenario, would things be different if the police officer had a tip that a man with a brown bag had a gun? Would that give him a reason to snatch the bag from your hand? The answer is that a certain level of information needs to be obtained that balances the need for police investigation with a need for privacy. Probable cause is the legal standard that allows police to arrest you or to search and seize you and your property. Probable cause is necessary for both arrest warrants and search warrants. Probable cause is a level of evidence.

YOUR THOUGHTS

Can a police officer insist that you must stop and identify yourself for any reason? Are you "seized" in this situation under the Fourth Amendment? Does the police officer have wide latitude to stop you, or does the officer need to demonstrate that this is "reasonable" based on circumstances surrounding the stop?

For probable cause to exist, a police officer must have trustworthy information sufficient to convince a reasonable person that a crime has occurred and that you committed the crime. If a police officer has probable cause, it means that the officer knows facts or circumstances that if truthful would be enough for a reasonable person to believe that you had either committed a crime or had evidence of a crime. Probable cause is more than a mere suspicion or hunch. However, the Supreme Court has never given a precise definition, choosing to judge situations on a case-by-case basis.

YOUR THOUGHTS

How much evidence should a police officer have before arresting you for a crime? How much evidence should a police officer have before searching your house or belongings? How sure should the police be before acting? How would you verify that they were sure?

What is the probability of probable cause? How sure must police be that a crime is being committed? What level of probability (1–99 percent) would you assign to each level of proof? The Court refuses to play the numbers game. What do you think?

Totality of Circumstances Test

In *Illinois v. Gates,* a nosy neighbor reported the suspicious activities of Sue and Lance Gates to the police.[16] In a letter written to the local chief of police, the anonymous neighbor accused the couple of dealing drugs. Based on this information and after watching the couple for a while, the police requested a search warrant from the local magistrate judge. Drugs were recovered. At trial, Lance Gates challenged the warrant, arguing that there was no probable cause for the search. Do you think the information in the letter was trustworthy?

> Probable cause is not a very apt term; it has little to do with probability and nothing whatever with causality. But it is the term chosen by the Framers to describe the degree of suspicion requisite for the government to move into the citizen's private spaces. It means 'damn good reason to believe,' that's all.
>
> —H. Richard Uviller, *Virtual Justice: The Flawed Prosecution of Crime in America*
> (New Haven, Conn.: Yale University Press, 1996), 49

ILLINOIS, PETITIONER
V.
LANCE GATES

Supreme Court of the United States
No. 81-430.
Argued October 13, 1982.
Reargued March 1, 1983.
Decided June 8, 1983.

Justice REHNQUIST delivered the opinion of the Court.

Respondents Lance and Susan Gates were indicted for violation of state drug laws after police officers, executing a search warrant, discovered marijuana and other contraband in their automobile and home. . . .

II

. . . Bloomingdale, Ill., is a suburb of Chicago located in DuPage County. On May 3, 1978, the Bloomingdale Police Department received by mail an anonymous handwritten letter which read as follows:

"This letter is to inform you that you have a couple in your town who strictly make their living on selling drugs. They are Sue and Lance Gates, they live on Greenway, off Bloomingdale Rd. in the condominiums. Most of their buys are done in Florida. Sue his wife drives their car to Florida, where she leaves it to be loaded up with drugs, then Lance flies down and drives it back. Sue flies back after she drops the car off in Florida. May 3 she is driving down there again and Lance will be flying down in a few days to drive it back. At the time Lance drives the car back he has the trunk loaded with over $100,000.00 in drugs. Presently they have over $100,000.00 worth of drugs in their basement.

They brag about the fact they never have to work, and make their entire living on pushers.

I guarantee if you watch them carefully you will make a big catch. They are friends with some big drugs dealers, who visit their house often.

Lance & Susan Gates

Greenway in Condominiums"

The letter was referred by the Chief of Police of the Bloomingdale Police Department to Detective Mader, who decided to pursue the tip. Mader learned, from the office of the Illinois Secretary of State, that an Illinois driver's license had been issued to one Lance Gates, residing at a stated address in Bloomingdale. He contacted a confidential informant, whose examination of certain financial records revealed a more recent address for the Gateses, and he also learned from a police officer assigned to O'Hare Airport that "L. Gates" had made a reservation on Eastern Airlines flight 245 to West Palm Beach, Fla., scheduled to depart from Chicago on May 5 at 4:15 p.m.

Mader then made arrangements with an agent of the Drug Enforcement Administration for surveillance of the May 5 Eastern Airlines flight. The agent later reported to Mader that Gates had boarded the flight, and that federal agents in Florida had observed him arrive in West Palm Beach and take a taxi to the nearby Holiday Inn. They also reported that Gates went to a room registered to one Susan Gates and that, at 7:00 a.m. the next morning, Gates and an unidentified woman left the motel in a Mercury bearing Illinois license plates and drove northbound on an interstate highway frequently used by travelers to the Chicago area. In addition, the DEA agent informed Mader that the license plate number on the Mercury was registered to a Hornet station wagon owned by Gates. The agent also advised Mader that the driving time between West Palm Beach and Bloomingdale was approximately 22 to 24 hours.

Mader signed an affidavit setting forth the foregoing facts, and submitted it to a judge of the Circuit Court of DuPage County, together with a copy of the anonymous letter. The judge of that court thereupon issued a search warrant for the Gateses' residence and for their automobile. The judge, in deciding to issue the warrant, could have determined that the *modus operandi* of the Gateses had been substantially corroborated. As the anonymous letter predicted, Lance Gates had flown from Chicago to West Palm Beach late in the afternoon of May 5th, had checked into a hotel room registered in the name of his wife, and, at 7:00 a.m. the following morning, had headed north, accompanied by an unidentified woman, out of West Palm Beach on an interstate highway used by travelers from South Florida to Chicago in an automobile bearing a license plate issued to him.

At 5:15 a.m. on March 7th, only 36 hours after he had flown out of Chicago, Lance Gates, and his wife, returned to their home in Bloomingdale, driving the car in which they had left West Palm Beach some 22 hours earlier. The Bloomingdale police were awaiting them, searched the trunk of the Mercury, and uncovered approximately 350 pounds of marijuana. A search of the Gateses' home revealed marijuana, weapons, and other contraband. . . .

The Illinois Supreme Court concluded—and we are inclined to agree—that, standing alone, the anonymous letter sent to the Bloomingdale Police Department would not provide the basis for a magistrate's determination that there was probable cause to believe contraband would be found in the Gateses' car and home. The letter provides virtually nothing from which one might conclude that its author is either honest or his information reliable; likewise, the letter gives absolutely no indication of the basis for the writer's predictions regarding the Gateses' criminal activities. Something more was required, then, before a magistrate could conclude that there was probable cause to believe that contraband would be found in the Gateses' home and car. . . .

The Illinois Supreme Court also properly recognized that Detective Mader's affidavit might be capable of supplementing the anonymous letter with information sufficient to permit a determination of probable cause. . . .

We agree with the Illinois Supreme Court that an informant's "veracity," "reliability" and "basis of knowledge" are all highly relevant in determining the value of his report. We do not agree, however, that these elements should be understood as entirely separate and independent requirements to be rigidly exacted in every case, which the opinion of the Supreme Court of Illinois would imply. Rather, as detailed below, they should be understood simply as closely intertwined issues that may usefully illuminate the commonsense, practical question whether there is "probable cause" to believe that contraband or evidence is located in a particular place.

III

This totality of the circumstances approach is far more consistent with our prior treatment of probable cause than is any rigid demand that specific "tests" be satisfied by every informant's tip. Perhaps the central teaching of our decisions bearing on the probable cause standard is that it is a "practical, nontechnical conception." *Brinegar v. United States,* 338 U.S. 160, 176 (1949). "In dealing with probable cause, . . . as the very name implies, we deal with probabilities. These are not technical; they are the factual and practical considerations of everyday life on which reasonable and prudent men, not legal technicians, act." *Id.,* at 175. . . .

As these comments illustrate, probable cause is a fluid concept—turning on the assessment of probabilities in particular factual contexts—not readily, or even usefully, reduced to a neat set of legal rules. . . .

IV

. . . [S]tanding alone, the facts obtained through the independent investigation of Mader and the DEA at least suggested that the Gateses were involved in drug trafficking. In addition to being a popular vacation site, Florida is well-known as a source of narcotics and other illegal drugs. . . . Lance Gates' flight to Palm Beach, his brief, overnight stay in a motel, and apparent immediate return north to Chicago in the family car, conveniently awaiting him in West Palm Beach, is as suggestive of a pre-arranged drug run, as it is of an ordinary vacation trip.

In addition, the magistrate could rely on the anonymous letter, which had been corroborated in major part by Mader's efforts. . . . The corroboration of the letter's predictions that the Gateses' car would be in Florida, that Lance Gates would fly to Florida in the next day or so, and that he would drive the car north toward Bloomingdale all indicated, albeit not with certainty, that the informant's other assertions also were true. "Because an informant is right about some things, he is more probably right about other facts," . . . including the claim regarding the Gateses' illegal activity. . . .

Finally, the anonymous letter contained a range of details relating not just to easily obtained facts and conditions existing at the time of the tip, but to future actions of third parties ordinarily not easily predicted. The letter writer's accurate information as to the travel plans of each of the Gateses was of a character likely obtained only from the Gateses themselves, or from someone familiar with their not entirely ordinary travel plans. If the informant had access to accurate information of this type a magistrate could properly conclude that it was not unlikely that he also had access to reliable information of the Gateses' alleged illegal activities.

But, as discussed previously . . . probable cause does not demand the certainty we associate with formal trials. It is enough that there was a fair probability that the writer of the anonymous letter had obtained his entire story either from the Gates or someone they trusted. And corroboration of major portions of the letter's predictions provides just this probability. It is apparent, therefore, that the judge issuing the warrant had a "substantial basis for . . . conclud[ing]" that probable cause to search the Gateses' home and car existed.

POINTS TO PONDER

- Do you understand the totality of circumstances standard set out by the Court? If you do not, you are not alone. Thousands of judges have wrestled over the question. How would you make it clearer?
- Were you convinced that the details of the letter along with the future actions gave the police reason to believe that the Gateses were involved in crime? If you were the magistrate judge, would you have signed the warrant? What if you were wrong, and the Gateses were on vacation?
- Argue why the facts are just as likely to suggest a business trip or vacation as a drug deal. Without the neighbor's letter, would there be enough suspicious information to support a finding of probable cause?
- How do you think the determination of probable cause is affected by issues of class, gender, and race? Should those factors ever play into the probability of guilt?

EXERCISE 3.1. How would you evaluate trustworthy information required for probable cause? Ask yourself the following questions.

- *Who:* Who is providing the information? Is this person reliable? Is he believable? Do you trust him?
- *How:* How did the person get the information? Did he obtain it personally? Did the person overhear it?
- *What:* Are the details in the information believable? Can you verify the details? Are there self-verifying details? Is the information corroborated by anyone else?

The Warrant Requirement

Search warrants and arrest warrants are legal documents that allow the police to interfere with your reasonable expectation of privacy. To get a warrant, a police officer must go to a judge and swear under criminal penalty for lying that there is probable cause to believe

> "The point of the Fourth Amendment, which often is not grasped by zealous officers, is not that it denies law enforcement the support of the usual inferences which reasonable men draw from evidence. Its protection consists in requiring that those inferences be drawn by a neutral and detached magistrate instead of being judged by the officer engaged in the often competitive enterprise of ferreting out crime."
>
> —*Johnson v. United States*, 333 U.S. 10, 13–14 (1948)

that either you committed a crime or that evidence of a crime is in your possession. In essence, warrants allow police to search you or arrest you.

A warrant is a legal document that has four important elements.

1. It is signed by a judicial officer, such as a judge or magistrate.
2. It recounts facts and circumstances that present probable cause under a totality of circumstances.
3. The facts are sworn to be the truth by a police officer.
4. The facts and circumstances are particular to a specific person or place to be searched.

Each of these requirements must be in a warrant for it to be valid. (See box on page 98.)

Why are warrants required? The answer dates back to the founding of the United States. When England ruled the American colonies, British officials used "general warrants" to search colonialist homes and seize colonialist goods. General warrants were not particularized to a person or place to be searched. These general warrants were open-ended and gave the British officials unbounded powers to interfere with the actions of the Americans. The drafters of the U.S. Constitution added the warrant requirement in the Fourth Amendment as a response to this interference.

Warrants must specify the particular person to be arrested or place to be searched. Thus they are not unbounded. The warrant requirement also limits police interference because police must appeal to an independent and neutral judicial officer for approval. The power of the warrant is the power of the court and not the individual officer. Thus, in the rush to solve crimes, police are required to get a second opinion before acting on their suspicions. This second opinion acts as a means to secure individual liberty.

POINTS TO PONDER

- Does the probable cause standard of a warrant satisfy you? Is it a sufficient check on police? Is it too restrictive for police? How would you change it?
- Who gets to decide if there is probable cause? How can the judge determine if the information is trustworthy? After all, the judicial officer was not present and has no firsthand knowledge. How could the judicial officer verify the police officer's sworn statement? What if the police officer is mistaken? What if she lies?

SUPERIOR COURT OF THE DISTRICT OF COLUMBIA
SEARCH WARRANT

TO: _____.

(Specific Law Enforcement Officer or Classification of Officer of the Metropolitan Police Department)

Affidavit, herewith attached, having been made before me by _____ that he has probable cause to believe that on the (person) (premises) (vehicle) (object) known as _____in the District of Columbia, there is now being concealed certain property, _____

which is _____ and as I am satisfied that there is probable cause to believe that the property so described is being concealed on the above designated (person) (premises) (vehicle) (object) and that the foregoing grounds for issuance of the warrant exist.

YOU ARE HEREBY AUTHORIZED within 10 days of the date of issuance of this warrant to search in the daytime/at any time of the day or night, the designated (person) (premises) (vehicle) (object) for the property specified and if the property be found there.

YOU ARE COMMANDED TO SEIZE IT, TO WRITE AND SUBSCRIBE an inventory of the property seized, to leave a copy of this warrant and return to file, a further copy of this warrant and return with the Court on the next Court day after its execution.

ISSUED this _____   _____

                                              Judge, Superior Court of the District of Columbia

---

RETURN

I received the above detailed warrant on _____, 20_____ and have executed it as follows:

On _____, 20_____, at _____ A.M./P.M., I searched the (person) (premises) (vehicle) (object) described in the warrant and I left a copy of the warrant and return with _____ properly posted.
(name of person searched or owner, occupant, custodian or person present at place of search)

The following is an inventory of the property taken pursuant to this warrant.

_____

_____

This inventory was made in the presence of

_____

I swear that this is a true and detailed account of all property taken by me under this warrant.

                                              _____

                                              Executing Officer

Subscribed and sworn to before me this _____ day of _____, 20_____.

                                              _____

                                              Judge, Superior Court of the District of Columbia

- In the quote from *Johnson v. United States,* what did the judge mean by the phrase "the often competitive enterprise of ferreting out crime"? Why would the police be competitive? Isn't it a good thing that they are competitive?
- What do you think of the following quote from a Chicago police officer?

> The search warrant is the most complicated and most dangerous thing you can do in the CPD [Chicago Police Department]. A warrant is the most power an officer has—it's a document that gives you the right to knock someone's door down. Doing a search warrant is a real art. First of all, to get it approved, it has to go before a state's attorney, and they scrutinize them pretty good. In addition to that, you have to have the expertise to get the people in there who are sharp enough to get into position, get the place within thirty seconds, get the dope, bring it back, arrest all these people, and have the finesse to put it down on paper, bring it to court, and then testify before the judge—and not blow the case. There are all these steps you have to do. You leave one of those out, and *you're* out. The whole thing for nix. Nothing. It's gone.
> —Connie Fletcher[17]

Notes

1. *Olmstead v. United States,* 277 U.S. 438, 478 (1928).
2. *Katz v. United States,* 389 U.S. 347 (1967).
3. See Center for Civic Education, "Lesson 6: What Are the Possible Consequences of Privacy? Foundations of Democracy: Authority, Privacy, Responsibility, and Justice," available at http://www. civiced.org/fod_ms_priv06_tg.html.
4. *Greenwood v. California,* 486 U.S. 35 (1988).
5. *Bond v. United States,* 529 U.S. 334 (2000).
6. *United States v. Place,* 462 U.S. 696 (1983).
7. *California v. Ciraolo,* 476 U.S. 207 (1986).
8. *Florida v. Riley,* 488 U.S. 445 (1989).
9. *Dow Chemical Company v. United States,* 476 U.S. 227 (1986).
10. *Kyllo v. United States,* 533 U.S. 27 (2001).
11. *Arizona v. Hicks,* 480 U.S. 321, 324 (1987).
12. *United States v. Mendenhall,* 446 U.S. 544 (1980).
13. David Cole, *No Equal Justice: Race and Class in the American Criminal Justice System* (New York: New Press, 1999), p. 16.
14. Cole, *No Equal Justice,* p. 16.
15. Cole, *No Equal Justice,* p. 16.
16. *Illinois v. Gates,* 462 U.S. 213 (1983).
17. Connie Fletcher, *What Cops Know* (New York: Pocket Books, 1990), pp. 216–217.

Additional Sources

Allen, Ronald, and Richard Kuhns. *Constitutional Criminal Procedure: An Examination of the Fourth, Fifth, and Sixth Amendments and Related Areas.* 2d ed. Boston, Mass.: Little Brown, 1991.

Amsterdam, Anthony. "Perspectives on the Fourth Amendment." *Minnesota Law Review* 58 (1974): 349.

Dressler, Joshua. *Understanding Criminal Procedure.* New York: Matthew Bender, 1991.

Kamisar, Yale, Wayne LaFave, and others. *Modern Criminal Procedure: Cases Comments Questions*. 9th ed. New York: West Publishing Company, 1999.

LaFave, Wayne. *Search and Seizure: A Treatise on the Fourth Amendment*. 3d ed. New York: West Publishing Company, 1996.

Miller, Marc, and Ronald White. *Teachers' Manual Criminal Procedures: Cases, Statutes, and Executive Materials*. 2d ed. New York: Aspen Publishers, 2003.

Tomkovicz, James J., and Welsh White. *Criminal Procedure: Constitutional Constraints Upon Investigation and Proof*. 3d ed. New York: Matthew Bender, 1998.

EXCEPTIONS SWALLOW THE RULE: WARRANTLESS SEARCHES

4

"When the right of privacy must reasonably yield to the right of search is, as a rule,
to be decided by a judicial officer, not by a policeman or a Government enforcement agent."
JUSTICE ROBERT H. JACKSON, *JOHNSON V. UNITED STATES* (1948)

The basic constitutional rule is that what makes a police search of your body and your belongings reasonable is a search warrant. Without a warrant, any evidence found during a search can be thrown out during trial. So, under the Fourth Amendment, before searching or apprehending you, the police must first go to a judge and get a search warrant based on probable cause that a reason exists for you to be searched, seized, or arrested.

If this rule were always in force, it would be easy to remember: Police searches and seizures without warrants would be unconstitutional. But, no such luck. The law is much more complicated than that.

The U.S. Supreme Court has carved out a series of large **exceptions** to the warrant requirement, which give the police power to arrest and search people even when they do not have a warrant. The number of exceptions is so large and their range is so broad that it is fair to say that the exceptions to the warrant requirement have swallowed large parts of the rule.

If you think of the warrant requirement as cheese, it is not American cheese but Swiss cheese. There are large holes all over it—and probably more holes than cheese. The warrant requirement still has protective power when you are at home and there is no emergency and no one consents to a police search. But the majority of searches and seizures happen today without warrants. These are the so-called warrantless searches.

Six main exceptions to the warrant requirement rule justify warrantless searches. The first four are intended to help the police gather evidence when they have probable cause to search but obtaining a warrant would be impractical, impossible, or dangerous for them. The last two drop not only the warrant requirement but the probable cause requirement, too.

The first exception is the "hot pursuit" exception, more formally known as the "emergency exception." In felony cases, when police have probable cause but no warrant and they are chasing a fleeing suspect or are concerned about the destruction of evidence, courts have allowed them to make entries directly into people's homes to pursue suspects even on a warrantless basis.

The second exception is the "plain view" doctrine, which allows police who are lawfully present somewhere to seize property when they see evidence of a crime right in front of their eyes. The reason for this exception is that courts do not want to penalize police for **inadvertent** discovery of other crimes or **contraband** found during the regular course of police investigation.

The third exception is for searches that occur during a criminal arrest. The reason for this "search incident to an arrest" exception is principally to protect officers from weapons or dangerous objects that suspects might have on their persons during an arrest.

The fourth exception is the "automobile exception," which grants police the power to search cars and other motor vehicles, as well as the things inside those vehicles, without a warrant so long as probable cause to search is present.

The fifth exception is for "consensual searches." Such searches take place when the police ask people to allow a search of their home, car, or body and they voluntarily and knowingly waive their rights and allow police to search. The assumption behind the consent exception is that people are freely waiving their right to keep the police from searching their private property or person.

Finally, the sixth exception allows police stops based on "reasonable suspicion." "Reasonable suspicion" describes a level of evidence less than probable cause. This exception is perhaps the most important exception to the warrant rule. Stops and searches based on reasonable suspicion are probably the most common and contested of the exceptions to the warrant requirement.

Exception 1: Hot Pursuit

Police regularly handle emergencies. Many times they act on a moment's notice to stop a crime or protect people in the community from danger. A suspect could escape, evi-

What should a police officer do when faced with a situation that requires immediate action to arrest or search but there is no warrant? Should he arrest or search anyway? Should he get a warrant? Does it depend on the crime?

dence could get destroyed, or innocent people could get hurt. Because of the need for police to act in these emergency situations, the Supreme Court introduced an exception to the Fourth Amendment's warrant requirement for cases in which police are in hot pursuit of suspects fleeing into a house or private residence. The clearest case of an emergency exception comes when the police are notified of a crime in progress and start to chase a suspect.

Consider the fictional case of sixteen-year-old Harold. Armed with a gun, he holds up a 7-11 and makes off with $363. The teen suspect runs down an alley, while the store employees call the police. Just a few blocks away, two neighbors see Harold running frantically into his house, clutching a big wad of cash, and they call the police, too. The police arrive quickly on the street in several patrol cars and stop at the suspect's door. They knock. When Harold's mother responds, they tell her they are investigating a crime. Although she does not invite them in and they have no warrant, they enter anyway. The police spread out through the house and find Harold pretending to be asleep upstairs in his bedroom. They discover a pistol in a flush tank in the bathroom as well as extra ammunition in Harold's bedroom. The police arrest Harold and introduce all these items into evidence against him. Harold tries to get the evidence excluded and his case thrown out on the grounds that the search of his home was illegal because the police had no search warrant or arrest warrant that would have allowed them entry.

Was this an emergency? Under the Supreme Court's precedents, almost certainly yes. The facts of Harold's case largely mirror the facts of *Warden, Maryland Penitentiary v. Hayden,* which involved a similar problem with an adult suspect.[1] In *Hayden,* the Court found that

> [t]he police were informed that an armed robbery had taken place, and that the suspect had entered 2111 Cocoa Lane less than five minutes before they reached it. They acted reasonably when they entered the house and began to search for a man of the description they had been given and for weapons which he had used in the robbery or might use against them. The Fourth Amendment does not require police officers to delay in the course of an investigation if to do so would gravely endanger their lives or the lives of others. Speed here was essential, and only a thorough search of the house for persons and weapons could have insured that Hayden was the only man present and that the police had control of all weapons which could be used against them or to effect an escape.

Does this analysis seem convincing to you? Should the police have had to get a search warrant from a judge or, under these circumstances, would that just be silly?

The hot pursuit doctrine kicks in when the police are chasing a potentially dangerous criminal in the course of a serious crime. Hot pursuit applies only to felonies. But what if the apparent crime is a minor one, such as a simple traffic offense, and the police have time to get a proper warrant? Can the police still benefit from the hot pursuit exception to avoid getting a warrant?

Imagine the case of Billie Jean, a seventeen-year-old Wisconsin girl who was driving her pickup truck home from her senior prom, where she drank some beers with friends behind the school. After changing speeds and veering from side to side, she swerved the truck off the road and came to a stop in an open field. No damage was done to any person or property. A neighbor, Carol Davis, saw the vehicle's zig-zag movements and became concerned. Fearing that the driver might get back on the highway, Carol drove her minivan up behind the truck to block it from the road. Another passerby stopped at the scene, and Carol asked her to call the police. Before the police arrived, Billie Jean emerged from her truck, approached Carol's minivan, and asked her for a ride home. Carol suggested that they wait for assistance in removing or repairing the pickup truck. Billie Jean then walked away from the scene and vanished.

When the police arrived, they questioned Carol, who described what she had seen, noting that the driver was a teenaged girl who seemed very sick. The officer checked the motor vehicle registration of Billie Jean's abandoned truck and learned that it was registered to Billie Jean's parents. They lived just a short distance from the scene, and therefore easily within walking distance.

Without securing any type of warrant, the police went directly to Billie Jean's home, arriving about 1 a.m. When her mother answered the door, two police officers briskly gained entry into the house by saying they needed to come in. Proceeding to Billie Jean's bedroom, they found her lying in bed. When the police began to question her, they noticed her bloodshot eyes and slurred speech. At this point, she was placed under arrest. She later was prosecuted and convicted for driving a motor vehicle while under the influence of alcohol. Billie Jean appealed her conviction on the grounds that the search of her house and the officers' ability to find her were based on an illegal warrantless search of the home. Was the search illegal or was it a fair application of the hot pursuit exception?

In a similar case, *Welsh v. Wisconsin,* the Supreme Court found that the hot pursuit exception was not designed for cases in which the underlying crime is "relatively minor"—such as a simple traffic offense.[2] The Court did not view it as constitutionally reasonable to waive the warrant requirement and give police the power to enter people's homes when only suspicion exists of a lesser offense. Moreover, because Welsh had

---

YOUR THOUGHTS

Should police be required to get a warrant in cold pursuit types of cases, such as when they know that a suspect is in a certain location and cannot leave to go somewhere else?

---

already arrived home and had left his car at the scene of the accident, he posed little remaining threat to public safety. The Court ruled that

> [o]n the facts of this case, . . . the claim of hot pursuit is unconvincing because there was no immediate or continuous pursuit of the petitioner from the scene of a crime. Moreover, because the petitioner had already arrived home, and had abandoned his car at the scene of the accident, there was little remaining threat to the public safety. Hence, the only potential emergency claimed by the State was the need to ascertain the petitioner's blood-alcohol level.

The minor nature of the crime was not enough.

POINTS TO PONDER

- The terms "emergency," "exigency," and "hot pursuit" have been used to describe the same type of immediate and pressing urgency. How do courts know when the police were acting on an emergency basis? What facts make an emergency?
- If the police had gone to get an arrest or search warrant in *Hayden,* what would have happened to the evidence? When the police got to the front door, what were their options? What if they had surrounded the house and waited for a search warrant? Consider the same questions about the *Welsh* case. Do you get different answers?
- The *Welsh* case involved a warrantless search of a house based on a suspected traffic offense. The Supreme Court held that the search was unconstitutional because of the relatively minor nature of the offense. Further, the Court reasoned that the only potential **exigency** was the need to get a blood alcohol level test from Welsh.

  Compare the *Welsh* case with *Schmerber v. California.*[3] In *Schmerber,* a suspect was arrested for driving under the influence of alcohol. He was brought to a hospital. At the hospital, the arresting police officer ordered that a doctor take a blood sample from Schmerber to test his blood alcohol level. The doctor did so, and the results revealed alcohol in Schmerber's bloodstream. Schmerber challenged the blood test saying that sticking a needle in his arm and withdrawing blood was a search and the removal of blood was a **seizure**. Do you agree? Was the Fourth Amendment violated?

  The Supreme Court held that the blood alcohol test was a search and seizure. However, it was a permissible search and seizure under the emergency exception to the warrant requirement. The Court said that because the police officer had probable cause to arrest Schmerber for driving under the influence, he could order the test. The emergency was that the alcohol in Schmerber's blood could have been lost by the time the officer obtained a warrant. Thus, the Court held that the warrantless search and seizure were justified.

  Do you agree? What is the difference between *Welsh* and *Schmerber?* Is it just that in *Welsh* the police entered a house, and in *Schmerber* they ordered that blood be drawn? Which is more intrusive? Does *Schmerber* mean that police can take other evidence from your person if they think it will help solve a crime? Hair? DNA? Fingerprints? It seems like the police may have this power.

Exception 2: Plain View

The plain view doctrine allows police to take and use evidence of crime that they observe firsthand even if they had no warrant to look for it. The theory is that so long as police have not illegally entered certain premises, they should not be required to ignore evidence of crime that they can plainly see.

Suppose officers are searching your house for a stolen television. Because there is no emergency, they obtain a valid search warrant, based upon probable cause, to look for the television in your home. While searching, they discover a bag of cocaine on your dining room table. Should the officers be required to ignore the cocaine because the search warrant was issued for a TV? Should the officers have to go back to court and request a second search warrant to seize the drugs? In general, the answer to these questions is no. Courts will allow this type of accidental discovery of evidence plainly in the view of officers, permitting the unexpected seizure of the evidence to take place without a warrant.

For the police to use the plain view doctrine, they must be lawfully on the scene in the first place, and the evidence officers find in plain view must be something obviously incriminating (for example, illegal drugs). Why must the police be lawfully present on the premises to get the benefit of the plain view doctrine? The theory is that, otherwise, police could justify illegal searches after the fact by simply finding incriminating evidence. In almost every case that gets to court, some incriminating evidence has been seized by police officers (otherwise no need for a criminal trial would exist). The real question is how the police came to acquire the evidence. If the police accidentally found it while legitimately looking for something else, the court would have no reason to punish them for that discovery. However, if the police were acting unconstitutionally in the first place, courts do not want to reward the illegality through the use of the plain view exception. Consider the imaginary case involving Bonnie and Claude to see how this problem might be resolved.

Bonnie and Claude are teenagers who have gone wayward. They have dropped out of high school and are living together on the outskirts of Chicago—and on the margins of society. One night they break into a home and tie up the husband and wife they find in the master bedroom and rob them of jewelry and cash. During this encounter, enough conversation takes place to enable the victims to identify their attackers' voices. The identification was partially confirmed by a next-door neighbor who saw the robbers leaving the scene.

Sergeant Lazarus, an experienced cop, investigated the crime and determined that there was probable cause to search Bonnie and Claude's suburban apartment for the pro-

---

YOUR THOUGHTS

Should police officers who are searching a house have to ignore obvious criminal evidence that they find by accident? For example, what if the search warrant specifies drugs but the police find guns?

---

ceeds of the robbery. So he went to court to ask for a search warrant. The warrant issued by the magistrate authorized a search for the stolen jewelry and money, including three specifically described antique rings. Executing the warrant, Lazarus searched their residence, but he did not find any of the stolen property. However, during the course of the search, he discovered a firearm sitting in plain view on the coffee table and seized it. Although the police did not have enough evidence to charge Bonnie and Claude for the robbery, they did charge them for possession of illegal firearms. They were convicted but appealed their convictions on the grounds that the seizure of the firearm was unconstitutional.

Do you think the evidence (the firearm) should be admitted or excluded as evidence? The Supreme Court found in a similar case, *Horton v. California,* that the weapons evidence accidentally discovered was admissible under the plain view exception. Given that the officers were lawfully present **pursuant** to a search warrant and came upon the guns inadvertently, they were allowed to seize the evidence of firearms crimes and introduce it in court later. "In this case," Justice John Paul Stevens wrote, "the items seized from petitioner's home were discovered during a lawful search authorized by a valid warrant. When they were discovered, it was immediately apparent to the officer that they constituted incriminating evidence."

POINTS TO PONDER

- The plain view exception allows officers to seize incriminating items without a warrant. Does it make sense?
- What if the evidence in the *Horton* case had been in a closet? Or in a safe? Or written in a diary? Should that evidence have remained hidden? How would the police have obtained that evidence?
- The *Horton* case involved a search of a house with a valid search warrant. What about plain view on the street? Or in a car? If an officer sees contraband in plain view, shouldn't he be able to seize it? What if the officer is not sure whether or not she sees contraband?
- What if the criminal evidence does not appear in "plain view" but within "plain smell" or "plain sound" or "plain touch"? Imagine that the police have a warrant to search someone's apartment for stolen government documents but smell marijuana burning. Can they find it and make appropriate seizures and arrests? The Court says yes, finding that what matters is the inadvertent discovery of evidence within "plain access to the senses."

Exception 3: Search Incident to an Arrest

Arrests precede prosecutions for breaking the law. Arrests are commonplace in the American criminal justice system. According to the Federal Bureau of Investigation, law enforcement authorities around the country made a total of 13.6 million criminal arrests in 2003. Usually if a person is arrested, police officers handcuff and take him to the police station to be processed and charged. Meantime, as part of the arrest itself, the suspect is usually thoroughly searched by the police.

After an arrest, should police officers be allowed to freely search a person, his clothes, and belongings before that person is taken to the police station? Should they be allowed to search his house as well? If not, why not?

Because police officers are taking you into their custody, courts allow them the freedom to search you after placing you under arrest. Usually this means that police can search your clothes, body, and the area immediately around where you were arrested for weapons or illegal items. Sometimes this area is called your wingspan, because it includes everywhere on your body and nearby that you might be able to reach. The reason for the search is to protect officers and other arrestees from any dangerous weapons or objects that you might have in your possession. Many times, additional evidence unrelated to the search for dangerous weapons is found during these searches. Courts have allowed such searches as exceptions to the warrant rule because of a practical concern with officer safety. But courts do not think that the arrest of a suspect justifies a much broader sweep of the premises. In *Chimel v. California,* the Court drew the line.[4]

—•—

TED STEVEN CHIMEL, PETITIONER,
V.
STATE OF CALIFORNIA

Supreme Court of the United States
No. 770.
Argued March 27, 1969.
Decided June 23, 1969.
Rehearing Denied Oct. 13, 1969.

Mr. Justice STEWART delivered the opinion of the Court.

This case raises basic questions concerning the permissible scope under the Fourth Amendment of a search incident to a lawful arrest.

The relevant facts are essentially undisputed. Late in the afternoon of September 13, 1965, three police officers arrived at the Santa Ana, California, home of the petitioner with a warrant authorizing his arrest for the burglary of a coin shop. The officers knocked on the door, identified themselves to the petitioner's wife, and asked if they might come inside. She ushered them into the house, where they waited 10 or 15 minutes until the petitioner returned home from work.

When the petitioner entered the house, one of the officers handed him the arrest warrant and asked for permission to 'look around.' The petitioner objected, but was advised that 'on the basis of the lawful arrest,' the officers would nonetheless conduct a search. No search warrant had been issued.

Accompanied by the petitioner's wife, the officers then looked through the entire three-bedroom house, including the attic, the garage, and a small workshop. In some rooms the search was relatively cursory. In the master bedroom and sewing room, however, the officers directed the petitioner's wife to open drawers and 'to physically move contents of the drawers from side to side so that (they) might view any items that would have come from (the) burglary.' After completing the search, they seized numerous items—primarily coins, but also several medals, tokens, and a few other objects. The entire search took between 45 minutes and an hour.

At the petitioner's subsequent state trial on two charges of burglary, the items taken from his house were admitted into evidence against him, over his objection that they had been unconstitutionally seized. . . . *This brings us directly to the question whether the warrantless search of the petitioner's entire house can be constitutionally justified as incident to that arrest.* . . .

When an arrest is made, it is reasonable for the arresting officer to search the person arrested in order to remove any weapons that the latter might seek to use in order to resist arrest or effect his escape. Otherwise, the officer's safety might well be endangered, and the arrest itself frustrated. In addition, it is entirely reasonable for the arresting officer to search for and seize any evidence on the arrestee's person in order to prevent its concealment or destruction. And the area into which an arrestee might reach in order to grab a weapon or evidentiary items must, of course, be governed by a like rule. A gun on a table or in a drawer in front of one who is arrested can be as dangerous to the arresting officer as one concealed in the clothing of the person arrested. There is ample justification, therefore, for a search of the arrestee's person and the area 'within his immediate control'—construing that phrase to mean the area from within which he might gain possession of a weapon or destructible evidence.

There is no comparable justification, however, for routinely searching any room other than that in which an arrest occurs—or, for that matter, for searching through all the desk drawers or other closed or concealed areas in that room itself. Such searches, in the absence of well-recognized exceptions, may be made only under the authority of a search warrant. The 'adherence to judicial processes' mandated by the Fourth Amendment requires no less.

. . . Application of sound Fourth Amendment principles to the facts of this case produces a clear result. The search here went far beyond the petitioner's person and the area from within which he might have obtained either a weapon or something that could have been used as evidence against him. There was no constitutional justification, in the absence of a search warrant, for extending the search beyond that area. The scope of the search was, therefore, 'unreasonable' under the Fourth and Fourteenth Amendments and the petitioner's conviction cannot stand.

- Does the Court's decision in *Chimel* concerning the search of the person make sense? What interests are being protected by the search? Safety? Preventing destruction of evidence? What other reasons would you give to allow police to search?
- Under the Court's decision in *Chimel*, only the search of the person was permissible. Why couldn't police also search the house? What if illegal contraband was in the house? Do you agree with the Court's reasoning?
- What if you are arrested with people standing next to you? Should the police be allowed to search them incident to your arrest?

Exception 4: Automobile Exception

The automobile exception deals with searches and seizures that police officers conduct in people's cars, but the exception has been extended to cover most other moving vehicles as well, such as motorcycles and boats. Courts have given much less Fourth Amendment protection to cars and other vehicles of transportation than to the home.

Over the years, the Supreme Court has offered three main reasons for reducing the level of Fourth Amendment protections people get in cars.

Over the years, courts have determined that people have fewer privacy rights in their cars than in their homes. The Supreme Court has found that police may search automobiles without obtaining a search warrant as long as there is probable cause to do so. *Source: R. Michael Jenkins/Congressional Quarterly Inc.*

What protections should people have in their car? What do people keep in their cars? Where are cars kept? Should people have an expectation of privacy in the things they keep in the car? Does it depend on what they are doing or carrying? Compare the expectation of privacy you would have in your home with what you have in your car and on the street. Which area is most private?

First, cars are mobile. As a result, a police officer may find it hard to get a warrant before a suspicious car disappears. This reasoning follows the logic of the emergency exception.[5]

Second, the "extensive regulation of motor vehicles" weakens the legitimate expectation that things in one's cars will be kept private. Because cars often get into accidents and more police-citizen contacts involve automobiles than homes, people have to expect greater police interference in their cars. Think of your local meter maid as a point of police-citizen contact.[6]

Third, because automobiles have to travel on public roads and are thus constantly exposed to public examination, they lose a heightened expectation of privacy. This reasoning follows the logic of the plain view exception, because the Court assumes that a car's occupants and its contents are plainly visible. Because a car's "function is transportation, and it seldom serves as one's residence or the repository of personal effects," by definition it deserves less protection than a home.[7]

The Supreme Court ruled in March 2004 that border agents, such as those shown here in California, can dismantle and search a car's gas tank without reasonable suspicion or probable cause. *Source: Lenny Ignelzi/AP Wide World Photos*

POINTS TO PONDER

- The Supreme Court has held that you have a lesser expectation of privacy for things in your car than on the street. Does this make sense to you? Why would you have a lesser expectation of privacy in a locked car compared with a locked backpack?[8]
- Do police ever need to search a car without a warrant? Why couldn't they impound the car (take the keys away or disable the car) and wait for a judge to sign a search warrant? Why create an exception when officers can easily get a warrant in most cases?
- Do you agree with the statement that cars "seldom serve as one's residence or the repository of personal effects"? Do some people sleep in cars? What if you are moving and are transporting all of your personal effects to your new home? What about family vacations?
- What about mobile homes? The automobile exception applies to almost all modes of transportation (cars, motorcycles, boats, planes). But a mobile home usually serves as a residence and holds personal effects. Should it fall under the automobile exception?

> The Supreme Court confronted this situation in *California v. Carney*, when a mobile home was searched without a warrant under the automobile exception.[9] The owners thought it should be given the higher privacy treatment of a home. But the Court determined that, in this case, the mobile home was being used for transportation and not simply as a residence. As a result, it was more like a car than a house. The Court upheld the warrantless search by police.
>
> Do you think that the fact that the mobile home was being used for transportation negates the reasonable expectation of privacy that the owners had in it as a home?

Automobile Exception in Practice

Americans love the open road. As Bruce Springsteen sings, Americans were "born to run," and their cars have been their favorite vehicles of escape. But the desire for freedom in cars does not mean that Americans have the same privacy rights driving as they have in their homes. In fact, the Court has made it easier for police to search cars than homes. The general rule is that when a police officer has probable cause to arrest the driver of a vehicle (even for a traffic violation), he can also search the passenger compartment of the car without a warrant. However, not all traffic stops give police the power to arrest. If the stop is merely for a ticketable (not arrestable) traffic offense, police can search the car only if they have additional probable cause that the car contains something illegal.

Consider a real-life example. In the early morning hours of May 8, 1992, Robert Wilkins and his aunt, uncle, and cousin were in a rental car going from Chicago to Washington, D.C. They had just attended the funeral of a family member. The vehicle was pulled over by a Maryland state trooper. It was alleged that the driver of the car was doing sixty miles an hour in a forty-mile-an-hour zone. The state trooper requested the driver's identification and the registration for the car. He then requested that the driver consent to a full search of the car. Robert Wilkins, a Harvard-educated lawyer and public defender

> Probable cause to arrest = Power to search car
> Traffic offense or ticket = No car search without further probable cause

in the District of Columbia, informed the police officer that he had no right to search the car without arresting the driver. Because there was no probable cause to arrest, there was no justification to search the car. The trooper was not amused by this lesson in the Fourth Amendment. He explained to Wilkins, who was a passenger in the car, that such searches were routine and said that if Wilkins and his family had nothing to hide, they should not have a problem with a search. Another police officer joined the group. Wilkins and his family still refused to allow the search. They wanted to go on their way. The troopers wanted to search the car. Faced with this standoff, the troopers kept the family detained on the side of the road until the police could bring a drug-sniffing dog to the scene. This took thirty minutes. Wilkins and family were ordered out of the car even though it was raining. They were made to wait on the side of the highway in the rain. A "plain view search" was conducted. Nothing illegal was seen. A dog-sniff search was conducted. No drugs were found. Eventually the police allowed them to go with a $105 speeding ticket.[10]

Review the following six questions and answers, based on this automobile stop, about the protections of the Fourth Amendment.

1. Did the police have grounds to stop the car?

Answer: Yes, the state trooper had probable cause to believe that a traffic offense had been committed. If the allegation that the driver was going twenty miles over the speed limit was correct, then sufficient probable cause existed for the traffic stop.

2. Did Robert Wilkins and his family have a reasonable expectation of privacy in the car?

Answer: Yes, but a limited expectation of privacy because of the Supreme Court's automobile rationale. The Wilkins family had an expectation that its car would not be searched without additional probable cause.

3. Did the police have a right to search the car?

Answer: No, Wilkins was correct that the only justification for the stop of his car was for a ticketable traffic offense, nothing more. As a result, there was no further justification to search the car.

4. Can the police ask you to consent to a search?

Answer: Yes, police can always ask you for permission to search your car.

5. Could the police take a look into the car from outside?

Answer: Yes, this is a plain view search. From this vantage point, the police are allowed to see if anything obviously illegal is present.

6. Could the police bring a drug-sniffing dog to the scene?

Answer: Yes, the appearance of drug-sniffing dogs is not considered a search for the purposes of the Fourth Amendment.

- Do you think that the police acted correctly? Is this good police work? Didn't they stay within the constitutional bounds allowed by the Supreme Court? Did the police conduct themselves in an honorable way? If not, which part of the operation bothers you most? The stop? The request to search? The request for consent? The plain view search? The dog? The rain?
- Does it change your thinking about the case to know that the Wilkins family was African American? The incident spurred a major class action lawsuit by the American Civil Liberties Union (ACLU) against the state police for racial profiling. Because of the lawsuit, new procedures were put in place to monitor racial profiling. Statistics show that African Americans were far more likely to be stopped by the police than whites. According to statistics from the ACLU, more than 63 percent of drivers forced out of their cars by state troopers in 2000 were minorities.[11] This figure is vastly disproportionate to the 36 percent of Maryland State residents in that year who were minorities.[12]

The Problem with Pretext

The general rule is that the police, if lawfully arresting you in a car, can search you, your car, and your belongings in the car. In addition, if you are lawfully stopped for a traffic offense, police are allowed to ask you questions, do a plain view search of the interior of the car, and ask for your consent to search the remainder of the car. (You are not obligated to give that consent.)

In a 1998 incident that exposed the pervasiveness of racial profiling nationwide, New Jersey police stopped *(left to right)* Danny Reyes, Keyshon Moore, Leroy Grant, and Rayshawn Brown while they were traveling on the New Jersey Turnpike. When their vehicle rolled backwards, police opened fire, wounding three of the young men. The state agreed to pay them $12.9 million in compensation. *Source: Shawn Baldwin/AP Wide World Photos*

Many people are afraid about the power that the automobile exception gives to the police. The problem is that hundreds of laws and regulations regulate driving. For example, you can be lawfully pulled over if you fail to properly signal before a turn, fail to wear a seatbelt, go two miles over the speed limit, improperly change lanes, drive with headlights out, have a crack in the windshield, and so on. The result is that the police can cite any of hundreds of reasons to pull a person over in a traffic stop, and a good number of reasons to search your car. Not surprisingly, some police officers use traffic stops to advance criminal investigations that are really about other things. These are called pretextual stops.

What do you think of the following statements from police officers?[13]

You can always get a guy legitimately on a traffic violation if you tail him for a while, and then a search can be made.

You don't have to follow a driver very long before he will move to the other side of the yellow line and then you can arrest and search him for driving on the wrong side of the highway.

In the event that we see a suspicious automobile or occupant and wish to search the person or the car, or both, we will usually follow the vehicle until the driver makes a technical violation of a traffic law. Then we have the means of making a legitimate search.

Should pretext stops be allowed or are they unconstitutional? The Supreme Court addressed this question in *Whren v. United States.*[14] *Whren* involved a car that turned without signaling in violation of a traffic regulation. However, this traffic violation was not the real reason that the police were interested in stopping the car. Although the police had something else on their minds, they used the stop as justification for a plain view search.

———

MICHAEL A. WHREN AND JAMES L. BROWN, PETITIONERS,
V.
UNITED STATES

Supreme Court of the United States
No. 95-5841.
Argued April 17, 1996.
Decided June 10, 1996.

Justice SCALIA delivered the opinion of the Court.

In this case we decide whether the temporary detention of a motorist who the police have probable cause to believe has committed a civil traffic violation is inconsistent with the Fourth

Amendment's prohibition against unreasonable seizures unless a reasonable officer would have been motivated to stop the car by a desire to enforce the traffic laws.

I

On the evening of June 10, 1993, plainclothes vice-squad officers of the District of Columbia Metropolitan Police Department were patrolling a "high drug area" of the city in an unmarked car. Their suspicions were aroused when they passed a dark Pathfinder truck with temporary license plates and youthful occupants waiting at a stop sign, the driver looking down into the lap of the passenger at his right. The truck remained stopped at the intersection for what seemed an unusually long time—more than 20 seconds. When the police car executed a U-turn in order to head back toward the truck, the Pathfinder turned suddenly to its right, without signaling, and sped off at an "unreasonable" speed. The policemen followed, and in a short while overtook the Pathfinder when it stopped behind other traffic at a red light. They pulled up alongside, and Officer Ephraim Soto stepped out and approached the driver's door, identifying himself as a police officer and directing the driver, petitioner Brown, to put the vehicle in park. When Soto drew up to the driver's window, he immediately observed two large plastic bags of what appeared to be crack cocaine in petitioner Whren's hands. Petitioners were arrested, and quantities of several types of illegal drugs were retrieved from the vehicle.

. . . At a pretrial **suppression** hearing, they challenged the legality of the stop and the resulting seizure of the drugs. They argued that the stop had not been justified by probable cause to believe, or even reasonable suspicion, that petitioners were engaged in illegal drug-dealing activity; and that Officer Soto's asserted ground for approaching the vehicle—to give the driver a warning concerning traffic violations—was pretextual. . . .

II

The Fourth Amendment guarantees "[t]he right of the people to be secure in their persons, houses, papers, and effects, against unreasonable searches and seizures." Temporary detention of individuals during the stop of an automobile by the police, even if only for a brief period and for a limited purpose, constitutes a "seizure" of "persons" within the meaning of this provision. . . . An automobile stop is thus subject to the constitutional **imperative** that it not be "unreasonable" under the circumstances. As a general matter, the decision to stop an automobile is reasonable where the police have probable cause to believe that a traffic violation has occurred. . . .

Petitioners accept that Officer Soto had probable cause to believe that various provisions of the District of Columbia traffic code had been violated. See 18 D.C. Mun. Regs. §§ 2213.4 (1995) ("An operator shall . . . give full time and attention to the operation of the vehicle"); 2204.3 ("No person shall turn any vehicle . . . without giving an appropriate signal"); 2200.3 ("No person shall drive a vehicle . . . at a speed greater than is reasonable and prudent under the conditions"). They argue, however, that "in the unique context of civil traffic regulations" probable cause is not enough. Since, they contend, the use of automobiles is so heavily and minutely regulated that total compliance with traffic and safety rules is nearly impossible, a police officer will almost invariably be able to catch any given motorist in a technical violation. This creates the temptation to use traffic stops as a means of investigating other law violations, as to which no probable cause or even **articulable** suspicion exists. Petitioners, who are both black, further contend that police officers might decide which motorists to stop based on decidedly impermissible factors, such as the race of the car's occupants. To avoid this danger, they say, the Fourth Amendment test for traffic stops should be, not the normal one . . . of whether probable cause existed to justify the stop; but rather, whether a police officer, acting reasonably, would have made the stop for the reason given. . . .

A

. . . We think [our] cases **foreclose** any argument that the constitutional reasonableness of traffic stops depends on the actual motivations of the individual officers involved. We of course agree with petitioners that the Constitution prohibits selective enforcement of the law based on considerations such as race. But the constitutional basis for objecting to intentionally discriminatory application of laws is the Equal Protection Clause, not the Fourth Amendment. Subjective intentions play no role in ordinary, probable-cause Fourth Amendment analysis.

B

Recognizing that we have been unwilling to entertain Fourth Amendment challenges based on the actual motivations of individual officers, petitioners **disavow** any intention to make the individual officer's subjective good faith the touchstone of "reasonableness." They insist that the standard they have put forward—whether the officer's conduct **deviated** materially from usual police practices, so that a reasonable officer in the same circumstances would not have made the stop for the reasons given—is an "objective" one.

. . . Petitioners' proposed standard may not use the word "pretext," but it is designed to combat nothing other than the perceived "danger" of the pretextual stop, albeit only indirectly and over the run of cases. Instead of asking whether the individual officer had the proper state of mind, the petitioners would have us ask, in effect, whether (based on general police practices) it is plausible to believe that the officer had the proper state of mind. . . .

[P]olice enforcement practices, even if they could be practicably assessed by a judge, vary from place to place and from time to time. We cannot accept that the search and seizure protections of the Fourth Amendment are so variable, . . . and can be made to turn upon such trivialities. . . .

* * *

Here the District Court found that the officers had probable cause to believe that petitioners had violated the traffic code. That rendered the stop reasonable under the Fourth Amendment, the evidence thereby discovered admissible, and the upholding of the convictions by the Court of Appeals for the District of Columbia Circuit correct. The judgment is *Affirmed.*

- Do you agree that the traffic offense was a good enough justification for the stop? Was the real reason for stopping the car the traffic offense, or was it something else?
- What do you think of pretextual stops as a law enforcement tactic? Are they justified?
- The Supreme Court mentions the "temptation to use traffic stops as a means of investigating other law violations." Do you think that officers are tempted to misuse traffic stops?
- What role did race play in this case, if any? How about the age of the suspects?
- Do you understand the Court's ruling that the officer's subjective motivations for the traffic stop should not be a factor, and that instead an evaluation of the stop should be based only on its objective reasonableness? Why shouldn't a police officer's actual reasons for stopping the car matter?

Exception 5: Consensual Searches

Searches based on consent are conducted with the permission of the person searched. For example, a police officer asks you, "Can I search your car?" If you answer yes, you have consented to the search. The Supreme Court has held that consent searches are reasonable and do not violate the Fourth Amendment ban on unreasonable searches and seizures.

Would you be surprised to know that the vast majority of searches are **consensual**? Some scholars have even estimated that 98 percent of warrantless searches are based on the consent of the person being searched.[15]

Why would anyone consent to give up his Fourth Amendment protections? What causes people to give up their rights? Are there good reasons to cooperate with police even if you know they may find contraband on you?

The standard for consent requires that the permission be voluntarily given and not the result of duress or **coercion**. This means that the consent cannot be obtained by virtue of any pressure put on you by the police. Agreement cannot be forced. As the Supreme Court stated in *Schneckloth v. Bustamonte*:

> [W]hen the subject of a search is not in custody and the State attempts to justify a search on the basis of his consent, the Fourth and Fourteenth Amendments require that it demonstrate that the consent was in fact voluntarily given, and not the result of duress or coercion, **express** or **implied**. Voluntariness is a question of fact to be determined

from all the circumstances, and while the subject's knowledge of a right to refuse is a factor to be taken into account, the prosecution is not required to demonstrate such knowledge as a **prerequisite** to establishing a voluntary consent.[16]

In the *Bostick* case, discussed in chapter 3, the issue was whether someone was seized after police officers boarded a passenger bus. The Supreme Court decided Bostick was not seized. It also assumed that Bostick's consent to his search was voluntary. Bostick was on an enclosed bus, confronted by two armed officers, who asked directly if they could search him. If you review the case, you will see that the justices do not address the issue of consent as a problem.

What if Bostick were a young boy traveling alone on a bus and the two officers approached him and then asked to search him? Would the same standard of consent be used? Consider a case from the District of Columbia to find an answer.

————

IN RE J. M., APPELLANT

District of Columbia Court of Appeals
No. 90-FS-183.
Argued En Banc Feb. 28, 1992.
Decided Dec. 30, 1992.

ON REHEARING EN BANC

FARRELL, Associate Judge:

. . . On October 31, 1989, Detective Donald Zattau and a team of Metropolitan Police officers were at the Greyhound-Trailways bus station in Northeast Washington, D.C. Their assignment was to question, and presumably search if they had cause or obtained consent, passengers arriving in or passing through Washington from New York City. At about 2:30 a.m. a bus arrived from New York en route to Wilmington, North Carolina. After the driver announced a ten-minute rest stop, Detective Zattau and two other officers boarded the bus dressed in civilian attire. Using the bus speaker system, Zattau announced their identity and purpose, explaining that they were part of a drug interdiction group that interviewed passengers arriving from New York because it was a "source supply of drugs," and in the past they had found that drugs were transported by bus passengers. After questioning other passengers, Zattau approached J. M., who was seated three-quarters of the way to the rear next to a window.

The detective introduced himself and, in a conversational voice, asked J. M.'s point of origin and destination and if he could see his bus ticket; he also asked if J. M. had heard the announcement over the speaker system, to which the youth replied that he had and understood it. Zattau asked if J. M. was carrying drugs or weapons, and when J. M. replied no, the detective asked if he could search the bag J. M. was carrying with him. J. M. consented, and the search revealed nothing. Zattau then asked if J. M. had drugs or weapons on his person; when J. M. said no, the officer asked if he would mind if he patted him down. In response J. M. turned toward the officer and raised his arms while still seated. Zattau patted him down and felt a hard object on his right side next to his rib cage. He lifted the shirt and discovered a plastic bag containing crack cocaine taped to J. M.'s body. J. M. was arrested.

J. M. testified that he was fourteen years old at the time of his arrest and fifteen at the time of the trial one and a half months later. He lived in Brooklyn, New York, and attended ninth grade. He acknowledged that he had consented to the search of his bag because he knew it contained nothing illegal and feared that if he did not consent, the police would become suspicious and investigate. He denied, however, that he had given Zattau permission to frisk him, asserting that the officer "just started patting me down." He made no effort to stop the frisk because if he had done so, the officers "would have got[ten] more suspicious at me." . . .

The trial judge denied the motion to suppress. . . .

II

We confront in this case two conceptually distinct yet, in practice, often overlapping issues. First, at the time Detective Zattau asked for and received appellant's consent to a pat-down search, did the totality of the officer's conduct amount to a seizure under the Fourth Amendment? Second, assuming appellant was not seized, was his consent to the pat-down voluntary so as to make the search reasonable under the Fourth Amendment? . . . The "crucial test" for determining whether a person has been seized "is whether, taking into account all of the circumstances surrounding the encounter, the police conduct would 'have communicated to a *reasonable person* that he was not at liberty to ignore the police presence and go about his business.' " By contrast, the issue of whether a person freely consented to a search "focuses on the particular individual rather than on a hypothetical reasonable person." . . . In that inquiry, all of the circumstances must be considered including *both* the nature of the police conduct and "the possibly vulnerable subjective state of the person who consents," . . . as "[t]he very object of the inquiry . . . [is] the nature of a person's subjective understanding." . . .

III

We first conclude that J. M. was not seized when Detective Zattau asked him questions and asked permission to search his bag and then pat him down. In reaching that conclusion, we do not on this record consider the fact that J. M. was fourteen years old and hence possibly vulnerable to coercion in a way an adult would not have been. We cannot do so because the Supreme Court has taught that the test for whether a person has been seized "is designed to assess the coercive effect of *police conduct* . . . and that while that test is flexible enough to be applied to the whole range of police conduct in an equally broad range of settings, it calls for consistent application from one police encounter to the next, *regardless of the particular individual's response to the actions of the police.* The test's objective standard—looking to the reasonable man's interpretation of the conduct in question—allows the police to determine in advance whether the conduct contemplated will implicate the Fourth Amendment. . . .

IV

The conclusion that J. M. was not seized does not end the inquiry, however. When the police patted him down, there unquestionably was a search of his person, which the government seeks to justify on the ground that he voluntarily consented. . . . When the issue is voluntariness of a consent, "characteristics of the accused" become relevant . . . and may even be decisive. Among the factors

. . . cited as significant are "the youth of the accused; his lack of education; or his low intelligence," and related to these may be "the lack of any advice to the accused of his constitutional rights." "[A]ccount must be taken of subtly coercive police questions, as well as the possibly vulnerable subjective state of the person who consents."

. . . As with the fact of custody, it seems to us almost self-evident that a trial judge deciding the issue of consent by a youth must be sensitive to the heightened danger of coercion in this setting. Correspondingly, our own responsibilities as a reviewing court permit us to require that in such cases the trial judge make explicit findings on the record concerning the effect of age and relative immaturity on the voluntariness of the defendant's consent. These findings (which need not be in writing) are particularly necessary when it is conceded, as in this case, that the youth was not told he could withhold consent, for even in the adult context the Supreme Court has explained that advice of that right may be "highly relevant" to the voluntariness issue and may "substantially lessen the probability that [the police] conduct could reasonably have appeared to [the person] to be coercive." . . .

. . . [W]e cannot properly discharge our review function on the basis of the findings apparent on the record.

V

We accordingly remand this case to the trial court for further consideration of that issue.

POINTS TO PONDER

- The judges could not make a decision about consent on the facts they had in front of them (those "on the record"). If you were the judge, could you have made the decision? Did J. M. consent to the search? Even if he said "Yes, go ahead and search me," would that be voluntary consent? Does your view depend on his age? The time of night? The way the police acted?
- In examining a consent search, what would you look at to determine if it was freely and voluntarily given? Psychological pressure? The nature of the interaction? Age, race, class, gender, power? How would those factors inform your decision?[17]
- Do you think that consent searches allow the police to exploit popular ignorance about the Constitution? Now that you have been informed of your rights, would you readily give them up? If so, under what circumstances?[18]
- How are courts supposed to know that someone has consented? Usually the only people on the scene are the suspect and the police officer. What if one of them lies? What do you think of the following statement by Chief of Police Joseph D. McNamara, a former police chief of Kansas City, Missouri, and San Jose, California? "[H]undreds of thousands of police officers swear under oath that the drugs were in plain view or that the defendant gave consent to a search. This may happen occasionally but it defies belief that so many drug users are careless enough to leave illegal drugs where the police can see them or so dumb as to give cops consent to search them when they possess drugs." [19]
- Does the idea of a consent search take into account the reality of police-citizen encounters?

If police see someone acting suspiciously, should they have to wait until the person commits a crime before they check it out? Or should they be able to approach the person and ask him questions? What if the person is armed and dangerous? Can the police search the person? Can they frisk for weapons?

Exception 6: Reasonable Suspicion

The language of the Fourth Amendment speaks of probable cause, but what about police-citizen encounters that involve less evidence of wrongdoing than probable cause? The vast majority of such encounters are governed by a lesser standard called reasonable suspicion. What is reasonable suspicion? Under what circumstances is this lesser standard used for police searches?

The most famous case about reasonable suspicion is *Terry v. Ohio*.[20] In *Terry*, the Supreme Court lessened the Fourth Amendment restrictions on policing, allowing police officers to stop and seize people without having full probable cause to search. What that means is that police can stop people if a reasonable suspicion exists that they are engaged in a criminal act. Reasonable suspicion means that specific, particularized facts show that criminal activity is afoot. This power, however, allows police only to stop—but not arrest—the person. Such a police stop also includes the right to conduct a brief frisk (a patting down of the clothing area) to search for weapons.

Heightened security measures after September 11, 2001, have raised concerns about balancing homeland security and privacy rights. Here, members of a bomb squad search a truck in 2004 at Purdue University in West Lafayette, Indiana. The operation required a massive evacuation and the closure of several streets. Nothing was found. *Source: Michael Heinz/AP Wide World Photos*

JOHN W. TERRY, PETITIONER,
V.
STATE OF OHIO

Supreme Court of the United States
No. 67.
Argued Dec. 12, 1967.
Decided June 10, 1968.

Mr. Chief Justice WARREN delivered the opinion of the Court.

This case presents serious questions concerning the role of the Fourth Amendment in the confrontation on the street between the citizen and the policeman investigating suspicious circumstances. . . .

At the hearing on the motion to suppress this evidence, Officer McFadden testified that while he was patrolling in plain clothes in downtown Cleveland at approximately 2:30 in the afternoon of October 31, 1963, his attention was attracted by two men, Chilton and Terry, standing on the corner of Huron Road and Euclid Avenue. He had never seen the two men before, and he was unable to say precisely what first drew his eye to them. However, he testified that he had been a policeman for 39 years and a detective for 35 and that he had been assigned to patrol this vicinity of downtown Cleveland for shoplifters and pickpockets for 30 years. He explained that he had developed routine habits of observation over the years and that he would 'stand and watch people or walk and watch people at many intervals of the day.' He added: 'Now, in this case when I looked over they didn't look right to me at the time.'

His interest aroused, Officer McFadden took up a post of observation in the entrance to a store 300 to 400 feet away from the two men. 'I get more purpose to watch them when I seen their movements,' he testified. He saw one of the men leave the other one and walk southwest on Huron Road, past some stores. The man paused for a moment and looked in a store window, then walked on a short distance, turned around and walked back toward the corner, pausing once again to look in the same store window. He rejoined his companion at the corner, and the two conferred briefly. Then the second man went through the same series of motions, strolling down Huron Road, looking in the same window, walking on a short distance, turning back, peering in the store window again, and returning to confer with the first man at the corner. The two men repeated this ritual alternately between five and six times apiece—in all, roughly a dozen trips. At one point, while the two were standing together on the corner, a third man approached them and engaged them briefly in conversation. This man then left the two others and walked west on Euclid Avenue. Chilton and Terry resumed their measured pacing, peering and conferring. After this had gone on for 10 to 12 minutes, the two men walked off together, heading west on Euclid Avenue, following the path taken earlier by the third man.

By this time Officer McFadden had become thoroughly suspicious. He testified that after observing their elaborately casual and oft-repeated reconnaissance of the store window on Huron Road, he suspected the two men of 'casing a job, a stick-up,' and that he considered it his duty as a police officer to investigate further. He added that he feared 'they may have a gun.' Thus, Officer McFadden followed Chilton and Terry and saw them stop in front of Zucker's store to talk to the same man who had conferred with them earlier on the street corner. Deciding that the situation was ripe for direct action, Officer McFadden approached the three men, identified himself as a police officer and asked for their names. At this point his knowledge was confined to what he had observed. He was not acquainted with any of the three men by name or by sight, and he had received no information concerning them from any other source. When the men 'mumbled something' in response to his inquiries, Officer McFadden grabbed petitioner Terry, spun him around so that they were facing the other two, with Terry between McFadden and the others, and patted down the outside of his clothing. In the left breast pocket of Terry's overcoat Officer McFadden felt a pistol. He reached inside the overcoat pocket, but was unable to remove the gun. At this point, keeping Terry between himself and the others, the officer ordered all three men to enter Zucker's store. As they went in, he removed Terry's overcoat completely, removed a .38-caliber revolver from the pocket and ordered all three men to face the wall with their hands raised. Officer McFadden proceeded to pat down the outer clothing of Chilton and the third man, Katz. He discovered another revolver in the outer pocket of Chilton's overcoat, but no weapons were found on Katz. The officer testified that he only patted the men down to see whether they had weapons, and that he did not put his hands beneath the outer garments of either Terry or Chilton until he felt their guns. So far as appears from the record, he never placed his hands beneath Katz' outer garments. Officer McFadden seized Chilton's gun, asked the proprietor of the store to call a police wagon, and took all three men to the station, where Chilton and Terry were formally charged with carrying concealed weapons.

I

. . . Unquestionably petitioner was entitled to the protection of the Fourth Amendment as he walked down the street in Cleveland. . . . The question is whether in all the circumstances of this on-the-street encounter, his right to personal security was violated by an unreasonable search and seizure.

We would be less than candid if we did not acknowledge that this question thrusts to the fore difficult and troublesome issues regarding a sensitive area of police activity—issues which have never before been squarely presented to this Court. Reflective of the tensions involved are the practical and constitutional arguments pressed with great vigor on both sides of the public debate over the power of the police to 'stop and frisk'—as it is sometimes **euphemistically** termed—suspicious persons.

On the one hand, it is frequently argued that in dealing with the rapidly unfolding and often dangerous situations on city streets the police are in need of an escalating set of flexible responses, graduated in relation to the amount of information they possess. For this purpose it is urged that distinctions should be made between a 'stop' and an 'arrest' (or a 'seizure' of a person), and between a 'frisk' and a 'search.' Thus, it is argued, the police should be allowed to 'stop' a person and detain him briefly for questioning upon suspicion that he may be connected with criminal activity. Upon suspicion that the person may be armed, the police should have the power to 'frisk' him for weapons. If the 'stop' and the 'frisk' give rise to probable cause to believe that the suspect has committed a crime, then the police should be empowered to make a formal 'arrest,' and a full incident 'search' of the person. . . .

On the other side the argument is made that the authority of the police must be strictly circumscribed by the law of arrest and search as it has developed to date in the traditional jurisprudence of the Fourth Amendment. . . . Courts which sit under our Constitution cannot and will not be made party to lawless invasions of the constitutional rights of citizens by permitting **unhindered** governmental use of the fruits of such invasions.

. . . Street encounters between citizens and police officers are incredibly rich in diversity. They range from wholly friendly exchanges of pleasantries or mutually useful information to hostile confrontations of armed men involving arrests, or injuries, or loss of life. Moreover, hostile confrontations are not all of a piece. Some of them begin in a friendly enough manner, only to take a different turn upon the injection of some unexpected element into the conversation. Encounters are initiated by the police for a wide variety of purposes, some of which are wholly unrelated to a desire to prosecute for crime. . . .

Having thus roughly sketched the perimeters of the constitutional debate over the limits on police investigative conduct in general and the background against which this case presents itself, we turn our attention to the quite narrow question posed by the facts before us: whether it is always unreasonable for a policeman to seize a person and subject him to a limited search for weapons unless there is probable cause for an arrest. . . .

II

Our first task is to establish at what point in this encounter the Fourth Amendment becomes relevant. That is, we must decide whether and when Officer McFadden 'seized' Terry and whether and when he conducted a 'search.'

. . . It is quite plain that the Fourth Amendment governs 'seizures' of the person which do not eventuate in a trip to the station house and prosecution for crime—'arrests' in traditional terminology. It must be recognized that whenever a police officer accosts an individual and restrains his freedom to walk away, he has 'seized' that person. And it is nothing less than sheer torture of the English language to suggest that a careful exploration of the outer surfaces of a person's clothing all over his or her body in an attempt to find weapons is not a 'search.' Moreover, it is simply fantastic to urge that such a procedure performed in public by a policeman while the citizen stands helpless, perhaps facing a wall with his hands raised, is a 'petty indignity.' It is a serious intrusion upon the sanctity of the person, which may inflict great indignity and arouse strong resentment, and it is not to be undertaken lightly.

In this case there can be no question, then, that Officer McFadden 'seized' petitioner and subjected him to a 'search' when he took hold of him and patted down the outer surfaces of his clothing. . . .

III

In order to assess the reasonableness of Officer McFadden's conduct as a general proposition, it is necessary 'first to focus upon the governmental interest which allegedly justifies official intrusion upon the constitutionally protected interests of the private citizen,' for there is 'no ready test for determining reasonableness other than by balancing the need to search (or seize) against the invasion which the search (or seizure) entails.' . . . And in making that assessment it is imperative that the facts be judged against an objective standard: would the facts available to the officer at the moment of the seizure or the search 'warrant a man of reasonable caution in the belief' that the action taken was appropriate? . . . Anything less would invite intrusions upon constitutionally guaranteed rights based on nothing more substantial than inarticulate hunches, a result this Court has consistently refused to sanction.

Applying these principles to this case, we consider first the nature and extent of the governmental interests involved. One general interest is of course that of effective crime prevention and detection; it is this interest which underlies the recognition that a police officer may in appropriate circumstances and in an appropriate manner approach a person for purposes of investigating possibly criminal behavior even though there is no probable cause to make an arrest. It was this legitimate investigative function Officer McFadden was discharging when he decided to approach petitioner and his companions. He had observed Terry, Chilton, and Katz go through a series of acts, each of them perhaps innocent in itself, but which taken together warranted further investigation. . . . It would have been poor police work indeed for an officer of 30 years' experience in the detection of thievery from stores in this same neighborhood to have failed to investigate this behavior further.

The **crux** of this case, however, is not the propriety of Officer McFadden's taking steps to investigate petitioner's suspicious behavior, but rather, whether there was justification for McFadden's invasion of Terry's personal security by searching him for weapons in the course of that investigation. We are now concerned with more than the governmental interest in investigating crime; in addition, there is the more immediate interest of the police officer in taking steps to assure himself that the person with whom he is dealing is not armed with a weapon that could unexpectedly and fatally be used against him. Certainly it would be unreasonable to require that police officers take unnecessary risks in the performance of their duties. . . .

In view of these facts, we cannot blind ourselves to the need for law enforcement officers to protect themselves and other prospective victims of violence in situations where they may lack probable cause for an arrest. When an officer is justified in believing that the individual whose suspicious behavior he is investigating at close range is armed and presently dangerous to the officer or to others, it would appear to be clearly unreasonable to deny the officer the power to take necessary measures to determine whether the person is in fact carrying a weapon and to neutralize the threat of physical harm.

We must still consider, however, the nature and quality of the intrusion on individual rights which must be accepted if police officers are to be conceded the right to search for weapons in situations where probable cause to arrest for crime is lacking. Even a limited search of the outer clothing for weapons constitutes a severe, though brief, intrusion upon cherished personal security, and it must surely be an annoying, frightening, and perhaps humiliating experience. Petitioner contends that such an intrusion is permissible only incident to a lawful arrest, either for a crime involving the possession of weapons or for a crime the commission of which led the officer to investigate in the first place. However, this argument must be closely examined. . . .

Our evaluation of the proper balance that has to be struck in this type of case leads us to conclude that there must be a narrowly drawn authority to permit a reasonable search for weapons for the protection of the police officer, where he has reason to believe that he is dealing with an armed and dangerous individual, regardless of whether he has probable cause to arrest the individual for a crime. The officer need not be absolutely certain that the individual is armed; the issue is whether a reasonably prudent man in the circumstances would be warranted in the belief that his safety or that of others was in danger. . . . And in determining whether the officer acted reasonably in such circumstances, due weight must be given, not to his inchoate and unparticularized suspicion or 'hunch,' but to the specific reasonable inferences which he is entitled to draw from the facts in light of his experience.

IV

We must now examine the conduct of Officer McFadden in this case to determine whether his search and seizure of petitioner were reasonable, both at their inception and as conducted. He had observed Terry, together with Chilton and another man, acting in a manner he took to be preface to a 'stick-up.' We think on the facts and circumstances Officer McFadden detailed before the trial judge a reasonably prudent man would have been warranted in believing petitioner was armed and thus presented a threat to the officer's safety while he was investigating his suspicious behavior. The actions of Terry and Chilton were consistent with McFadden's hypothesis that these men were contemplating a daylight robbery—which, it is reasonable to assume, would be likely to involve the use of weapons—and nothing in their conduct from the time he first noticed them until the time he confronted them and identified himself as a police officer gave him sufficient reason to negate that hypothesis. Although the trio had departed the original scene, there was nothing to indicate abandonment of an intent to commit a robbery at some point. Thus, when Officer McFadden approached the three men gathered before the display window at Zucker's store he had observed enough to make it quite reasonable to fear that they were armed; and nothing in their response to his hailing them, identifying himself as a police officer, and asking their names served to dispel that reasonable belief. We cannot say his decision at that point to seize Terry and pat his clothing for weapons was the product of a volatile or inventive imagination, or was undertaken simply as an act of harassment; the record evidences the tempered act of a policeman who in the course of an investigation had to make a quick decision as to how to protect himself and others from possible danger, and took limited steps to do so.

The scope of the search in this case presents no serious problem in light of these standards. Officer McFadden patted down the outer clothing of petitioner and his two companions. He did not place his hands in their pockets or under the outer surface of their garments until he had felt weapons, and then he merely reached for and removed the guns. He never did invade Katz' person beyond the outer surfaces of his clothes, since he discovered nothing in his patdown which might have been a weapon. Officer McFadden confined his search strictly to what was minimally necessary to learn whether the men were armed and to disarm them once he discovered the weapons. He did not conduct a general exploratory search for whatever evidence of criminal activity he might find.

V

We conclude that the revolver seized from Terry was properly admitted in evidence against him. At the time he seized petitioner and searched him for weapons, Officer McFadden had reasonable grounds to believe that petitioner was armed and dangerous, and it was necessary for the protection of himself and others to take swift measures to discover the true facts and neutralize the threat of harm if it materialized. The policeman carefully restricted his search to what was appropriate to the discovery of the particular items which he sought. Each case of this sort will, of course, have to be decided on its own facts. We merely hold today that where a police officer observes unusual conduct which leads him reasonably to conclude in light of his experience that criminal activity may be afoot and that the persons with whom he is dealing may be armed and presently dangerous, where in the course of investigating this behavior he identifies himself as a policeman and makes reasonable inquiries, and where nothing in the initial stages of the encounter serves to dispel his reasonable fear for his own or others' safety, he is entitled for the protection of himself and others in the area to conduct a carefully limited search of the outer clothing of such persons in an attempt to discover weapons which might be used to assault him. Such a search is a reasonable search under the Fourth Amendment, and any weapons seized may properly be introduced in evidence against the person from whom they were taken.

Affirmed.

POINTS TO PONDER

- Having read the opinion, are you certain what "reasonable suspicion" means? What does it mean when a "police officer observes unusual conduct which leads him reasonably to conclude in light of his experience that criminal activity may be afoot"? How are police officers supposed to decide whether they have reasonable suspicion? How are courts supposed to decide whether suspicion is reasonable or not?
- What factors should be a part of a finding of reasonable suspicion? What do you consider suspicious? Is it the same thing that a police officer might consider suspicious? Is that the same that a judge would consider suspicious?
- How do issues of race, class, geography, age, or appearance affect the determination of reasonable suspicion? Should these factors be legitimate in creating reasonable suspicion? What are the risks of allowing these factors to be used by police?
- Part of the Supreme Court's rationale in *Terry* for not requiring probable cause was that Detective McFadden was an experienced police officer. What if McFadden had been a rookie? Should the individual police officer's level of experience affect your rights under the Fourth Amendment?
- Review the following sworn testimony of Detective McFadden in the suppression hearing of the *Terry* case. The trial judge is asking the questions.

  > Q: In your thirty-nine years of experience as an officer . . . [h]ave you ever had any experience in observing the activities of individuals in casing a place?
  > A: To be truthful with you, no.
  > Q: You never observed anybody casing a place?
  > A: No.
  > Q: During your entire tenure as a police officer, during your 39 years as a police officer, how many men have you had occasion to arrest when you had observed them and felt as though they might pull a stick-up?
  > A: To my recollection, I wouldn't know, I don't know if I had, I don't remember any.[21]

What experience did McFadden have that was relevant to finding reasonable suspicion? Was the Court correct to rely on his experience?

- Reasonable suspicion does not have a precise definition. How would you determine what level of suspicion is enough to stop someone on the street?

Levels of Suspicion of Criminal Activity on the Street Required to Stop and Frisk

●————————●————————————●————————————————●————————●
No suspicion   Hunch   Reasonable suspicion   Probable cause   Certainty

Refining the Definition of Reasonable Suspicion

The reasonable suspicion standard allows police far greater opportunity to stop and frisk people on the street. In this way it decreases the liberty protections of the Fourth Amendment. But for the same reason, it is also a valuable crime-solving tool that has resulted in tens of thousands of arrests and fewer drugs and guns on the streets. In that sense, it increases security and perhaps freedom, too.

Over the years, the Supreme Court has made the definition of "reasonable suspicion" very broad by deferring to the "reasonable" discretion of police officers on the streets. Police are entitled to follow up on their observations and intuitions about the apparently anxious behavior of persons being searched as well as the character of the neighborhood.

Consider the situation the Court faced in *Illinois v. Wardlow*.[22]

YOUR THOUGHTS

In a high crime area, is seeing the police and running away sufficient reasonable suspicion to justify a stop?

—-—

ILLINOIS, PETITIONER,
V.
WILLIAM AKA SAM WARDLOW

Supreme Court of the United States
No. 98-1036.
Argued Nov. 2, 1999.
Decided Jan. 12, 2000.

Chief Justice REHNQUIST delivered the opinion of the Court.

. . . On September 9, 1995, Officers Nolan and Harvey were working as uniformed officers in the special operations section of the Chicago Police Department. The officers were driving the last car of a four car caravan converging on an area known for heavy narcotics trafficking in order to investigate drug transactions. The officers were traveling together because they expected to find a crowd of people in the area, including lookouts and customers.

As the caravan passed 4035 West Van Buren, Officer Nolan observed respondent Wardlow standing next to the building holding an opaque bag. Respondent looked in the direction of the officers and fled. Nolan and Harvey turned their car southbound, watched him as he ran through the gangway and an alley, and eventually cornered him on the street. Nolan then exited his car and stopped respondent. He immediately conducted a protective patdown search for weapons because in his experience it was common for there to be weapons in the near vicinity of narcotics transactions. During the frisk, Officer Nolan squeezed the bag respondent was carrying and felt a heavy, hard object similar to the shape of a gun. The officer then opened the bag and discovered a .38-caliber handgun with five live rounds of ammunition. The officers arrested Wardlow.

This case, involving a brief encounter between a citizen and a police officer on a public street, is governed by the analysis we first applied in *Terry [v. Ohio]*. In *Terry*, we held that an officer may, consistent with the Fourth Amendment, conduct a brief, investigatory stop when the officer has a reasonable, articulable suspicion that criminal activity is afoot. . . . While "reasonable suspicion" is a less demanding standard than probable cause and requires a showing considerably less than preponderance of the evidence, the Fourth Amendment requires at least a minimal level of objective justification for making the stop. . . . The officer must be able to articulate more than an "inchoate and unparticularized suspicion or 'hunch' " of criminal activity.

Nolan and Harvey were among eight officers in a four-car caravan that was converging on an area known for heavy narcotics trafficking, and the officers anticipated encountering a large number of people in the area, including drug customers and individuals serving as lookouts. . . . It was in this context that Officer Nolan decided to investigate Wardlow after observing him flee. An individual's presence in an area of expected criminal activity, standing alone, is not enough to support a reasonable, particularized suspicion that the person is committing a crime. . . . But officers are not required to ignore the relevant characteristics of a location in determining whether the circumstances are sufficiently suspicious to warrant further investigation. Accordingly, we have previously noted the fact that the stop occurred in a "high crime area" among the relevant contextual considerations in a *Terry* analysis. . . .

In this case, moreover, it was not merely respondent's presence in an area of heavy narcotics trafficking that aroused the officers' suspicion, but his unprovoked flight upon noticing the police. Our cases have also recognized that nervous, evasive behavior is a pertinent factor in determining reasonable suspicion. . . . Headlong flight—wherever it occurs—is the consummate act of evasion: It is not necessarily indicative of wrongdoing, but it is certainly suggestive of such. In reviewing the propriety of an officer's conduct, courts do not have available empirical studies dealing with inferences drawn from suspicious behavior, and we cannot reasonably demand scientific certainty from judges or law enforcement officers where none exists. Thus, the determination of reasonable suspicion must be based on commonsense judgments and inferences about human behavior. . . . We conclude Officer Nolan was justified in suspecting that Wardlow was involved in criminal activity, and, therefore, in investigating further. . . .

It is so ordered.

Justice STEVENS, with whom Justice SOUTER, Justice GINSBURG, and Justice BREYER join, concurring in part and dissenting in part. . . .

. . . The question in this case concerns "the degree of suspicion that attaches to" a person's flight—or, more precisely, what "commonsense conclusions" can be drawn respecting the motives behind that flight. A pedestrian may break into a run for a variety of reasons—to catch up with a friend a block or two away, to seek shelter from an impending storm, to arrive at a bus stop before the bus leaves, to get home in time for dinner, to resume jogging after a pause for rest, to avoid contact with a bore or a bully, or simply to answer the call of nature—any of which might coincide with the arrival of an officer in the vicinity. A pedestrian might also run because he or she has just sighted one or more police officers. . . .

In addition to these concerns, a reasonable person may conclude that an officer's sudden appearance indicates nearby criminal activity. And where there is criminal activity there is also a substantial element of danger—either from the criminal or from a confrontation between the criminal and the police. These considerations can lead to an innocent and understandable desire to quit the vicinity with all speed.

Among some citizens, particularly minorities and those residing in high crime areas, there is also the possibility that the fleeing person is entirely innocent, but, with or without justification, believes that contact with the police can itself be dangerous, apart from any criminal activity associated with the officer's sudden presence. . . . For such a person, unprovoked flight is neither "aberrant" nor "abnormal." . . . Moreover, these concerns and fears are known to the police officers themselves, and are validated by law enforcement investigations into their own practices. Accordingly, the evidence supporting the reasonableness of these beliefs is too pervasive to be dismissed as random or rare, and too persuasive to be disparaged as inconclusive or insufficient. . . .

II

Guided by that totality-of-the-circumstances test, the Court concludes that Officer Nolan had reasonable suspicion to stop respondent. . . . In this respect, my view differs from the Court's. The entire justification for the stop is articulated in the brief testimony of Officer Nolan. Some facts are perfectly clear; others are not. This factual insufficiency leads me to conclude that the Court's judgment is mistaken.

. . . I am not persuaded that the mere fact that someone standing on a sidewalk looked in the direction of a passing car before starting to run is sufficient to justify a forcible stop and frisk.

POINTS TO PONDER

- What facts did the Supreme Court find suspicious? Are you persuaded that the officers had reasonable suspicion to stop and frisk? What was the suspect doing? Would his behavior create reasonable suspicion to stop him in all neighborhoods? What about a very wealthy neighborhood? What about on a college campus?
- Do you agree that "unprovoked flight" gives sufficient reasonable suspicion to stop? Which side is more persuasive on the reasons that people run, the majority or the dissent?

- The Supreme Court describes the area as a high drug neighborhood. Do you think that a neighborhood's reputation should help to establish reasonable suspicion to stop all of the people who live or work there? Is there a problem with using that standard? Doesn't it make sense?
- The reason the police stopped Wardlow was that he ran in a high drug neighborhood. The officers' suspicion was thus that he had drugs. Does it trouble you that no drugs were found on Wardlow?

A Reasonable Search

At 9:00 a.m. on April 16, 1999, a police officer named Randall Goins in Phoenix, Arizona, received a radio transmission report from a school security guard stationed at Alhambra High School. The guard told him that a high school student was showing a gun to fellow students at a market near school. The officer quickly went to meet the security guard, who pointed out to him with binoculars where the student was standing in front of a neighborhood mom-and-pop store.

Officer Goins went closer and began to follow the suspect, "an Hispanic male teenager wearing baggy white pants and an untucked blue shirt." [23] Officer Goins never saw a gun but got out of his patrol car and yelled at the juvenile, "Hey, you," catching his attention. Then Officer Goins drew his gun and held it to his side so the teenager could not see it. He motioned the youngster to come over to his car, which he did, with his hands over his head. The officer asked, "Do you have a gun?" The young man, Roy L., replied, "Yeah." Officer Goins lowered his gun and asked the young man to place his hands on the patrol car, which he did. He patted down Roy L.'s exterior clothing with his left hand and felt what he recognized to be the handle of a revolver-type firearm in the right front pants pocket. "Is this a gun?" he asked. Roy L. answered, "Yes, it is." Officer Goins lifted up his shirt and found a stainless steel six-shot revolver sticking out of his pocket. He removed the weapon, finished the frisk, and placed Roy L. under arrest for carrying a concealed weapon.

Officer Goins handcuffed Roy L., asked his age, which was sixteen, and drove him to the police office at school where he proceeded to read him his "juvenile *Miranda* rights." [24] Roy L. said that he understood his rights and then declined to have his parents present during his interrogation. Roy L. told the officer that he had taken the gun from his father's truck that morning because he had been threatened at gunpoint by a rival gangster the day before. He was charged with being a minor in possession of a firearm in violation of Arizona State law.

At trial, Roy L. tried to get all of the evidence against him suppressed by arguing that the initial search and seizure was unreasonable under the Fourth Amendment because Officer Goins had no reasonable suspicion of criminal activity. Specifically, he argued that a hearsay rumor from an unidentified student does not give rise to sufficient suspicion to justify a *Terry* stop. Roy L. argued that the officer did not have sufficient reason to stop him or question him. But the district court, in *In re Roy L.*, found that an informant's tip can provide an adequate basis for a police stop when the tip seems reliable.[25] The Arizona Court of Appeals emphasized that "the tipster was not simply an anonymous telephone informant but a fellow student who had personally given the information about the juvenile to the guard." [26] When Officer Goins went to investigate, Roy L. was clearly trying to avoid him, which gave Goins all the suspicion he needed to stop and frisk. The fact that Officer Goins asked about the gun before informing Roy L. of his *Miranda* rights did not make this part of the encounter unlawful because the court saw it as a valid part of the investigation before Roy L. was in custody. Meantime, the frisk of Roy L. was clearly proper to dispel the suspicion that he was armed and dangerous and to secure the situation. Under *Terry*, the police may lawfully frisk a person for weapons if the officer reasonably suspects that the person may be armed and presently dangerous to the officer or other people.

Thus, the evidence flowing from the stop, frisk, and arrest was admitted into evidence. Roy L. was prosecuted and convicted.

Should the police be able to stop and frisk students based on reports that they get from other students that they are armed and dangerous? Why or why not?

Realities of Reasonable Suspicion

The law of reasonable suspicion speaks of objective, individualized, and specific facts that would give police a reason to stop you. But how has the *Terry* standard worked in practice? Consider how the multiple ambiguities of the Fourth Amendment play out through two descriptions of police-citizen encounters.

> It was 72 degrees and sunny in Homestead, a town just south of Pittsburgh, whose better days saw steel mills ablaze and streets busy with people on their way to well-paying jobs. . . .
>
> At 3:10 in the afternoon, the police and the young black men standing on Amity are playing the usual cat-and-mouse game. Two officers in a cruiser drive slowly past the men and stare, silently sending the word: don't hang too long. The men shrug the police off, walking casually away, but only until the car is out of sight. Then they re-group.
>
> The game continues for the rest of the day and into the night. Police drive quietly by three more times. On the fourth pass, they order the men to move on or "someone's going to jail." Finally, two of the men give it up and leave for home. On the way, police stop and search them. An officer notices a marijuana cigarette on the sidewalk and asks where it came from. The men say they don't know. The police let them go.
>
> A half-hour later, officers stop three more of the original group on Amity Street and pat them down. No arrest is made. But the message has been sent.[27]

> Roll call was particularly lively as the 7th District's evening shift prepared to hit the street on the Sunday before Memorial Day. . . . Prompted by a news item that day, we fell into a discussion of racism, bias and hate crimes. As the watch commander that evening, I put in my two-cents' worth on what constitutes a hate crime under the D.C. code and how a victim's perception of events can influence whether a crime is classified as bias- or hate-related.
>
> Less than two hours later, I made an arrest and I thought back to our roll call discussion. I didn't consider my actions to be motivated by bias or racism. But the young man I took into custody felt that he was the victim of a hate crime and that I was the perpetrator. What happened in those few minutes on that afternoon helps explain the fragile and fraying relationship between the Metropolitan Police Department and the community.
>
> Watch commanders act as shift supervisors for a district and do not normally answer specific calls for police service. On this afternoon, I was driving in a marked car and heard

a call on the police radio about "subjects shooting guns" in the 400 block of Valley Avenue SE. It was typical of many 911 calls—no descriptions, no citizens willing to be called back for more information. An anonymous tip. Not much to go on.

I was the first officer to drive into the block. Because of the vagueness of the dispatcher's call, I had to be prepared for anything—from a false report to a shootout. People were out on their porches, enjoying the beautiful spring weather as I drove slowly down the block. I pulled the car alongside the only person on the sidewalk—a young black man in his late teens or early twenties, dressed in a T-shirt, sweat pants and sneakers.

"Sir," I said, "did you hear any gunshots?"

He stopped and stared at me, but said nothing. I asked him again, and he started to walk away. As a white police officer working east of the Anacostia River, I'm used to rebuffs. But this young man seemed scared and nervous. I parked my car and walked toward him. During my 10 years on the force, I have been in such situations hundreds of times. The young man could have been concealing a weapon. Or he could have been just a local resident exercising his right not to talk to the police. But to my trained eyes, his behavior seemed suspicious. I had to make a choice, so I decided to frisk him. Before I could get closer, he ran.

I chased him through an alley. He headed back to the street and ran up the steps of a house. Two other officers, who had also heard the radio call, pulled into the block and saw the chase. Before we could catch up, the young man used a set of keys to unlock the door with his left hand. His right hand was grabbing at his waistband. I could not tell if he had a gun, but his motion to his waist put me on guard.

As the three of us ran up the steps, the door shut and the lock turned. I radioed the dispatcher to send more officers. In a matter of minutes, an attempt to get information had escalated into a possible siege. We knocked on the door, hoping to defuse the situation. Suddenly, the door opened. "You have no reason to stop me!" the young man yelled at us.

He held no weapon, and both his hands were visible. Although he posed no immediate threat, I still wanted to investigate the original call that had brought us to the block. Because he had run when I first tried to question him, I decided to handcuff him until I could get to the bottom of things. As I reached for him, he pushed my hand away. His natural response was to resist, which only increased our determination to detain him.

As we tried to secure him, he struggled to get free. I broke a fingernail in the scuffle, and the young man was bleeding from a scrape on his left forearm.

Two other lieutenants arrived. Because I was out of breath and impatient, I was glad that they were there to talk to the owner of the house, who was understandably flustered. She was the young man's aunt, and she refused to believe that her nephew could have had anything to do with guns. But we needed to search the house to resolve it. I paged an on-call prosecutor to start the proper procedures for a search warrant. But before he answered the page, the woman agreed to sign a Consent to Search form.

We found no gun. Even though we had no evidence that the young man had ever had a weapon, he had technically committed the crime of assault on a police officer. Although he had not attacked me, he had run away and resisted my attempts to question him. D.C. law states that any interference with or impediment of public safety personnel is a felony. There is no misdemeanor charge of "resisting" a police officer, as there are in other jurisdictions. Just felony APO [assault on police officer].

Later at the station, I asked the detective sergeant to interview the arrestee. Although it wasn't the case of the century, I wanted to get his version of events on paper. I had to anticipate the possibility of a formal complaint. The scrape on his arm and my broken fingernail, while minor injuries, were also factors: Once blood is drawn, an officer is advised to make a record.

The young man declined to give a formal statement, but told the sergeant he wanted to talk to me. Through the bar of the holding cell, he told me he works every day, had never been in trouble and was tired of being stopped by the police. When he saw me in my police car, he said, he thought I was a "skinhead cop who was going to whip my [his] ass just for being black." He recited the slights and humiliations that he had suffered at the hands of uniformed police. I felt as if he saw my white uniform as nothing more than a fancy sheet and the patch we wear that says "Justitia Omnibus" (a Latin phrase meaning Justice for All) as a sad joke.

A lot of things ran through my mind as I thought about how to respond, even the old hoary cliche "some of my best friends. . . ." I considered telling him that my wife (who also is white) and I have adopted two foster children, one black and the other biracial. But it didn't seem the place or time for such a discussion. I looked at him and could see his fury. So I just told him that I had worked in Southeast for many years and that people who know me would tell him that I didn't beat people or stop them without a reason.

Later in the day, the young man's family came to the station and asked to speak with me. There were three relatives: the young man's grandmother, who was dressed in church clothes and a stylish hat, and a male cousin and a young aunt who appeared to be in their twenties. They listened as I recounted the story and showed them the APO statute in the D.C. code. They were respectful, and did not yell or berate me. I told them why I chased the young man, and his reasons for running away.

"He's probably right," his grandmother said.

"Ma'am," I replied, "you think I'm a racist who wanted to beat your grandson?"

"I don't know you," she said. "You could be." She told me she knew many young people in the District who are scared of police officers. As the father of two young children of color, her point hit home.

Again, my mind filled with things I wanted to say. But throwing platitudes at her about my happy rainbow family didn't seem appropriate either. Why should she care about my background or beliefs? There was as much anger and bitterness in her voice as there had been in her grandson's. I was just the white guy who was ruining her grandson's future by giving him an arrest record.

I sympathized with her. She had lived in this city a long time and had seen a city police department empowered to keep the peace contribute to the disorder of her community through brutality, corruption, incompetence and indifference—a kind of lost generation as far as police-community relations were concerned. I told her I had a lot of years left on the force and I hoped that by the time I retired, young black men—including my kids—will not be so terrified of officers trying to do their jobs. But her grandson had to spend the night in jail, and I got to go home.

The next day, I went to court. This is the "papering" stage, where an arrest lives or dies. A prosecutor reviews the paperwork and interviews the arresting officer. The screener on Memorial Day was a longtime veteran of the U.S. Attorney's office. After hearing my story, he let out a sigh. "Well, Crane, you weren't assaulted and he didn't attack you, so we don't have much, do we?" I agreed, and the charge was dropped. . . .

I came away from this incident with another arrest booked to my badge number and two hours of comp time for the time I spent at the court. The young man has an arrest record, his fingerprints will be forwarded to the FBI and his name will be entered into the National Crime Information Center's database. Whether he will stop for other officers in the future, I can't say. He might just decide to run faster.[28]

- In both descriptions, the police used their power to stop suspicious people. Does this power give the police too much license to interfere in the lives of young citizens?
- What reasonable suspicion did the police officer have about the young man in Washington, D.C.? In your opinion, did the officer violate the Fourth Amendment?
- Do you think that the Fourth Amendment adequately protects young people from arbitrary or unfair police practices? Could anything be done to protect them more?
- What is your view of the "fragile and fraying relationship between the Metropolitan Police Department and the community" in Washington? Doesn't Lieutenant Crane present a sympathetic story?
- Do you think Lieutenant Crane did the right thing? What could he have done differently?
- What do you think the young man in the story thought about his constitutional rights?

Exclusionary Rule Review

A violation of the Fourth Amendment is remedied by the exclusionary rule—the evidence is excluded at trial. So what happens when there is a Fourth Amendment violation and evidence to exclude?

In chapter 3, you were asked to imagine that your friend handed you stolen DVDs just before the police arrived on your street. You ran inside your house, and the police broke in. You were searched. Your house was searched. Your room was searched. The DVDs were seized. You were seized and charged with receiving stolen property. Your friend ran away and escaped arrest.

At trial, the DVDs are the crucial evidence against you. The only reason the police have the DVDs is that they took them from you as part of a search and seizure. Thus, before trial a Fourth Amendment hearing (called a motions hearing) is held to figure out if your Fourth Amendment rights were violated. The question for the court is whether your Fourth Amendment rights were violated before the police obtained the evidence. If there was a Fourth Amendment violation, the evidence will be suppressed. If the search and seizure were constitutional, the evidence will come in against you. Remember, you might still win at trial, but the first issue a court needs to address at the Fourth Amendment hearing is whether your constitutional rights were violated.

Does the Fourth Amendment apply? Consider the following questions and answers.

Were police (or governmental agents) involved? Yes, police officers are government agents. Keep in mind that the Constitution protects you from the acts of government agents.

Did you have a reasonable expectation of privacy in your house? In your person? In the property in your possession? Yes, you almost always have a reasonable expectation of privacy in your house. You also almost always have a reasonable expectation of privacy in your person. Because you were found in the house, you also would have a reasonable

What should happen when the Fourth Amendment is violated and there is evidence to exclude?

expectation of privacy in not being physically searched in the house. You also would have a reasonable expectation of privacy in any property in your room or on your person.

Is the evidence (the DVDs) a person, house, paper, or effect under the Fourth Amendment? Yes, the DVDs are effects—the residual category of things in the Fourth Amendment.

Did the police actions constitute a Fourth Amendment search? In entering your house, there was a search. In entering your room, there was a search. In opening the sock drawer, there was a search. In looking through your pockets and sweatshirt, there were additional searches of your person.

Did the police seize anything? Yes, the DVDs and you.

Did the police have a warrant? No. This was a warrantless search and seizure.

If there was no warrant, did the police have probable cause to arrest? Probably not. When the police rounded the block, they had information that a stolen DVD or two existed. They clearly suspected your friend as having possession of the stolen DVDs. When they came into the block, they saw you with possession of a DVD, but not necessarily one of the stolen DVDs. This may be enough for probable cause to arrest you, because your friend could have handed you a stolen DVD. However, you might have possession of a DVD for many innocent reasons, and nothing indicates that the DVD in your hands was stolen. Furthermore, the police officers had no other corroborating evidence to think that you were involved in the crime. You were not seen at the scene of the crime, and no other information about you was available that connected you to the DVD. Probably, if that is all the evidence the police had against you, there would not be enough evidence to arrest you for the crime.

If there was no probable cause, did the police have reasonable suspicion to stop you? Probably yes. Under the same analysis, the police might not have enough to arrest you, but they would likely have enough evidence to stop you under the standard set out in *Terry*. The reasonable suspicion necessary to justify a stop would consist of your presence near someone suspected of a crime, the appearance that you might have the object of the crime (the DVDs) in your hands, and your flight from the sight of the police. A stop based on reasonable suspicion would likely be permitted.

If the police had reasonable suspicion, but not probable cause, do any of the exceptions to the warrant requirement apply to allow them to search you in your house? You were stopped in your house after the police knocked down the door. Usually, for police to enter the house, they need a warrant. Here, without a warrant, the only justification would be the emergency exception. The question for the court would be whether the pursuit was hot enough to justify smashing down your door. The court would consider the danger to the community (minimal) and the seriousness of the offense (also minimal).

While some courts could allow a search based on an emergency exception argument, others would find that police should have obtained a warrant. If the court found a Fourth Amendment violation, the DVDs would be excluded.

If the search of the house was valid, was the search of your person valid? Assume that police are in your room because they are following up on an emergency situation (the hot pursuit of you). They see you in the room. They search your pockets and sweatshirt. But they also claim that they see a DVD sticking out from your sweatshirt. Under the plain view exception to the warrant requirement, they can seize what they believe is contraband. A court faced with this situation would likely say that if the police were lawfully in your room, and they can see the evidence in plain view, they can seize it without violating the Constitution. If they could see it only after searching you without a warrant, the evidence would be suppressed as the result of an unconstitutional search.

Did you consent to the search of the sock drawer? They asked you if they could search the sock drawer. If you said yes, they could look in the drawer without any constitutional concerns. You would have given them permission to search and thus waived your Fourth Amendment rights. If you did not give them permission, you could argue that to the judge. If the judge believed you, the evidence would be suppressed.

Will the evidence be excluded? You be the judge. What do you think of the above analysis? What other arguments could be made on both sides?

POINTS TO PONDER

- The exclusionary rule normally requires judges to exclude evidence that the government has obtained in an unlawful way. Do you think it makes sense?
- Discuss the pros and cons of the exclusionary rule. In the pros category, the rule establishes the principle that constitutional rights must be respected; creates a penalty for violation of the Fourth Amendment by preventing the government from profiting from its own wrongdoing, thus increasing the chances that law enforcement officers will not violate it in the future; and creates accountability of police officers to the court system. In the cons category, the rule keeps relevant evidence out of trial; sometimes allows guilty people to go free; shifts attention from the truth of what happened to police behavior; sometimes hides the truth; prioritizes the constitutional protection of the individual over the safety or interests of the community; and does not deter police misconduct when police do not need to use evidence in court.
- Can you brainstorm more reasons for or against the rule?
- How does the exclusionary rule influence police work? How does it influence police work when there is no evidence to suppress?
- Are there other ways to control police action that do not also affect the safety or security of the community? For example, you could sue a police officer who violated your rights or sue the police department. Or police officers could face employment sanctions or dismissal for violating constitutional rights. Would these options work better? Is there confidence that they will endure?

Notes

1. *Warden, Maryland Penitentiary v. Hayden,* 387 U.S. 294 (1967).
2. *Welsh v. Wisconsin,* 466 U.S. 740 (1984).
3. *Schmerber v. California,* 384 U.S. 757 (1966).
4. *Chimel v. California,* 395 U.S. 752 (1969).
5. *Carroll v. United States,* 267 U.S. 132 (1925).
6. *Cady v. Dombrowski,* 413 U.S. 433 (1973).
7. *Cardwell v. Lewis,* 417 U.S. 583 (1974).
8. Joseph D. Grano, "Rethinking the Fourth Amendment Warrant Requirement for Warrantless Searches," *Journal of Criminal Law and Criminology* 74 (1983): 172.
9. *California v. Carney,* 471 U.S. 386 (1985).
10. David A. Harris, " 'Driving While Black' and All Other Traffic Offenses: The Supreme Court and Pretextual Traffic Stops," *Journal of Criminal Law and Criminology* 87 (1997): 544, 563–564. See also David Cole, *No Equal Justice: Race and Class in the American Criminal Justice System* (New York: New Press, 1999).
11. American Civil Liberties Union, "Citing Continued Police Denial of Racial Profiling, ACLU Renews Call for Federal Traffic Stops Law," May 16, 2001, available at http://www.aclu.org/Racial Equality/RacialEquality.cfm?ID=7264&c=133 (accessed November 8, 2004).
12. U.S. Census Bureau, "Maryland QuickFacts," July 9, 2004, available at http://quickfacts. census.gov/qfd/states/24000.html (accessed November 8, 2004).
13. Lawrence F. Tiffany and others, *Detection of Crime* (Chicago, Ill.: American Bar Foundation, 1967), p. 31, quoted in David A. Harris, " 'Driving While Black' and All Other Traffic Offenses: The Supreme Court and Pretextual Traffic Stops," *Journal of Criminal Law and Criminology 87 (1997):* 544, 563–564.
14. Whren v. United States, 517 U.S. 806 (1996).
15. Joshua Dressler, *Understanding Criminal Procedure* (New York: Matthew Bender, 1991), sec. 88, p. 177.
16. *Schneckloth v. Bustamonte,* 412 U.S. 218 (1973).
17. Lourdes Rosado, "Minors and the Fourth Amendment: How Juvenile Status Should Invoke Different Standards for Searches and Seizures on the Street," *New York University Law Review* 71 (1996): 762, 763.
18. Robert Ward, "Consenting to a Search and Seizure in Poor and Minority Neighborhoods: No Place for a 'Reasonable Person,' " *Howard Law Journal* 36 (1993): 239.
19. Joseph D. McNamara, "Has the Drug War Created an Officer Liars' Club?" *L.A. Times,* February 11, 1996, p. M1, reprinted in Tracey Maclin, "Race and the Fourth Amendment," *Vanderbilt Law Review* 51 (1998): 333, 393 n. 39.
20. *Terry v. Ohio,* 392 U.S. 1 (1968).
21. "Defendant's Bill of Exceptions, *State v. Terry* and *State v. Chilton,*" Nos. 79,491 and 79,432, reprinted in "*State of Ohio v. Richard D. Chilton* and *State of Ohio v. John W. Terry:* The Suppression Hearing and Trial Transcripts," *St. John's Law Review* 72 (1998): 1387, 1420, 1477. Also reprinted in Tracey Maclin, "*Terry v. Ohio's* Fourth Amendment Legacy: Black Men and Police Discretion," *St. John's Law Review* 72 (1998): 1271, 1273.
22. *Illinois v. Wardlow,* 528 U.S. 673 (2000).
23. *In re Roy L.,* 197 Ariz. 441, 444 (2000) (Court of Appeals of Arizona, Division One).
24. *In re Roy L.,* 197 Ariz. 444.
25. *In re Roy L.,* 197 Ariz. 441.

26. *In re Roy L.*, 197 Ariz. 444.

27. Quoted from Ann Belser, "Suspect Black Men Are Subject to Closer Scrutiny from Patrolling Police, And the Result Is Often More Fear, Antagonism between Them," *Pittsburgh Post-Gazette,* May 5, 1996, p. A15. See also Maclin, "Race and the Fourth Amendment," 333, 392 n. 1; Maclin, *"Terry v. Ohio*'s Fourth Amendment Legacy."

28. James O. Crane, "Outlook: Shackled by Mistrust: A Chase, an Arrest, and a Cop's Uncomfortable Questions," *Washington Post,* June 21, 1998. Reprinted with the permission of James O. Crane.

Additional Sources

Allen, Ronald, and Richard Kuhns. *Constitutional Criminal Procedure: An Examination of the Fourth, Fifth, and Sixth Amendments and Related Areas.* 2d ed. Boston, Mass.: Little Brown, 1991.

Amsterdam, Anthony. "Perspectives on the Fourth Amendment." *Minnesota Law Review* 58 (1974): 349.

Dressler, Joshua. *Understanding Criminal Procedure.* New York: West Publishing Company, 1991, secs. 28-54.

Kamisar, Yale, Wayne LaFave, and others. *Modern Criminal Procedure: Cases, Comments, Questions.* 9th ed. New York: West Publishing Company, 1999.

LaFave, Wayne. *Search and Seizure: A Treatise on the Fourth Amendment.* 3d ed. New York: West Publishing Company, 1996.

Miller, Marc, and Ronald White. *Teachers' Manual Criminal Procedures: Cases, Statutes, and Executive Materials.* 2d ed. New York: Aspen Publishers, 2003.

Tomkovicz, James J., and Welsh White. *Criminal Procedure: Constitutional Constraints upon Investigation and Proof.* 3d ed. New York: Matthew Bender, 1998.

SCHOOL SEARCHES

5

I n the ideal school, teachers and administrators never search students and students never give their schools any reason to suspect them of wrongdoing. The focus is purely on teaching and learning.

But American schools are not utopian intellectual communes. While it may take a village to raise a child, as the African proverb made famous by Hillary Rodham Clinton goes, it takes just a few children to raise hell in a school. And many schools today are beset by serious violence, disorder, drug dealing, and crime.

So what are the rules governing official school searches of students and their belongings for drugs, weapons, and other harmful things?

On the one hand, some people defending student rights think that school authorities should be forced to go to court and prove probable cause and then get a search warrant from a judge before ever searching anyone or anything at school.

On the other hand, some people, invoking the doctrine of *in loco parentis* (in the place of the parent), say schools should simply have the right to search students and their property however they want and whenever they want.

But the U.S. Supreme Court has refused to side with either of these polar opposite positions, which assert, in one case, that students have all the same rights at school as they have elsewhere and, in the other, that they essentially have no rights at all because the schools are acting in the place of the parents.

In *New Jersey v. T. L. O.,* the Court found that school authorities need not obtain search warrants or even show probable cause to search students at school. But they cannot simply search whenever they want. In carrying out searches and discipline, school officials act as representatives of the state, not merely as **surrogates** of the parents. When it comes to the bodies and personal belongings of students, schools can search without a warrant only so long as they have a reasonable suspicion to think that the students are breaking the law or the rules of the school community.

YOUR THOUGHTS

Do you have the same Fourth Amendment privacy rights inside school as you have outside?

Do schools and police need to get search warrants based on probable cause to search your body and belongings at school?

When do schools have the authority to compel students to submit to drug tests?

The Court, alarmed by high levels of drug use on campus, has gone even further to allow urinalysis drug testing of student athletes and other students involved in extracurricular activities even without reasonable suspicion.

It is also generally assumed by lower courts that schools can place metal detectors at entrances and conduct searches of student lockers, which are school property, whenever they choose to do so.

The bottom line is that students have some Fourth Amendment rights at school but not many. In theory, this particular balance struck by the Court increases security for students and teachers while reducing student liberty and privacy. Is this a good trade-off?

Are schools secure? Do students feel free or restricted at school? How much educational time is consumed by security investigations, metal detector lines, locker searches, drug testing, dog sniffs, automobile searches, suspension hearings, and the whole apparatus of discipline and punishment at school? Is there any alternative?

The Marshall-Brennan Constitutional Literacy Project is working to heighten students' understanding of the Bill of Rights. The project Web site is www.wcl.american.edu/wethestudents. *Source: www.CartoonStock.com*

POINTS TO PONDER

- On a scale of 1-10, with 1 being the lowest and 10 being the highest, define the expectation of privacy you believe you have against inspection and surveillance by school authorities in the following areas and items.
    School locker in main hallway
    Gym locker in girls' locker room
    Backpack
    Bathroom stall with closed door
    Hallways
    Purse in school locker
    Desk in classroom
    Clothing, including pockets and underwear, that you are wearing
    Clothing that you are not wearing
    Bodily fluids such as urine and blood?

Search of Belongings

Because the privacy interests of schoolchildren are outweighed by the substantial need of teachers and administrators to maintain order in the schools, the Supreme Court has dropped the requirement of probable cause and a search warrant when schools are investigating violations of school rules and criminal laws.

Standard for Searches

New Jersey v. T. L. O. established a lower standard for official searches by school authorities: reasonable suspicion.

NEW JERSEY
V.
T. L. O.

Supreme Court of the United States
No. 83-712.
Decided January 15, 1985.

JUSTICE WHITE delivered the opinion of the Court. . . .

I

On March 7, 1980, a teacher at Piscataway High School in Middlesex County, N.J., discovered two girls smoking in a lavatory. One of the two girls was the respondent T. L. O., who at that time was a 14-year-old high school freshman. Because smoking in the lavatory was a violation of a school rule, the teacher took the two girls to the Principal's office, where they met with Assistant Vice Principal Theodore Choplick. In response to questioning by Mr. Choplick, T. L. O.'s companion admitted that she had violated the rule. T. L. O., however, denied that she had been smoking in the lavatory and claimed that she did not smoke at all.

Mr. Choplick asked T. L. O. to come into his private office and demanded to see her purse. Opening the purse, he found a pack of cigarettes, which he removed from the purse and held before T. L. O. as he accused her of having lied to him. As he reached into the purse for the cigarettes, Mr. Choplick also noticed a package of cigarette rolling papers. In his experience, possession of rolling papers by high school students was closely associated with the use of marihuana. Suspecting that a closer examination of the purse might yield further evidence of drug use, Mr. Choplick proceeded to search the purse thoroughly. The search revealed a small amount of marihuana, a pipe, a number of empty plastic bags, a substantial quantity of money in one-dollar bills, an index card that appeared to be a list of students who owed T. L. O. money, and two letters that implicated T. L. O. in marihuana dealing.

Mr. Choplick notified T. L. O.'s mother and the police, and turned the evidence of drug dealing over to the police. At the request of the police, T. L. O.'s mother took her daughter to police headquarters, where T. L. O. confessed that she had been selling marihuana at the high school. On the basis of the confession and the evidence seized by Mr. Choplick, the State brought delinquency charges against T. L. O. in the Juvenile and Domestic Relations Court of Middlesex County. Contending that Mr. Choplick's search of her purse violated the Fourth Amendment, T. L. O. moved to suppress the evidence found in her purse as well as her confession, which, she argued, was **tainted** by the allegedly unlawful search. The Juvenile Court denied the motion to suppress. Although the court concluded that the Fourth Amendment did apply to searches carried out by school officials, it held that a school official may properly conduct a search of a student's person if the official has a reasonable suspicion that a crime has been or is in the process of being committed, *or* reasonable cause to believe that the search is necessary to maintain school discipline or enforce school policies.

Applying this standard, the court concluded that the search conducted by Mr. Choplick was a reasonable one. The initial decision to open the purse was justified by Mr. Choplick's well-founded suspicion that T. L. O. had violated the rule forbidding smoking in the lavatory. Once the purse was open, evidence of marihuana violations was in plain view, and Mr. Choplick was entitled to conduct a thorough search to determine the nature and extent of T. L. O.'s drug-related activities. Having denied the motion to suppress, the court on March 23, 1981, found T. L. O. to be a delinquent and on January 8, 1982, sentenced her to a year's probation. . . .

. . . [W]e are satisfied that the search did not violate the Fourth Amendment.

II

In determining whether the search at issue in this case violated the Fourth Amendment, we are faced initially with the question whether that Amendment's prohibition on unreasonable searches and seizures applies to searches conducted by public school officials. We hold that it does. . . . In carrying out searches and other disciplinary functions pursuant to such policies, school officials act as representatives of the State, not merely as surrogates for the parents, and they cannot claim the parents' immunity from the strictures of the Fourth Amendment.

III

To hold that the Fourth Amendment applies to searches conducted by school authorities is only to begin the inquiry into the standards governing such searches. Although the underlying command of the Fourth Amendment is always that searches and seizures be reasonable, what is reasonable depends on the context within which a search takes place. The determination of the standard of reasonableness governing any specific class of searches requires "balancing the need to search against the invasion which the search entails." On one side of the balance are arrayed the individual's legitimate expectations of privacy and personal security; on the other, the government's need for effective methods to deal with breaches of public order.

We have recognized that even a limited search of the person is a substantial invasion of privacy. We have also recognized that searches of closed items of personal luggage are intrusions on protected privacy interests, for "the Fourth Amendment provides protection to the owner of every container that conceals its contents from plain view." A search of a child's person or of a closed purse or other bag carried on her person, no less than a similar search carried out on an adult, is undoubtedly a severe violation of **subjective** expectations of privacy.

To receive the protection of the Fourth Amendment, an expectation of privacy must be one that society is "prepared to recognize as legitimate." The State of New Jersey has argued that because of the pervasive supervision to which children in the schools are necessarily subject, a child has virtually no legitimate expectation of privacy in articles of personal property "unnecessarily" carried into a school. This argument has two factual premises: (1) the fundamental incompatibility of expectations of privacy with the maintenance of a sound educational environment; and (2) the minimal interest of the child in bringing any items of personal property into the school. Both premises are severely flawed.

Although this Court may take notice of the difficulty of maintaining discipline in the public schools today, the situation is not so dire that students in the schools may claim no legitimate expectations of privacy. We have recently recognized that the need to maintain order in a prison is such that prisoners retain no legitimate expectations of privacy in their cells, but it goes almost without saying that "[the] prisoner and the schoolchild stand in wholly different circumstances, separated by the harsh facts of criminal conviction and incarceration." We are not yet ready to hold that the schools and the prisons need be equated for purposes of the Fourth Amendment.

Nor does the State's suggestion that children have no legitimate need to bring personal property into the schools seem well anchored in reality. Students at a minimum must bring to school not only the supplies needed for their studies, but also keys, money, and the necessaries of personal hygiene and grooming. In addition, students may carry on their persons or in purses or wallets such nondisruptive yet highly personal items as photographs, letters, and diaries. Finally, students may have perfectly legitimate reasons to carry with them articles of property needed in connection with extracurricular or recreational activities. In short, schoolchildren may find it necessary to carry with them a variety of legitimate, noncontraband items, and there is no reason to conclude that they have necessarily waived all rights to privacy in such items merely by bringing them onto school grounds.

Against the child's interest in privacy must be set the substantial interest of teachers and administrators in maintaining discipline in the classroom and on school grounds. Maintaining order in the classroom has never been easy, but in recent years, school disorder has often taken particularly ugly forms: drug use and violent crime in the schools have become major social problems. Even in schools that have been spared the most severe disciplinary problems, the preservation of order and a proper educational environment requires close supervision of schoolchildren, as well as the enforcement of rules against conduct that would be perfectly permissible if undertaken by an adult. . . .

How, then, should we strike the balance between the schoolchild's legitimate expectations of privacy and the school's equally legitimate need to maintain an environment in which learning can take place? It is evident that the school setting requires some easing of the restrictions to which searches by public authorities are ordinarily subject. The warrant requirement, in particular, is unsuited to the school environment: requiring a teacher to obtain a warrant before searching a child suspected of an infraction of school rules (or of the criminal law) would unduly interfere with the maintenance of the swift and informal disciplinary procedures needed in the schools. Just as we have in other cases dispensed with the warrant requirement when "the burden of obtaining a warrant is likely to frustrate the governmental purpose behind the search," we hold today that school officials need not obtain a warrant before searching a student who is under their authority.

The school setting also requires some modification of the level of suspicion of illicit activity needed to justify a search. Ordinarily, a search—even one that may permissibly be carried out without a warrant—must be based upon "probable cause" to believe that a violation of the law has occurred. However, "probable cause" is not an irreducible requirement of a valid search. . . .

We join the majority of courts that have examined this issue in concluding that the accommodation of the privacy interests of schoolchildren with the substantial need of teachers and administrators for freedom to maintain order in the schools does not require strict adherence to the requirement that searches be based on probable cause to believe that the subject of the search has violated or is violating the law. Rather, the legality of a search of a student should depend simply on the reasonableness, under all the circumstances, of the search. Determining the reasonableness of any search involves a twofold inquiry: first, one must consider "whether the . . . action was justified at its **inception**"; second, one must determine whether the search as actually conducted "was reasonably related in scope to the circumstances which justified the interference in the first place." Under ordinary circumstances, a search of a student by a teacher or other school official will be "justified at its inception" when there are reasonable grounds for suspecting that the search will turn up evidence that the student has violated or is violating either the law or the rules of the school. Such a search will be permissible in its scope when the measures adopted are reasonably related to the objectives of the search and not excessively intrusive in light of the age and sex of the student and the nature of the infraction.

This standard will, we trust, neither unduly burden the efforts of school authorities to maintain order in their schools nor authorize unrestrained intrusions upon the privacy of schoolchildren. By focusing attention on the question of reasonableness, the standard will spare teachers and school administrators the necessity of schooling themselves in the niceties of probable cause and permit them to regulate their conduct according to the dictates of reason and common sense. At the same time, the reasonableness standard should ensure that the interests of students will be invaded no more than is necessary to achieve the legitimate end of preserving order in the schools.

IV

. . . The incident that gave rise to this case actually involved two separate searches, with the first—the search for cigarettes—providing the suspicion that gave rise to the second—the search for marihuana. Although it is the fruits of the second search that are at issue here, the validity of the search for marihuana must depend on the reasonableness of the initial search for cigarettes, as there would have been no reason to suspect that T. L. O. possessed marihuana had the first search not taken place. Accordingly, it is to the search for cigarettes that we first turn our attention.

The New Jersey Supreme Court pointed to two grounds for its holding that the search for cigarettes was unreasonable. First, the court observed that possession of cigarettes was not in itself illegal or a violation of school rules. Because the contents of T. L. O.'s purse would therefore have "no direct bearing on the infraction" of which she was accused (smoking in a lavatory where smoking was prohibited), there was no reason to search her purse. Second, even assuming that a search of T. L. O.'s purse might under some circumstances be reasonable in light of the accusation made against T. L. O., the New Jersey court concluded that Mr. Choplick in this particular case had no reasonable grounds to suspect that T. L. O. had cigarettes in her purse. At best, according to the court, Mr. Choplick had "a good hunch."

Both these conclusions are implausible. T. L. O. had been accused of smoking, and had denied the accusation in the strongest possible terms when she stated that she did not smoke at all. Surely it cannot be said that under these circumstances, T. L. O.'s possession of cigarettes would be irrelevant to the charges against her or to her response to those charges. T. L. O.'s possession of cigarettes, once it was discovered, would both corroborate the report that she had been smoking and undermine the credibility of her defense to the charge of smoking. To be sure, the discovery of the cigarettes would not prove that T. L. O. had been smoking in the lavatory; nor would it, strictly speaking, necessarily be inconsistent with her claim that she did not smoke at all. But it is universally recognized that evidence, to be relevant to an inquiry, need not conclusively prove the ultimate fact in issue, but only have "any tendency to make the existence of any fact that is of consequence to the determination of the action more probable or less probable than it would be without the evidence." The relevance of T. L. O.'s possession of cigarettes to the question whether she had been smoking and to the credibility of her denial that she smoked supplied the necessary "**nexus**" between the item searched for and the infraction under investigation. Thus, if Mr. Choplick in fact had a reasonable suspicion that T. L. O. had cigarettes in her purse, the search was justified despite the fact that the cigarettes, if found, would constitute "mere evidence" of a violation.

Of course, the New Jersey Supreme Court also held that Mr. Choplick had no reasonable suspicion that the purse would contain cigarettes. This conclusion is puzzling. A teacher had reported that T. L. O. was smoking in the lavatory. Certainly this report gave Mr. Choplick reason to suspect that T. L. O. was carrying cigarettes with her; and if she did have cigarettes, her purse was the obvious place in which to find them. Mr. Choplick's suspicion that there were cigarettes in the purse . . . was the sort of "common-sense [conclusion] about human behavior" upon which "practical people"—including government officials—are entitled to rely. . . . It cannot be said that Mr. Choplick acted unreasonably when he examined T. L. O.'s purse to see if it contained cigarettes.

Our conclusion that Mr. Choplick's decision to open T. L. O.'s purse was reasonable brings us to the question of the further search for marihuana once the pack of cigarettes was located. The suspicion upon which the search for marihuana was founded was provided when Mr. Choplick observed a package of rolling papers in the purse as he removed the pack of cigarettes. Although T. L. O. does not dispute the reasonableness of Mr. Choplick's belief that the rolling papers indicated the presence of marihuana, she does contend that the scope of the search Mr. Choplick conducted exceeded permissible bounds when he seized and read certain letters that implicated T. L. O. in drug dealing. This argument, too, is unpersuasive. The discovery of the rolling papers concededly gave rise to a reasonable suspicion that T. L. O. was carrying marihuana as well as cigarettes in her purse. This suspicion justified further exploration of T. L. O.'s purse, which turned up more evidence of drug-related activities: a pipe, a number of plastic bags of the type commonly used to store marihuana, a small quantity of marihuana, and a fairly substantial amount of money. Under these circumstances, it was not unreasonable to extend the search to a separate zippered compartment of the purse; and when a search of that compartment revealed an index card containing a list of "people who owe me money" as well as two letters, the inference that T. L. O. was involved in marihuana trafficking was substantial enough to justify Mr. Choplick in examining the letters to determine whether they contained any further evidence. In short, we cannot conclude that the search for marihuana was unreasonable in any respect. . . .

The judgment of the Supreme Court of New Jersey is

Reversed.

JUSTICE STEVENS, with whom JUSTICE MARSHALL joins, and with whom JUSTICE BRENNAN joins as to Part I, concurring in part and dissenting in part. . . .

III

. . . In this case, Mr. Choplick overreacted to what appeared to be nothing more than a minor infraction—a rule prohibiting smoking in the bathroom of the freshmen's and sophomores' building. It is, of course, true that he actually found evidence of serious wrongdoing by T. L. O., but no one claims that the prior search may be justified by his unexpected discovery. As far as the smoking infraction is concerned, the search for cigarettes merely tended to corroborate a teacher's eyewitness account of T. L. O.'s violation of a minor regulation designed to channel student smoking behavior into designated locations. Because this conduct was neither unlawful nor significantly disruptive of school order or the educational process, the invasion of privacy associated with the forcible opening of T. L. O.'s purse was entirely unjustified at its inception.

. . . Although I agree that school administrators must have broad latitude to maintain order and discipline in our classrooms, that authority is not unlimited.

IV

The schoolroom is the first opportunity most citizens have to experience the power of government. Through it passes every citizen and public official, from schoolteachers to policemen and prison guards. The values they learn there, they take with them in life. One of our most cherished ideals is the one contained in the Fourth Amendment: that the government may not intrude on the personal privacy of its citizens without a warrant or compelling circumstance. The Court's decision today is a curious moral for the Nation's youth. . . .

I respectfully dissent.

POINTS TO PONDER

- Do you agree with the majority in this case that schools could not be functional institutions if administrators needed to go to court to get search warrants before searching students' belongings? Why or why not?
- If schools do not have to seek warrants to search students, should the schools then be able to turn over evidence of crime they find—drugs and guns, for example—to state prosecutors? Right now, they can do that and the students can be prosecuted. Does that make sense?

T. L. O. Review

The Court in *T. L. O.* applied a two-part test to determine the reasonableness of any search: (1) whether the search was justified when it began; and (2) whether the search that took place was reasonably related in scope to its original purpose. A search of a student ordinarily would be justified when reasonable grounds exist for suspecting that it would produce evidence that the student has violated or is violating either the law or the rules of the school. Such a search would be reasonable in its scope when the measures adopted are reasonably related to the purpose of the search and not overly intrusive in light of the age and gender of the student and the nature of the infraction.

Consider the following hypothetical situations.

Jenny Jefferson borrows a CD from her friend Carmela Costas, promising to return it after she has had a chance to burn it. After two weeks pass, Carmela gets impatient and asks Jenny about the CD. Jenny promises to return it soon, but Carmela is so upset she loudly complains about it in class. Mr. Williams, the teacher, gets tired of hearing about

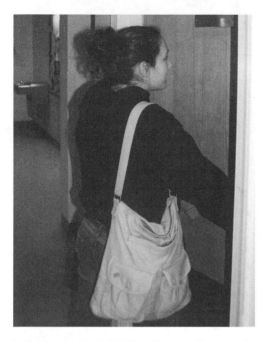

In *New Jersey v. T. L. O.* (1985), the Supreme Court found that school authorities need not obtain a search warrant or show probable cause to search a student at school. The authorities must, however, have a reasonable suspicion that the student is breaking the law or the rules of the school. *Source: Daniel Gossett*

it and asks Jenny to open her bag so that he can look for the CD and give it back to Carmela. Before Carmela can respond, Mr. Williams grabs the bag, opens it, and, while he is fishing around, finds not only the CD but also a small bag of marijuana. He refers her to the police officer at the school, and drug charges are brought against her. Using *T. L. O.*, do you think Mr. Williams violated Jenny's Fourth Amendment rights by searching her bag? Why or why not?

Johnny Walkman, an Eagle Scout, brings to school in his backpack a pocketknife that he had with him on a camping trip. Walking through the metal detector at the front door of his school, the pocketknife sets off the alarm. Johnny says, "Oh, no, I forgot about my pocketknife! Let me go give it to my Mom. She's right outside in the car." The security guard says, "Not so fast," and opens up his backpack to find both the knife and a pornographic magazine. The school then suspends Johnny for ten days for bringing a weapon and indecent sexual material to school. Was the search of Johnny's backpack a lawful one?

On the morning of a big math test, Rachelle Forest goes to the girls' bathroom and sees Tomika Henry putting something in her sweater. She thinks Tomika is hiding some math information and has long suspected that Tomika cheats. In fact, Tomika was just putting on some underarm antiperspirant, but Rachelle rushes to tell the math teacher, Mr. Desmel, of her suspicions and he calls the principal, Art Szienz. They take Tomika to the office and demand she take off her sweater, t-shirt, and bra, all to be examined by Ms. Efficiel, the deputy principal. Ms. Efficiel finds nothing and asks Tomika to lift her arms. Finding no hidden answers, Ms. Efficiel says, "I'm sorry, Tomika. That Rachelle lets her imagination run wild some times. You can get dressed and go take your math test." Tomika thinks this search was unlawful and wants to sue. Was this a reasonable search or an unlawful one?

YOUR THOUGHTS

Imagine your dream was to make your school's soccer team. If you had to sign a form consenting to random drug testing to join the team, would you sign it? Why or why not?

Drug Testing and After-School Activities

James Acton was a seventh-grade student who wanted to play football, and his parents refused to sign a drug-testing consent form required by the school district for participation on all athletic teams. The Supreme Court ruled on whether a school can subject students who want to play on sports teams to mandatory random drug testing without any suspicion that they are using drugs. What did the Court say?

—•—

VERNONIA SCHOOL DISTRICT 47J, PETITIONER
V.
WAYNE ACTON, ET UX., ETC.

Supreme Court of the United States
No. 94-590.
Decided June 26, 1995.

JUSTICE SCALIA delivered the opinion of the Court.

The Student Athlete Drug Policy adopted by School District 47J in the town of Vernonia, Oregon, authorizes random urinalysis drug testing of students who participate in the District's school athletics programs. We **granted certiorari** to decide whether this violates the Fourth and Fourteenth Amendments to the United States Constitution.

I

A

Petitioner Vernonia School District 47J (District) operates one high school and three grade schools in the logging community of Vernonia, Oregon. As elsewhere in small-town America, school sports play a prominent role in the town's life, and student athletes are admired in their schools and in the community.

Drugs had not been a major problem in Vernonia schools. In the mid-to-late 1980's, however, teachers and administrators observed a sharp increase in drug use. Students began to speak out about their attraction to the drug culture, and to boast that there was nothing the school could do about it. Along with more drugs came more disciplinary problems. Between 1988 and 1989 the number of disciplinary referrals in Vernonia schools rose to more than twice the number reported in the early 1980's, and several students were suspended. Students became increasingly rude during class; outbursts of profane language became common.

Not only were student athletes included among the drug users but, as the District Court found, athletes were the leaders of the drug culture. This caused the District's administrators particular concern, since drug use increases the risk of sports-related injury. Expert testimony at the trial confirmed the **deleterious** effects of drugs on motivation, memory, judgment, reaction, coordination, and performance. The high school football and wrestling coach witnessed a severe sternum injury suffered by a wrestler, and various omissions of safety procedures and misexecutions by football players, all attributable in his belief to the effects of drug use.

Initially, the District responded to the drug problem by offering special classes, speakers, and presentations designed to deter drug use. It even brought in a specially trained dog to detect drugs, but the drug problem persisted. . . . They held a parent "input night" to discuss the proposed Student Athlete Drug Policy (Policy), and the parents in attendance gave their unanimous approval. The school board approved the Policy for implementation in the fall of 1989. Its expressed purpose is to prevent student athletes from using drugs, to protect their health and safety, and to provide drug users with assistance programs.

B

The Policy applies to all students participating in interscholastic athletics. Students wishing to play sports must sign a form consenting to the testing and must obtain the written consent of their parents. Athletes are tested at the beginning of the season for their sport. In addition, once each week of the season the names of the athletes are placed in a "pool" from which a student, with the supervision of two adults, blindly draws the names of 10% of the athletes for random testing. Those selected are notified and tested that same day, if possible.

The student to be tested completes a specimen control form which bears an assigned number. Prescription medications that the student is taking must be identified by providing a copy of the prescription or a doctor's authorization. The student then enters an empty locker room accompanied by an adult monitor of the same sex. Each boy selected produces a sample at a urinal, remaining fully clothed with his back to the monitor, who stands approximately 12 to 15 feet behind the student. Monitors may (though do not always) watch the student while he produces the sample, and they listen for normal sounds of urination. Girls produce samples in an enclosed bathroom stall, so that they can be heard but not observed. After the sample is produced, it is given to the monitor, who checks it for temperature and tampering and then transfers it to a vial.

If a sample tests positive, a second test is administered as soon as possible to confirm the result. If the second test is negative, no further action is taken. If the second test is positive, the athlete's parents are notified, and the school principal convenes a meeting with the student and his parents, at which the student is given the option of (1) participating for six weeks in an assistance program that includes weekly urinalysis, or (2) suffering suspension from athletics for the remainder of the current season and the next athletic season. The student is then retested prior to the start of the next athletic season for which he or she is eligible. The Policy states that a second offense results in automatic imposition of option (2); a third offense in suspension for the remainder of the current season and the next two athletic seasons.

C

In the fall of 1991, . . . James Acton, then a seventh grader, signed up to play football at one of the District's grade schools. He was denied participation, however, because he and his parents refused to sign the testing consent forms. The Actons filed suit. . . . After a bench trial, the District Court entered an order denying the claims on the merits and dismissing the action. The United States Court of Appeals for the Ninth Circuit reversed, holding that the Policy violated both the Fourth and Fourteenth Amendments and Article I, § 9, of the *Oregon Constitution*. We granted certiorari.

. . . As the text of the Fourth Amendment indicates, the ultimate measure of the constitutionality of a governmental search is "reasonableness." . . .

We have found . . . "special needs" to exist in the public school context. There, the warrant requirement "would unduly interfere with the maintenance of the swift and informal disciplinary procedures [that are] needed," and "strict adherence to the requirement that searches be based on probable cause" would undercut "the substantial need of teachers and administrators for freedom to maintain order in the schools." The school search we approved in *T. L. O.*, while not based on probable cause, *was* based on individualized *suspicion* of wrongdoing. As we explicitly acknowledged, however, " 'the Fourth Amendment imposes no irreducible requirement of such suspicion.' " We have upheld suspicionless searches and seizures to conduct drug testing of railroad personnel involved in train accidents; to conduct random drug testing of federal customs officers who carry arms or are involved in drug interdiction; and to maintain automobile checkpoints looking for illegal immigrants and contraband, and drunk drivers.

The first factor to be considered is the nature of the privacy interest upon which the search here at issue intrudes. The Fourth Amendment does not protect all subjective expectations of privacy, but only those that society recognizes as "legitimate." . . . Central, in our view, to the present case is the fact that the subjects of the Policy are (1) children, who (2) have been committed to the temporary custody of the State as schoolmaster.

Traditionally at common law, and still today, unemancipated minors lack some of the most fundamental rights of self-determination—including even the right of liberty in its narrow sense, *i. e.*, the right to come and go at will. They are subject, even as to their physical freedom, to the control of their parents or guardians. When parents place minor children in private schools for their education, the teachers and administrators of those schools stand *in loco parentis* over the children entrusted to them. In fact, the tutor or schoolmaster is the very prototype of that status. . . .

In *T. L. O.* we rejected the notion that public schools, like private schools, exercise only parental power over their students, which of course is not subject to constitutional constraints. . . . But while denying that the State's power over schoolchildren is formally no more than the delegated power of their parents, *T. L. O.* did not deny, but indeed emphasized, that the nature of that power is custodial and tutelary, permitting a degree of supervision and control that could not be exercised over free adults. . . . [W]hile children assuredly do not "shed their constitutional rights . . . at the schoolhouse gate," the nature of those rights is what is appropriate for children in school.

Fourth Amendment rights, no less than First and Fourteenth Amendment rights, are different in public schools than elsewhere; the "reasonableness" inquiry cannot disregard the schools' custodial and tutelary responsibility for children. For their own good and that of their classmates, public school children are routinely required to submit to various physical examinations, and to be vaccinated against various diseases. . . . Particularly with regard to medical examinations and procedures, therefore, "students within the school environment have a lesser expectation of privacy than members of the population generally."

Legitimate privacy expectations are even less with regard to student athletes. School sports are not for the bashful. They require "suiting up" before each practice or event, and showering and changing afterwards. Public school locker rooms, the usual sites for these activities, are not notable for the privacy they afford. The locker rooms in Vernonia are typical: No individual dressing rooms are provided; shower heads are lined up along a wall, unseparated by any sort of partition or curtain; not even all the toilet stalls have doors. As the United States Court of Appeals for the Seventh Circuit has noted, there is "an element of 'communal undress' inherent in athletic participation."

There is an additional respect in which school athletes have a reduced expectation of privacy. By choosing to "go out for the team," they voluntarily subject themselves to a degree of regulation even higher than that imposed on students generally. In Vernonia's public schools, they must submit to a preseason physical exam (James testified that his included the giving of a urine sample, App. 17), they must acquire adequate insurance coverage or sign an insurance waiver, maintain a minimum grade point average, and comply with any "rules of conduct, dress, training hours and related matters as may be established for each sport by the head coach and athletic director with the principal's approval." Somewhat like adults who choose to participate in a "closely regulated industry," students who voluntarily participate in school athletics have reason to expect intrusions upon normal rights and privileges, including privacy.

IV

Having considered the scope of the legitimate expectation of privacy at issue here, we turn next to the character of the intrusion that is complained of. We recognized in *Skinner* that collecting the samples for urinalysis intrudes upon "an excretory function traditionally shielded by great privacy." We noted, however, that the degree of intrusion depends upon the manner in which production of the urine sample is monitored. Under the District's Policy, male students produce samples at a urinal along a wall. They remain fully clothed and are only observed from behind, if at all. Female students produce samples in an enclosed stall, with a female monitor standing outside listening only for sounds of tampering. These conditions are nearly identical to those typically encountered in public restrooms, which men, women, and especially school children use daily. Under such conditions, the privacy interests compromised by the process of obtaining the urine sample are in our view negligible.

The other privacy-invasive aspect of urinalysis is, of course, the information it discloses concerning the state of the subject's body, and the materials he has ingested. In this regard it is significant that the tests at issue here look only for drugs, and not for whether the student is, for example, epileptic, pregnant, or diabetic. Moreover, the drugs for which the samples are screened are standard, and do not vary according to the identity of the student. And finally, the results of the tests are disclosed only to a limited class of school personnel who have a need to know; and they are not turned over to law enforcement authorities or used for any internal disciplinary function. . . .

The General Authorization Form that [the Actons] refused to sign, which refusal was the basis for James's exclusion from the sports program, said only. . . : "I . . . authorize the Vernonia School District to conduct a test on a urine specimen which I provide to test for drugs and/or alcohol use. I also authorize the release of information concerning the results of such a test to the Vernonia School District and to the parents and/or guardians of the student." While the practice of the District seems to have been to have a school official take medication information from the student at the time of the test, that practice is not set forth in, or required by, the Policy, which says simply: "Student athletes who . . . are or have been taking prescription medication must provide verification (either by a copy of the prescription or by doctor's authorization) prior to being tested." It may well be that, if and when James was selected for random testing at a time that he was taking medication, the School District would have permitted him to provide the requested information in a confidential manner—for example, in a sealed envelope delivered to the testing lab. Nothing in the Policy contradicts that, and when respondents choose, in effect, to challenge the Policy on its face, we will not assume the worst. Accordingly, we reach the same conclusion as in *Skinner:* that the invasion of privacy was not significant.

V

Finally, we turn to consider the nature and immediacy of the governmental concern at issue here, and the **efficacy** of this means for meeting it. . . . [T]he District Court held that because the District's program also called for drug testing in the absence of individualized suspicion, the District "must demonstrate a 'compelling need' for the program." . . . It is a mistake, however, to think that the phrase "compelling state interest," in the Fourth Amendment context, describes a fixed, minimum quantum of governmental concern, so that one can dispose of a case by answering in isolation the question: Is there a compelling state interest here? Rather, the phrase describes an interest that appears *important enough* to justify the particular search at hand, in light of other factors that show the search to be relatively intrusive upon a genuine expectation of privacy. Whether that relatively high degree of government concern is necessary in this case or not, we think it is met.

That the nature of the concern is important—indeed, perhaps compelling—can hardly be doubted. Deterring drug use by our Nation's schoolchildren is at least as important as enhancing efficient enforcement of the Nation's laws against the importation of drugs. . . . School years are the time when the physical, psychological, and addictive effects of drugs are most severe. "Maturing nervous systems are more critically impaired by intoxicants than mature ones are; childhood losses in learning are lifelong and profound"; "children grow chemically dependent more quickly than adults, and their record of recovery is depressingly poor." And of course the effects of a drug-infested school are visited not just upon the users, but upon the entire student body and faculty, as the educational process is disrupted. In the present case, moreover, the necessity for the State to act is magnified by the fact that this evil is being visited not just upon individuals at large, but upon children for whom it has undertaken a special responsibility of care and direction. Finally, it must not be lost sight of that this program is directed more narrowly to drug use by school athletes, where the risk of immediate physical harm to the drug user or those with whom he is playing his sport is particularly high. Apart from psychological effects, which include impairment of judgment, slow reaction time, and a lessening of the perception of pain, the particular drugs screened by the District's Policy have been demonstrated to pose substantial physical risks to athletes. Amphetamines produce an "artificially induced heart rate increase, peripheral vasoconstriction, blood pressure increase, and masking of the normal fatigue response," making them a "very dangerous drug when used during exercise of any type." Marijuana causes "irregular blood pressure responses during changes in body position," "reduction in the oxygen-carrying capacity of the blood," and "inhibition of the normal sweating responses resulting in increased body temperature." Cocaine produces "vasoconstriction[,] elevated blood pressure," and "possible coronary artery spasms and myocardial infarction."

As for the immediacy of the District's concerns: We are not inclined to question . . . the District Court's conclusion that "a large segment of the student body, particularly those involved in interscholastic athletics, was in a state of rebellion," that "disciplinary actions had reached 'epidemic proportions,' " and that "the rebellion was being fueled by alcohol and drug abuse as well as by the student's misperceptions about the drug culture." . . .

As to the efficacy of this means for addressing the problem: It seems to us self-evident that a drug problem largely fueled by the "role model" effect of athletes' drug use, and of particular danger to athletes, is effectively addressed by making sure that athletes do not use drugs. Respondents argue that a

"less intrusive means to the same end" was available, namely, "drug testing on suspicion of drug use."
We have repeatedly refused to declare that only the "least intrusive" search practicable can be reasonable under the Fourth Amendment. Respondents' alternative entails substantial difficulties—if it is
indeed practicable at all. It may be impracticable, for one thing, simply because the parents who are
willing to accept random drug testing for athletes are not willing to accept accusatory drug testing for
all students, which transforms the process into a badge of shame. Respondents' proposal brings the risk
that teachers will impose testing arbitrarily upon troublesome but not drug-likely students. It generates
the expense of defending lawsuits that charge such arbitrary imposition, or that simply demand greater
process before accusatory drug testing is imposed. And not least of all, it adds to the ever-expanding
diversionary duties of schoolteachers the new function of spotting and bringing to account drug abuse,
a task for which they are ill prepared, and which is not readily compatible with their vocation. In many
respects, we think, testing based on "suspicion" of drug use would not be better, but worse.

VI

Taking into account all the factors we have considered above—the decreased expectation of privacy,
the relative unobtrusiveness of the search, and the severity of the need met by the search—we conclude Vernonia's Policy is reasonable and hence constitutional. . . .
   It is so ordered.

JUSTICE O'CONNOR, with whom JUSTICE STEVENS and JUSTICE SOUTER join, dissenting.

   The population of our Nation's public schools, grades 7 through 12, numbers around 18 million. By the reasoning of today's decision, the millions of these students who participate in interscholastic sports, an overwhelming majority of whom have given school officials no reason whatsoever to suspect they use drugs at school, are open to an intrusive bodily search. . . .
   For most of our constitutional history, mass, suspicionless searches have been generally considered *per se* unreasonable within the meaning of the Fourth Amendment. . . . I dissent.

I
A

. . . [W]hat the Framers of the Fourth Amendment most strongly opposed, with limited exceptions
wholly inapplicable here, were general searches—that is, searches by general warrant, by writ of
assistance, by broad statute, or by any other similar authority. . . .
   Perhaps most telling of all, as reflected in the text of the Warrant Clause, the particular way the
Framers chose to curb the abuses of general warrants—and by implication, *all* general searches—was not
to impose a novel "evenhandedness" requirement; it was to retain the individualized suspicion requirement contained in the typical general warrant, but to make that requirement meaningful and enforceable, for instance, by raising the required level of individualized suspicion to objective probable cause. . . .
   Protection of privacy, not evenhandedness, was then and is now the touchstone of the Fourth
Amendment.
   . . . [C]ertainly monitored urination combined with urine testing is more intrusive than some
personal searches we have said trigger Fourth Amendment protections in the past. Finally, the collection and testing of urine is, of course, a search of a person, one of only four categories of suspect
searches the Constitution mentions by name.

Thus, it remains the law that the police cannot, say, subject to drug testing every person entering or leaving a certain drug-ridden neighborhood in order to find evidence of crime. And this is true even though it is hard to think of a more compelling government interest than the need to fight the scourge of drugs on our streets and in our neighborhoods. . . .

II

. . . I do not believe that suspicionless drug testing is justified on these facts. But even if I agreed that some such testing were reasonable here, I see two other Fourth Amendment flaws in the District's program. First, and most serious, there is virtually no evidence in the record of a drug problem at the Washington Grade School, which includes the seventh and eighth grades, and which Acton attended when this litigation began. . . .

Second, even as to the high school, I find unreasonable the school's choice of student athletes as the class to subject to suspicionless testing—a choice that appears to have been driven more by a belief in what would pass constitutional muster . . . than by a belief in what was required to meet the District's principal disciplinary concern. . . .

[I]t seems to me that the far more reasonable choice would have been to focus on the class of students found to have violated published school rules against severe disruption in class and around campus—disruption that had a strong nexus to drug use, as the District established at trial. Such a choice would share two of the virtues of a suspicion-based regime: testing dramatically fewer students, tens as against hundreds, and giving students control, through their behavior, over the likelihood that they would be tested. Moreover, there would be a reduced concern for the accusatory nature of the search, because the Court's feared "badge of shame" would already exist, due to the antecedent accusation and finding of severe disruption. . . .

III

It cannot be too often stated that the greatest threats to our constitutional freedoms come in times of crisis. But we must also stay mindful that not all government responses to such times are hysterical overreactions; some crises are quite real, and when they are, they serve precisely as the compelling state interest that we have said may justify a measured intrusion on constitutional rights. . . . Having reviewed the record here, I cannot avoid the conclusion that the District's suspicionless policy of testing all student athletes sweeps too broadly, and too imprecisely, to be reasonable under the Fourth Amendment.

POINTS TO PONDER

- What were Justice O'Connor's main points in her dissenting opinion? Do you think schools must wait until an obvious drug problem exists before it can take action?
- Why do schools care about an individual student's drug use? Should schools be able to intrude upon students' choices about their bodies and minds outside of school?
- Do you agree with the majority that random drug testing of student athletes is reasonable? What about random drug testing of students on the chess team? What about random drug testing of cheerleaders or

student council representatives? What about random drug testing of team coaches? What about random drug testing of all teachers?

- Do you agree that student athletes are role models for the rest of the student body? Why or why not? Does that give schools more power to reduce their privacy rights?
- How are urinalysis drug searches invasive? Is it the embarrassment associated with going to the bathroom in public or the "chemical window" opened onto your body and activities? What kinds of information can be revealed in a urinalysis test? Pregnancy? Sickness? Drug and alcohol use? Cholesterol levels? Do some research in your school library or science class about what information can be revealed as a result of these tests.

Drug Testing for All Students?

Many people thought that the *Acton* case would lead to drug-testing policies against student athletes only and not other students. Yet a number of high schools decided to press further and test students involved in any competitive extracurricular activity. Is that constitutional?

BOARD OF EDUCATION OF INDEPENDENT SCHOOL DISTRICT NO. 92 OF POTTAWATOMIE COUNTY ET AL., PETITIONERS V. LINDSAY EARLS ET AL.

Supreme Court of the United States
No. 01-332.
Decided June 27, 2002.

JUSTICE THOMAS delivered the opinion of the Court.

The Student Activities Drug Testing Policy implemented by the Board of Education of Independent School District No. 92 of Pottawatomie County (School District) requires all students who participate in competitive extracurricular activities to submit to drug testing. Because this Policy reasonably serves the School District's important interest in detecting and preventing drug use among its students, we hold that it is constitutional.

I

The city of Tecumseh, Oklahoma, is a rural community located approximately 40 miles southeast of Oklahoma City. The School District administers all Tecumseh public schools. In the fall of 1998, the School District adopted the Student Activities Drug Testing Policy (Policy), which requires all middle and high school students to consent to drug testing in order to participate in any extracurricular activity. In practice, the Policy has been applied only to competitive extracurricular activities **sanctioned** by the Oklahoma Secondary Schools Activities Association, such as the Academic Team, Future Farmers of America, Future Homemakers of America, band, choir, pom pom, cheerleading, and athletics. Under the Policy, students are required to take a drug test before participating in an

Lindsay Earls of Tecumseh, Oklahoma, challenged her high school's compulsory random drug testing of students involved in competitive extracurricular activities. In 2002, after Earls had graduated and enrolled in Dartmouth College, the Supreme Court upheld such drug-testing policies as a reasonable way to deter drug use. *Source: Lee Mariner/AP Wide World Photos*

extracurricular activity, must submit to random drug testing while participating in that activity, and must agree to be tested at any time upon reasonable suspicion. The urinalysis tests are designed to detect only the use of illegal drugs, including amphetamines, marijuana, cocaine, opiates, and barbituates, not medical conditions or the presence of authorized prescription medications.

At the time of their suit, both respondents attended Tecumseh High School. Respondent Lindsay Earls was a member of the show choir, the marching band, the Academic Team, and the National Honor Society. Respondent Daniel James sought to participate in the Academic Team. Together with their parents, Earls and James . . . alleged that the Policy violates the Fourth Amendment as incorporated by the Fourteenth Amendment and requested injunctive and declarative relief. They also argued that the School District failed to identify a special need for testing students who participate in extracurricular activities, and that the "Drug Testing Policy neither addresses a proven problem nor promises to bring any benefit to students or the school." . . .

II

. . . In *Vernonia,* this Court held that the suspicionless drug testing of athletes was constitutional. The Court, however, did not simply authorize all school drug testing, but rather conducted a fact-specific balancing of the intrusion on the children's Fourth Amendment rights against the promotion of legitimate governmental interests. Applying the principles of *Vernonia* to the somewhat different facts of this case, we conclude that Tecumseh's Policy is also constitutional.

A

We first consider the nature of the privacy interest allegedly compromised by the drug testing. . . .

A student's privacy interest is limited in a public school environment where the State is responsible for maintaining discipline, health, and safety. Schoolchildren are routinely required to submit to physical examinations and vaccinations against disease. Securing order in the school environment sometimes requires that students be subjected to greater controls than those appropriate for adults.

Respondents argue that because children participating in nonathletic extracurricular activities are not subject to regular physicals and communal undress, they have a stronger expectation of privacy than the athletes tested in *Vernonia*. This distinction, however, was not essential to our decision in *Vernonia*, which depended primarily upon the school's custodial responsibility and authority.

In any event, students who participate in competitive extracurricular activities voluntarily subject themselves to many of the same intrusions on their privacy as do athletes. Some of these clubs and activities require occasional off-campus travel and communal undress. All of them have their own rules and requirements for participating students that do not apply to the student body as a whole. . . . We therefore conclude that the students affected by this Policy have a limited expectation of privacy.

B

Next, we consider the character of the intrusion imposed by the Policy. Urination is "an excretory function traditionally shielded by great privacy." But the "degree of intrusion" on one's privacy caused by collecting a urine sample "depends upon the manner in which production of the urine sample is monitored."

Under the Policy, a faculty monitor waits outside the closed restroom stall for the student to produce a sample and must "listen for the normal sounds of urination in order to guard against tampered specimens and to insure an accurate chain of custody." The monitor then pours the sample into two bottles that are sealed and placed into a mailing pouch along with a consent form signed by the student. This procedure is virtually identical to that reviewed in *Vernonia*, except that it additionally protects privacy by allowing male students to produce their samples behind a closed stall. . . .

In addition, the Policy clearly requires that the test results be kept in confidential files separate from a student's other educational records and released to school personnel only on a "need to know" basis. Respondents nonetheless contend that the intrusion on students' privacy is significant because the Policy fails to protect effectively against the disclosure of confidential information and, specifically, that the school "has been careless in protecting that information: for example, the Choir teacher looked at students' prescription drug lists and left them where other students could see them." But the Choir teacher is someone with a "need to know," because during off-campus trips she needs to know what medications are taken by her students. Even before the Policy was enacted the choir teacher had access to this information. In any event, there is no allegation that any other student did see such information. . . .

Moreover, the test results are not turned over to any law enforcement authority. Nor do the test results here lead to the imposition of discipline or have any academic consequences. Rather, the only consequence of a failed drug test is to limit the student's privilege of participating in extracurricular activities. Indeed, a student may test positive for drugs twice and still be allowed to participate in extracurricular activities. After the first positive test, the school contacts the student's parent or guardian for a meeting. The student may continue to participate in the activity if within five days of the meeting the student shows proof of receiving drug counseling and submits to a second drug test in two weeks. For the second positive test, the student is suspended from participation in all extracurricular activities for 14 days, must complete four hours of substance abuse counseling, and must submit to monthly drug tests. Only after a third positive test will the student be suspended from participating in any extracurricular activity for the remainder of the school year, or 88 school days, whichever is longer.

Given the minimally intrusive nature of the sample collection and the limited uses to which the test results are put, we conclude that the invasion of students' privacy is not significant.

C

Finally, this Court must consider the nature and immediacy of the government's concerns and the efficacy of the Policy in meeting them. . . . The drug abuse problem among our Nation's youth has hardly abated since *Vernonia* was decided in 1995. In fact, evidence suggests that it has only grown worse. As in *Vernonia*, "the necessity for the State to act is magnified by the fact that this evil is being visited not just upon individuals at large, but upon children for whom it has undertaken a special responsibility of care and direction." . . .

Additionally, the School District in this case has presented specific evidence of drug use at Tecumseh schools. . . .

Respondents consider the **proffered** evidence insufficient and argue that there is no "real and immediate interest" to justify a policy of drug testing nonathletes. We have recognized, however, that "[a] demonstrated problem of drug abuse . . . [is] not in all cases necessary to the validity of a testing regime," but that some showing does "shore up an assertion of special need for a suspicion-less general search program." The School District has provided sufficient evidence to shore up the need for its drug testing program. . . .

Given the nationwide epidemic of drug use, and the evidence of increased drug use in Tecumseh schools, it was entirely reasonable for the School District to enact this particular drug testing policy. . . .

We also reject respondents' argument that drug testing must presumptively be based upon an individualized reasonable suspicion of wrongdoing because such a testing regime would be less intrusive. In this context, the Fourth Amendment does not require a finding of individualized suspicion, and we decline to impose such a requirement on schools attempting to prevent and detect drug use by students. Moreover, we question whether testing based on individualized suspicion in fact would be less intrusive. Such a regime would place an additional burden on public school teachers who are already tasked with the difficult job of maintaining order and discipline. A program of individualized suspicion might unfairly target members of unpopular groups. The fear of lawsuits resulting from such targeted searches may chill enforcement of the program, rendering it ineffective in combating drug use. In any case, this Court has repeatedly stated that reasonableness under the Fourth Amendment does not require employing the least intrusive means, because "the logic of such elaborate less-restrictive-alternative arguments could raise insuperable barriers to the exercise of virtually all search-and-seizure powers." . . .

III

Within the limits of the Fourth Amendment, local school boards must assess the desirability of drug testing schoolchildren. In upholding the constitutionality of the Policy, we express no opinion as to its wisdom. Rather, we hold only that Tecumseh's Policy is a reasonable means of furthering the School District's important interest in preventing and deterring drug use among its schoolchildren. Accordingly, we reverse the judgment of the Court of Appeals. . . .

Student Name: _____

            Last   **First**   **Middle**

Current Grade Level: _____

Industrial Independent School District
Student Drug Testing Consent Form

Statement of Purpose and Intent

Participation in school sponsored extra-curricular activities at the Industrial Independent School District is a privilege. Activity Students carry a responsibility to themselves, their fellow students, their parents, and their school to set the highest possible examples of conduct, which includes avoiding the use or possession of illegal drugs.

Drug use of any kind is incompatible with participation in extra-curricular activities on behalf of the Industrial Independent School District. For the safety, health, and well being of the student of the District, the Industrial Independent School District has adopted the attached Activity Student Drug Testing Procedures and the Student Drug Testing Consent for use by all participating students at the middle school and high school levels.

All Driving Students must also participate in the Student Drug Testing Program in order to have the privilege of driving to and from and to have the privilege of parking on school grounds or within 300 feet of the school.

Participation in Extra-Curricular Activities

Each Activity Student and Driving Student shall be provided with a copy of the Student Drug Testing Procedures and Student Drug Testing Consent, which shall be read, signed and dated by the student, parent or custodial guardian, and coach/sponsor before such student shall be eligible to practice or participate in any interscholastic activities. The consent shall be to provide a urine sample: a) as part of their annual physical or for eligibility for participation; b) as chosen by the random selection basis; and c) at any time requested based on reasonable suspicion to be tested for illegal or performance-enhancing drugs. No student shall be allowed to practice or participate in any activity governed by the procedures unless the student has retuned the properly signed Student Drug Testing Consent.

                                 * * * * * * * * * * *

I understand after having read the "Student Drug Testing Procedures" and "Student Drug Testing Consent," that, out of care for my safety and health, the Industrial Independent School District enforces the rules applying to the consumption or possession of illegal and performance-enhancing drugs. As a member of an Industrial extra-curricular interscholastic activity and/or as a driving student, I realize that the personal decision that I make daily in regard to the consumption or possession of illegal or performance-enhancing drugs may affect my health and well being as well as the possible endangerment of those around me and reflect upon any organization with which I am associated. If I choose to violate school policy regarding the use or possession of illegal or performance-enhancing drugs any time while I am involved in in-season or off-season activities and/or while participating as a driving student, I understand upon determination of that violation I will be subject to the restrictions on my participation as outlined in the Policy.

_____   _____
Signature of Student   Date

We have read and understood the Industrial Independent School District "Student Drug Testing Procedures" and "Student Drug Testing Consent." We desire that the student named above participate in the extra-curricular interscholastic programs and/or be designated as a driving student of the Industrial Independent School District and we hereby voluntarily agree to be subject to its terms. We accept the method of obtaining urine samples, testing and analysis of such specimens, and all other aspects of the program. We further agree and consent to the disclosure of the sampling, testing and results as provided in this program.

_____ _____ _____
Signature of Parent or Custodial Guardian   Date   Contact Phone Number

_____ _____
Signature of Coach/Sponsor/Principal   Date

Source: Available at http://www.iisd1.org/iisd_handouts/DrugTestingProceduresStudents_new.pdf (accessed January 19, 2004).

JUSTICE GINSBURG, with whom JUSTICE STEVENS, JUSTICE O'CONNOR, and JUSTICE SOUTER join, dissenting.

. . . Today, the Court relies upon *Vernonia* to permit a school district with a drug problem its superintendent repeatedly described as "not . . . major," to test the urine of an academic team member solely by reason of her participation in a nonathletic, competitive extracurricular activity—participation associated with neither special dangers from, nor particular predilections for, drug use.

"The legality of a search of a student," this Court has instructed, "should depend simply on the reasonableness, under all the circumstances, of the search." Although " 'special needs' inhere in the public school context," those needs are not so expansive or malleable as to render reasonable any program of student drug testing a school district elects to install. The particular testing program upheld today is not reasonable, it is capricious, even perverse: Petitioners' policy targets for testing a student population least likely to be at risk from illicit drugs and their damaging effects. I therefore dissent.

I

A

. . . The *Vernonia* Court concluded that a public school district facing a disruptive and explosive drug abuse problem sparked by members of its athletic teams had "special needs" that justified suspicionless testing of district athletes as a condition of their athletic participation.

. . . *Vernonia* cannot be read to endorse invasive and suspicionless drug testing of all students upon any evidence of drug use, solely because drugs jeopardize the life and health of those who use them. Many children, like many adults, engage in dangerous activities on their own time; that the children are enrolled in school scarcely allows government to monitor all such activities. . . .

Nationwide, students who participate in extracurricular activities are significantly less likely to develop substance abuse problems than are their less-involved peers. Even if students might be deterred from drug use in order to preserve their extracurricular eligibility, it is at least as likely that other students might forgo their extracurricular involvement in order to avoid detection of their drug use. Tecumseh's policy thus falls short doubly if deterrence is its aim. . . .

To summarize, this case resembles *Vernonia* only in that the School Districts in both cases conditioned engagement in activities outside the obligatory curriculum on random subjection to urinalysis. The defining characteristics of the two programs, however, are entirely dissimilar. The Vernonia district sought to test a subpopulation of students distinguished by their reduced expectation of privacy, their special susceptibility to drug-related injury, and their heavy involvement with drug use. The Tecumseh district seeks to test a much larger population associated with none of these factors. It does so, moreover, without carefully safeguarding student confidentiality and without regard to the program's untoward effects. A program so sweeping is not sheltered by *Vernonia;* its unreasonable reach renders it impermissible under the Fourth Amendment. . . .

- In *Acton,* the Court held that there was special reason to test student athletes for drug use because their sports activities are inherently dangerous and because they are role models to the whole student body. What is the special reason to test young people in other after-school activities?
- What do you think about the majority's argument that random drug testing of students is no more intrusive than requiring them to be vaccinated?
- Is drug use a big problem in your school? What can be done about it?
- Is drug testing an effective policy? Do you think the threat of random drug testing would make students think twice before using drugs? This is the idea of testing having a deterrent value.

Strip Searches

What is a reasonable search depends on the context within which it takes place. A school's need to search must be balanced against the invasion of student privacy that the search requires.

The Fourth Amendment does not protect expectations of privacy that are unreasonable. For a person to receive the protection of the Fourth Amendment, an expectation of privacy must be one that society is prepared to recognize as legitimate. Although no Supreme Court cases deal with the issue of strip searches in schools, at least one federal court of appeals has considered the issue, along with several state courts of appeals. Compare the facts in *Doe v. Renfrow, Thomas ex rel. Thomas v. Roberts,* and *Holmes v. Montgomery,* and decide whether you think circumstances ever could exist under which strip searches in schools would be reasonable.

According to the Department of Health and Human Services report entitled *Monitoring the Future: National Results on Adolescent Drug Use, Overview of Key Findings* (2001, table 1), the number of twelfth graders using one or more illicit drugs increased from 48.4 percent in 1995 to 53.9 percent in 2001. The number of twelfth graders reporting they had used marijuana jumped from 41.7 percent to 49.0 percent during that same period. In light of these statistics, should school administrators have more leeway in instituting measures that invade student privacy?

DOE V. RENFROW

United States Court of Appeals, Seventh Circuit
Argued April 3, 1980.
Decided July 18, 1980.

PER CURIAM

[Petitioner Diane Doe is a thirteen-year-old student at Highland Junior High School in Highland, Indiana, a community of approximately thirty thousand residents. Highland has one junior high school and one senior high school, located in adjacent buildings. There are 2,780 students total enrolled in the two schools.]

On the morning of March 23, 1979, [Doe] went to her first-period class as usual. Shortly before 9:15, when the class was scheduled to adjourn, Doe's teacher ordered everyone to remain seated until further notice. An assistant principal, accompanied by a police-trained German shepherd, a dog handler, and a uniformed police officer, then entered the classroom as one of six teams conducting simultaneous raids at the Highland schools. For the next 2-1/2 hours, Doe and her classmates were required to sit quietly in their seats with their belongings in view and their hands upon their desks. They were forbidden to use the washroom unless accompanied by an escort. Uniformed police officers and school administrators were stationed in the halls. Guards were posted at the schoolhouse doors. While no student was allowed to leave the schoolhouse, representatives of the press and other news media, on invitation of the school authorities, were permitted to enter the classrooms to observe the proceedings.

The dogs were led up and down each aisle of the classroom, from desk to desk, and from student to student. Each student was probed, sniffed, and inspected by at least 1 of the 14 German shepherds detailed to the school. When the search teams assigned to Doe's classroom reached Doe, the police dog pressed forward, sniffed at her body and repeatedly pushed its nose and muzzle into her legs. The uniformed officer then ordered Doe to stand and empty her pockets, apparently because the dog "alerted" to the presence of drugs. However, no drugs were found. After Doe emptied her pockets, the dogs again sniffed her body and again it apparently "alerted." Doe was then escorted to the nurses' office for a more thorough physical inspection.

Doe was met at the nurse's office by two adult women, one a uniformed police officer. After denying that she had ever used marihuana, Doe was ordered to strip. She did so, removing her clothing in the presence of the two women. The women then looked over Doe's body, inspected her clothing, and touched and examined the hair on her head. Again, no drugs were found. Doe was subsequently allowed to dress and was escorted back to her classroom.

Each of the 2,780 students present at Highland Junior and Senior High Schools that day was subjected to the mass detention and general exploratory search. Eleven students, including Doe, were subjected to body searches. Although the police dogs "alerted" 50 times, no junior high school students, and only 17 senior high school students, were found to be in possession of contraband. This contraband included marihuana, drug "paraphernalia," and three cans of beer. . . .

It does not require a constitutional scholar to conclude that a nude search of a thirteen-year-old child is an invasion of constitutional rights of some magnitude. More than that: it is a violation of any known principle of human decency. Apart from any constitutional readings and rulings, simple common sense would indicate that the conduct of the school officials in permitting such a nude search was not only unlawful but outrageous under "settled indisputable principles of law."

[The court] accords immunity to school officials who act in good faith *and within the bounds of reason*. We suggest as strongly as possible that the conduct herein described exceeded the "bounds of reason" by two and a half country miles. It is not enough for us to declare that the little girl involved was indeed deprived of her constitutional and basic human rights. We must also permit her to seek damages from those who caused this humiliation and did indeed act as though students "shed at the schoolhouse door rights guaranteed by . . . any . . . constitutional provision." . . .

SWYGERT, Circuit Judge, dissenting. . . .

I am deeply troubled by this court's holding that the dragnet inspection of the entire student body of the Highland Senior and Junior High Schools by trained police dogs and their dog-handlers did not [itself] constitute a search under the Fourth Amendment. No doctrine of *in loco parentis* or diminished constitutional rights for children in a public school setting excuses this alarming invasion by police and school authorities of the constitutional rights of thousands of innocent children.

POINTS TO PONDER

- Judge Swygert considered not only the individual strip search but the dragnet dog-sniff search to be unlawful. What do you think about a police offensive in which dogs are brought to do a thorough search of everyone and everything at school? Is that lawful? Keep Judge Swygert's views in mind as we discuss locker searches later in the chapter.
- Why does the Court say that a strip search of a student violates the basic principles of human decency? What are those principles? What is so upsetting about a strip search?

In a Georgia Court of Appeals case called *Thomas ex rel. Thomas v. Roberts,* a group of schoolchildren sued their teacher, an officer of the county police, their school's assistant principal, the school's principal, the school district, and the county, alleging that they were subject to unconstitutional strip searches. In this case, a class of fifth-grade students was strip searched in October 1996 after an envelope containing $26 disappeared from the teacher's desk. The boys were taken into the boys' bathroom in groups of four or five and asked to drop their pants. Some of the boys dropped both their pants and their underwear. Officer Billingslea, a male, searched the boys. As each boy dropped his pants, Billingslea visually inspected the boys' underwear to ensure that the money was not inside. The girls were taken into the girls' bathroom in groups of four or five at a time. Their female teacher, Ms. Morgan, then asked the girls to lower their pants and lift their dresses or shirts. Most of the girls were asked to lift their bras and expose their breasts to ensure that the money was not hidden under their bras.

The United States District Court for the Northern District of Georgia decided in favor of the school and the students appealed. The Eleventh Circuit Court of Appeals held that the strip searches of schoolchildren, which were conducted without individualized suspicion, were unreasonable. Although the limited search of students from another classroom for the stolen funds was reasonable, the county could be held liable for its officer's unconstitutional conduct.

In *Holmes v. Montgomery*, the Kentucky Court of Appeals in 2003 decided in favor of two young women who sued their school for violating their Fourth Amendment rights by strip searching them. On November 17, 1998, during a middle school physical education class, a student reported missing a pair of shorts. The classroom teachers told the students they would be given five minutes to return the missing shorts, but no one turned them in. After the students were given an additional five minutes, the teacher brought in a security guard and an assistant principal, who informed the students they would be searched to find the shorts. The students were taken in pairs to a locker room and searched. The students were forced to expose their underwear by raising their shirts above their bras and by lowering their pants below their knees.

Applying the logic from *T. L. O.* and *Doe v. Renfrow*, the Court agreed that the strip search violated the Fourth Amendment rights of the young women, especially in light of the fact that the school board policy stated, "In no instance shall the school official strip search any student."

POINTS TO PONDER

- Does your school policy mention strip searches?
- Do you think teachers or administrators at your school should be able to conduct strip searches? Why or why not?
- React to this statement: Given the presence of guns and other weapons in far too many schools, strip searches may be necessary under certain circumstances to maintain the health and safety of the student population in certain schools.
- You are the principal of a large urban high school that shows signs of gang activity, including graffiti on the walls of the school and rival gang fights in the school parking lot. Lately, gang activity has increased and parents have called you asking what your plans are to step up security. A respected teacher informs you that he overheard several students in his remedial math class talking about how easy it is to bring stun guns, which are legal in your state, to school. You are worried about this and decide that something needs to be done. Would it be OK to gather all the students you suspect are gang members in the gym, based on their clothing and dress, and strip search them? If not, what can you do to stop this problem before someone gets hurt?

Transit Authority police officer Tom Kolbert and Roggie, a narcotics-detecting dog, inspect student lockers at John F. Kennedy High School in 1999 in Cheektowaga, New York. Courts have found that dog-sniff searches do not require warrants. *Source: David Duprey/AP Wide World Photos*

Locker Searches

The Supreme Court has not definitively ruled on locker searches, but lower courts have applied the principles of other Supreme Court rulings to legal disputes involving locker searches. Generally, the courts are finding that schools may search lockers that they allow students to use even without reasonable suspicion but may not search the personal student items inside the lockers unless there is reasonable suspicion.

Suppression Hearing

The leaders of Lakeview High School believe their school has a serious drug problem. Teachers see students passing small packages to each other in the hallways and bringing beepers and telephones to school, against the rules. Many students contact a student

---

YOUR THOUGHTS

Do you keep any private personal items in your locker that you do not want anyone else to see even though they are lawful?

Does the locker you use belong to you or the school or both?

What kinds of expectations of privacy do you have in your locker?

---

assistance program to get counseling for drug abuse problems. Parents express concern about peer pressure brought on their children to try drugs. And some teachers say that certain students at school are flashing large wads of money in class.

Increasingly anxious about the situation, the principal of Lakeview High School decides to conduct unannounced searches of all student lockers. The principal escorts two police officers and a trained drug dog around the school to each of the twelve hundred student lockers in the school. The dog handler takes the dog to each locker. When the dog barks at a locker, an officer, along with school officials, opens the locker and searches everything inside it—backpacks, purses, clothes, gym bags—and also any lockers next to it.

The police find marijuana, a pipe, a roach clip, and rolling papers in a gym bag in the locker of Michael Grant, an eighteen-year-old senior at Lakeview. Michael's lawyer introduces a suppression motion against all the evidence when criminal charges are brought against his client. Michael argues that the mass, suspicionless search of lockers, including his, violated his Fourth Amendment rights and that even if the school could open his locker without suspicion, it could not open his zipped gym bag. The government says that the school needed no reasonable suspicion to search its own lockers and that the barking dog provided reasonable suspicion to search Michael's gym bag. How would you rule on his motion?

Commonwealth of Pennsylvania v. Cass

In a case similar to Michael Grant's, the highest court in Pennsylvania denied a student's motion to suppress evidence of drug use found in his school locker.

———

COMMONWEALTH OF PENNSYLVANIA V. CASS

Supreme Court of Pennsylvania
Decided, Jan. 7, 1998.

Justice CAPPY.

This case presents the question of what level of protection public school students are entitled to during a school wide search under the Fourth Amendment to the United States Constitution and Article I, Section 8 of the Pennsylvania Constitution. For the reasons that follow we find that public school students have a limited expectation of privacy while in the school environment. In balancing this limited privacy interest against the need to maintain a safe and secure environment for all public school students, we find that public school students are subject to a search by school officials when the decision to search is reasonable given all the circumstances present at the inception of the search and the search itself is reasonably limited in its scope to the objective which initially prompted the search. Applying this principle, we reverse the decision of the Superior Court.

The actions which prompted this appeal occurred on April 12, 1994 at the Harborcreek High School in Harborcreek Township, Erie County, Pennsylvania. The school principal announced to the students that morning that a safety inspection would be conducted. The students were to remain in their classes until the inspection was completed. The inspection was in actuality a search of all the student lockers, 2,000 in number, for the presence of drugs and/or drug paraphernalia. In order to expedite the search process, the principal enlisted the aid of two police officers and a trained drug dog. The methodology for the search was that the Erie police officer who was designated as the dog handler would take the dog to each locker in the school accompanied by school officials. When the dog "alerted" to a particular locker, the other officer, along with school officials, would open that locker, and any lockers adjacent thereto, and search the contents. Based upon the alerts by the dog, a total of 18 lockers were searched during the inspection. Appellee's locker was the only one of the 18 lockers searched which was found to contain contraband. The search of appellee's locker resulted in the seizure of a small amount of marijuana, a pipe, a roach clip and rolling papers. Appellee was subject to a ten-day out of school suspension and required to attend counseling. In addition, appellee was charged criminally with possession of a small amount of marijuana and possession of drug paraphernalia. In connection with the criminal charges, appellee filed a motion to suppress the items seized from his locker during the safety inspection.

At the suppression hearing the school principal testified that the search was undertaken due to concerns which had arisen over the preceding months indicating that drugs were being sold within the school. The principal offered several reasons for his heightened concern as to drug activity within the school: information received from unnamed students; observations from teachers of suspicious activity by the students, such as passing small packages between themselves in the hallways; increased use of the student assistance program for counseling students with drug problems; calls from concerned parents; observation of a growing number of students carrying beepers; students in possession of large amounts of money; and increased use of pay phones by students. The principal also testified that he had observed students exhibiting physical signs of drug use such as dilated pupils while in the school nurse's office. Armed with this information the principal decided upon the course of conduct described above as the most efficient method of searching the 2,000 lockers in the school. The principal testified that he had not received any specific information implicating appellee as being involved in drug activity. The parties all agree that the search, as undertaken, was a general search as opposed to a particularized search which would have focused on a certain student or, in this case, a certain locker. The principal also offered in support of his decision to undertake this generalized search the Harborcreek school code which provides as follows:

School authorities may search a student's locker and seize any illegal materials. Prior to a locker search a student shall be notified and given an opportunity to be present. However, where school authorities have a reasonable suspicion that the locker contains materials which pose a threat to the health, welfare, and safety of students in the school, students' lockers may be searched without prior warning.

Upon considering all the evidence presented by the Commonwealth, the trial court granted the motion to suppress. The trial court held that probable cause was not required before school officials could conduct a search of a students' locker and that a search of a student locker would be valid upon a showing of reasonable suspicion. Applying the reasonable suspicion standard to the facts in this case, the trial court concluded that the search at issue did not meet the necessary legal standard. Although the trial court recognized the good intentions of the principal . . . the court concluded that "good intentions" alone could not justify the sweeping search which was undertaken here in the absence of some level of articulable suspicion. The court found the principal's generalized suspicions to fall short of an objective reasonable belief that would justify the search. The Superior Court affirmed the decision of the trial court. This court granted the Commonwealth's Petition for Allowance of Appeal, and for the reasons that follow, now reverse. . . .

Based on the holding of *Acton*, we conclude that the search at Harborcreek High School, as conducted, was a practical means to effectuate the principal's compelling concerns over possible drug use, that it was minimally intrusive as it affected a limited privacy interest of the students, and thus, it was compatible with the Fourth Amendment. Accordingly, we hold that the trial court erred in granting the motion to suppress under the Fourth Amendment. . . .

ZAPPALA, Justice, dissenting.

The Court today holds that Pennsylvania law enforcement officials may utilize a drug detection dog to conduct a general sweep of students' school lockers and thereafter search particular lockers to investigate criminal wrongdoing without probable cause to believe that any individual student is in possession of illegal narcotics. The Court reaches this result through an erroneous analysis of governing constitutional law. I must therefore dissent. . . .

To characterize the locker search in this case as a search by school officials is to engage in subterfuge. Appellee's school locker was searched by police officers and the contraband seized as a result thereof formed the basis of a criminal prosecution. This case does not present the question of what degree of scrutiny is appropriate when reviewing a constitutional challenge to a search conducted by school officials on school property; rather, it presents the question of what degree of scrutiny is appropriate when reviewing a constitutional challenge to an evidentiary search conducted by police officers on school property. . . .

The Fourth Amendment sets the minimum level of protection from unreasonable searches and seizures below which the states may not fall. In determining whether a search violates the Fourth Amendment, the initial question is whether the prohibition against unreasonable searches and seizures applies to the search at issue. . . .

While the decisions in *T. L. O.* and *Vernonia* are instructive generally, the critical distinction between those cases and the instant case is that the searches in *T. L. O.* and *Vernonia* were conducted by school officials, whereas the search conducted in the instant case was conducted by police officers. . . .

In the instant case, before actually opening and searching Appellee's locker, the police conducted a canine sniff of all the lockers at Harborcreek High School. In *Commonwealth v. Johnston,* this Court stated, "we believe that the majority view of the United States Supreme Court would be that [a] canine sniff [carried out on private property and directed at the closed door of a private area] would not constitute a search." Thus, a canine sniff of lockers at a public school does not constitute a search under the Fourth Amendment.

The inquiry then becomes whether the subsequent search of Appellee's locker constitutes a search subject to the requirements of the Fourth Amendment. In *T. L. O.*, the Court observed:

We do not address the question, not presented by this case, whether a schoolchild has a legitimate expectation of privacy in lockers, desks, or other school property provided for the storage of school supplies. . . .

[T]he Court in *T. L. O.* explicitly limited its holding by stating:

[We do not] express any opinion on the standards (if any) governing searches of such areas by school officials or by other public authorities acting at the request of school officials.

The Court re-emphasized this limitation by further stating:

We here consider only searches carried out by school authorities acting alone and on their own authority. This case does not present the question of the appropriate standard for assessing the legality of searches conducted by school officials in conjunction with or at the behest of law enforcement agencies, and we express no opinion on that question.

The Court in *Vernonia* also implicitly acknowledged this distinction:

Despite the fact that, like routine school physicals and vaccinations . . . the search here is undertaken for prophylactic and distinctly *non* punitive purposes (protecting student athletes from injury, and deterring drug use in the student population) . . . the dissent would nonetheless lump this search together with "evidentiary" searches, which generally require probable cause. . . .

Thus, the United States Supreme Court has not spoken on the appropriate standard in a public school setting for assessing the legality of an evidentiary search conducted by police officers and forming the basis of a criminal prosecution, as in the instant case. However, the preceding quotation seems to suggest that "evidentiary" searches conducted by law enforcement officials for the purposes of investigating criminal conduct require probable cause. . . .

For the foregoing reasons, I would affirm the Order of the Superior Court. I therefore respectfully dissent.

Locker-Sniffing Dogs

Compare the outcome in *Cass* with the outcome in *Zamora v. Pomeroy*. In *Zamora*, the Tenth Circuit Court of Appeals found that a student's civil rights were not violated when he was transferred to another school after marijuana was found in his locker during a warrantless search conducted when trained police dogs alerted.

In *New Jersey v. T. L. O.*, the Supreme Court specifically declined to consider the issue of whether a student has a legitimate expectation of privacy in lockers, desks, or other school property provided for the storage of school supplies. The Court also did not address what standards, if any, govern searches of such areas if conducted by school officials or other public authorities acting at the request of school officials. However, some federal courts have found that students do not have a legitimate expectation of privacy in school lockers.

ZAMORA V. POMEROY

United States Court of Appeals, Tenth Circuit.
Argued and Submitted Nov. 19, 1980.
Decided Jan. 26, 1981.

WILLIAM E. DOYLE, Circuit Judge.

This civil action was brought by the mother of an allegedly aggrieved high school student who maintains that his civil rights were violated. . . . The source of the claim is the conducting of a warrantless search of his school locker. That search revealed the presence of marijuana and the alternate contentions are that it was unlawful to use "sniffer" dogs to discover the drug, and that after discovery of it a warrant was essential to the opening of the locker and the removal of the marijuana.

The search . . . was a general investigation. The Assistant District Attorney of the county in question contacted Mr. Worley, then Assistant Principal of the Roswell High School [RHS] about conducting a search of the school lockers, using so-called "sniffer" dogs, which dogs would be available to them some time in the future. At that time no specific persons were suspected of possessing marijuana at Roswell High. . . .

Before the first locker was opened, Sergeant Keller inquired as to whether a search warrant should be obtained. One of the school authorities replied that a search warrant was not necessary because a consent to search had been signed by the students. In any event, no search warrant was ever obtained by the police officers or by the defendants. . . .

In the course of searching the lockers in the Roswell High School, a so-called "hit" was made by one of the dogs. It was the locker of plaintiff-appellant Zamora. The locker was opened and a substance which proved to be marijuana was found therein. Besides the substance and a leather strap, nothing else was found; neither books, clothes nor school supplies were in the locker. The marijuana was taken from the locker and given to Worley. He tested the substance and concluded that it was marijuana. Some little time after the test Vidal Zamora was taken from his classes and was questioned about the substance that had been found in his locker. . . . Zamora denied any wrong-doing and denied that the marijuana was in his possession. He said that he was not using that locker, but was using one in what was called the Vo-Core Building. Vidal was called out of class a second time. He contends that he was pressured by the defendant to confess that the alleged marijuana was his. On one occasion during the questioning, Vidal discovered that Worley was using an electronic recording device, although permission had not been asked to record his statement. It is also pointed out that he was not warned about self-incrimination. The relevance of this failure is questionable, because this procedure is not criminal in nature.

During the time Vidal was being questioned by Worley, he was given the impression, so it is maintained by counsel for Zamora, that it was his obligation to prove his innocence; and he was not told that he could confer with counsel.

Soon after these happenings, the appellant Vidal was transferred from Roswell High School to the District's Educational Services Center [ESC], another high school within the city which did not have the academic standing of Roswell High. An objection is made to the fact that Mrs. Zamora, the mother of the boy in question, did not receive notice through the mails as to what was happening. . . . Worley said that he could not get hold of her on the telephone because she did not have a telephone, and he did not mail a notice to her because he did not have an address for her.

On December 23rd the semester ended and school let out for Christmas. Mrs. Zamora sought to contact Worley during the Christmas vacation and was unable to do so. She finally contacted one Dan Gomez, an Assistant Principal, and asked about Vidal's problem. Gomez informed her that Worley was out of town and would not be back until the end of the Christmas vacation. On January 4th, Mrs. Zamora finally spoke to the defendant Worley, and she then asked why her son had been "expelled" from school, and inquired as to what was needed to get her son back into school. At that time a meeting was arranged with the defendants Worley and [school principal] Mallory at Worley's office.

On January 9, 1978, Mrs. Zamora went to the offices of the Southern New Mexico Legal Services, and obtained counsel. Also on January 9th they were given an appointment with the principal. . . . At the meeting the Zamoras were informed by the defendants, so it is charged, that he had to prove his innocence in order to avoid being expelled from school; that a substance alleged to be marijuana was found in his locker and that the search of the lockers was legal. The point was made that there was no opportunity for **cross-examination**, etc., and the meeting was ended in a short time. The plaintiffs argue that Vidal was expelled from the high school. The order transferred him to the Educational Services Center. . . .

The defendants' side of the case brings out the fact that Zamora was enrolled in a special program for students who were potential drop-outs; that the courses given to him were easier ones than were offered average students. . . . It was brought out that during his high school career, Vidal's attendance was poor, and that he had a history of disruptive conduct and insubordination.

During the 1977–1978 school year the State Board of Education Regulation 77-3 was in effect. It prohibited the sale, possession, transportation or use of marijuana on school premises, and had a provision with regard to search of lockers, which said general searches of school property, including lockers and school buses, may be conducted at any time with or without the presence of students. . . . The administration policy on lockers was published in the student handbook, a copy of which was given to each student. It was stated that lockers remain under the jurisdiction of the school, notwithstanding the fact that they were assigned to individual students; that the school reserved the right to inspect all lockers at any time; that the students were to assume the full responsibility for security of the lockers, were to make certain that they were locked after being opened, and that the combination should not be given to a friend. . . .

Although the search of the lockers and the use of the dogs was brought about through the District Attorney, the District Attorney assured the school officials that he was not doing it in any official capacity; that no charges or arrests would be made as a result of the demonstration; and that if marijuana was found the decision as to action against the offender would be left to the school authorities. The search (so it is argued) was performed under the sole control and direction of Mallory, and not the Assistant District Attorneys, who were there just as observers. . . .

The evening after the inquiry Vidal advised his mother that he had been called into the office and charged by school officials with having marijuana in his locker, and that it could lead to his being suspended. He discussed with her what had occurred, but was unable to explain how the marijuana got into his locker. Worley and another Assistant Principal, Mr. Gomez, conferred with Vidal on Monday, December 19th. Vidal was advised that the matter was still being investigated, and that no evidence had come to light to support his innocence; and that Vidal would be held responsible unless he produced further evidence. Vidal was specifically asked to come up with further evidence and witnesses to support his innocence; he failed to provide it. He was advised that if he was suspended he would have a right to appeal the matter, and would have a hearing, and it was explained how an appeal would be carried out. . . .

On February 28, 1978, a special meeting was held by the Board of Education, and that body approved what had been done. Vidal attended ESC during the spring semester, continuing the same academic courses that he had taken at RHS the previous semester, including counseling and guidance. Upon arriving there he was tested in order to ascertain his level of achievement and competence, and was thereafter instructed accordingly. He was given full credit for all courses taken in the past. Vidal became a senior at RHS the next fall and has since graduated from RHS. He was never prosecuted nor was other action taken of a legal nature. . . .

II

Inasmuch as the school had assumed joint control of the locker it cannot be successfully maintained that the school did not have a right to inspect it. Therefore, the search was legal once the probability existed that there was contraband inside of the locker. We fail to see that there was any violation of Vidal Zamora's rights under the Fourth Amendment. As a result of this, it cannot be seriously challenged that the school had reasonable cause to search the locker. Whether the **fruits of such a search** could be used in a criminal action we need not decide. An annotation . . . summarizes this question on locker searching, as follows:

> A few cases involving searches of lockers assigned to high school students have been decided not on the distinction between the school officials searching the lockers as a private individual or as a government agent. . . , but rather on the view that the student's possession of the locker was exclusive only as against fellow students and not as against school officials, who because of their quasi-parental relationship to the students had the right and perhaps even the duty to inspect such lockers. Under this view, school officials may inspect student lockers themselves or consent to such an inspection by law enforcement officers.

The particular relationship between Vidal and the school authorities serves to distinguish this case from the search and seizure cases which are relied on by the plaintiff-appellant.

The basic theory is that although a student has rights under the Fourth Amendment, these rights must yield to the extent that they interfere with the school administration's fundamental duty to operate the school as an educational institution and that a reasonable right to inspect is necessary in the performance of its duties, even though it may infringe, to some degree, on a student's Fourth Amendment rights. The courts which have considered this question have noted that the doctrine in loco parentis expands the authority to school officials, even to the extent that it may conflict with the rules set forth in the Fourth Amendment. Some cases have gone so far as to say that the school authorities have an affirmative duty to search the lockers.

The logical explanation for all of this is that the school authorities have, on behalf of the public, an interest in these lockers and a duty to police the school, particularly where possible serious violations of the criminal laws exist. There is no merit in the contention that a school locker is the property of the student who occupies it pro tem.

In this case the appellant has acknowledged that the locker in question was assigned to him. He necessarily knew that it was a violation of school policy to have drugs on the premises. The school retained control and access to all lockers, and maintained a confidential file of all lockers and the combinations thereto. Both Worley and Mallory retained master keys to all lockers. The evidence shows that Vidal was given a handbook containing the regulations bearing on lockers, and that he was aware of the rules. Finally, the authorities hold that a school official need only have reasonable cause or reasonable suspicion in order to search a student or his locker. . . .

We affirm.

YOUR THOUGHTS

Although schools have a duty to protect children in their care, some argue that young people in crime-ridden neighborhoods carry weapons only for self-protection and protection of younger siblings and relatives. How can violence be kept out of schools while keeping students safe when they are not in school? Is carrying a weapon a good way to keep safe? Does gun control reduce violence or increase it?

Metal Detectors and the Constitution

In the wake of numerous incidents of school violence across America, over the past ten years many public schools have introduced metal detectors as a way to keep guns, knives, and other weapons out. Does your school district use metal detectors? Are they an effective deterrent? Do they violate your freedom from unreasonable searches and seizures?

The U.S. Supreme Court has not considered the issue of metal detectors in schools, but a number of lower courts have decided that metal detectors do not violate students' Fourth Amendment rights.

In Hancock, Michigan, a police officer uses a hand-held metal detector to search middle school students arriving for classes. Courts have generally allowed metal detectors at school entrances on a warrantless basis. *Source: Marshall Anderson/AP Wide World Photos*

Does your school place metal detectors at the entrances?

Do you think metal detectors violate your right to privacy?

What about hand-held wands that guards use at their discretion to wave over the bodies of students?

Do metal detectors stop students from bringing guns and knives to school?

IN RE LATASHA W.

California Court of Appeal, Second District
January 27, 1998.

NEAL, Associate Justice

Summary

Random metal detector weapon searches of high school students do not violate the Fourth Amendment constitutional ban on unreasonable searches and seizures.

Facts and Proceedings Below

Appellant is a high school student. Before appellant enrolled, her high school had instituted a written policy for daily weapons searches, in order to protect students and staff. The searches were to be made at random, and persons to be searched selected on neutral criteria. Parents and students were given notice before institution of this practice, and again at frequent intervals. Searches were conducted using a hand-held metal detector, waved next to the student's person. Students were asked to open jackets or pockets to reveal items which triggered the detector. The day appellant was searched the assistant principal determined that those students who entered the attendance office without hall passes, and those who were late, within a half-hour after 8:09 a.m., would be searched. Appellant was one of eight to ten students who met these criteria and were searched. After the metal detector beeped, she was asked to open her pocket, revealing a knife.

Appellant was charged in a juvenile court petition with the crime of bringing on school grounds a knife with a blade longer than 2.5 inches. The trial court denied appellant's motion to suppress the knife as unlawfully seized, sustained the petition, and ordered appellant home on probation.

This appeal followed. Appellant challenges only the ruling denying her motion to suppress.

..

Discussion

We find no California case addressing the propriety of a search such as occurred here, but courts in other states have upheld against Fourth Amendment challenge similar searches of students without individualized suspicion. . . . The school cases just cited are part of a larger body of law holding that "special needs" administrative searches, conducted without individualized suspicion, do not violate the Fourth Amendment where the government need is great, the intrusion on the individual is limited, and a more rigorous standard of suspicion is unworkable.

The searches involved here met the standard for constitutionality. The need of schools to keep weapons off campuses is substantial. Guns and knives pose a threat of death or serious injury to students and staff. The California Constitution, article I, section 28, subdivision (c), provides that students and staff of public schools have "the inalienable right to attend campuses which are safe, secure and peaceful."

The searches in the present case were minimally intrusive. Only a random sample of students was tested. Students were not touched during the search, and were required to open pockets or jackets only if they triggered the metal detector.

Finally, no system of more suspicion-intense searches would be workable. Schools have no practical way to monitor students as they dress and prepare for school in the morning, and hence no feasible way to learn that individual students have concealed guns or knives on their persons, save for those students who brandish or display the weapons. And, by the time weapons are displayed, it may well be too late to prevent their use.

The search here did not violate the Fourth Amendment.

Disposition

The judgment is affirmed.

POINTS TO PONDER

- Your parents are involved in the Parent-Teacher Association at your school, where there is considerable concern that students' fears for their personal safety are interfering with their education. At the next monthly meeting, the hot topics on the agenda are whether metal detectors and guards should be posted at all entrances to the school, whether a new identification (ID) system should be imposed whereby students are required to wear their photo ID badges around their necks at all time, and how to raise money for these potential new security measures. Using facts about your own school district, prepare a memorandum outlining arguments in favor of and against installation of metal detectors and guards in your school and adoption of the new ID system. If you do not like this plan, what do you suggest instead?
- Many schools have stationed police officers in the hallways or at the front door, or they patrol on campus. Oftentimes these officers are involved in searches of student lockers, belongings, and bodies. Should the school still get to search students without a warrant and on the lesser reasonable suspicion standard if police officers are present and involved? The Supreme Court has not ruled on this question, but other courts have been allowing schools to conduct their searches even with the involvement of police officers. Resulting evidence can be used in criminal prosecutions. Is this fair or is it an end run around the Fourth

Amendment? Or is it so critical to straighten kids out if they are causing trouble at school that their constitutional rights are secondary?

- The following lyrics are from Bruce Springsteen's song "41 Shots": Lena gets her son ready for school / She says "On these streets Charles / You've got to understand the rules / If an officer stops you / Promise me that you'll always be polite, that you'll never ever run away / Promise Mama you'll keep your hands in sight" / Is it a gun, is it a knife / Is it a wallet, this is your life / It ain't no secret / It ain't no secret / No secret my friend / You can get killed just for living / In your American skin.

    What do you think of the mother's statement "Promise Mama you'll keep your hands in sight." Is it the responsibility of young people to protect themselves from the police or is it the responsibility of the police to protect young people? How is the presence of police in the school setting different from their presence on the street?

Additional Sources

Arbetman, Lee, and Edward O'Brien. *Street Law.* St. Paul, Minn.: West Educational Publishing, 1999.

Cole, David. *No Equal Justice: Race and Class in the American Criminal Justice System.* New York: New Press, 1999.

LaFave, Wayne R. *Search and Seizure.* 2d ed. St. Paul, Minn.: West Publishing, 1987.

Raskin, Jamin B. *We the Students: Supreme Court Cases for and about Students.* 2d ed. Washington, D.C.: CQ Press, 2003.

FIFTH AMENDMENT: PRIVILEGE AGAINST SELF-INCRIMINATION

6

Imagine you broke your mother's favorite glass bowl in the kitchen at home. You are about to clean it up but hear your parents arriving at the front door. Guilty and surprised, you run upstairs to join your four brothers and sisters. You do your best to blend in. Your parents enter the house and discover the broken glass. They yell for everyone to come downstairs. The children line up and your father asks, "Who did this?" Everyone is silent.

Your parents then ask each of you directly: "Did you do this?" When you are singled out, you are panicky and about to cry.

"Did you break the glass bowl?" your father asks.

What do you say?

You essentially have three choices.

1. You can tell the truth—say you did it—and face the consequences.
2. You can lie and hope against hope that the lie will be believed. If your lie is discovered or you break down, you may be punished both for the glass and for lying.
3. You can say nothing or else simply say that you have nothing to say. You tell them you are going to remain silent.

In a family, getting away with option 3 is unlikely. If your parents ask you whether you broke the glass bowl, and you say you choose to remain silent, your parents would probably look at you as if you are crazy and conclude that you did it. In most families— at least in healthy families—parents expect children to give them an honest answer to a direct question. In the family context, your practical choice usually comes down to telling the truth or lying.

But the situation is not the same in police investigations of crime. There you do have a constitutional right to remain silent and your silence cannot count against you. This is part of the meaning of the Fifth Amendment:

No person shall be compelled, in any criminal case, to be a witness against himself.

The Fifth Amendment protects you against compelled self-incrimination. This is a fancy way of saying that the government cannot force you to confess to committing a crime (to incriminate yourself), to be a witness against yourself, or to make any statements that could later be used against you at trial. When the government questions you, you have a right to remain silent if your statements would put you at risk of **prosecution**.

The Screaming Eagle

It all started as an idea for a silly prank. You and your two best friends, TJ and Brian, are preparing for high school graduation and want go out with a bang. Your plan is to sneak your school's eagle mascot costume—an oversized bright-green screaming eagle, complete with feathers—out of the principal's office, cause a schoolwide mystery about its disappearance, and then have one of you wear it to the graduation ceremony. All of this was just talk, but then, one day just a week before graduation, you arrive at school and find that three police officers are looking around and questioning students. Before you know it, your school principal enters your math class and pulls you out. He leads you to his office, where two police officers are seated at a conference table.

"You are under investigation for breaking and entering, conspiracy and theft in the second degree," an officer says after you sit down. "We've already spoken to TJ and Brian and they both say it was your idea, you were the ringleader. Now tell us where the costume is."

You realize that TJ and Brian, or at least one of them, got into the principal's office and took the costume. You cannot believe that police are involved and that a full-blown criminal investigation is under way.

"I don't know where the mascot is," you say honestly.

"Well, you were involved in this crime, weren't you?" the officer asks.

Now, what are your choices?

1. You can tell the truth and face the consequences.
2. You can lie and potentially create bigger problems for yourself.
3. You can say that, given this is a criminal investigation, you choose to remain silent and not talk to the police without first consulting with a lawyer.

In this context, unlike the family situation, option #3 is a viable option and it may be the best option. The Fifth Amendment gives you the right to stop answering questions.

Assume that the government brings a criminal prosecution against you and Brian. TJ, meanwhile, has struck a deal. He will testify that it was your idea and that Brian broke into the principal's office. All he did, TJ will say, was act as a lookout. In return for his cooperation, TJ will not be prosecuted but will have to take summer school classes to graduate.

At trial, because you are a defendant, the Fifth Amendment gives you the right not to testify. If you testified truthfully, you would have to admit that it was your idea. This might not be bad if you could show that it was just an idea and not part of a conspiracy, but the government might be able to show you intended to form a conspiracy that actually took a step toward commission of a crime. If you take the stand and lie, you could face further trouble, including a perjury prosecution because all witnesses in court are sworn to tell the truth under pain of criminal penalty.

You can also decide to remain silent and not to testify. This might make sense given that you will not be tempted to perjure yourself (that is, lie) and it will force the government to make the case against you by proving beyond a reasonable doubt that you were involved in a conspiracy. Your lawyer can attack the state's case by arguing that your involvement was limited to throwing out a bunch of ideas long before a real crime or conspiracy to commit one took place. Your lawyer can cross-examine TJ and any other witnesses to try to discredit their testimony. Moreover, because you have a Fifth Amendment right not to testify, the prosecutors cannot comment on your decision to exercise it and the jury will not be allowed to draw any negative inferences or conclusions from your decision to remain silent during trial.

Not Taking the Stand

Many defendants whose cases go to trial do not take the stand and testify in their own defense. This is part of their Fifth Amendment right. In his double murder trial, former professional football player O. J. Simpson declined to take the stand. He ended up being acquitted. In her trial on charges of conspiracy, obstruction of justice, and lying about stock deals, former chief executive officer and chairman of a multimedia company Martha Stewart chose not to take the stand. She was convicted.

A key reason people choose not to testify at their own trials is that this is the only way to avoid being cross-examined by the government's prosecutors. If you take the stand, you have to answer whatever questions they have for you. Thus, criminal defendants have to take the bitter with the sweet. So if you are guilty or you have something to hide or you have contradictions in your story, you have to be careful about taking the stand to testify. It is easy to be demolished as a witness if you are not telling the whole truth and nothing but the truth. Because jurors and judges are not supposed to hold it against you if you elect not to take the stand, it often makes more sense not to testify, and defendants frequently reach that conclusion with their lawyers. The judge instructs the jurors that declining to testify is not evidence of guilt and may not be held against defendants.

People who are not guilty may also have good reasons to decline to testify at their own trials. Some people do not want to implicate friends or relatives. Some people get extremely nervous and make bad witnesses. Some people have had criminal, legal, or medical problems in their past that they do not want to testify about in public. So no one should assume that a defendant who sits it out is guilty. Judges correctly instruct jurors not to make that assumption.

Do you think jurors can be fair about defendants who elect to exercise their Fifth Amendment rights? If you were a juror, would you have special suspicions about a criminal defendant who refused to testify on his own behalf? How would you control those suspicions?

The Purposes and Values Served by the Fifth Amendment

Why does the U.S. Constitution give people the right not to testify against themselves when they have relevant information about a crime to share? The basic principle of the

American justice system is that anyone who is **subpoenaed** (or called) to court must show up and give truthful testimony. Why should an exception be made when your testimony relates to your own conduct and potential guilt?

The U.S. Supreme Court in *Murphy v. Waterfront Commission of New York Harbor* gave this authoritative overview of the purposes of the exception.[1]

> The privilege against self-incrimination 'registers an important advance in the development of our liberty'—one of the great landmarks in man's struggle to make himself civilized. . . . It reflects many of our fundamental values and most noble aspirations: our unwillingness to subject those suspected of crime to the cruel trilemma of **self-accusation**, perjury or contempt; our preference for an **accusatorial** rather than an inquisitorial system of criminal justice; our fear that self-incriminating statements will be **elicited** by inhumane treatment and abuses; our sense of fair play which dictates 'a fair state-individual balance by requiring the government to leave the individual alone until good cause is shown for disturbing him and by requiring the government in its contest with the individual to shoulder the entire load'; our respect for the inviolability of the human personality and of the right of each individual 'to a private enclave where he may lead a private life'; our distrust of **self-deprecatory** statements; and our realization that the privilege, while sometimes 'a shelter to the guilty,' is often 'a protection to the innocent.'

Consider the specific values and purposes discussed by the Court in *Murphy v. Waterfront Commission of New York Harbor.*

The privilege keeps suspects from being forced to choose among self-accusation, perjury, and contempt.

Why shouldn't people have to choose between telling the truth or being punished for not telling the truth? Shouldn't people face the consequences of lying or concealing the truth?

The privilege reinforces the adversarial and accusatorial basis of the U.S. system. This means that there are two sides in a criminal case: the prosecution and the accused. The prosecution must prove guilt beyond a reasonable doubt; the accused does not have to prove anything. The framers of the Constitution were as suspicious of government officials as

Chief Justice Earl Warren previously served as district attorney, state attorney general, and governor of California. The Warren Court upheld many constitutional protections for millions of Americans, including many criminal defendants. *Source: Library of Congress*

of criminal defendants. The prosecution thus cannot force people to participate in their own criminal prosecution.

Why is an **adversarial** system of justice desirable? Wouldn't it be better to let the court go after the truth and force everyone to testify? What if the most valuable information would come from the suspect?

The privilege recognizes that the government will sometimes obtain confessions or self-incriminating statements by inhumane treatment, such as physical or psychological abuse and even torture.

Why shouldn't the government take advantage of a suspect's ignorance or weakness to find out what happened? Why should any limits be placed on what police and prosecutors can do? What is wrong with torture and trickery? What if the crime is very bad, such as mass murder or terrorism?

The privilege stops government from taking advantage of false or untrustworthy confessions that may have been coerced. It thus protects the innocent.

Why are coerced confessions thought of as untrustworthy? Is it worth shielding the guilty to protect the innocent? Why or why not?

Protections against Self-Incrimination

People make statements at many points along the way of a police investigation that can be self-incriminating. Suspects cast doubt on their own innocence and give the police valuable information from the first moment they interact with them. Thus, the Supreme Court has determined that before any confession or incriminating statement made while you are in police custody can be used against you in court, you must first have been informed by the police of your Fifth Amendment right against self-incrimination. This means that the police must "read you your rights" before questioning you. This is the

MIRANDA WARNINGS
What are your rights under the Fifth Amendment in a police setting?

- You have the right to remain silent. You are not required to say anything or answer any questions. Anything you say can be used against you in a court of law.
- You have the right to talk to a lawyer before you are questioned and have a lawyer with you during questioning.
- If you cannot afford a lawyer, one will be appointed for you.
- If you want to answer questions without a lawyer present, you will still have the right to stop answering at any point until you talk to a lawyer

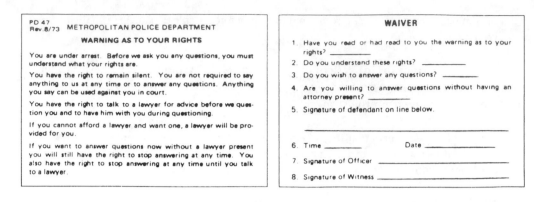

Miranda v. Arizona (1996) resulted in the now-mandatory Miranda warnings. Officers in many jurisdictions carry Miranda waiver cards that willing suspects can sign to speak without having counsel present.

famous *Miranda* warnings seen so often on television. The name comes from a Supreme Court case *Miranda v. Arizona.*[2]

After being advised of your rights, you might still choose to speak. This is called a waiver of your Fifth Amendment rights. You can always choose to confess. But a waiver of rights must be made voluntarily, knowingly, and intelligently. You have to understand the rights you are giving up by speaking with the police, and you cannot be forced through violence, threats, or trickery to surrender your right to remain silent or to talk to a lawyer. But what are your rights exactly?

Consider the warnings as they might apply in the screaming eagle case. Imagine the police have singled you out for arrest for suspicion of stealing the school mascot costume.

Four uniformed police officers arrive at school to arrest you and place you under arrest. They give you no *Miranda* warnings, but they handcuff you. They transport you in the back seat of a police car to the local police station. You are fingerprinted, photographed, and asked your name and address. The police then place you in a small room and leave you there. You are alone. You are not given food or water. You are not allowed to leave. After an hour, three large policemen come in to question you about the disappearance of the screaming eagle costume. You are not allowed a phone call. You are not provided a lawyer. The three officers begin questioning you. They ask you about your involvement in the crime. They do not give *Miranda* warnings or explain your right to remain silent or your right to a lawyer. They keep questioning you, some acting tough and mean, even threatening; others are gentle and forgiving. Upset, isolated, and hopeful that by cooperating you will get better treatment from the nice officers, you tell them everything you know about the crime, including your own involvement. You confess it was all your idea to start with and you drew up the plans.

The police did not give you *Miranda* warnings and therefore never told you that you have a right to see an attorney, including an appointed one, or that you have a right to

Custody = Arrested or the formal equivalent of arrest
Interrogation = Questioning

What protections should you have when you are being questioned by the police? Should police be required to tell you about your rights to a lawyer and to remain silent before questioning you? Why? Why should they do anything that might interfere with you telling them the truth?

remain silent. This failure to warn makes any statements obtained from you **inadmissible** in court, meaning the court would not let the government introduce any such statements against you.

What information did you lack that would have been useful to you before spilling your guts? Would it have helped to know you were allowed to consult a lawyer or to remain silent?

The type of police questioning described in the screaming eagle case was at issue in the famous case of *Miranda v. Arizona.* That case defined the meaning and the rules of custodial interrogation. It is custodial because you are under arrest and have been taken into custody by the police. It is interrogation because you are being interrogated, or asked questions, by police. The Court decided that you have a right to the *Miranda* warnings if you are being held in custody and questioned. The remedy for a violation of this rule ordinarily is exclusion of the confession or statements obtained unlawfully in this manner.

The *Miranda* Case

Miranda v. Arizona is one of the most celebrated Supreme Court cases of all time. It defines the operation of the Fifth Amendment and the privilege against self-incrimination when people are taken into police custody.

The case arose when Ernesto Miranda was arrested and charged with the rape and kidnapping of a woman in Arizona. He was brought

Ernesto Miranda's original conviction was overturned by the Supreme Court because he was never informed by police of his rights to remain silent and talk to a lawyer. His case led to the well-known *Miranda* warnings. *Source: AP Wide World Photos*

into the police station and interrogated. During the many hours he was questioned, he made several incriminating statements that were used by the prosecution to convict him. He appealed his conviction, claiming that use of his confession was a violation of his rights under the Fifth Amendment. The Supreme Court used the case to discuss the nature of custodial interrogation and the protections that must be afforded those who are subject to police questioning of this type.

—·—

ERNESTO A. MIRANDA, PETITIONER,
V.
STATE OF ARIZONA.

Supreme Court of the United States
Nos. 759-761, 584.
Argued Feb. 28, March 1 and 2, 1966.
Decided June 13, 1966.
Rehearing Denied No. 584 Oct. 10, 1966.

Mr. Chief Justice WARREN delivered the opinion of the Court.

The cases before us raise questions which go to the roots of our concepts of American criminal **jurisprudence**: the restraints society must observe consistent with the Federal Constitution in prosecuting individuals for crime. More specifically, we deal with the admissibility of statements obtained from an individual who is subjected to custodial police interrogation and the necessity for procedures which assure that the individual is accorded his privilege under the Fifth Amendment to the Constitution not to be compelled to incriminate himself.

1.

An understanding of the nature and setting of this in-custody interrogation is essential to our decisions today. The difficulty in depicting what transpires at such interrogations stems from the fact that in this country they have largely taken place **incommunicado**. From extensive factual studies undertaken in the early 1930's, including the famous Wickersham Report to Congress by a Presidential Commission, it is clear that police violence and the 'third degree' flourished at that time. In a series of cases decided by this Court long after these studies, the police resorted to physical brutality—beatings, hanging, whipping—and to sustained and protracted questioning incommunicado in order to extort confessions. . . .

The examples given above are undoubtedly the exception now, but they are sufficiently widespread to be the object of concern. Unless a proper limitation upon custodial interrogation is achieved—such as these decisions will advance—there can be no assurance that practices of this nature will be eradicated in the foreseeable future. . . .

Again we stress that the modern practice of in-custody interrogation is psychologically rather than physically oriented. As we have stated before, . . . this Court has recognized that coercion can be mental as well as physical, and that the blood of the accused is not the only hallmark of an unconstitutional inquisition. . . .

Interrogation still takes place in privacy. Privacy results in secrecy and this in turn results in a gap in our knowledge as to what in fact goes on in the interrogation rooms. A valuable source of information about present police practices, however, may be found in various police manuals and texts which document procedures employed with success in the past, and which recommend various other effective tactics. These texts are used by law enforcement agencies themselves as guides. . . .

The officers are told by the manuals that the 'principal psychological factor contributing to a successful interrogation is privacy—being alone with the person under interrogation.'

To highlight the isolation and unfamiliar surroundings, the manuals instruct the police to display an air of confidence in the suspect's guilt and from outward appearance to maintain only an interest in confirming certain details. The guilt of the subject is to be posited as a fact. The interrogator should direct his comments toward the reasons why the subject committed the act, rather than court failure by asking the subject whether he did it. Like other men, perhaps the subject has had a bad family life, had an unhappy childhood, had too much to drink, had an unrequited desire for women. The officers are instructed to minimize the moral seriousness of the offense, to cast blame on the victim or on society. These tactics are designed to put the subject in a psychological state where his story is but an elaboration of what the police purport to know already—that he is guilty. Explanations to the contrary are dismissed and discouraged. . . .

When the techniques described above prove unavailing, the texts recommend they be alternated with a show of some hostility. One ploy often used has been termed the 'friendly-unfriendly' or the 'Mutt and Jeff' act:

> 'In this technique, two agents are employed. Mutt, the relentless investigator, who knows the subject is guilty and is not going to waste any time. He's sent a dozen men away for this crime and he's going to send the subject away for the full term. Jeff, on the other hand, is obviously a kindhearted man. He has a family himself. He has a brother who was involved in a little scrape like this. He disapproves of Mutt and his tactics and will arrange to get him off the case if the subject will cooperate. He can't hold Mutt off for very long. The subject would be wise to make a quick decision. The technique is applied by having both investigators present while Mutt acts out his role. Jeff may stand by quietly and demur at some of Mutt's tactics. When Jeff makes his plea for cooperation, Mutt is not present in the room.'

The interrogators sometimes are instructed to induce a confession out of trickery. The technique here is quite effective in crimes which require identification or which run in series. In the identification situation, the interrogator may take a break in his questioning to place the subject among a group of men in a line-up. 'The witness or complainant (previously coached, if necessary) studies the line-up and confidently points out the subject as the guilty party.' Then the questioning resumes 'as though there were now no doubt about the guilt of the subject.' A variation on this technique is called the 'reverse line-up':

> 'The accused is placed in a line-up, but this time he is identified by several **fictitious** witnesses or victims who associated him with different offenses. It is expected that the subject will become desperate and confess to the offense under investigation in order to escape from the false accusations.'

The manuals also contain instructions for police on how to handle the individual who refuses to discuss the matter entirely, or who asks for an attorney or relatives. The examiner is to concede him the right to remain silent. 'This usually has a very undermining effect. First of all, he is disappointed in his expectation of an unfavorable reaction on the part of the interrogator. Secondly, a concession of this right to remain silent impresses the subject with the apparent fairness of his interrogator.' After this psychological conditioning, however, the officer is told to point out the incriminating significance of the suspect's refusal to talk:

> 'Joe, you have a right to remain silent. That's your privilege and I'm the last person in the world who'll try to take it away from you. If that's the way you want to leave this, O.K. But let me ask you this. Suppose you were in my shoes and I were in yours and you called me in to ask me about this and I told you, 'I don't want to answer any of your questions.' You'd think I had something to hide, and you'd probably be right in thinking that. That's exactly what I'll have to think about you, and so will everybody else. So let's sit here and talk this whole thing over.' . . .

From these representative samples of interrogation techniques, the setting prescribed by the manuals and observed in practice becomes clear. In essence, it is this: To be alone with the subject is essential to prevent distraction and to deprive him of any outside support. The aura of confidence in his guilt undermines his will to resist. He merely confirms the preconceived story the police seek to have him describe. Patience and persistence, at times relentless questioning, are employed. To obtain a confession, the interrogator must 'patiently maneuver himself or his quarry into a position from which the desired objective may be attained.' When normal procedures fail to produce the needed result, the police may resort to deceptive **stratagems** such as giving false legal advice. It is important to keep the subject off balance, for example, by trading on his insecurity about himself or his surroundings. The police then persuade, trick, or cajole him out of exercising his constitutional rights.

Even without employing brutality, the 'third degree' or the specific stratagems described above, the very fact of custodial interrogation exacts a heavy toll on individual liberty and trades on the weakness of individuals.

In the cases before us today, given this background, we concern ourselves primarily with this interrogation atmosphere and the evils it can bring. . . .

It is obvious that such an interrogation environment is created for no purpose other than to **subjugate** the individual to the will of his examiner. This atmosphere carries its own badge of intimidation. To be sure, this is not physical intimidation, but it is equally destructive of human dignity. The current practice of incommunicado interrogation is at odds with one of our Nation's most cherished principles—that the individual may not be compelled to incriminate himself. Unless adequate protective devices are employed to dispel the compulsion inherent in custodial surroundings, no statement obtained from the defendant can truly be the product of his free choice.

From the foregoing, we can readily perceive an intimate connection between the privilege against self-incrimination and police custodial questioning. . . .

III

We have concluded that without proper safeguards the process of in-custody interrogation of persons suspected or accused of crime contains **inherently** compelling pressures which work to undermine the individual's will to resist and to compel him to speak where he would not otherwise do so freely. In order to combat these pressures and to permit a full opportunity to exercise the privilege against self-incrimination, the accused must be adequately and effectively apprised of his rights and the exercise of those rights must be fully honored.

. . . At the outset, if a person in custody is to be subjected to interrogation, he must first be informed in clear and unequivocal terms that he has the right to remain silent. For those unaware of the privilege, the warning is needed simply to make them aware of it—the threshold requirement for an intelligent decision as to its exercise. More important, such a warning is an absolute prerequisite in overcoming the inherent pressures of the interrogation atmosphere. It is not just the subnormal or woefully ignorant who succumb to an interrogator's imprecations, whether implied or expressly stated, that the interrogation will continue until a confession is obtained or that silence in the face of accusation is itself damning and will bode ill when presented to a jury. Further, the warning will show the individual that his interrogators are prepared to recognize his privilege should he choose to exercise it.

The warning of the right to remain silent must be accompanied by the explanation that anything said can and will be used against the individual in court. This warning is needed in order to make him aware not only of the privilege, but also of the consequences of forgoing it. It is only through an awareness of these consequences that there can be any assurance of real understanding and intelligent exercise of the privilege. Moreover, this warning may serve to make the individual more acutely aware that he is faced with a phase of the adversary system—that he is not in the presence of persons acting solely in his interest.

The circumstances surrounding in-custody interrogation can operate very quickly to overbear the will of one merely made aware of his privilege by his interrogators. Therefore, the right to have counsel present at the interrogation is indispensable to the protection of the Fifth Amendment privilege under the system we **delineate** today. Our aim is to assure that the individual's right to choose between silence and speech remains unfettered throughout the interrogation process. . . . Thus, the need for counsel to protect the Fifth Amendment privilege comprehends not merely a right to consult with counsel prior to questioning, but also to have counsel present during any questioning if the defendant so desires.

An individual need not make a pre-interrogation request for a lawyer. While such request affirmatively secures his right to have one, his failure to ask for a lawyer does not constitute a waiver. No effective waiver of the right to counsel during interrogation can be recognized unless specifically made after the warnings we here delineate have been given. The accused who does not know his rights and therefore does not make a request may be the person who most needs counsel.

Accordingly we hold that an individual held for interrogation must be clearly informed that he has the right to consult with a lawyer and to have the lawyer with him during interrogation under the system for protecting the privilege we delineate today.

If an individual indicates that he wishes the assistance of counsel before any interrogation occurs, the authorities cannot rationally ignore or deny his request on the basis that the individual does not have or cannot afford a retained attorney. The financial ability of the individual has no relationship to the scope of the rights involved here. The privilege against self-incrimination secured by the Constitution applies to all individuals. The need for counsel in order to protect the privilege exists for the indigent as well as the affluent. In fact, were we to limit these constitutional rights to those who can retain an attorney, our decisions today would be of little significance. The cases before us as well as the vast majority of confession cases with which we have dealt in the past involve those unable to retain counsel. . . .

In order fully to apprise a person interrogated of the extent of his rights under this system then, it is necessary to warn him not only that he has the right to consult with an attorney, but also that if he is indigent a lawyer will be appointed to represent him. Without this additional warning, the admonition of the right to consult with counsel would often be understood as meaning only that he can consult with a lawyer if he has one or has the funds to obtain one. The warning of a right to counsel would be hollow if not couched in terms that would convey to the indigent—the person most often subjected to interrogation—the knowledge that he too has a right to have counsel present. . . .

Once warnings have been given, the subsequent procedure is clear. If the individual indicates in any manner, at any time prior to or during questioning, that he wishes to remain silent, the interrogation must cease. At this point he has shown that he intends to exercise his Fifth Amendment privilege; any statement taken after the person invokes his privilege cannot be other than the product of compulsion, subtle or otherwise. Without the right to cut off questioning, the setting of in-custody interrogation operates on the individual to overcome free choice in producing a statement after the privilege has been once invoked. If the individual states that he wants an attorney, the interrogation must cease until an attorney is present. At that time, the individual must have an opportunity to confer with the attorney and to have him present during any subsequent questioning. If the individual cannot obtain an attorney and he indicates that he wants one before speaking to police, they must respect his decision to remain silent.

The warnings required and the waiver necessary in accordance with our opinion today are, in the absence of a fully effective equivalent, prerequisites to the admissibility of any statement made by a defendant.

IV

A recurrent argument made in these cases is that society's need for interrogation outweighs the privilege. . . . The whole thrust of our foregoing discussion demonstrates that the Constitution has prescribed the rights of the individual when confronted with the power of government when it provided in the Fifth Amendment that an individual cannot be compelled to be a witness against himself. That right cannot be abridged. . . .

In announcing these principles, we are not unmindful of the burdens which law enforcement officials must bear, often under trying circumstances. We also fully recognize the obligation of all citizens to aid in enforcing the criminal laws. This Court, while protecting individual rights, has always given ample latitude to law enforcement agencies in the legitimate exercise of their duties. The limits we have placed on the interrogation process should not constitute an undue interference with a proper system of law enforcement. As we have noted, our decision does not in any way preclude police from carrying out their traditional investigatory functions.

We reverse.

- Some people think that the *Miranda* warnings make law enforcement too much of a game. They ask why the police should have to throw up obstacles to their own pursuit of the truth. Others think that the warnings are a requirement of justice and that, without them, people can be pressured into making confessions, many of which may be false. What do you think?
- Some scholars think the *Miranda* warnings make the criminal justice system fairer for people who have little education or understanding of the law.[3] Thus, someone with a law degree and someone who learned his rights only from being advised by the police would be in the same situation. Do you agree?
- Some defense lawyers say the *Miranda* warnings have failed to protect people in practice because police tactics have simply changed to get around them. How would police do that? What if they read the warnings quickly? Or yell them out harshly? What if they were mixed in with warnings or sarcastic comments from other police officers?
- Do you think differences in age, gender, race, ethnicity, class, or wealth influence people's ability to exercise their Fifth Amendment rights?
- Why is custodial interrogation necessarily coercive? The Supreme Court in *Oregon v. Mathiason* stated that "any interview of one suspected of a crime by a police officer will have coercive aspects to it, simply by virtue of the fact that the police officer is part of a law enforcement system which may ultimately cause the suspect to be charged with a crime." [4] How is being questioned by the police different from being questioned by a teacher or your parents? Anything you say to your parents or teachers or principals can be used against you, but they have no obligation to give you the *Miranda* warnings.
- The warnings are considered constitutional procedural safeguards—rules designed to protect you. Why is it necessary to have procedural safeguards? The Supreme Court in *Miranda* held that "the prosecution may not use statements, whether exculpatory or inculpatory, stemming from custodial interrogation of the defendant unless it demonstrates the use of procedural safeguards effective to secure the privilege against self-incrimination." [5] Do those procedural safeguards have to be in the form of the *Miranda* warnings? What if an officer in the screaming eagle case gave you his own personalized version of the *Miranda* warnings: "Hey, dude, you've seen TV and you've got your rights. So you can shut up if you want or even find a lawyer, but here's my question. . . ."? Would that be sufficient warning?

Juveniles and the *Miranda* Warnings

Miranda applies to young people, too. Like adults, juveniles must be warned of their Fifth Amendment rights if any of their statements are to be used against them in court. But the big question is whether juveniles can truly understand the *Miranda* warnings. Can they appreciate what it means to surrender their right to counsel and their right to silence when they start talking to the police during a criminal investigation? The Supreme Court does not bend over backward to make special exceptions for young people who have been properly advised of their *Miranda* rights. If they have been fairly warned, the Supreme Court is not about to cut them any special breaks.

The Michael C. Case: Juvenile Waiver

Michael C. was sixteen and a half years old when he was arrested and questioned about a murder. When the police asked him whether he wanted to consult a lawyer, he asked to speak with his probation officer. The request was denied. He did not follow up by asking to speak with a lawyer or a parent but proceeded to make self-incriminating statements. Later he tried to get his statements suppressed on the grounds that the police questioning should have stopped when he asked to speak with his probation officer. The Court rejected this argument and found that *Miranda* was followed and the privilege respected.

Michael C. also argued that his statements could not have been voluntary given his tender

John Lee Malvo was charged with being one of two snipers who killed ten people and wounded several others in the Washington, D.C., area in fall 2002. After his arrest, Malvo asked Virginia police, "Do I get to see my attorneys?" and signed a *Miranda* waiver with an "X," saying that to sign his name would be incriminating. An interrogation ensued, and Malvo confessed. Malvo's defense attorneys argued that his confession should be suppressed because he was interrogated without a lawyer present. Shown here leaving Fairfax County juvenile court in Virginia in November 2002, Malvo is now serving a life sentence for the shootings he committed as a minor. *Source: Brendan McDermid/Reuters/Landov*

age and immaturity. Although the Court took these factors into account in assessing the voluntariness of his statements, it found that a sixteen-and-a-half-year-old with his experience in the criminal justice system could be expected not to be coerced or tricked to talk in an ordinary police interrogation.

YOUR THOUGHTS

Should juveniles be read different *Miranda* warnings? Should special juvenile *Miranda* warnings be devised to make sure that they understand their rights? How should police handle custodial questioning when the suspect is a juvenile? How can it be determined that juveniles understand these rights? How can it be determined that they waived their rights knowingly and voluntarily? Write out one or two paragraphs to compose a special juvenile *Miranda* warning.

KENNETH F. FARE, ETC., PETITIONER,
V.
MICHAEL C.

Supreme Court of the United States
No. 78-334.
Argued Feb. 27, 1979.
Decided June 20, 1979.
Rehearing Denied Oct. 1, 1979.

Mr. Justice BLACKMUN delivered the opinion of the Court.

I

Respondent Michael C. was implicated in the murder of Robert Yeager. The murder occurred during a robbery of the victim's home on January 19, 1976. A small truck registered in the name of respondent's mother was identified as having been near the Yeager home at the time of the killing, and a young man answering respondent's description was seen by witnesses near the truck and near the home shortly before Yeager was murdered.

On the basis of this information, Van Nuys, Cal., police took respondent into custody at approximately 6:30 p.m. on February 4. Respondent then was $16^1/_2$ years old and on probation to the Juvenile Court. He had been on probation since the age of 12. Approximately one year earlier he had served a term in a youth corrections camp under the supervision of the Juvenile Court. He had a record of several previous offenses, including burglary of guns and purse snatching, stretching back over several years.

Upon respondent's arrival at the Van Nuys station house two police officers began to **interrogate** him. The officers and respondent were the only persons in the room during the interrogation. The conversation was tape-recorded. One of the officers initiated the interview by informing respondent that he had been brought in for questioning in relation to a murder. The officer fully advised respondent of his *Miranda* rights. The following exchange then occurred, as set out in the opinion of the California Supreme Court, *In re Michael C.*, 579 P.2d 7, 8 (1978) (emphasis added by that court):

"Q. . . . Do you understand all of these rights as I have explained them to you?
"A. Yeah.
"Q. Okay, do you wish to give up your right to remain silent and talk to us about this murder?
"A. What murder? I don't know about no murder.
"Q. I'll explain to you which one it is if you want to talk to us about it.
"A. Yeah, I might talk to you.
"Q. Do you want to give up your right to have an attorney present here while we talk about it?
"A. *Can I have my probation officer here?*
"Q. Well I can't get a hold of your probation officer right now. You have the right to an attorney.
"A. How I know you guys won't pull no police officer in and tell me he's an attorney?
"Q. Huh?

"A. [How I know you guys won't pull no police officer in and tell me he's an attorney?]

"Q. Your probation officer is Mr. Christiansen.

"A. Yeah.

"Q. Well I'm not going to call Mr. Christiansen tonight. There's a good chance we can talk to him later, but I'm not going to call him right now. If you want to talk to us without an attorney present, you can. If you don't want to, you don't have to. But if you want to say something, you can, and if you don't want to say something you don't have to. That's your right. You understand that right?

"A. Yeah.

"Q. Okay, will you talk to us without an attorney present?

"A. Yeah I want to talk to you."

Respondent thereupon proceeded to answer questions put to him by the officers. He made statements and drew sketches that incriminated him in the Yeager murder.

Largely on the basis of respondent's incriminating statements, probation authorities filed a petition in Juvenile Court alleging that respondent had murdered Robert Yeager. . . .

Respondent thereupon moved to suppress the statements and sketches he gave the police during the interrogation. He alleged that the statements had been obtained in violation of *Miranda* in that his request to see his probation officer at the outset of the questioning constituted an **invocation** of his Fifth Amendment right to remain silent, just as if he had requested the assistance of an attorney. . . .

II

The rule the Court established in *Miranda* is clear. In order to be able to use statements obtained during custodial interrogation of the accused, the State must warn the accused prior to such questioning of his right to remain silent and of his right to have counsel, retained or appointed, present during interrogation. . . .

The rule in *Miranda,* however, was based on this Court's perception that the lawyer occupies a critical position in our legal system because of his unique ability to protect the Fifth Amendment rights of a client undergoing custodial interrogation. Because of this special ability of the lawyer to help the client preserve his Fifth Amendment rights once the client becomes enmeshed in the adversary process, the Court found that "the right to have counsel present at the interrogation is indispensable to the protection of the Fifth Amendment privilege under the system" established by the Court. *Id.* at 469. Moreover, the lawyer's presence helps guard against overreaching by the police and ensures that any statements actually obtained are accurately transcribed for presentation into evidence. *Id.,* at 470. . . .

A probation officer is not in the same posture with regard to either the accused or the system of justice as a whole. Often he is not trained in the law, and so is not in a position to advise the accused as to his legal rights. . . . Moreover, the probation officer is the employee of the State which seeks to prosecute the alleged offender. He is a peace officer, and as such is allied, to a greater or lesser extent, with his fellow peace officers. He owes an obligation to the State, notwithstanding the obligation he may also owe the juvenile under his supervision. In most cases, the probation officer is duty bound to report wrongdoing by the juvenile when it comes to his attention, even if by communication from the juvenile himself.

. . . We thus believe it clear that the probation officer is not in a position to offer the type of legal assistance necessary to protect the Fifth Amendment rights of an accused undergoing custodial interrogation that a lawyer can offer. . . . We hold, therefore, that it was error to find that the request by respondent to speak with his probation officer *per se* constituted an invocation of respondent's Fifth Amendment right to be free from compelled self-incrimination. It therefore was also error to hold that because the police did not then cease interrogating respondent the statements he made during interrogation should have been suppressed.

III

Miranda further recognized that after the required warnings are given the accused, "[i]f the interrogation continues without the presence of an attorney and a statement is taken, a heavy burden rests on the government to demonstrate that the defendant knowingly and intelligently waived his privilege against self-incrimination and his right to retained or appointed counsel."

. . . [T]he determination whether statements obtained during custodial interrogation are admissible against the accused is to be made upon an inquiry into the totality of the circumstances surrounding the interrogation, to ascertain whether the accused in fact knowingly and voluntarily decided to forgo his rights to remain silent and to have the assistance of counsel. . . .

This totality-of-the-circumstances approach is adequate to determine whether there has been a waiver even where interrogation of juveniles is involved. . . . The totality approach permits— indeed, it mandates—inquiry into all the circumstances surrounding the interrogation. This includes evaluation of the juvenile's age, experience, education, background, and intelligence, and into whether he has the capacity to understand the warnings given him, the nature of his Fifth Amendment rights, and the consequences of waiving those rights. . . .

The transcript of the interrogation reveals that the police officers conducting the interrogation took care to ensure that respondent understood his rights. They fully explained to respondent that he was being questioned in connection with a murder. They then informed him of all the rights delineated in *Miranda,* and ascertained that respondent understood those rights. There is no indication in the record that respondent failed to understand what the officers told him. Moreover, after his request to see his probation officer had been denied, and after the police officer once more had explained his rights to him, respondent clearly expressed his willingness to waive his rights and continue the interrogation.

Further, no special factors indicate that respondent was unable to understand the nature of his actions. He was a $16^{1}/_{2}$ -year-old juvenile with considerable experience with the police. He had a record of several arrests. He had served time in a youth camp, and he had been on probation for several years. He was under the full-time supervision of probation authorities. There is no indication that he was of insufficient intelligence to understand the rights he was waiving, or what the consequences of that waiver would be. He was not worn down by improper interrogation tactics or lengthy questioning or by trickery or **deceit**.

On these facts, we think it clear that respondent voluntarily and knowingly waived his Fifth Amendment rights.

The Supreme Court has developed neither a special warning for juveniles nor a clear test of whether juveniles have waived their rights knowingly and voluntarily. Instead, the Court has said that judges will independently review each juvenile interrogation producing a confession to determine whether, under the totality of circumstances, the decision to waive was voluntary and knowing.

POINTS TO PONDER

- Michael C. waived his *Miranda* rights, namely, the right to keep silent and consult with a lawyer. The decision may have cost him his liberty because his resulting confession was used against him in trial. Can you think of reasons that Michael may not have asked for a lawyer?
- Do you think Michael C.'s waiver of his rights was voluntary? Was it knowing; that is, did he really know what he was doing? Do you think he would do it again?
- Some research has been done on juveniles and *Miranda* warnings. Consider the following information.

    Research shows that *Miranda* warnings are not well understood by children, especially those fourteen and under or young adults with low intelligence scores. This can mean that young people do not comprehend the words used or appreciate the concepts behind the words and do not see their practical meaning.[6]

    Research shows that sometimes juveniles agree to things that they do not fully understand or agree to things out of confusion about what they mean.[7]

    Research shows that about 90 percent of juveniles who were asked to make statements by police in felony cases waived their rights to silence and counsel. The rate for adult waiver is about 60 percent.[8] Do these statistics suggest that *Miranda* is an effective warning for young people? Do many young people assume that remaining silent will just get them into more trouble?

    Research shows that juveniles tend to think less about the long-term consequences of their actions. Sometimes this results in the juveniles telling truthful things to the police that will ultimately hurt them, and sometimes it results in juveniles telling police false things simply to appease them and end an uncomfortable situation.[9]

    Research shows that some juveniles are more susceptible to suggestive questioning by police officers. Sometimes the use of leading questions (questions that include the desired answer, such as "You were certainly at the store at 4:35, weren't you?") can get juveniles to agree to things that are factually inaccurate. In addition, sometimes the tactic of confronting the juvenile with false evidence or false statements can convince him to give up on claiming innocence.[10]

    Research shows that juveniles are at a profound disadvantage in confronting adult authority figures such as police, prosecutors, or even parents because young people are taught to obey these figures and not to contradict them.[11]

- Are the regular *Miranda* warnings adequate for juveniles? Should a special warning be designed for juveniles? How would you write it?
- What about juveniles who do not speak English as a first language? What if they are from another country? Should people from other countries be granted added protection when it comes to *Miranda*?[12]

The *Haley* Case

Just because a juvenile is given *Miranda*-type warnings does not mean that a confession produced by custodial interrogation will be valid and admissible. Imagine that the police read a young person his *Miranda* rights and then proceed to threaten to beat him up or kill him by dropping him off a bridge if he does not confess. A resulting confession would surely not be admissible even though one of the officers read the *Miranda* warning first.

Consider the Supreme Court case of *Haley v. Ohio.* John Haley was fifteen years old when police woke him up at midnight and arrested him on suspicion of murder. John was taken to the police station and questioned by police officers for more than six hours straight. From midnight to 6:30 am, the police took turns interrogating him. Five or six policemen questioned him in relay teams of one or two officers, constantly firing questions at the boy. They did not allow him to see a lawyer or his parents, nor did they allow him to sleep. They confronted him with statements allegedly made by other boys with whom he was supposed to have done the crime. Haley also testified that he was physically beaten by the police during this time. After the initial interrogation session, the police then kept him isolated for three days. He eventually signed a typed confession to the murder which included a *Miranda*-style warning and waiver at the top of the page (even though these events took place before *Miranda*). Haley's written confession was preceded by these words:

> "We want to inform you of your constitutional rights, the law gives you the right to make this statement or not, as you see fit. It is made with the understanding that it may be used at a trial in court either for or against you or anyone else involved in this crime with you, of your own free will and accord, you are under no force or duress or compulsion and no promises are being made to you at this time whatsoever." [13]

The Supreme Court ruled that John Haley's confession was unconstitutional under the Due Process Clause of the Fourteenth Amendment. The Court took into account in its decision the suspect's age, maturity, and capacity to resist adult authority and assert one's rights.

FACTORS TO CONSIDER IN EVALUATING THE EFFECTIVENESS OF THE *MIRANDA* WARNINGS AND A JUVENILE'S DECISION TO WAIVE HIS RIGHTS

- Juvenile suspect's age and experience
- Juvenile suspect's level of education
- Juvenile suspect's personal background
- Juvenile suspect's intelligence
- Juvenile suspect's experience with police
- Juvenile's mental and physical condition during time of questioning
- Custodial environment: whether they were in custody, time of day custody took place, treatment during custody
- Juvenile suspect's capacity to understand the warnings
- Juvenile suspect's ability to understand consequences of waiving rights
- Presence of family or lawyer at time of being questioned

What transpired would make us pause for careful inquiry if a mature man were involved. And when, as here, a mere child—and easy victim of the law—is before us, special care in scrutinizing the record must be used. Age 15 is a tender and difficult age for a boy of any race. He cannot be judged by the more exacting standards of maturity. That which would leave a man cold and unimpressed can overawe a lad in his early teens. This is the period of great instability which the crisis of adolescence produces. . . . [W]e cannot believe that a lad of tender years is a match for the police in such a contest. He needs counsel and support if he is not to become a victim of fear, then of panic.[14]

The Court also observed that just because a juvenile is warned of his constitutional rights does not necessarily mean that he understands them or that the police have not manipulated or coerced him into confessing.

[W]e are told that this boy was advised of his constitutional rights before he signed the confession and that, knowing them, he nevertheless confessed. That assumes, however that a boy of fifteen, without aid of counsel, would have a full appreciation of that advice and that on the facts of this record had a freedom of choice.[15]

POINTS TO PONDER

- John Haley signed the confession but the Court found that it did not constitute a valid waiver of rights. Why not?
- The *Haley* decision was handed down in 1948, long before the *Miranda* case came to the Court. Do you think the decision would be the same today assuming Haley had been given the *Miranda* warnings and signed the same statement?

What Is Custody?

The *Miranda* protections come into play when someone is in custody. The Supreme Court defined in *Miranda* the custodial setting as the time "after a person has been taken into custody or otherwise deprived of his freedom of action in any significant way."[16] In other words, the warning is required when someone under police control is being questioned.

Courts have determined that a person is in custody when he is arrested or his freedom is limited in a way similar to being arrested. Legal custody, the Supreme Court said in *Berkemer v. McCarty,* is found "as soon as a suspect's freedom of action is curtailed to a degree associated with formal arrest."[17]

The courts look to a "reasonable person" standard to define when custody takes place. Would a reasonable person understand himself to be in the custody of the police? Custody clearly takes place when a formal arrest has been made. When not, the court, as described in *Stansbury v. California,* looks to all of the facts and circumstances sur-

What does it mean to be under police control? What does it mean for someone to be taken into custody? If it does not mean formal arrest, when is someone in custody?

rounding the questioning and asks "how a reasonable man in the suspect's position would have understood his situation." [18]

Under U.S. law, police can ask questions that may be used against you as long as you are not in custody. You are not in custody if police merely ask you questions on the street. This is true even if they are uniformed, armed, and in an official police car. This is true even though police may suspect you of a crime. This is true even though police may be investigating a crime and trying to get you to admit things that are incriminating. You are not in custody until you are arrested or somehow in a situation that is the equivalent of being arrested.

You are also not in custody if you voluntarily meet with police and answer questions. This is true even if you are being questioned in a police station. This is true even if you are the sole suspect in a case. As long as you have appeared voluntarily and are not under formal arrest, police can ask you questions and your statements can be used against you.

You are also not in custody during a traffic stop. This is true even if the officer is in uniform, gets you out of the car, and suspects you of a crime. You are not in custody even if the officer asks you questions meant to trick you into incriminating yourself. During a traffic stop, your statements are not statements made in custody unless you have been arrested.

Exercises: Custody or Not?

The following fictional cases involving young people who confess without *Miranda* warnings are based on Supreme Court decisions involving adults. Here, you are the judge and must decide whether the juvenile suspects were in police custody when they made their confessions (or incriminating statements). If they were not in custody at the time they confessed, the police were not required to advise them of their *Miranda* rights and their confessions would be allowed into evidence. If they were in custody, the failure to give *Miranda* warnings should lead to suppression of their statements. In a suppression hearing, you the judge would hear motions to suppress (exclude, keep out) evidence on the grounds that the evidence was obtained unlawfully, in violation of the defendant's constitutional rights.

Midnight Raid. Jimmy Lee, age sixteen, got into a fight at a club with another young man who he thought was flirting with his girlfriend. The other man was found dead outside the club at closing time. The police went to Jimmy Lee's house at 4:00 a.m., were admitted by a relative staying at the house, and woke Jimmy up in his bedroom. Standing over him, armed and angry, the police questioned Jimmy. He told them that he had been at the club earlier in the evening, that there had been some kind of a fight, and that he owned a pistol. At no point did the police read him his *Miranda* rights. Later when Jimmy was prosecuted for murder, his lawyer moved to suppress introduction of Jimmy's statements on the grounds that he had not been given the *Miranda* warnings and thus using his statements in court would violate his Fifth Amendment rights. But the government denied Jimmy was ever in custody within the meaning of the *Miranda* decision. The legal question is whether Jimmy was in custody for purposes of the Fifth Amendment when he was asked questions at his home by the officers. How would you decide this motion? Was he in custody or not?

Uninvited Guest. Joe Johnson, age fifteen, had a house party while his parents were away for the weekend. When a local drug dealer showed up uninvited, Joe and his friends decided to rob the dealer of his money. The robbery did not go off as planned, and Joe's friend Bryant shot the dealer and killed him. After sending Bryant home, Joe called the police and, when they arrived, told them that Bryant had killed the drug dealer and then hidden his gun in Joe's backyard. The police promptly found the gun. Joe agreed to accompany the police back to the station and talk to them about the night's events. The police questioning produced a complete statement from Joe about the robbery plan and the killing. But the police never read Joe his *Miranda* rights, either at his home or down at the police station. Joe was arrested a week later and charged with aiding the murder. His lawyer moved to suppress his statements to the police on the grounds that he was never given the *Miranda* warnings. The government responded that he was never in custody when speaking to the police because he always spoke to them voluntarily. How would you decide this case? Do you allow his statements in or not?

While You Were Out. Skip Billings, sixteen, was suspected of burglary in connection with a rash of break-ins at homes in Los Angeles. Acting on a tip, the police went to Skip's home and left a business card with Skip's parents asking him to call them. The next day he called and set up a meeting at the state police patrol headquarters. Skip took the bus to the office to meet with the officer. They shook hands, and Skip was escorted into an office. The investigating officer and Skip sat across a table from each other. The officer told him he was not under arrest but that he was suspected of the burglaries. The officer told Skip that his fingerprints were discovered on the scene and were now in police possession. This was not true, but because of this suggestion, Skip confessed to the burglaries. After Skip's confession, the police officer then read him his *Miranda* rights. When Skip was prosecuted, his lawyer moved to suppress the statements on the grounds that Skip had not been properly advised of his *Miranda* rights before he confessed. As the judge in this case, would you allow his confession in as evidence or not?

Answers: Custody or Not?

Each of the three fictional cases involving juveniles who confess to crimes without having been told their *Miranda* rights mirrors a real-life Supreme Court case that centered around an adult in a similar situation. The court cases offer an answer to the question of whether the defendant was in custody or not.

Midnight Raid. In *Orozco v. Texas,* the Court found that the at-home questioning of Orozco by police in the middle of the night did involve custody.[19] Even though Orozco was at his own home and not in a police station, the police were still in control and it clearly remained a coercive environment. Even the police admitted that he was not free to leave. The situation was thus the equivalent of a custodial interrogation at the police station.

Uninvited Guest. In *California v. Beheler,* the Supreme Court found that defendant Beheler was not in custody when the questioning took place.[20] Because Beheler had initiated the contact with the police and voluntarily accompanied the police to the station, he was not deprived of his freedom in a way that is equivalent to arrest. Because he was never forced to remain in the presence of police officers and was not forced to answer any questions, he was not in custody for purposes of the Fifth Amendment. Therefore, the police did not have to give him the warnings. His self-incriminating statements were allowed into evidence.

While You Were Out. In *Oregon v. Mathiason,* the Supreme Court rejected Mathiason's motion to suppress his statements.[21] The Supreme Court said Mathiason was not in custody because he had voluntarily met with the police and freely answered their questions. He was not under arrest and could have left the police station at any time. Thus, because he could have left during the conversation with police and was not being kept against his will, he was not in custody for Fifth Amendment purposes and there was no need to read the *Miranda* warnings.

POINTS TO PONDER

- How did your decisions as a judge ruling on suppression motions compare with those of the Supreme Court?
- In Skip Billings's case, do you agree that a person who receives a business card from the police and proceeds to call and set up a meeting at headquarters is not in custody for Fifth Amendment purposes? Do most young people know that if they meet voluntarily with police and are not in custody, anything they say to the police can be used against them in court and the police do not have to give them the *Miranda* warnings?
- Looking at the above cases, what common elements of custody were important to your determinations? Did it matter if the suspect was questioned at home or at the police stations? Did it matter if the suspects were invited to the police station or simply came on their own initiative? Did it matter if several officers were questioning them? Did it matter how the officers treated them—whether they were given a cup of coffee or a glass of water? Did it matter that they were told they were not under arrest? That they were handcuffed or kept behind locked doors?

Pull Over, Jack

The controversies about police custody examined so far relate to what happens at a police station or the suspect's home. What about interrogation on the road? Many people are familiar with being pulled over by police for a traffic violation. In a traffic stop, a person's freedom of movement is clearly limited by a law enforcement officer who may be asking

You are sixteen and had your driver's license for a few months when you are pulled over driving with a group of your friends. The police begin asking questions about why your front right headlight is broken and what you know about a local robbery. Are you in custody during a routine traffic stop?

questions that could lead to self-incrimination. But are you in custody? Should the police have to give *Miranda* warnings?

In *Berkemer v. McCarty*, the Supreme Court found that an ordinary traffic stop does not create a situation of custodial interrogation. Thus, *Miranda* warnings do not have to be given so long as the motorist is not placed under arrest.

—

HARRY J. BERKEMER, SHERIFF OF FRANKLIN COUNTY, OHIO, PETITIONER
V.
RICHARD N. MCCARTY.

Supreme Court of the United States
No. 83-710.
Argued April 18, 1984.
Decided July 2, 1984.

Justice MARSHALL delivered the opinion of the Court.

. . . [D]oes the roadside questioning of a motorist detained pursuant to a traffic stop constitute custodial interrogation for the purposes of the doctrine enunciated in *Miranda*?

I

A

On the evening of March 31, 1980, Trooper Williams of the Ohio State Highway Patrol observed respondent's car weaving in and out of a lane on Interstate Highway 270. After following the car for two miles, Williams forced respondent to stop and asked him to get out of the vehicle. When respondent complied, Williams noticed that he was having difficulty standing. At that point, "Williams concluded that [respondent] would be charged with a traffic offense and, therefore, his freedom to leave the scene was terminated." . . . However, respondent was not told that he would be taken into custody. Williams then asked respondent to perform a field sobriety test, commonly known as a "balancing test." Respondent could not do so without falling.

While still at the scene of the traffic stop, Williams asked respondent whether he had been using intoxicants. Respondent replied that "he had consumed two beers and had smoked several joints of marijuana a short time before." . . . Respondent's speech was slurred, and Williams had difficulty understanding him. Williams thereupon formally placed respondent under arrest and transported him in the patrol car to the Franklin County Jail.

At the jail, respondent was given an intoxilyzer test to determine the concentration of alcohol in his blood. The test did not detect any alcohol whatsoever in respondent's system. Williams then resumed questioning respondent in order to obtain information for inclusion in the State Highway Patrol Alcohol Influence Report. Respondent answered affirmatively a question whether he had been drinking. When then asked if he was under the influence of alcohol, he said, "I guess, barely." . . . Williams next asked respondent to indicate on the form whether the marihuana he had smoked had been treated with any chemicals. In the section of the report headed "Remarks," respondent wrote, "No ang[el] dust or PCP in the pot. Rick McCarty." . . .

At no point in this sequence of events did Williams or anyone else tell respondent that he had a right to remain silent, to consult with an attorney, and to have an attorney appointed for him if he could not afford one.

III

To assess the admissibility of the self-incriminating statements made by respondent prior to his formal arrest, we are obliged to address . . . [an] issue concerning the scope of our decision in *Miranda:* whether the roadside questioning of a motorist detained pursuant to a routine traffic stop should be considered "custodial interrogation." . . .

It must be acknowledged at the outset that a traffic stop significantly curtails the "freedom of action" of the driver and the passengers, if any, of the detained vehicle. Under the law of most States, it is a crime either to ignore a policeman's signal to stop one's car or, once having stopped, to drive away without permission. . . . Certainly few motorists would feel free either to disobey a directive to pull over or to leave the scene of a traffic stop without being told they might do so. . . .

Thus, we must decide whether a traffic stop exerts upon a detained person pressures that sufficiently impair his free exercise of his privilege against self-incrimination to require that he be warned of his constitutional rights.

Two features of an ordinary traffic stop mitigate the danger that a person questioned will be induced "to speak where he would not otherwise do so freely," *Miranda v. Arizona,* 384 U.S., at 467. First, detention of a motorist pursuant to a traffic stop is presumptively temporary and brief. The vast majority of roadside detentions last only a few minutes. A motorist's expectations, when he sees a policeman's light flashing behind him, are that he will be obliged to spend a short period of time answering questions and waiting while the officer checks his license and registration, that he may then be given a citation, but that in the end he most likely will be allowed to continue on his way. In this respect, questioning incident to an ordinary traffic stop is quite different from stationhouse interrogation, which frequently is prolonged, and in which the detainee often is aware that questioning will continue until he provides his interrogators the answers they seek. *See id.,* at 451.

Second, circumstances associated with the typical traffic stop are not such that the motorist feels completely at the mercy of the police. To be sure, the aura of authority surrounding an armed, uniformed officer and the knowledge that the officer has some discretion in deciding whether to issue a citation, in combination, exert some pressure on the detainee to respond to questions. But other aspects of the situation substantially offset these forces. Perhaps most importantly, the typical traffic stop is public, at least to some degree. Passersby, on foot or in other cars, witness the interaction of officer and motorist. This exposure to public view both reduces the ability of an unscrupulous policeman to use illegitimate means to elicit self-incriminating statements and diminishes the motorist's fear that, if he does not cooperate, he will be subjected to abuse. The fact that the detained motorist typically is confronted by only one or at most two policemen further mutes his sense of vulnerability. In short, the atmosphere surrounding an ordinary traffic stop is substantially less "police dominated" than that surrounding the kinds of interrogation at issue in *Miranda* itself, *see* 384 U.S., at 445, 491-498, and in the subsequent cases in which we have applied *Miranda*.

. . . It is settled that the safeguards prescribed by Miranda become applicable as soon as a suspect's freedom of action is curtailed to a "degree associated with formal arrest." *California v. Beheler,* 463 U.S. 1121, 1125 (1983) (per curiam). If a motorist who has been detained pursuant to a traffic stop thereafter is subjected to treatment that renders him "in custody" for practical purposes, he will be entitled to the full panoply of protections prescribed by *Miranda. See Oregon v. Mathiason,* 429 U.S. 492, 495 (1977) (per curiam).

Turning to the case before us, we find nothing in the record that indicates that respondent should have been given *Miranda* warnings at any point prior to the time Trooper Williams placed him under arrest. For the reasons indicated above, we reject the contention that the initial stop of respondent's car, by itself, rendered him "in custody." And respondent has failed to demonstrate that, at any time between the initial stop and the arrest, he was subjected to restraints comparable to those associated with a formal arrest. Only a short period of time elapsed between the stop and the arrest. At no point during that interval was respondent informed that his detention would not be temporary. Although Trooper Williams apparently decided as soon as respondent stepped out of his car that respondent would be taken into custody and charged with a traffic offense, Williams never communicated his intention to respondent. A policeman's unarticulated plan has no bearing on the question whether a suspect was "in custody" at a particular time; the only relevant inquiry is how a reasonable man in the suspect's position would have understood his situation. Nor do other aspects of the interaction of Williams and respondent support the contention that respondent was exposed to "custodial interrogation" at the scene of the stop. From aught that appears in the stipulation of facts, a single police officer asked respondent a modest number of questions and requested him to perform a simple balancing test at a location visible to passing motorists. Treatment of this sort cannot fairly be characterized as the functional equivalent of formal arrest.

We conclude, in short, that respondent was not taken into custody for the purposes of *Miranda* until Williams arrested him. Consequently, the statements respondent made prior to that point were admissible against him.

Accordingly, the judgment of the Court of Appeals is *Affirmed.*

- The Supreme Court says that a traffic stop is not custody for two basic reasons. First, traffic stops usually are only temporary. But what if the stop is not temporary? What if the police keep you there for two hours and call for a drug-sniffing dog? Should this kind of traffic stop also be considered noncustodial? Second, people do not feel completely at the mercy of the police during most traffic stops. Is this true? Is it always true? Do other motorists feel that they can get involved and challenge something that is happening? What if no other passengers are in the area? What if the stop takes place late at night or on a deserted street? What if numerous officers are on the scene and just one driver? What if they pull their guns on you?
- Do members of certain groups—young people, racial minorities, people who do not speak English as a first language—find traffic stops more intimidating? Can the Supreme Court justices identify with the subjective experiences with the police that most Americans have had?

What Is Interrogation?

The custodial interrogation that triggers the requirement of the *Miranda* warnings has two parts: police custody and interrogation. Custody has been discussed. Now consider what interrogation means in this context. Interrogation means questioning, but what type of questioning? When is questioning taking place? The easiest case is described in the *Miranda* decision itself: lengthy, difficult, repeated, and constant questions by law enforcement officials directed at a suspect. But what happens when the police do not ask direct questions? What if they have a conversation amongst themselves that the suspect overhears? If confessions follow in ambiguous situations such as that, are they admissible in court if the police failed to read the suspect his *Miranda* rights?

YOUR THOUGHTS

What does police interrogation mean to you? Does interrogation always require questions? Are there different ways people obtain information from each other? What about tricks to elicit information or statements? Is that interrogation?

The Supreme Court has determined that interrogation means more than simply questioning a suspect. The Court, in *Rhode Island v. Innis,* interpreted the term *interrogation* to mean any questions, words, or actions initiated by the police that the police should know is likely to lead to an incriminating response from the suspect.

> [T]he term interrogation under *Miranda* refers not only to express questioning, but also to any words or actions on the part of the police (other than those normally attendant to

arrest and custody) that the police should know are reasonably likely to elicit an incriminating response from the suspect. The latter portion of this definition focuses primarily upon the perceptions of the suspect, rather than the intent of the police. This focus reflects the fact that the *Miranda* safeguards were designed to vest a suspect in custody with an added measure of protection against coercive police practices, without regard to objective proof of the underlying intent of the police. A practice that the police should know is reasonably likely to evoke an incriminating response from a suspect thus amounts to interrogation. But, since the police surely cannot be held accountable for the unforeseeable results of their words or actions, the definition of interrogation can extend only to words or actions on the part of the police officers that they should have known were reasonably likely to elicit an incriminating response.[22]

This definition of interrogation has four basic elements.

1. **Words or Actions.** You must have words or actions initiated by police officers. Words can be direct questions, indirect questions, or comments in the presence of the accused person, which are the functional equivalent of questioning. Actions can be anything from showing a suspect evidence (the murder weapon, for example), or pictures of the victim, or anything the police think might get the suspect to react.
2. **Likely to Elicit an Incriminating Response.** The words or actions must be reasonably likely to get the suspect to respond. For example, asking about the weather or inquiring if the person wants a lawyer or a cup of coffee are not designed to get someone to confess. Usually, the subject matter must be connected in some way to the crime at issue. By incriminating response, the court means any response, whether inculpatory or exculpatory (meaning tending to support guilt or tending to support innocence, respectively), that the prosecution may seek to introduce at trial. Courts do not care whether the statement helps or hurts the suspect, only that it was made in response to the police officer's words or actions.
3. **Looked at through the Perceptions of the Suspect.** The determination of whether a word or action was reasonably likely to get the suspect to respond must be looked at from the suspect's point of view. So, courts try to think about what was going through the head of the accused person and figure out how a person in that situation would react. This analysis may involve the age, education, maturity, and experience of the accused.
4. **Police Should Have Known.** Courts look to see if the response by a suspect should have been foreseen by the police. For example, if police said or did something specifically to elicit an incriminating response, courts will find that the police should have known that their conduct would result in that response. If police should have known that the person would say something incriminating, courts have ruled that the police should have read the suspect his *Miranda* rights. If the police have no reason to know that something they are doing would produce an incriminating response, then the *Miranda* warnings are not required.

Exercises: Interrogation or Not?

The following are hypothetical cases involving juveniles. You are the judge and must determine whether custodial interrogation took place and thus, whether the *Miranda* warnings were necessary. If there was custodial interrogation and *Miranda* warnings were necessary, the confessions would be suppressed. If they were not, the confessions would be allowed into evidence.

Mary Hartman. Mary Hartman, sixteen, was arrested on suspicion of marijuana dealing at her high school. She was picked up after soccer practice by two police officers and arrested. But she was not read her *Miranda* rights. On the way to the police station, the two officers began discussing the case in voices loud enough for Mary to hear from the back seat. This was their dialogue.

Officer Adams: We've got to find who sold that pot to that kid.

Officer Brown: Yeah, he looks really messed up.

Officer Adams: He could die.

Officer Brown: If we could trace the pot back to where it came from, we could figure out what they put into it. Maybe PCP or acid or—

Officer Adams: Could have been rat poison.

Officer Brown: If the person who sold him those drugs has any feeling at all, he or she would be like a hero. . . .

Officer Adams: Besides, it could keep them out of a lot more trouble.

At that point, Mary leaned forward and said, "I sold it to him, I admit it. I'll take you to the guy who sold it to me."

The officers then drive to the home of Mary's supplier and arrested him as well. Later, when Mary is prosecuted for distribution of marijuana, her lawyer moves to suppress her statements in the police car and all of the evidence against her that came from it. You have to decide whether what took place in the car was custodial interrogation. Mary was definitely taken into custody, but was she subject to an interrogation? Did the officers' dialogue constitute a kind of questioning (in the absence of *Miranda* warnings)?

Joey Bones and the Prison Informant. Joey Bones, seventeen, was being held in a juvenile detention facility in Baltimore, Maryland, on drug charges when someone named him as a murder suspect in an unrelated crime. To find out what Joey knew, the police placed an undercover government agent, Rafferty, in Joey's cell in the hopes that he might confess to the murder. Rafferty, who was twenty-one, told people he was seventeen and doing time for assault. He was supposed to get to know Joey, become his buddy, and then find out about the unsolved crime. One day Rafferty told Joey all about a (fictional) murder and then asked Joey whether he had ever killed someone. Joey then made a number of statements about the unsolved crime and bragged about having shot the victim, thus clearly implicating himself. Rafferty heard the comments, wrote them down, and reported them to the police investigating the murder. Joey was prosecuted for murder. At trial, he challenges the use of the self-incriminating statements he made to the undercover agent on Fifth Amendment grounds, arguing that he was in custody at the time (being in jail) and was being asked questions by a law enforcement officer (even though he did not know it was a law enforcement officer at the time). Do you agree? Would you suppress his statements on the grounds that he had not been given the *Miranda* warnings?

Tiny Tim and the Terrible Two. Tiny Tim is picked up on charges of burglary and rides in the back of the police car. In front, the following conversation takes place.

Officer Gomez (pretending to whisper): If the kid cops to the burglary plea, we should go easy on him. If not, let's throw in some drug charges. We must have a ton of cocaine back at the station and we can drop it on him.

Officer Darrell: Great idea. If he cooperates, we go easy. If he plays hardball, let's throw the kitchen sink at him.

At this point, Tim blurts out, "All right, all right, I admit the burglary, just don't make anything up about drugs 'cause my Dad'll kill me."

Without *Miranda* warnings, is the confession admissible? As the judge, how do you rule?

Answers: Interrogation or Not?

Two of the three fictional cases involving juveniles who were questioned by the police are similar to real-life Supreme Court cases that centered around an adult. In those cases, the Court offers an answer to the question of whether the defendant was subject to custodial interrogation or not.

Mary Hartman. In *Rhode Island v. Innis,* the Supreme Court majority found that the custodial conversation between two officers was not the functional equivalent of custodial interrogation.[23] The Court held that the police officers could not have known that their conversation—in which they speculated that a missing murder weapon might be found by a child and pose a danger to his life—would necessarily result in Innis's confession. The Court observed that the conversation was between two fellow officers, and no questions were directed specifically at Innis. Furthermore, the Court reasoned that the officers could not have known that Innis would blurt out his confession because of their comments. Thus, it did not count as interrogation for purposes of the Fifth Amendment. Dissenting justices thought this analysis was artificial and ignored the fact that the whole conversation seemed geared to elicit a confession. Following *Innis,* a court would probably find that Mary Hartman had not been interrogated, but room for disagreement on this complex issue clearly exists.

Joey Bones and the Prison Informant. In *Illinois v. Perkins,* the Court found that the undercover agent's questions did not constitute interrogation within the meaning of the Fifth Amendment because this was not the kind of situation that *Miranda* was meant to guard against.[24] *Miranda* was simply designed to protect people from being forced to confess in a police-dominated atmosphere where they might be afraid and intimidated. Because Perkins did not know the undercover agent in his cell was a police officer, the Court reasoned that he could not have been afraid of him and the power of the police. Though Perkins was in the custody of the state and being asked questions by a law enforcement agent, he was not in police custody and did not know he was being questioned by a police officer. This was not true custodial interrogation. The Court reasoned that "when an incarcerated person speaks freely to someone whom he believes to be a fellow inmate," the protections of *Miranda* do not apply. The Court determined this was trickery not coercion, and trickery—at least this kind—is allowed. Should it be the same with respect to juveniles? The Court has not addressed this question. What's your answer? In the meantime, people in jail who have something to hide need to remain ever suspicious and vigilant about their cell mates.

Tiny Tim and the Terrible Two. The fictional account is not based on a Supreme Court case. However, these facts could certainly arise. Based on previous cases, do you think such a confession should be allowed? Why or why not?

The Dangers of False Confession

The Supreme Court in *Miranda* was concerned about the "interrogation environment" because it believed that police questioning of suspects in custody, without warnings, would "subjugate the individual to the will of his examiner" and thus violate the Fifth Amendment principle that protects against self-incrimination. See *Rhode Island v. Innis.*[25] The Court, in *Miranda,* recognized that interrogation involves "inherently compelling pressures which work to undermine the individual's will to resist and to compel him to speak where he would not otherwise do so freely." [26] Do people confess to crimes they did not commit? It sounds silly, but you would be surprised.

Michael Crowe, 14, confessed to murdering his own sister after several days of police interrogation. He was not allowed to see his parents or a lawyer. On the first day of questioning police told him that if he just confessed, the police would help him and give him a lighter sentence. Michael maintained his innocence. On the second day, the police told him they had scientific evidence against him and that he had failed a lie detector test. Michael began breaking under the pressure. Michael insisted to police that he couldn't remember killing his sister. Police kept interrogating him. Eventually, Michael signed a confession because he believed that the police had overwhelming evidence against him. DNA evidence proved Michael absolutely innocent.[27]

Allen Jacob Chesnet, 16, confessed to murdering a neighbor. The circumstances of his prosecution demonstrate the danger of false confessions. Allen had been sitting on his porch having just cut himself with a tool. Because of the cut, he was bleeding. A local news reporter investigating the murder down the street noticed his injury and told the police. Based on this report, Allen became a suspect. He was interrogated at police headquarters, where he was shown pictures of the victim, the crime scene, and told that his DNA matched the blood found on the scene. Police kept demanding that he confess. After more interrogation, Allen began to cry and then confessed to the murder telling the police what he thought they wanted to hear. His confession matched some of the details from the pictures he had been shown. However, his blood did not match the evidence on the scene, and his story while having some of the details correct, did not match the rest of the physical evidence. Eventually, he was released despite his confession.[28]

Even older people can be subject to the pressures of the interrogation environment. Corethian Bell, 24, confessed to killing his own mother after two days of interrogation during which, it was alleged, he was roughed up and told he failed a lie detector test. Bell had even called the police to report the murder, only to find himself the lead suspect. Because the police were unaware that he was mildly mentally retarded and suffered from mental illness, the questioning was intense—so intense that after fifty hours of questioning Bell gave a taped videotaped confession. Fortunately, forensic evidence did not match Bell, and he was released after seventeen months in jail.[29]

Professor Saul Kassin, a psychology professor at Williams College and expert in false confessions has stated: "What happens over time is that the suspect gets tired, and there is an intensification of techniques. The suspect is getting the message that denial is not the escape, so they can offer something else." [30] Other experts have explained that confessions of the guilty and innocent alike result from the same pressures. "Police elicit the decision to confess from the guilty by leading them to believe that the evidence against them is overwhelming, that their fate is certain (whether or not they confess), and that there are advantages that follow if they confess. Investigators elicit the decision to confess from the innocent in one of two ways: either by leading them to believe that their situation, though unjust, is hopeless and will only be improved by confessing; or by persuading them that they probably committed a crime about which they have no memory and that confessing is the proper and optimal course of action." [31] Many times, individuals with mental health problems or slow learners are more vulnerable to making a false confession.

POINTS TO PONDER

- Studies have shown that perhaps at least one in four suspects arrested for a crime is innocent.[32] If those suspects are subjected to overly harsh questioning, what is the possibility that they will confess?
- Courts have allowed police to use all sorts of tricks to question suspects. Which of the following do you think is a fair police practice?

> You are told by the police that an eyewitness has identified you when no one has.
>
> You are connected to what you are told is a polygraph (lie detector) machine and then told you failed the test, but it is not a real polygraph.
>
> You are shown a piece of evidence that the police claim has your fingerprint or DNA on it. It is not real.
>
> Police convince your wife or girlfriend to get you to talk and then record the conversation.
>
> You are in a juvenile detention center and the police send in an undercover agent who dresses as a priest. You confess your crimes to him. He then gives the information to the police.
>
> The police make an agreement with your friend that, if he truthfully testifies against you in court for drug dealing, he will not be prosecuted for his own role in the operation.

- What should the limits be for police? In fact, all these practices are permissible.
- What solutions can you propose to prevent false confessions? Would videotaping confessions be helpful? Would having a neutral party be helpful? What other things can you imagine would be helpful?

The Central Park jogger story is a recent high profile false confessions case. As teenagers, Antron McCray, Kevin Richardson, Yusef Salaam, Raymond Santana, and Kharey Wise were convicted of a brutal attack of a female jogger in Central Park. After aggressive interviewing by police, each gave a detailed videotaped statement implicating the rest. The jury did not have a chance to see the tactics employed by the police, but it used the tapes to convict all five young men, who served out their sentences but were later exonerated when their convictions were overturned.

On the night of April 19, 1989, a twenty-eight-year-old jogger was brutally attacked and raped in Central Park. When she recovered, she had no memory of the assault. Initial police investigations quickly focused on a group of African American and Latino youths who were in police custody for a series of other attacks perpetrated in the park that night.

After prolonged periods of police interrogation, McCray, Richardson, Salaam, Santana, and Wise confessed to being involved in the attacks. At the time, the defendants were between fourteen and sixteen years of age. Richardson, McCray, Sanatana, and Wise gave videotaped confessions.

The confessions were presented as evidence though they differed in the time, location, and participants of the rape. At trial, the prosecutors also presented forensic evidence, including hair found on one of the defendants that resembled that of the victim and a hair found on the victim's clothing that was believed to have originated from one of the defendants. Also presented as evidence was a rock found near the scene of the crime with blood and hair on it, evidence that was believed to have come from the victim.

In 1990 all five teenagers were convicted, in two separate trials, of charges stemming from the attack. In early 2002, Matias Reyes, a convicted murderer and rapist, admitted that he alone was responsible for the attack on the Central Park jogger. Reyes had already committed another rape near Central Park days earlier in 1989, using the same modus operandi. The victim of that rape had described the rapist as having fresh stitches in his chin, and an investigator quickly linked Reyes to this description. Although the police had Reyes's name on file, they failed to connect Reyes to the rape and assault of the Central Park jogger.

Eventually, the evidence from the crime was subjected to DNA testing. The DNA profile obtained from the spermatozoa found in the rape kit matched the profile of Reyes. Mitochondrial DNA testing on the hairs found on one of the defendants revealed that the hairs were not related to the victim or the crime. Further testing on hairs found on the victim also matched Reyes. Neither blood nor the hair found on the rock matched the victim. The evidence corroborates Reyes's confession to the crime and is consistent with the other crimes committed by Reyes. He is currently serving a life sentence for those crimes.

The investigation of the convictions of the five teenagers raised questions regarding police coercion and false confessions, as well as the vulnerability of juveniles during police interrogations. In retrospect, these young men clearly did not know where, how, or when the attack took place.[33]

Following the Manhattan district attorney's recommendation to release the five men, all of their convictions were overturned on December 19, 2002. McCray served six years in a New York State prison for a crime he did not commit. Salaam served six and a half years for a crime he did not commit. Richardson served six and a half years for a crime he did not commit. Santana spent eight years in prison for a crime he did not commit. Wise served eleven and a half years in prison for a crime he did not commit.

Notes

1. *Murphy v. Waterfront Commission of New York Harbor,* 378 U.S. 52, 55 (1964) (citations omitted).

2. *Miranda v. Arizona,* 384 U.S. 436 (1966).

3. Gerald M. Caplan, "Questioning Miranda," *Vanderbilt Law Review* 38 (1985): 1417.

4. *Oregon v. Mathiason,* 429 U.S. 492, 495 (1977).

5. *Miranda v. Arizona,* 384 U.S. 436, 444.

6. Barbara Kaban and Ann E. Tobey, "When Police Question Children," *Journal of the Center for Children and the Courts* 1 (1999): 151; Lisa M. Krzewinski, "But I Didn't Do It: Protecting the Rights of Juveniles During Interrogation," *Boston College Third World Law Journal* 22 (2002): 355; Jennifer J. Walters, "Illinois' Weakened Attempt to Prevent False Confessions by Juveniles: The Requirement of Counsel for the Interrogation of Some Juveniles," *Loyola University Chicago Law Journal* 33 (2002): 487, 506–509.

7. Krzewinski, "But I Didn't Do It," 360.

8. Walters, "Illinois' Weakened Attempt to Prevent False Confessions by Juveniles," 487, 503, n. 164, citing Thomas Grisso, "Juveniles' Waiver of Rights: Legal and Psychological Competence," *Loyola University of Chicago Law Journal* 38 (1981).

9. Krzewinski, "But I Didn't Do It," 355, 361.

10. Krzewinski, "But I Didn't Do It," 355, 359.

11. Krzewinski, "But I Didn't Do It," 355, 361.

12. Floralynn Einesman, "Confessions and Culture: The Interaction of Miranda and Diversity," *Journal of Criminal Law and Criminology* 90 (1999): 1.

13. *Haley v. Ohio,* 332 U.S. 596, 599 (1948).

14. *Haley v. Ohio,* 332 U.S. 596, 599-600.

15. *Haley v. Ohio,* 332 U.S. 596, 601.

16. *Miranda v. Arizona,* 384 U.S. 436, 444.

17. *Berkemer v. McCarty,* 468 U.S. 420, 440 (1984).

18. *Stansbury v. California,* 511 U.S. 318, 322 (1994).

19. *Orozco v. Texas,* 394 U.S. 324, 325-326 (1969).

20. *California v. Beheler,* 463 U.S. 1121 (1983).

21. *Oregon v. Mathiason,* 429 U.S. 492, 493 (1977).

22. *Rhode Island v. Innis,* 446 U.S. 291, 301 (1980).

23. *Rhode Island v. Innis,* 446 U.S. 291, 293-294.

24. *Illinois v. Perkins,* 496 U.S. 292 (1990).

25. *Rhode Island v. Innis,* 446 U.S. 291, 299.

26. *Miranda v. Arizona,* 384 U.S. 436, 467.

27. Nashiba Boyd, " 'I Didn't Do It, I Was Forced To Say That I Did': The Problem of Coerced Juvenile Confessions, and Proposed Federal Legislation To Prevent Them," *Howard Law Journal* 47 (Winter 2004): 395; see also Mark Sauer, "TV Looks at Police Methods in Stephanie Crowe Murder Case," *San Diego Union-Tribune,* April 9, 2001, E6; Steve Irsay, "Fear Factor: How Far Can Police Go to Get a Confession?" at http://www.courttv.com/movie/crowe/fear.html.

28. Steven A. Drizen and Richard A. Leo, "The Problems of False Confessions in a Post-DNA World," *North Carolina Law Review* 82 (2004): 891, 969.

29. Kirsten Scharnberg and Steve Mills, "DNA Voids Murder Charge," *Chicago Tribune,* January 5, 2002.

30. Susan Saulny, "Why Confess to What you Didn't Do?" *New York Times,* December 8, 2002.

31. Nashiba Boyd, " 'I Didn't Do It, I Was Forced To Say That I Did': The Problem of Coerced Juvenile Confessions, and Proposed Federal Legislation To Prevent Them," *Howard Law Journal* 47 (Winter 2004): 395; Richard J. Ofshe and Richard A. Leo, "The Decision to Confess Falsely: Rational Choice and Irrational Action," *Denver University Law Review* 74 (1997): 979, 985.

32. See Edward Connors and others, *Convicted by Juries, Exonerated by Science: Case Studies in the Use of DNA Evidence to Establish Innocence after Trial* (Washington, D.C.: National Institute of Justice, 1996), p. 20, available at http://www.ncjrs.org/pdffiles/dnaevid.pdf (accessed January 20, 2005).

33. Innocence Project, "Case Profiles," at http://www.innocenceproject.org/case/index.php (accessed March 16, 2005).

Additional Sources

Allen, Ronald, and Richard Kuhns. *Constitutional Criminal Procedure: An Examination of the Fourth, Fifth, and Sixth Amendments and Related Areas*. 2d ed. Boston, Mass.: Little Brown, 1991.

Dressler, Joshua. *Understanding Criminal Procedure*. New York: West Publishing Company, 1991, secs. 28-54.

Kamisar, Yale, Wayne LaFave, and others. *Modern Criminal Procedure: Cases, Comments, Questions*. 9th ed. New York: West Publishing Company, 1999.

LaFave, Wayne. *Search and Seizure: A Treatise on the Fourth Amendment*. 3d ed. New York: West Publishing Company, 1996.

Miller, Marc, and Ronald White. *Teachers' Manual Criminal Procedures: Cases, Statutes, and Executive Materials*. 2d ed. New York: Aspen Publishers, 2003.

Tomkovicz, James J., and Welsh White. *Criminal Procedure: Constitutional Constraints upon Investigation and Proof*. 3d ed. New York: Matthew Bender, 1998.

7 SIXTH AMENDMENT: RIGHT TO COUNSEL

In all criminal prosecutions, the accused shall . . . have the assistance of counsel for his defense.

U.S. CONSTITUTION, AMENDMENT VI

Most people get into some kind of trouble at some point. The problem might be relatively trivial: Your parents accuse you of stealing cookies or your teacher says you have been interrupting the class. These things will not go to court. But it might be more serious: you are accused of shoplifting by a storeowner or your school accuses you of cheating on a test or selling marijuana. Or it might be something truly terrible: you are accused of murder by the government or sexual assault by a person you met at a party.

In the U.S. system of justice and in Americans' way of thinking, a legal process against you for commission of a crime is fair only if you have the presence of a lawyer to represent you. Although criminal defendants retain the right to defend themselves, this course of action is disfavored.

Why do you need a lawyer? Why can't you represent yourself—especially if you are not guilty of what you are being charged with?

Imagine you have been accused of shoplifting candy bars and cookies from a convenience store. You were with some kids who committed the offense, but you did not participate. Why can't you go to court and explain that your friends did it but not you? Sure, you ate some of the cookies and candy later on, but it was never your decision to take any in the first place. Why don't you just represent yourself?

There are a number of reasons.

The first reason you need a lawyer is that you do not know the process. You need to have someone explain to you how the legal proceeding will take place, when you can speak, and how to discuss what happened. Should you testify? Should you not? Will you have to testify against your friends? What if you don't want to? Your lawyer will explain the rules of the court, of procedure and evidence, and the different dynamics of the process. Your lawyer should help you figure out how to dress for court (conservatively), how to address the judge (politely and respectfully), and how to conduct yourself there (with dignity and calm). Your lawyer also will lead you through the complicated and delicate question of whether to enter into a plea bargain, in which you agree to plead "guilty" (or responsible) in return for certain kinds of consideration, such as a lesser charge or lighter punishment.

The second reason you need a lawyer is that you do not know the law. Did you aid and abet the crime? You have to know what **aiding and abetting** is to figure that out. Were you an **accessory after the fact**? Again, it takes someone with legal knowledge to figure this out and argue against it. What about the rules of evidence? Will the prosecutors be able to bring up the fact that you were convicted of shoplifting last year? How can you stop them from bringing in that evidence? You need to understand the law as well as the process to develop your strategy in court.

The third reason you need a lawyer is that you may be so nervous and ashamed of being in the situation—even if you are not guilty—that it may be hard for you to think straight and speak clearly. Your lawyer can reassure you, comfort you, help you understand what is going on, and help you express yourself clearly. He can make sure that you do not get lost in the shuffle or in the maze of legal jargon.

The fourth reason you need a lawyer is that putting on your case involves more than your personal testimony before the judge. Your case does not involve only your testimony. Your lawyer will need to cross-examine witnesses against you, which means asking critical questions of the police, the store owner, and others who may be testifying against you. Your lawyer will object to the introduction of evidence against you and submit different kinds of motions to the judge. Your lawyer also will have to make an opening statement to tell your basic story to the court and a closing statement to remind the judge or jury of the basic theory of why you are not guilty.

The fifth reason you need a lawyer is that if you lose in court, you will need someone to appeal your case to an appellate court or even the Supreme Court.

In the best of all worlds, your lawyer will be your confidante, your adviser, and your overall champion if you get into trouble. No one wants to be caught up with the law, but if that is where you are, you are in much better shape with a good lawyer than without one.

The Right to Legal Counsel

The U.S. Supreme Court in *Johnson v. Zerbst* stated: "The Sixth Amendment stands as a constant **admonition** that if the constitutional safeguards it provides be lost, justice will not 'still be done.' It embodies a realistic recognition of the obvious truth that the average defendant does not have the professional legal skill to protect himself when brought before a **tribunal** with power to take his life or liberty, wherein the prosecution is presented by experienced and learned counsel." [1]

In every criminal trial, a lawyer stands with the person accused. The defense lawyer advises the accused about his legal rights and ensures that his interests are fully protected. This is what is meant by a right to counsel.

Sometimes lawyers are highly paid private attorneys, sometimes they are public defenders, and sometimes they are private lawyers appointed by the court for people who could not otherwise afford their services. But in every criminal case today, a lawyer stands in court with the person or persons accused of a crime.

This has not always been the case.

Role of Legal Counsel

What does a defense lawyer do? The best way to understand what a defense lawyer does is to follow the path of a simple criminal case.

Imagine that you are eighteen years old and need a new pair of socks. You go to a department store. You find a pair that you like in the sock section, take it off the rack, and then head to the cash register. Because the checkout line in the sock department is too long, you decide to find another cash register. On your way, you duck into the bathroom. You come out with the socks tucked under your arm and are immediately stopped by store security and arrested for attempted shoplifting. The store security officer informs you that because you had taken the socks, concealed them under your arm, had not paid for them, had avoided the nearest cash register, looked suspicious when you entered the bathroom, and still had the socks concealed, he had reason to arrest you. He shows you a copy of the criminal statute that defines "shoplifting" as "taking or concealing possession of personal property of another that was offered for sale knowingly and with the intent to appropriate the property without complete payment for it." The guard refuses to listen to your explanation that you were going to pay for the socks. The police also refuse to listen to you, explaining they must accept the accusations of the store security officer. You are handcuffed, placed in a police car, and taken to a police station. After a night in jail, you meet your court-appointed lawyer. She explains that she has been appointed by the court to represent you and that she has your best interests at heart.

Initial Meeting: Establishment of an Attorney-Client Relationship

Famed defense attorney Clarence Darrow once said:

> Strange as it may seem, I grew to like to defend men and women charged with crime. It soon came to be something more than the winning or losing of a case. I sought to learn why one goes one way and another takes an entirely different road. I became vitally interested in the causes of human conduct. This meant more than the quibbling with lawyers and juries. I was dealing with life, with its hopes and fears, its aspirations, and despairs. With me it was going to the foundation of motive and conduct and adjustments

---

YOUR THOUGHTS

How should a lawyer behave in the first meeting with a client?

---

for human beings, instead of blindly talking of hatred and vengeance, and that subtle, indefinable quality that men call "justice" and of which nothing really is known.[2]

A good defense lawyer will tell you that she works for you and represents your interests.[3] This means she does not follow the government's approach to the case, or accept what the judge wants to happen, or even abide by what your mother wants her to do about the case. Her duty is only to her client: you.

Your lawyer will tell you that everything you tell her remains confidential, that she is forbidden to share anything she learns about your case with other people, and that you can tell her anything without fearing that she will tell anyone. This means you can tell her about the facts of the case without worrying that she will be forced by the court to testify against you. This is called the attorney-client privilege. This allows you to speak freely.

Your attorney will want some information about you. The information will be used to make your case, to win an acquittal, to gain a basic sense about the evidence against you, to get you out of jail if you are being held there, and to understand what your goals are in the case. In interviewing you, the lawyer will try to find out about your family background, your schooling, any prior experience you have had with the criminal justice system, and what happened to land you in trouble.[4] She will use this information to make arguments about your release and to begin an investigation of your case. You have just developed an attorney-client relationship.

In the initial meeting in the imaginary case, you might tell the lawyer about how you were trying to buy some socks when the security guard stopped you. You would explain that you live with your parents and attend the local high school. You would tell her that you have never been in trouble with the law and that you want the lawyer to call your mother and let her know you are all right. The lawyer will use all this information to help the judge understand that you are not a danger to the community, that you have family and friends nearby, and that you would show up to trial without fail.

Continuing Representation: Protection of Rights

Your attorney's principal goal is to protect your freedom and preserve your rights.[5] The U.S. Constitution provides you with rights against self-incrimination and illegal searches. Lawyers can protect these interests by filing written papers with the court (motions) and arguing your position to the judge. Your attorney's goal is to allow you to remain free from jail or the juvenile detention hall. Your lawyer will thus argue for your release back home and to the community.

Your attorney must keep you informed about the progress of your case.[6] After all, it is your case, and your liberty is at stake. Your attorney should make sure to explain the charges against you and the government's evidence. You need to have sufficient information to participate knowingly and intelligently in your defense. For example, you could provide names of witnesses, leads on possible evidence in the case, and ideas for defense strategies. Your attorney should remain in communication with you so that you can play a meaningful role in your own defense and make all the key decisions, such as whether to enter a plea bargain, together.

How should an attorney protect your rights before trial? What should he do on your behalf?

Pretrial Duties: Investigation and Advice

In the socks case, the evidence against you comes from one source—namely, what the security guard claims to have seen. Thus, the security guard and the kind of evidence he has against you must be investigated. Your attorney has a duty to scrutinize all of the alleged facts in the case.[7] Either the lawyer or her investigator should go to the scene of the crime and interview the witnesses, see if a videotape of the incident exists, and determine whether there is any reason to doubt the observations and conclusions of the security guard. For example, what if the guard admits to your lawyer that he saw you only for a few seconds before you came out of the bathroom? What if he admits that he did not watch you at any time in the socks department? What if the security guard was watching another young man who looked like you and was dressed like you and who disappeared into the bathroom minutes before you? What if this particular security guard has made ten false arrests in the past year in the hopes that he could get a better job at a bigger department store? What if he was disciplined recently for lying on his job application?

How should your attorney investigate your case? What should he do to prepare for trial?

Good lawyers do research and never stop looking for facts that will undermine the government's case.

Your lawyer has the duty of advising you of all of your legal options. For example, you could go to trial, you could plead guilty in the hopes of a lighter charge or sentence, or you might be eligible to enter a diversion program in which you would be required to complete some sort of alternative punishment. Depending on the jurisdiction where you are arrested and the offense charged, the options will vary. However, no matter where you are arrested, your lawyer should explain all of the available choices fully and patiently and then give you the final decision about what to do.[8]

Trial

Not every defendant goes to trial; most defendants choose to enter into a plea agreement.[9] But if you do go to trial, your lawyer seeks to win your acquittal by introducing enough evidence to prevent the government from proving beyond a reasonable doubt that you have committed the crime. Your lawyer's argument will take the form of an opening statement, which lays out the defense's theory of the case. When the prosecution puts on its case, your lawyer will question (cross-examine) the government witnesses in an effort to make the judge or jury doubt their story. Suppose the theory of your defense is that you did not have the intent to deprive the store of its property. You would want your lawyer to cross-examine the security guard about the many possible innocent explanations of your actions. How did he know you were not headed back to the cashier line? Was he reading your mind?

YOUR THOUGHTS

What makes a lawyer effective at trial? What are the responsibilities of a lawyer in trial?

When it is your lawyer's turn to present your case, you would want her to present evidence that supports your theory of the case—perhaps the store videotape, which shows you looking normal and not trying to hide anything. Your lawyer might also have you testify about your version of the events, although you do not have to. And that is sometimes risky because you will be cross-examined by the prosecutors. But you will make that decision with your lawyer in advance. Your lawyer would also be able to present a closing argument summarizing the evidence presented to the court in an effort to convince the judge or jury to believe your side. In short, the lawyer will be your advocate to present your side of the story and to battle the government as it tries to convince the judge or jury of your guilt.

Sentencing

After trial, if you are convicted, your lawyer will argue for the most lenient (least harsh) sentence.[10] This means the shortest jail or juvenile reformatory sentence and the most resources, such as drug or alcohol counseling, made available to you through probation (if a probation system is in place in your state). At sentencing, your lawyer will try to emphasize your positive attributes, your family ties, your friends, your accomplishments, your goals, and why you can be a contributing member of society in the future. In short, your lawyer will try to convince the judge that you should be given another opportunity to rehabilitate your life in the community.

YOUR THOUGHTS

What should a lawyer do at sentencing? What is the goal of sentencing? What should you and your lawyer do to prepare for sentencing? What is presented to the judge at sentencing?

A good defense lawyer will do all of the above things in every case. This is what the constitutional right to counsel should mean. But, does it work like that in the real world?

EXERCISE 7.1. The following excerpt from the movie *Slam* involves a conversation between an overworked defense lawyer and a young Washington, D.C., man caught with illegal drugs.[11] In the movie, the young rapper-poet hero, Raymond Joshua, was caught possessing marijuana and faces the decision of whether to accept a plea bargain and definitely go to jail or to go to trial, which offers the chance to avoid prison but also involves the risk of a much longer prison sentence if he is convicted. In his first meeting with his appointed defense lawyer, a real smooth talker, Raymond learns about what his options are. What do you think of this relationship between the lawyer and the accused? Is it good? Is the lawyer doing his job?

LAWYER:

Well, you can get a trial. They call that cop or rock. You can take the cop—we plead—or rock, which means we take you to trial. But if you lose, you're looking at ten. Mandatory. Ten. And you have to do 85 percent of ten. Which means eight and a half years.

RAY:

So wait, if I try to fight it, I have to serve more time for just trying to fight it?

LAWYER:

If you get found guilty, you would. And usually—

The success ratio of convictions in drug cases is about 90 to 95 percent. If they lock up ten people, nine, nine and a half go to jail. But the chances of beating it is like . . . trying to throw a snowball into an elephant's mouth, man, at a hundred feet. You can't make it. You are in trouble. You are a victim of—you are a casualty of war. You got two options—three: You can plead guilty to a simple possession, which is two or three years, you do eighteen months. You can go to trial and run the risk of doing ten years if you get found guilty. Or, you can cooperate, which means you can rat, snitch, blow the whistle on whoever you want to blow it on in order to get out.

RAY:

Cop-cooperate, which I'm not gonna do. You say I can't even fight it 'cause I'll serve more time. This doesn't make any . . . sense. None whatsoever, man. It doesn't make any sense at all. . . .

LAWYER:

I know it sounds like a lot of time, but most guys get a lot longer than that, man. The best I can do is try to get you two to three. Even if you were innocent I could only get you two to three. You are a victim brother. You're black, you're young, you come from the Southeast, you're in the inner city . . . you don't have a chance. Your best chance now is to see how little time can you get before you get back to society. It ain't about beating it. When they lock you up, you dead.

POINTS TO PONDER

- How do you react to this scene? Did the lawyer do what he was supposed to do? Did he establish a good attorney-client relationship? Did he establish trust? Did it seem that he had his client's best interests at heart? Was he zealously advocating Raymond's interests?
- Review what a good lawyer is supposed to do in every case. What did this lawyer do well? What did he do poorly? If you were to use these standards to grade the lawyer, how would he do? What could he improve? If you were given the opportunity to talk to the lawyer, what would you say about his manner and tone? Does he do a good job of describing the plea-bargain process?
- How would you feel if you were Raymond Joshua? Would you have a positive view of your lawyer? Would you see him as your champion?
- Would things have been different if Ray had a high-paid lawyer? How?

Role of the Defense

The defense counsel is supposed to have a singular purpose—to represent the expressed interests of his client to the exclusion of all other goals. This is an ethical duty. In many situations, the defense counsel and client are pitted against all of the power of the police, prosecutors, and the court system. Why does the lawyer have an important role?

Consider the following statement by Justice Byron R. White about the role of the defense counsel from *United States v. Wade.*

> [Defense counsel] must be and is interested in preventing the conviction of the innocent, but, absent a voluntary plea of guilty, we also insist that he defend his client whether he is innocent or guilty. The State has the obligation to present the evidence. Defense counsel need present nothing, even if he knows what the truth is. He need not furnish any witnesses to the police, or reveal any confidences of his client, or furnish any other information to help the prosecution's case. If he can confuse a witness, even a truthful one, or make him appear at a disadvantage, unsure or indecisive, that will be his normal course. Our interest in not convicting the innocent permits counsel to put the State to its proof, to put the State's case in the worst possible light, regardless of what he thinks or knows to be the truth. . . . In this respect, as part of our modified adversary system and as part of the duty imposed on the most honorable defense counsel, we countenance or require conduct, which in many instances has little, if any, relation to the search for truth.[12]

POINTS TO PONDER

- Do you agree that defense lawyers should try to confuse and undermine the state's case even if they know the state is presenting an accurate case? People who disagree with Justice White emphasize that defense lawyers are still officers of the court and should never try to cast doubt on prosecution evidence they know to be accurate. But Professor Alan Dershowitz of Harvard Law School has argued that every defendant deserves the best possible arguments against the government, as long as they are not dishonest, because the system is meant to be adversarial. Where do you come down on this question?
- The adversarial system is based on the idea that the government will present its case and witnesses, the defense will present its case and witnesses, and the judge and jury will be able to sort out the facts to figure out what really happened. Is this a good way for the courts to proceed? Many countries operate on a more inquisitorial model in which the judge and court themselves try to find evidence and facts. Are there any advantages to that system?
- If you were accused of a crime, what kind of lawyer would you want? Go back to the socks case. What would you want to see in your defense lawyer?
- Why shouldn't the defense lawyer have to be concerned with the truth? Is the societal interest in not convicting the innocent a good justification for letting defense lawyers do everything in their power, short of lying, to destroy the government's case?

Powell v. State of Alabama

In 1931 the state of Alabama charged nine black teenagers—the Scottsboro Boys—with raping two white females. Their mistreatment at the hands of the authorities led to multiple legal cases and to the Supreme Court's ruling in *Powell v. Alabama* (1932), which expanded the rights of poor people to representation. Prominent attorney Samuel Liebowitz, seated left with the Scottsboro Boys, handled their appeals. *Source: Brown Brothers, Sterling, Pennsylvania.*

The Sixth Amendment of the Constitution provides that counsel shall be available to the accused. One of the first cases to address the issue was also one of the most sensational cases in American history. It involved nine young African American men falsely accused of a crime who came to face the death penalty.

In a death penalty case, the state is threatening to take away not the defendant's liberty but his life. Thus, nothing could be more serious than a capital case. Yet, before 1932, a criminal defendant facing the death penalty had no constitutional right to an appointed lawyer, and many were sentenced to death without having the benefit of counsel.

It took the famous Scottsboro case for the Supreme Court to determine that a constitutional right to counsel exists in state death penalty trials.[13] In *Powell v. State of Alabama*, the Court held that it was a violation of due process for an individual to be deprived of his Sixth Amendment right to counsel in a capital case.[14]

The *Powell* case arose in Alabama in 1931.[15] Two white women traveling on a train accused nine African American men of raping them. At the time, the state of Alabama

---

YOUR THOUGHTS

If you are facing the death penalty for a crime, should you be entitled to a lawyer paid for by the state? Why? What benefit does a lawyer give you? Why should the state have to pay for it? Where in the Sixth Amendment does it say that the state should pay for your lawyer if you are too poor to afford one?

---

was racially segregated and the Deep South was marked by white supremacy and racial terror and violence. The accused were taken off the train by an all-white lynch mob. The police arrested the young men and held them in jail. Local officials scheduled a trial twelve days later. The accused men had no access to lawyers and could not communicate with their families. On the day of trial, local lawyers appeared in court on their behalf. Their lawyers never investigated the case, met with their clients only one half-hour before the trial started, did not cross-examine the government witnesses, and did not put on a closing argument. Each of the nine defendants was found guilty and sentenced to death.

The case attracted national attention because it was so obvious that the young men had not received anything like a fair trial. Lawyers from civil rights groups got involved in the defense of the now-famous Scottsboro Boys. The case was appealed up to the Supreme Court, which agreed that the accused had not received a fair trial because they had not been represented by competent appointed counsel. Thus, the Supreme Court reversed the convictions, holding that the death penalty sentences of the defendants violated due process. The Due Process Clause of the Fourteenth Amendment prohibits states from depriving individuals of "life, liberty, or property without due process of law." The Court found that people facing the electric chair or other forms of capital punishment must be represented by lawyers. If they are too poor to afford one, the state must provide counsel and pay for it.

———

POWELL ET AL.
V.
STATE OF ALABAMA

Supreme Court of the United States
Nos. 98—100.
Argued October 10, 1932.
Decided November 7, 1932.

Mr. Justice SUTHERLAND delivered the opinion of the Court.

These cases were argued together and submitted for decision as one case. The petitioners, hereinafter referred to as defendants, are [African Americans] charged with the crime of rape, committed upon the persons of two white girls. The crime is said to have been committed on March 25, 1931.

[T]he defendants were tried in three . . . groups, ... Each of the three trials was completed within a single day. Under the Alabama statute the punishment for rape is to be fixed by the jury, and in its discretion may be from ten years imprisonment to death. The juries found defendants guilty and imposed the death penalty upon all.

In this court the judgments are assailed upon the grounds that the defendants, and each of them, were denied due process of law and the equal protection of the laws, in contravention of the

Fourteenth Amendment, specifically as follows[:] . . . [T]hey were denied the right of counsel, with the accustomed incidents of consultation and opportunity of preparation for trial. . . .

The record shows that on the day when the offense is said to have been committed, these defendants, together with a number of other [African Americans], were upon a freight train on its way through Alabama. On the same train were seven white boys and the two white girls. A fight took place between the [African Americans] and the white boys, in the course of which the white boys, with the exception of one named Gilley, were thrown off the train. A message was sent ahead, reporting the fight and asking that every [African American] be gotten off the train. The participants in the fight, and the two girls, were in an open gondola car. The two girls testified that each of them was assaulted by six different [African Americans] in turn, and they identified the seven defendants as having been among the number. None of the white boys was called to testify, with the exception of Gilley, who was called in rebuttal.

Before the train reached Scottsboro, Ala., a sheriff's posse seized the defendants and two other [African American men]. Both girls and the [African Americans] then were taken to Scottsboro, the county seat. Word of their coming and of the alleged assault had preceded them, and they were met at Scottsboro by a large crowd. It does not sufficiently appear that the defendants were seriously threatened with, or that they were actually in danger of, mob violence; but it does appear that the attitude of the community was one of great hostility. The sheriff thought it necessary to call for the militia to assist in safeguarding the prisoners. . . . Soldiers took the defendants to Gadsden for safe-keeping, brought them back to Scottsboro for arraignment, returned them to Gadsden for safe-keeping while awaiting trial, escorted them to Scottsboro for trial a few days later, and guarded the courthouse and grounds at every stage of the proceedings. It is perfectly apparent that the proceedings, from beginning to end, took place in an atmosphere of tense, hostile, and excited public sentiment. During the entire time, the defendants were closely confined or were under military guard. The record does not disclose their ages, except that one of them was nineteen; but the record clearly indicates that most, if not all, of them were youthful, and they are constantly referred to as 'the boys.' They were ignorant and illiterate. All of them were residents of other states, where alone members of their families or friends resided.

[W]e confine ourselves, as already suggested, to the inquiry whether the defendants were in substance denied the right of counsel, and if so, whether such denial infringes the due process clause of the Fourteenth Amendment.

First. The record shows that immediately upon the return of the indictment defendants were arraigned and pleaded not guilty. Apparently they were not asked whether they had, or were able to employ, counsel, or wished to have counsel appointed; or whether they had friends or relatives who might assist in that regard if communicated with. That it would not have been an idle ceremony to have given the defendants reasonable opportunity to communicate with their families and endeavor to obtain counsel is demonstrated by the fact that very soon after conviction, able counsel appeared in their behalf. This was pointed out by Chief Justice Anderson in the course of his dissenting opinion. 'They were nonresidents,' he said, 'and had little time or opportunity to get in touch with their families and friends who were scattered throughout two other states, and time has demonstrated that they could or would have been represented by able counsel had a better opportunity been given by a reasonable delay in the trial of the cases judging from the number and activity of counsel that appeared immediately or shortly after their conviction.'

It is hardly necessary to say that the right to counsel being conceded, a defendant should be afforded a fair opportunity to secure counsel of his own choice. Not only was that not done here, but such designation of counsel as was attempted was either so indefinite or so close upon the trial as to amount to a denial of effective and substantial aid in that regard. This will be amply demonstrated by a brief review of the record. April 6, six days after indictment, the trials began. When the first case was called, the court inquired whether the parties were ready for trial. The state's attorney replied that he was ready to proceed. No one answered for the defendants or appeared to represent or defend them. . . .

It thus will be seen that until the very morning of the trial no lawyer had been named or definitely designated to represent the defendants.

Second. The question . . . which it is our duty, and within our power, to decide, is whether the denial of the assistance of counsel contravenes the due process clause of the Fourteenth Amendment to the Federal Constitution. . . .

The Sixth Amendment, in terms, provides that in all criminal prosecutions the accused shall enjoy the right 'to have the Assistance of Counsel for his defence.'

. . . It never has been doubted by this court, or any other so far as we know, that notice and hearing are preliminary steps essential to the passing of an enforceable judgment, and that they, together with a legally competent tribunal having jurisdiction of the case, constitute basic elements of the constitutional requirement of due process of law. . . .

What, then, does a hearing include? Historically and in practice, in our own country at least, it has always included the right to the aid of counsel when desired and provided by the party asserting the right. The right to be heard would be, in many cases, of little avail if it did not comprehend the right to be heard by counsel. Even the intelligent and educated layman has small and sometimes no skill in the science of law. If charged with crime, he is incapable, generally, of determining for himself whether the indictment is good or bad. He is unfamiliar with the rules of evidence. Left without the aid of counsel he may be put on trial without a proper charge, and convicted upon incompetent evidence, or evidence irrelevant to the issue or otherwise inadmissible. He lacks both the skill and knowledge adequately to prepare his defense, even though he have a perfect one. He requires the guiding hand of counsel at every step in the proceedings against him. Without it, though he be not guilty, he faces the danger of conviction because he does not know how to establish his innocence. If that be true of men of intelligence, how much more true is it of the ignorant and illiterate, or those of feeble intellect. If in any case, civil [or] criminal, a state or federal court were arbitrarily to refuse to hear a party by counsel, employed by and appearing for him, it reasonably may not be doubted that such a refusal would be a denial of a hearing, and, therefore, of due process in the constitutional sense. . . .

In the light of the facts outlined in the forepart of this opinion—the ignorance and illiteracy of the defendants, their youth, the circumstances of public hostility, the imprisonment and the close surveillance of the defendants by the military forces, the fact that their friends and families were all in other states and communication with them necessarily difficult, and above all that they stood in deadly peril of their lives—we think the failure of the trial court to give them reasonable time and opportunity to secure counsel was a clear denial of due process.

But passing that, and assuming their inability, even if opportunity had been given, to employ counsel, as the trial court evidently did assume, we are of opinion that, under the circumstances just stated, the necessity of counsel was so vital and imperative that the failure of the trial court to make an effective appointment of counsel was likewise a denial of due process within the meaning of the Fourteenth Amendment.

. . . To hold otherwise would be to ignore the fundamental postulate, . . . 'that there are certain immutable principles of justice which inhere in the very idea of free government which no member of the Union may disregard.' . . .

The judgments must be reversed and the causes remanded for further proceedings not inconsistent with this opinion.

Judgments reversed.

POINTS TO PONDER

- Do you think the Scottsboro Boys could have gotten a fair trial in Alabama? Why or why not? How do you think the accused felt when they were arrested?
- Why does the Supreme Court consider a lawyer important? What would you expect the lawyer's role to be at a hearing? What could a lawyer have done for these young men?
- What does the Supreme Court consider to be the basic elements of due process? What does the Court mean by "notice"? Why would notice be important? What does the Court mean by a "hearing"? Why is a hearing important?
- The Court makes some less than flattering assessments of the defendants in this case. Do you think the Court's decision would have been different if the defendants were wealthy and educated?
- How could the young men have gotten lawyers appointed for them? As the Court states, they were not from Alabama, they did not have money, and they did not have a way to communicate with their families. How could they have gotten a good lawyer?
- How much of a role do you think race and racism played in the case?

The recognition that legal counsel is necessary in a death penalty case meant that the Scottsboro Boys were granted another trial. A famed civil rights lawyer, Samuel Liebowitz, represented each of the defendants at the new trial. One of the two women victims recanted her story, meaning that she testified that no rape or incident had occurred. Liebowitz was able to cast grave doubt on the medical evidence, bolstering the argument that the women had made up the entire incident. Through questions on cross-examination, he effectively challenged each of the state's witnesses. Despite this strong defense, the all-white jury still convicted the first of the defendants. However, because the evidence had been so discredited at trial, the presiding judge threw out the jury's conviction for not being based on the evidence.

The victory was short-lived. The cases kept getting retried, and because of the racial discrimination and animosity in Alabama, the men could never get a fair trial. Over the next few years, the cases continued to be challenged, but all-white juries kept convicting the young men of a crime they had not committed. Eventually, four of the men were convicted of rape, charges were dropped against four of them, and one was convicted of assault after he stabbed a deputy on his way out of a courthouse.

Gideon v. Wainwright

The Supreme Court in *Powell* held that the Sixth Amendment and the Due Process Clause were violated when the accused did not have government-appointed counsel in a death

When New York attorney Samuel Liebowitz received a call . . . asking him whether he would defend the Scottsboro Boys in their new trials, he was considered by many to be the "new Clarence Darrow," the man to call if you were charged with a capital crime. In over fifteen years of criminal defense work, Liebowitz had represented seventy-eight persons charged with first-degree murder. [None of his clients had ever been convicted.] . . . In the courtroom, Liebowitz was known for his meticulous preparation, knowledge of the law, vibrant voice, and flamboyant style. . . .

After reading the record of the first trials and becoming convinced of the innocence of the Scottsboro Boys, Liebowitz accepted the . . . offer. He did so against the urgings of his wife and many friends who told him that the skin color of the defendants gave them no chance in the Alabama of the 1930's. He would work for the next four years on the cases without pay or reimbursement for most of his expenses.

Liebowitz quickly became an object of loathing around Decatur [Alabama] . . . . One national reporter overheard several people saying, "It'll be a wonder if he gets out of here alive." Five uniformed members of the National Guard were assigned to protect him during the trial, with another 150 available to defend against a possible lynch mob.

Liebowitz was stunned by the jury's guilty verdict in [Haywood] Patterson's 1933 trial. . . . Back in New York after the trial, Liebowitz vowed to defend the Boys "until hell freezes over." Speaking before enthusiastic audiences sometimes numbering in the thousands, he promised to take guilty verdicts to the Supreme Court and back until Alabama finally gives up. . . . Liebowitz's determined efforts won the affection of his clients. . . .

After his work on the Scottsboro Boys case was finished, Liebowitz returned to his New York practice, then was appointed to serve as a justice on the Supreme Court of New York. Liebowitz died in January, 1978.

—Douglas O. Linder, "The Trials of 'The Scottsboro Boys,' " available at http://www.law.umkc.edu/faculty/projects/FTrials/scottsboro/SB_bLieb.html (accessed January 29, 2005).

penalty case. What about cases in which imprisonment, but not death, is the punishment? The vast majority of cases do not involve the death penalty. What about the right to lawyers in these cases?

Up to 1963, people accused of crimes, even serious felonies, did not get a lawyer unless they could afford to hire one. The courts interpreted the Constitution's right to counsel language only as protecting the right to bring your own lawyer to trial, not as an affirmative requirement that the state provide a lawyer free of charge. This view changed when a poor, uneducated prisoner named Clarence Earl Gideon sat down in his jail cell and wrote a letter to the U.S. Supreme Court demanding that his conviction be reversed

---

YOUR THOUGHTS

Should people be entitled to get a free defense lawyer for all crimes? What about less serious crimes? Who should pay for the lawyer? Why should society pay for the defense of someone who allegedly broke the law?

---

because he did not have a lawyer at trial. The door thus was opened for any poor criminal defendant to have a government-appointed lawyer at a felony trial.

The Case. The story of Clarence Earl Gideon shows that individuals who stand up for their rights can make a difference in the justice system. Gideon was poor, carried a lengthy criminal record, and had no legal education. As he was described by Anthony Lewis, a famed news reporter who wrote a book on Gideon's case:

> [T]hose who had known [Gideon], even the men who had arrested him and those who were now his jailers, considered Gideon a perfectly harmless human being, rather likeable, but one tossed aside by life. Anyone meeting him for the first time would be likely to regard him as the most wretched of men. And yet a flame still burned in Clarence Earl Gideon. He had not given up caring about life or freedom; he had not lost his sense of injustice.[16]

While in prison, Clarence Earl Gideon penned this handwritten petition to the Supreme Court challenging his conviction. Because he was impoverished, Gideon had been unable to afford a defense attorney to represent him at trial. The Court took his case and ruled unanimously in 1963 that every state must provide lawyers to poor people charged with felony crimes. *Source: National Archives*

Gideon was accused of breaking into and trying to steal money from a poolroom in Florida. He was arrested and brought to trial in Florida State court. Because he was poor, he could not afford to hire a lawyer.[17]

The judge denied Gideon's request for a lawyer and forced him to represent himself. He was found guilty and sentenced to five years imprisonment. While he was in jail, he wrote the Supreme Court a letter asking the justices to overturn his conviction as a violation of due process, because he had been denied the right to counsel.

The Supreme Court received and read the letter. Because Gideon could not represent himself in front of the Supreme Court, the Court appointed Abe Fortas, a brilliant lawyer and future Supreme Court justice, to argue his case. After listening to Fortas's constitutional arguments, the Court decided in favor of Gideon, establishing the constitutional right to appointed counsel in all felony cases.[18]

The Ruling. The Court held that all persons, regardless of the financial situation, deserve a lawyer when charged with a felony offense.

CLARENCE EARL GIDEON, PETITIONER,

v.

LOUIE L. WAINWRIGHT, DIRECTOR, DIVISION OF CORRECTIONS

Supreme Court of the United States
No. 155.
Argued Jan. 15, 1963.
Decided March 18, 1963.

Mr. Justice BLACK delivered the opinion of the Court.

Petitioner was charged in a Florida state court with having broken and entered a poolroom with intent to commit a misdemeanor. This offense is a felony under Florida law. Appearing in court without funds and without a lawyer, petitioner asked the court to appoint counsel for him, where-upon the following colloquy took place:

> The COURT: Mr. Gideon, I am sorry, but I cannot appoint Counsel to represent you in this case. Under the laws of the State of Florida, the only time the Court can appoint Counsel to represent a Defendant is when that person is charged with a capital offense. I am sorry, but I will have to deny your request to appoint Counsel to defend you in this case.
> The DEFENDANT: The United States Supreme Court says I am entitled to be represented by Counsel.

Put to trial before a jury, Gideon conducted his defense about as well as could be expected from a layman. He made an opening statement to the jury, cross-examined the State's witnesses, presented witnesses in his own defense, declined to testify himself, and made a short argument 'emphasizing his innocence to the charge contained in the Information filed in this case.' The jury returned a verdict of guilty, and petitioner was sentenced to serve five years in the state prison. . . .

II

The Sixth Amendment provides, "In all criminal prosecutions, the accused shall enjoy the right * * * to have the Assistance of Counsel for his defence." We have construed this to mean that in federal courts counsel must be provided for defendants unable to employ counsel unless the right is competently and intelligently waived. . . .

[R]eason and reflection require us to recognize that in our adversary system of criminal justice, any person haled into court, who is too poor to hire a lawyer, cannot be assured a fair trial unless counsel is provided for him. This seems to us to be an obvious truth. Governments, both state and federal, quite properly spend vast sums of money to establish machinery to try defendants accused of crime. Lawyers to prosecute are everywhere deemed essential to protect the public's interest in an orderly society. Similarly, there are few defendants charged with crime, few indeed, who fail to hire the best lawyers they can get to prepare and present their defenses. That government hires lawyers to prosecute and defendants who have the money hire lawyers to defend are the strongest indications of the wide-spread belief that lawyers in criminal courts are necessities, not luxuries. The right of one charged with crime to counsel may not be deemed fundamental and essential to fair trials in some countries, but it is in ours. From the very beginning, our state and national constitutions and laws have laid great emphasis on procedural and substantive safeguards designed to assure fair trials before impartial tribunals in which every defendant stands equal before the law. This noble ideal cannot be realized if the poor man charged with crime has to face his accusers without a lawyer to assist him. . . .

The judgment is reversed and the cause is remanded to the Supreme Court of Florida for further action not inconsistent with this opinion.

Reversed.

Mr. Justice CLARK, concurring in the result.

. . . That the Sixth Amendment requires appointment of counsel in 'all criminal prosecutions' is clear, both from the language of the Amendment and from this Court's interpretation. See *Johnson v. Zerbst,* 304 U.S. 458, (1938). It is equally clear from the above cases, all decided after *Betts v. Brady,* 316 U.S. 455 (1942), that the Fourteenth Amendment requires such appointment in all prosecutions for capital crimes. The Court's decision today, then, does no more than erase a distinction which has no basis in logic and an increasingly eroded basis in authority.

. . . I must conclude here . . . that the Constitution makes no distinction between capital and noncapital cases. The Fourteenth Amendment requires due process of law for the deprival of 'liberty' just as for deprival of 'life,' and there cannot constitutionally be a difference in the quality of the process based merely upon a supposed difference in the sanction involved. How can the Fourteenth Amendment tolerate a procedure which it condemns in capital cases on the ground that deprival of liberty may be less onerous than deprival of life—a value judgment not universally accepted—or that only the latter deprival is irrevocable? I can find no acceptable rationalization for such a result, and I therefore concur in the judgment of the Court.

The Retrial. The Supreme Court reversed Gideon's conviction, giving him a second chance to prove his innocence at trial. This time Gideon had a lawyer, a good one named Fred Turner. At the retrial, Turner was able to undermine the two most damaging pieces of evidence against Gideon. Through cross-examination, he showed that the state's chief eyewitness was the likely thief. Gideon was found not guilty and allowed to leave the courtroom as a free man.

POINTS TO PONDER

- Today's robust Sixth Amendment right to counsel began with a letter from a prisoner, not a lawyer or a law professor. Does this suggest that Americans all have power to effect change in our system of rights under the Constitution?
- The Supreme Court bases its conclusion, in part, on the fact that the United States has an adversarial system that cannot work unless both sides are represented. In other words, the American system of justice

presumes two equal adversaries in court, the defense lawyer and the prosecutor. Do you agree? Why would it be important to have equal legal knowledge and power on both sides?

- The Supreme Court says that lawyers are necessities and not luxuries. Is that true in all kinds of cases, such as contracts, disputes over wills, parking ticket appeals, and divorces? If so, why is the right to appointed counsel limited to criminal cases?

- Why shouldn't someone accused of a crime have to pay for a lawyer? If you have money, you have to pay for a lawyer. Why should someone without money not have to pay for the same services? Why should you, or your parents, or other taxpayers have to pay for an impoverished defendant?

- What do you think of the "noble ideal" that poor men and women charged with crime should be in the same situation as rich men and women?

The result in *Gideon* was limited to felony cases. However, in subsequent cases, the Supreme Court has recognized a constitutional right to counsel in any and all cases in which the accused is facing imprisonment. In addition, the Court in *Douglas v. California* found a constitutional right to an appointed lawyer on a first criminal appeal.[19]

Following is an excerpt from a speech delivered by Attorney General Robert F. Kennedy to the New England Law Institute on November 1, 1963.

If an obscure Florida convict named Clarence Earl Gideon had not sat down in his prison cell with a pen and paper to write a letter to the Supreme Court, and if the Court had not taken the trouble to look for merit in that one crude petition among all the bundles of mail it must receive every day, the vast machinery of American law would have gone on functioning undisturbed.

But Gideon did write that letter; the Court did look into his case; he was retried with the help of competent defense counsel, found not guilty and released from prison after two years of punishment for a crime he did not commit—and the whole course of American legal history has been changed.

—Landmark Supreme Court Cases, "*Gideon v. Wainwright* (1963)," available at http://www.landmarkcases.org/gideon/home.html (accessed January 30, 2005).

Right to Counsel for Juveniles

The Sixth Amendment protects the right to counsel for adults. What about juveniles, people under the age of eighteen? Do young people charged with crimes in the juvenile justice system also have a constitutional right to appointed counsel?

The Supreme Court has said that juveniles are entitled to counsel and must be informed of their right to counsel in all juvenile delinquency hearings. A juvenile delinquency hearing is a legal proceeding, like a criminal trial, for persons under the age of eighteen. Being found delinquent in a juvenile case is the equivalent of being found guilty in an adult case. While juveniles can waive the right to counsel, meaning that they can give up the right to a lawyer, courts must at least give young people the option of having a lawyer present.

Born in Memphis, Tennessee, June 9, 1910, Abe Fortas was the youngest of five children. Because of his remarkable skills as a debater, he decided on a career in the law. [He] entered Yale Law School [and] became . . . editor-in-chief of the prestigious *Yale Law Journal.* He graduated second in his class in 1933.

In July 1965 President [Lyndon B.] Johnson . . . offered the post [of Supreme Court justice] informally to Fortas, who declined. Nevertheless, an insistent president nominated Fortas, without securing his acceptance.

[Fortas] provided the decisive fifth vote for Chief Justice Earl Warren's majority opinion in *Miranda v. Arizona* (1966), the landmark case that required law enforcement officers to inform suspects of their constitutional rights prior to questioning. Fortas was particularly concerned with expanding the rights of juveniles. Writing for the Court in 1967, he held in *In re Gault* that the privilege against self-incrimination and the right to counsel extended to juvenile court proceedings. He insisted that "under our Constitution, the condition of being a boy does not justify a kangaroo court."

In one of his last and most famous opinions, *Tinker v. Des Moines Independent Community School District* (1969), Fortas wrote that the wearing of black armbands by students protesting the Vietnam War was "closely akin" to the "pure speech" protected by the First Amendment. Consequently, such public expression of opinion was entitled to constitutional protection as a form of peaceful and nondisruptive "symbolic" speech as long as it did not violate the rights of others.

[Facing a scandal] Fortas resigned from the Court on May 14, 1969. In a letter to Chief Justice Warren, he denied any wrongdoing but explained that he wanted to let the Court "proceed with its vital work free from extraneous stress."

Excerpted from "Fortas, Abe, Supreme Court Historical Society Biography," CQ Electronic Library, CQ Supreme Court Collection. Originally published in *The Supreme Court Justices: Illustrated Biographies, 1789–1995,* ed. Clare Cushman (Washington, D.C.: CQ Press, 1995), available at http://library.cqpress.com/scc/scjbio-0012629725 (accessed March 14, 2005). Photo from the Collection of the Supreme Court of the United States.

Juveniles have not always had a right to counsel. This was true even though sometimes the punishments for juveniles were harsh and resulted in a lengthy loss of freedom. In *In Re Gault,* the Supreme Court decided that juveniles should have the right to legal counsel in all hearings that might result in the loss of their liberty.[20] For the Court, it was a matter of fundamental fairness necessary to ensure due process of law.

Should young people charged with crimes in the juvenile justice system be given free lawyers? What about if they are not facing jail time? The juvenile justice system developed differently from the adult system. Because juveniles were treated less harshly than adults, it was thought that they might not need the same legal protections in court. For example, if a young girl was caught stealing a candy bar, the legal system did not think it necessary to appoint a lawyer to defend her. The thought was that the judge could handle the punishment without the interference of a lawyer. Do you agree? Does it depend on the potential consequences? Does it depend on the type of crime?

The Case of Gerald Gault

Gerald Gault was fifteen years old when he found himself in the midst of what became one of the most important legal cases of the twentieth century.[21] Gerald and a friend were arrested after a female neighbor complained to police about an obscene phone call. Gerald and his friend were suspected of the call. Police took Gerald into custody without telling his parents or informing any family member. He spent the night in the juvenile detention hall. The next day, Gerald appeared before a juvenile judge. He was not represented by a lawyer. At the hearing, no witnesses appeared to testify against Gerald. The state did not provide any notice of the facts about why Gerald was arrested. No record was kept of the testimony. The judge asked Gerald some questions about the phone call. Gerald was never informed of his right to counsel, his right against self-incrimination, or any other rights. Based on Gerald's answers, the judge ordered a second hearing a week later. Gerald was sent to juvenile hall. At the second hearing, again the female neighbor did not appear. Despite conflicting evidence about Gerald's role in the phone call, he was found guilty

A defense attorney explains the right to counsel to a ten-year-old boy appearing at a hearing in a Milwaukee County Children's Courtroom in October 2002. *Source: Allen Fredrickson/Reuters/Landov*

(delinquent) and sent to the state juvenile reformatory for a period of six years, until he turned twenty-one.

Gerald challenged the constitutionality of these proceedings before the Supreme Court. The Court agreed that what happened to Gerald was "fundamentally unfair." It held that certain protections needed to be in place in juvenile delinquency hearings. At a minimum, the Court found, juveniles are entitled to assistance of counsel, notice of the charges against them, the right to confront witnesses against them, and the protection against self-incrimination.

—•—

APPLICATION OF PAUL L. GAULT AND MARJORIE GAULT, FATHER AND MOTHER OF GERALD FRANCIS GAULT, A MINOR, APPELLANTS

Supreme Court of the United States
No. 116.
Argued December 6, 1966.
Decided May 15, 1967.

Mr. Justice FORTAS delivered the opinion of the Court.

I

On Monday, June 8, 1964, at about 10 a.m., Gerald Francis Gault and a friend, Ronald Lewis, were taken into custody by the Sheriff of Gila County. . . . The police action on June 8 was taken as the result of a verbal complaint by a neighbor of the boys, Mrs. Cook, about a telephone call made to her in which the caller or callers made lewd or indecent remarks. It will suffice for purposes of this opinion to say that the remarks or questions put to her were of the irritatingly offensive, adolescent, sex variety.

At the time Gerald was picked up, his mother and father were both at work. No notice that Gerald was being taken into custody was left at the home. No other steps were taken to advise them that their son had, in effect, been arrested. Gerald was taken to the Children's Detention Home. When his mother arrived home at about 6 o'clock, Gerald was not there. Gerald's older brother was sent to look for him at the trailer home of the Lewis family. He apparently learned then that Gerald was in custody. He so informed his mother. The two of them went to the Detention Home. The deputy probation officer, Flagg, who was also superintendent of the Detention Home, told Mrs. Gault 'why Jerry was there' and said that a hearing would be held in Juvenile Court at 3 o'clock the following day, June 9. . . .

On June 9, Gerald, his mother, his older brother, and Probation Officers Flagg and Henderson appeared before the Juvenile Judge in chambers. Gerald's father was not there. He was at work out of the city. Mrs. Cook, the complainant, was not there. No one was sworn at this hearing. No transcript or recording was made. No memorandum or record of the substance of the proceedings was prepared. Our information about the proceedings and the subsequent hearing on June 15, derives entirely from the testimony of the Juvenile Court Judge, Mr. and Mrs. Gault and Officer Flagg at the habeas corpus proceeding [a separate review hearing] conducted two months later. From this, it appears that at the June 9 hearing Gerald was questioned by the judge about the telephone call. There was conflict as to what he said. His mother recalled that Gerald said he only dialed Mrs. Cook's number and handed the telephone to his friend, Ronald. Officer Flagg recalled that Gerald had admitted making the lewd remarks. Judge McGhee testified that Gerald 'admitted making one of these (lewd) statements.' At the conclusion of the hearing, the judge said he would 'think about it.' Gerald was taken back to the Detention Home. He was not sent to his own home with his parents. On June 11 or 12, after having been detained since June 8, Gerald was released and driven home. There is no explanation in the record as to why he was kept in the Detention Home or why he was released. At 5 p.m. on the day of Gerald's release, Mrs. Gault received a note signed by Officer Flagg. It was on plain paper, not letterhead. Its entire text was as follows:

Mrs. Gault:

Judge McGHEE has set Monday June 15, 1964 at 11:00 A.M. as the date and time for further Hearings on Gerald's delinquency
'/s/ Flagg'

At the appointed time on Monday, June 15, Gerald, his father and mother, Ronald Lewis and his father, and Officers Flagg and Henderson were present before Judge McGhee. Witnesses at the . . . proceeding differed in their recollections of Gerald's testimony at the June 15 hearing. Mr. and Mrs. Gault recalled that Gerald again testified that he had only dialed the number and that the other boy had made the remarks. Officer Flagg agreed that at this hearing Gerald did not admit making the lewd remarks. But Judge McGhee recalled that 'there was some admission again of some of the lewd statements. He—he didn't admit any of the more serious lewd statements.' Again, the complainant, Mrs. Cook, was not present. Mrs. Gault asked that Mrs. Cook be present 'so she could see which boy that done the talking, the dirty talking over the phone.' The Juvenile Judge said 'she didn't have to be present at that hearing.' The judge did not speak to Mrs. Cook or communicate with her at any time. Probation Officer Flagg had talked to her once—over the telephone on June 9.

At this June 15 hearing a 'referral report' made by the probation officers was filed with the court, although not disclosed to Gerald or his parents. This listed the charge as 'Lewd Phone Calls.' At the conclusion of the hearing, the judge committed Gerald as a juvenile delinquent to the State Industrial School 'for the period of his minority (that is, until 21), unless sooner discharged by due process of law.' An order to that effect was entered. It recites that 'after a full hearing and due deliberation the Court finds that said minor is a delinquent child, and that said minor is of the age of 15 years.'

II

. . . We do not in this opinion consider the impact of these constitutional provisions upon the totality of the relationship of the juvenile and the state. . . . We consider only the problems presented to us by this case. These relate to the proceedings by which a determination is made as to whether a juvenile is a 'delinquent' as a result of alleged misconduct on his part, with the consequence that he may be committed to a state institution. As to these proceedings, there appears to be little current dissent from the proposition that the Due Process Clause has a role to play. The problem is to ascertain the precise impact of the due process requirement upon such proceedings. . . .

[W]e confront the reality of that portion of the Juvenile Court process with which we deal in this case. A boy is charged with misconduct. The boy is committed to an institution where he may be restrained of liberty for years. It is of no constitutional consequence—and of limited practical meaning—that the institution to which he is committed is called an Industrial School. The fact of the matter is that, however euphemistic the title, a 'receiving home' or an 'industrial school' for juveniles is an institution of confinement in which the child is incarcerated for a greater or lesser time. . . .

In view of this, it would be extraordinary if our Constitution did not require the procedural regularity and the exercise of care implied in the phrase 'due process.' Under our Constitution, the condition of being a boy does not justify a kangaroo court.

. . . If Gerald had been over 18, he would not have been subject to Juvenile Court proceedings. For the particular offense immediately involved, the maximum punishment would have been a fine of $5 to $50, or imprisonment in jail for not more than two months. Instead, he was committed to custody for a maximum of six years. If he had been over 18 and had committed an offense to which such a sentence might apply, he would have been entitled to substantial rights under the Constitution of the United States as well as under Arizona's laws and constitution. . . .

We now turn to the specific issues which are presented to us in the present case.

III
NOTICE OF CHARGES

. . . No notice was given to Gerald's parents when he was taken into custody on Monday, June 8. On that night, when Mrs. Gault went to the Detention Home, she was orally informed that there would be a hearing the next afternoon and was told the reason why Gerald was in custody. The only written notice Gerald's parents received at any time was a note on plain paper from Officer Flagg delivered on Thursday or Friday, June 11 or 12, to the effect that the judge had set Monday, June 15, 'for further Hearings on Gerald's delinquency.'

. . . Notice, to comply with due process requirements, must be given sufficiently in advance of scheduled court proceedings so that reasonable opportunity to prepare will be afforded, and it must 'set forth the alleged misconduct with particularity.' . . .

IV
RIGHT TO COUNSEL

. . . There is no material difference in this respect between adult and juvenile proceedings of the sort here involved. In adult proceedings, this contention has been foreclosed by decisions of this Court. A proceeding where the issue is whether the child will be found to be 'delinquent' and subjected to the loss of his liberty for years is comparable in seriousness to a felony prosecution. The juvenile needs the assistance of counsel to cope with problems of law, to make skilled inquiry into the facts, to insist upon regularity of the proceedings, and to ascertain whether he has a defense and to prepare and submit it. The child 'requires the guiding hand of counsel at every step in the proceedings against him.' . . .

We conclude that the Due Process Clause of the Fourteenth Amendment requires that in respect of proceedings to determine delinquency which may result in commitment to an institution in which the juvenile's freedom is curtailed, the child and his parents must be notified of the child's right to be represented by counsel retained by them, or if they are unable to afford counsel, that counsel will be appointed to represent the child. . . .

Our first question, then, is whether Gerald's admission [about the lewd phone calls to the authorities] was improperly obtained and relied on as the basis of decision, in conflict with the Federal Constitution. . . . Specifically, the question is whether, in such a proceeding, an admission by the juvenile may be used against him in the absence of clear and unequivocal evidence that the admission was made with knowledge that he was not obliged to speak and would not be penalized for remaining silent. . . .

It would indeed be surprising if the privilege against self-incrimination were available to hardened criminals but not to children. The language of the Fifth Amendment, applicable to the States by operation of the Fourteenth Amendment, is unequivocal and without exception. And the scope of the privilege is comprehensive. . . .

It would be entirely unrealistic to carve out of the Fifth Amendment all statements by juveniles on the ground that these cannot lead to 'criminal' involvement. In the first place, juvenile proceedings to determine 'delinquency,' which may lead to commitment to a state institution, must be regarded as 'criminal' for purposes of the privilege against self-incrimination. . . .

We conclude that the constitutional privilege against self-incrimination is applicable in the case of juveniles as it is with respect to adults. . . .

The 'confession' of Gerald Gault was first obtained by Officer Flagg, out of the presence of Gerald's parents, without counsel and without advising him of his right to silence, as far as appears. . . .

For the reasons stated, the judgment of the Supreme Court of Arizona is reversed and the cause remanded for further proceedings not inconsistent with this opinion. It is so ordered.

Judgment reversed and cause remanded with directions.

A court convicted Gorman Roberts in 2002 for drowning a five-year-old autistic boy in Fort Lauderdale, Florida. In May 2004, an appellate court overturned Roberts' conviction, ruling that detectives did not inform Roberts, then a seventeen-year-old with an IQ of 67, that he could have an attorney present before and during questioning. After the state supreme court refused to hear the case in January 2005, prosecutors dropped the charges against Roberts, citing lack of evidence without the elicited statement. *Source: J. Pat Carter/AP Wide World Photos*

- Do you think the trial judge in *Gault* was fair in his sentencing of Gerald? Do you think that six years in the juvenile detention facility (the State Industrial School) was an appropriate punishment for the phone call?
- What would a lawyer have done during the hearing that Gerald was not able to do? Do you think there would have been a different outcome? Why?
- What does the Court mean by the term "due process"? What process was due to Gerald? Why are procedural protections important? Why did the Supreme Court compare the proceedings with a kangaroo court?
- What is the value of notice? What does it mean to have notice of a hearing?
- What does the "guiding hand of counsel" mean? Why did the Court think this was important?[22]

Juvenile Waiver of Right to Counsel

Juveniles have the right to counsel at a hearing to determine their delinquency (guilt) or innocence. They also have the choice to go forward without a lawyer. This is called waiving the right to counsel. It means that you face the judge alone, without a lawyer.

Why would someone waive a right to counsel in a case that might result in lengthy incarceration at a juvenile facility? Why would anyone give up his constitutional rights? What might happen during a court hearing that would cause a young person to give up those rights?

The answer is that many times juveniles do not know their rights or do not understand the consequences of waiving the right to an attorney. Moreover, sometimes judges do not encourage young people to have legal counsel. The result is that, oftentimes, free legal services are not made adequately available to juveniles.

In the following examples, trial courts found that a juvenile adequately waived the right to counsel. Do you agree with the trial court that a valid waiver of the right to counsel existed? Or was something else going on?

G. L. D. A young boy, G. L. D., was charged with a crime. When asked if he wanted a lawyer appointed to represent him, he initially told the court yes, he did want a lawyer. The judge then explained that because he wanted a lawyer to be appointed, he would

What do you think juveniles know about their right to a lawyer? How many juveniles know about it? Do you think misunderstanding or a lack of understanding of the Constitution may result in young people mistakenly giving up their rights?

have to give the guitar and amplifier he had in his possession to the court in partial payment for the lawyer's fee. Upon hearing that, the boy told the judge that he did not want a lawyer. The boy then proceeded without a lawyer and was found delinquent. He was sent to the state detention facility.[23] See *In re G. L. D.*, 442 So. 2d 401 (Fla. 2d DCA 1983).

R. S. B. A young boy, R. S. B., was charged with burglary. He appeared with his father in the juvenile court without a lawyer. The young man told the judge that he did not want to proceed without a lawyer. The father then explained how they had tried to get a lawyer and had spoken to three lawyers who all had conflicts for the hearing date. The father also explained that he hoped the court would appoint a public defender for his son. The court treated the absence of counsel as a waiver of counsel and went ahead with the full hearing. R. S. B. was found guilty and sent to a state detention facility.[24] See *In re R. S. B.*, 498 N.W. 2d 646 (SD 1993).

Carlos Rodriquez. At age fifteen, Carlos Rodriquez was arrested for a series of crimes. Police officers mistakenly told Carlos that his mother had the right to decide whether he should speak to police or have an attorney present. Carlos's mother decided he should waive his right to a lawyer. She did so after having a conversation in Spanish with police officers. Carlos did not speak Spanish as a first language. In addition, he had repeated eighth grade and dropped out of school in ninth grade. The question was whether Carlos had waived his right to an attorney. The trial court accepted the waiver as a valid one. See *State v. Rodriguez*, 559 S.E. 2d 435 (Ga. 2002).

N. M. N. M., a fifteen-year-old girl, was charged in a robbery. She appeared before the judge with her mother and the following conversation took place.

> Court: [N. M.], you have a number of rights that are guaranteed to you in this matter. The first of these rights that you have, you have the right to have an attorney. Do you wish to have an attorney in this case?
> [N. M.]: No.
> The Court: No what?
> [N. M.]: No sir, I don't, I don't need an attorney.
> The Court: Oh you don't, alright. Mom, you think your daughter needs a lawyer here?
> [Ms. Magness]: No sir she . . . she knows.
> The Court: All right, we'll show knowing lawful waiver of counsel in this matter.

POINTS TO PONDER

- In each case, the trial judge was satisfied with the waiver of the right to counsel. Do you agree? Why or why not?
- Did these children knowingly give up their right to counsel? Was it a fair choice? What does "knowing" mean in this situation? Does it take into account the reality of the situation?
- What are the other pressures on the juvenile?

- How do money and a family's financial ability to pay for a lawyer factor into a knowing waiver? Do you think that if G. L. D. had money to buy another guitar, he might have made a different decision? Had R. S. B.'s father hired his son a lawyer, would the proceeding have had a different result?
- What about the role of parents? Whose decision should it be when a juvenile waives the right to counsel, the youngster or the parents? Do you think that Carlos Rodriquez or N. M. felt that they could disagree with their parents? Do you think that most children would defer to the wishes of their parents?
- What rules should be in place before a juvenile gives up the right to a lawyer? Who should be consulted? Parents? Teachers? Lawyers? Do you need to talk with a lawyer before you give up a right to a lawyer?
- Do you fault the judge in these cases for allowing the children to proceed without a lawyer? Shouldn't the judge know the Constitution and know that the child probably does not know the Constitution? What incentive does the judge have to have the child proceed without a lawyer?
- Now that you know your rights, would you ever waive your right to a lawyer? When? How would you respond to the judge in each of the cases?

The court was satisfied with this waiver, and N. M. was sent to the state girls school for twenty-four months. The issue at hand was whether the waiver was valid. See *N. M. v. Indiana*, 791 N.E. 2d 802 (Ind. App. 2003).

In each of the juvenile waiver examples discussed above, the court of appeals decided that the juvenile in question had *not* knowingly or intelligently waived the right to counsel. In each case, the court of appeals reversed the decision of the trial court, saying that the issue was wrongly decided and ordered new hearings with counsel present. The courts obviously take the right to a lawyer very seriously.

Right to Effective Counsel

The Constitution grants all citizens the right to counsel in a criminal trial. But what kind of lawyer do you get? What if your lawyer is lazy, inexperienced, drunk, or incompetent? What if your lawyer sleeps through your trial? What if your lawyer is too busy with other cases and clients?

The answer given by the Supreme Court is that you are not entitled to a good lawyer or even a somewhat good lawyer. All that the Constitution protects against is having a legally ineffective lawyer. What does this mean? Why would the Supreme Court set the standard so low?

One of the justifications for this low standard for ineffectiveness is that otherwise it would be too easy for convicted defendants to claim their lawyer was bad and get a new trial on appeal. In every trial, defense lawyers make tactical decisions—some good, some bad—and the Supreme Court did not want appellate courts (higher courts) second-

---

YOUR THOUGHTS

Should the Sixth Amendment right to counsel mean that you get a good lawyer appointed by the state? Should the Constitution protect you against a bad lawyer?

---

guessing these decisions. Thus, the Sixth Amendment guarantees you a lawyer, but the quality of that lawyer need only be somewhat more than ineffective.

Test of Ineffectiveness

In *Strickland v. Washington,* the Supreme Court provided a two-part test for ineffective assistance of counsel.[25] Simply put, you must show that your lawyer made mistakes that other lawyers would not make and that these mistakes negatively affected the outcome of your trial. In lawyer terms, you must show deficient performance and prejudice.

Deficient Performance. To satisfy the first prong of this test, you must overcome the strong presumption that your lawyer's conduct falls within the wide range of reasonable professional assistance. What this means is that you have to show that your lawyer did things that no other lawyer would do or failed to do things that every other lawyer would do. For example, if your lawyer was asleep during trial, you have to show that it is uncommon for lawyers to sleep during trial and that such conduct is unprofessional. (That should not be too hard.)

Prejudice. To satisfy the second prong, you must show that a reasonable probability existed that, but for your lawyer's unprofessional errors, the result of the proceeding would have been different. This means that you have to show that the bad lawyering made a real difference. For example, if your lawyer fell asleep in trial, you have to show that sleeping caused him to miss the opportunity to object to a key piece of evidence that should not have been admitted but was vital to the government's case against you.

EXERCISE 7.2. To understand this standard, apply it to the following examples of ineffective assistance, which were taken from a dissent written by Justice Harry A. Blackmun in *McFarland v. Scott.*[26] Consider two questions: Do you think that the lawyers were ineffective? Do you think that their actions prejudiced their clients?

John Young was represented in his capital trial by an attorney who was addicted to drugs and who, a few weeks after Young's trial, was sent to jail himself on federal drug charges. The Court of Appeals for the Eleventh Circuit rejected Young's ineffective assistance of counsel claim, in *Young v. Zant.*[27] Young was executed in 1985.

John Smith and his codefendant, Rebecca Machetti, were sentenced to death by juries selected under the same flawed Georgia statute. Machetti's attorneys successfully challenged the statute under a Supreme Court decision, *Taylor v. Louisiana,* winning Machetti a new trial and ultimately a life sentence, in *Machetti v. Linahan.*[28] For some reason, Smith's counsel was completely unaware of the Supreme Court decision and failed to file the necessary objection at trial. See *Smith v. Kemp.*[29] Because of this failure, Smith did not get the benefit of the Court's change in the law and was executed in 1983.

Jesus Romero's attorney did not present any evidence at the sentencing phase of Romero's capital trial and delivered a closing argument totaling twenty-nine words. Although the attorney later was suspended (on different charges), Romero's ineffective assistance claim was rejected by the Court of Appeals for the Fifth Circuit, in *Romero v. Lynaugh.*[30] Romero was executed in 1992.

Larry Heath was represented on direct appeal by counsel who filed a six-page written argument before the Alabama Court of Criminal Appeals. The attorney failed to appear for oral argument before the Alabama Supreme Court and instead filed a one-page written argument citing a single case. The Eleventh Circuit, in *Heath v. Jones,* found no prejudice and thus no ineffective assistance of counsel.[31] Heath was executed in 1992.

James Messer, a mentally impaired defendant facing the death penalty, was represented by an attorney who at trial presented no defense, made no objections, and emphasized the horror of the crime in his closing statement. At the sentencing phase, the attorney presented no evidence of mental impairment, failed to introduce other substantial mitigating evidence, and repeatedly suggested in closing that death was the appropriate punishment in the case. The Eleventh Circuit refused to grant relief, in *Messer v. Kemp.*[32] Messer was executed in 1988.

POINTS TO PONDER

- Do you think the promise of *Gideon* has been realized in these cases? Is it enough to have a lawyer with you even if that lawyer is not doing his job?
- Many of the appeals courts did not seem to care about dismal performances by lawyers because the defendants seemed to be guilty. Should that sort of reasoning influence a court's judgment of whether a lawyer's performance was ineffective or not? Should anyone care about guilty people who have ineffective lawyers?
- Review the role of the defense lawyer. Did these defense lawyers do enough for their clients?
- What is your reaction to the following statement?

  The vice-president of the Georgia Trial Lawyers Association once described the standard for competence of counsel in Georgia counties and the "mirror test." You put a mirror under the court-appointed attorney's nose, and if the mirror clouds up, that's adequate counsel. His statement was prompted by instances such as one a couple of years ago when it was discovered on the second day of trial that the wrong defendant had been brought to court for trial. Defense counsel had failed to recognize that the person seated next to him at the counsel table was not his client; he had dismissed the man's repeated assertions of "not me" as protestations of innocence.[33]

Reality of Ineffective Counsel

In the above examples, the lawyers unquestionably did not do their jobs. Fortunately, some were removed from the practice of law. However, sometimes the system, not the person, contributes to the problem. Following is an excerpt from David Cole's *No Equal Justice: Race and Class in the American Criminal Justice System* about the New Orleans Public Defenders Office. Leonard Peart was charged with a series of serious criminal offenses.

A successful but overworked public defender named Rick Teissier was assigned to represent him. While the outcome of the case was unusual, it illustrates the problems facing overburdened and underfunded defense attorneys for the indigent.

At the time he was appointed, Teissier was handling seventy active felony cases. From January to August of that year, he had represented 418 defendants. He often wasn't even able to conduct an initial interview with his clients until they had been incarcerated for thirty to seventy days; at that point, the best thing to do was often to plead guilty in exchange for a sentence of the time they had already served. . . . He had at least one serious felony case set for trial for every trial date during 1991, and his office had only three investigators to cover some 7,000 cases a year. The Orleans Indigent Defender Program had a worse library than many prisons have, and no money to hire experts.

Everyone in Teissier's office was similarly overworked, as the local government sought to stretch as far as possible the limited dollars it was willing to spend on indigent defense. The public defender program was funded by receipts from traffic tickets, and when ticket collecting fell, so did the program's funding. Peart's case was the straw that finally broke Teissier's back. He took the unusual step of filing a pretrial motion asking the judge to declare his own legal assistance ineffective before trial. He argued that under these conditions it was simply impossible to provide Peart an effective defense. The trial judge agreed. . . . He declared the entire Orleans public defender system unconstitutional. . . .

On appeal, the Louisiana Supreme Court agreed that "because of excessive caseloads and insufficient support, indigent defendants are generally not provided effective assistance in New Orleans." It declined to find the entire defender system unconstitutional, reasoning that each case must be examined individually on its facts. But the court did hold that, absent a change in workloads and resources, it would apply a rebuttable presumption [courts could assume unless demonstrated otherwise] that indigent defendants represented by the Orleans public defender officer were receiving ineffective assistance of counsel. . . .[34]

POINTS TO PONDER

- Why do you think the public is unwilling to adequately fund lawyers for the poor? What can be done to change the situation?
- What does it say about the other parts of the system—the judge, prosecutor, jury—that a defense lawyer had to report himself as ineffective? Who should be making sure that legal assistance is not systematically ineffective?
- What should Teissier have done about his workload? What about the 418 defendants he had already represented that year? Could he have been effective representing those people?

A Quick Career Quiz

America has more than one million lawyers, which is why jokes about lawyers are so popular. Yet, too few lawyers are willing to represent poor people and young people accused of crimes. Would you be interested in such a career path?

Answer the following questions and find out whether you should think about going to law school.

1. Do you like to argue?
2. Are you interested in rules and exceptions?
3. Do you have a passion for justice?
4. Are you a little bit of a showboat and show-off?
5. Do you like drama?
6. How about prosecuting those who break our laws and make our communities unsafe?
7. Do you like to help other people with their problems?
8. Do you like to work hard?
9. Do you like writing?
10. Are you willing to study for three years and then take the bar exam, which would qualify you to practice law?

No matter what your score, you should consider the practice of law. Rent *The Paper Chase* to see what you think of law school. Remember, like Clarence Earl Gideon, with a little bit of studying you, too, can change the law.

Notes

1. *Johnson v. Zerbst*, 304 U.S. 458, 462-463 (1938).
2. Abbe Smith, "Rosie O'Neill Goes to Law School: The Clinical Education of the Sensitive New Age Public Defender," *Harvard Civil Rights—Civil Liberties Law Review* 28 (1993): 48. See also Clarence Darrow, *The Story of My Life* (New York: Charles Scribner's Sons, 1932), 75–76.
3. American Bar Association, Criminal Justice Section, Standards Committee, *ABA Standards for Criminal Justice*, 3d ed. (Chicago, Ill.: American Bar Association, 1993), sec. 4-3.1, available at http://www.abanet.org/crimjust/standards/func_blk.html#3.1.
4. American Bar Association, *ABA Standards for Criminal Justice*, sec. 4-3.2.
5. American Bar Association, *ABA Standards for Criminal Justice*, sec. 4-3.6.
6. American Bar Association, *ABA Standards for Criminal Justice*, sec. 4-3.8.
7. American Bar Association, *ABA Standards for Criminal Justice*, sec. 4-4.1.
8. American Bar Association, *ABA Standards for Criminal Justice*, secs. 4-6.1, 4.6.2.
9. American Bar Association, *ABA Standards for Criminal Justice*, secs. 4-5.2, 4-7.2, 4-7.4, 4-7.5, 4-7.6, 4-7.7.
10. American Bar Association, *ABA Standards for Criminal Justice*, secs. 4-8.1, 4-7.9.
11. *Slam*, directed by Marc Levin (Santa Monica, Calif.: Trimark Pictures, 1998).
12. *United States v. Wade*, 388 U.S. 218, 256058 (concurring in part).

13. Douglas O. Linder, "Famous American Trials: 'The Scottsboro Boys' Trials," 1999, available at http://www.law.umkc.edu/faculty/projects/Ftrials/scottsboro/scottsb.htm (accessed November 8, 2004).

14. *Powell v. State of Alabama*, 287 U.S 45 (1932).

15. Douglas O. Linder, "Without Fear or Favor: Judge James Edwin Horton and the Trial of the 'Scottsboro Boys,'" *University of Missouri at Kansas City Law Review* 68 (2000): 549.

16. Anthony Lewis, *Gideon's Trumpet* (New York: Vintage Books, 1964), p. 6.

17. National Association of Criminal Defense Lawyers, "Lesson Plan: Gideon at 40: Understanding the Right to Counsel," 2003, available at http://www.nacdl.org/public.nsf/Gideon Anniversary/lesson/$FILE/gideon_lesson_plan1-7.pdf (accessed November 9, 2004).

18. Barry Scheck and Sara Toft, "*Gideon*'s Promise and the Innocent Defendant," *Champion* (February 27, 2003): 38. See also Anthony Lewis, "To Realize *Gideon:* Competent Counsel with Adequate Resources," *Champion* (March 22, 1998): 20.

19. *Douglas v. California*, 372 U.S. 353 (1963).

20. *In Re Gault*, 387 U.S. 1 (1967).

21. "Juvenile Court Procedures," *Harvard Law Review* 81 (1967): 171.

22. Francine T. Sherman, "Thoughts on a Contextual View of Juvenile Justice Reform Drawn from Narratives of Youth," *Temple Law Review* 68 (1995): 1837.

23. Mary Berkheiser, "The Fiction of Juvenile Right to Counsel: Waiver in the Juvenile Courts," *Florida Law Review* 54 (2002): 577, 611.

24. Berkheiser, "The Fiction of Juvenile Right to Counsel," 613.

25. *Strickland v. Washington*, 466 U.S. 668, 685 (1984).

26. *McFarland v. Scott*, 512 U.S. 1256, 1260 (1984).

27. *Young v. Zant*, 727 F.2d 1489 (11th Cir. 1984).

28. *Taylor v. Louisiana*, 419 U.S. 522 (1975); *Machetti v. Linahan*, 679 F.2d 236 (11th Cir. 1982).

29. *Smith v. Kemp*, 715 F.2d 1459 (11th Cir. 1983).

30. *Romero v. Lynaugh*, 884 F.2d 871, 875 (5th Cir. 1989).

31. *Heath v. Jones*, 941 F.2d 1126, 1131 (11th Cir. 1991).

32. *Messer v. Kemp*, 760 F.2d 1080 (11th Cir. 1985) (Johnson, J., dissenting).

33. Stephen Bright, Stephan Kinnard, and David Webster, "Keeping Gideon from Being Blown Away: Prospective Challenges to Inadequate Representation May Be Our Best Hope," *4-WTR Criminal Justice* 10 (1990): 11.

34. David Cole, *No Equal Justice: Race and Class in the American Criminal Justice System* (New York: New Press, 1999), pp. 82-83.

Additional Sources

Bright, Stephen. "Counsel for the Poor: The Death Sentence Not for the Worst Crime But for the Worst Lawyer." *Yale Law Journal* 103 (1994): 1835.

Bright, Stephen, Stephan Kinnard, and David Webster. "Keeping Gideon from Being Blown Away: Prospective Challenges to Inadequate Representation May Be Our Best Hope." *4-WTR Criminal Justice* 10 (1990): 10–13, 46–48.

Caeti, Tory, Craig Hemmens, and Velmer Burton. "Juvenile Right to Counsel: A National Comparison of State Legal Codes." *American Journal of Criminal Law* 23 (1996): 611.

Feld, Barry. "Bad Kids: Race and the Transformation of the Juvenile Court." *Urban Lawyer* 31 (1999): 1033.

Fitzgerald, Wendy Anton. "Stories of Child Outlaws: On Child Heroism and Adult Power in Juvenile Justice." *Wisconsin Law Review* (1996): 495.

Lewis, Anthony. "The Silencing of Gideon's Trumpet." *New York Times Magazine,* April 20, 2003.

Shepard Jr., Robert E. "Youth in the Criminal Justice System: An ABA Task Force Report (A Summary of the White Paper)." Available at http://www.abanet.org/crimjust/juvjus/jjpolicies/YCJSReport.pdf. (accessed November 9, 2004).

Smith, Abbe. "Rosie O'Neill Goes to Law School: The Clinical Education of the Sensitive New Age Public Defender." *Harvard Civil Rights—Civil Liberties Law Review* 28, no. 1 (1993): 48.

Smith, Abbe. "The Calling of Criminal Defense." *Mercer Law Review* 50 (1999): 443.

Stahl, Marc. "The Impact of Counsel on Juvenile Delinquency Proceedings." *Journal of Criminal Law and Criminology* 84 (1993): 642.

Thibodeau, Jennifer. "Sugar and Spice and Everything Nice: Female Juvenile Delinquency and Gender Bias in Punishment and Behavior in Juvenile Courts." *William and Mary Journal of Women and the Law* 8 (2002): 489.

CRUEL AND UNUSUAL PUNISHMENT

8

"In America, teenagers under the age of 18 can't drink, vote, or sit on a jury. The public has come to believe that it takes children time to develop mentally, to mature fully before they can make decisions on their own. But in many death-penalty states, that reasoning changes if a teenager under the age of 18 commits murder. Prosecutors and victim's families contend that the child knew exactly what he or she was doing, and should be held fully accountable." KRIS AXTMAN[1]

The Death Penalty Today

In the United States, the death penalty has been available—and controversial—since the nation was founded. Today, its critics are chipping away at capital punishment, and the number of people sentenced to die has sharply declined in the new century. From 1994 to 2000, the death row population grew by an average of 296 people each year. In 2000, there were only 226 new death sentences. In 2001, the number fell to 155, the lowest recorded since 1973. The number of juveniles sentenced to die has also fallen, and the Supreme Court outright abolished the juvenile death penalty in 2005.

Why the sharp decline in death penalties being handed out by juries? One important factor has been media coverage about wrongful convictions of people on death row. These cases involve people convicted of murder but later determined to be innocent through the use of new DNA technologies to examine evidence that can conclusively refute the finding of guilt. Some people speculate that jurors, now very much aware that the justice system is not **infallible,** are fearful of putting an innocent person to death and as a result are choosing instead to sentence people to life in prison without the possibility of parole. Of the

---

YOUR THOUGHTS

- Is the death penalty sometimes appropriate punishment? When?
- Would you be willing to pull the switch on an electric chair?
- Does the age of a defendant matter? Is the death penalty a cruel and unusual punishment for someone who commits murder under the age of eighteen?
- Should the Supreme Court have banned the death penalty for juveniles?

Before the Supreme Court abolished the juvenile death penalty in *Roper v. Simmons* (2005), twenty of the thirty-eight states with capital punishment allowed juveniles to be sentenced to die. *Reuters/Landov*

thirty-eight states that have death penalty laws, thirty-six have life without parole statutes.

Another possible factor in the decline of death penalty sentencing is the reluctance of prosecutors to incur the high costs of litigating capital punishment cases. According to one estimate, prosecution costs in a non-capital case rarely exceed $10,000, but because of the large number of procedural safeguards built into death penalty cases, they can routinely reach $500,000 or more. Furthermore, a general **erosion** of support has occurred among the public for the death penalty as an answer to crime. With growing media attention on ineffective counsel in criminal cases, governors imposing **moratoriums** on the death penalty, and the U.S. Supreme Court's ban on the execution of people with mental retardation (*Atkins v. Virginia* [2002]), enthusiasm for the death penalty is slowly fading. Still, the death penalty remains an option in most states and is an important feature of the criminal justice landscape.

EXERCISE 8.1. People have argued for centuries about the morality of capital punishment. Most nations have banned the practice as uncivilized, but U.S. states, the federal government, and the military allow it.

If you oppose the death penalty, imagine that you are confronted by the families, friends, and loved ones of hundreds of people killed in a terrorist attack. Some of them want the death penalty for the people convicted of mass murder in the attack. Try to convince them that the death penalty is wrong or ineffective. What do you say? Do you lose any conviction that you are right in opposing the death penalty?

If you favor the death penalty, under what circumstances would you be willing to personally administer it to, for example, a convicted criminal who grew up in an abusive home and later in life, in cold blood, murdered his parents while they were asleep?

As of 2005, thirty-seven states allowed for death by lethal injection of a poison, ten by electrocution, five in a gas chamber, two by hanging, and two by firing squad. Some states offer more than one method.

- Would you be willing to inject the prisoner with the lethal substance?
- Would you pull the switch on the electric chair?
- Would you release the poison into the gas chamber?
- Would you pull the floor from beneath the person to be hanged?
- Would you participate as a shooter in a firing squad?

Write an essay about the thoughts and feelings you experience working through these hypotheticals.

The Death Penalty and Juveniles

The colonies and the states that would later form the United States have a long history of executing juveniles who murder. The first such execution of a convict under the age of eighteen took place in 1642 in Plymouth Colony, Massachusetts.

At the beginning of 2005, the laws of twenty states permitted executions of juveniles, but few engaged in the practice. In fact, a number of states had actively backed away from executing juvenile offenders. For example, in 1992 Indiana increased the minimum age for imposing the death penalty to eighteen. Montana did the same in 1999. Bills were introduced in ten state legislatures that would raise to eighteen the legal limit for imposition of capital punishment. Nonetheless, in the majority of states that permitted the death penalty, if a prosecutor decided that a juvenile had committed an especially terrible murder and demonstrated a lack of regard for human life, he or she could choose to seek the death penalty.

The juvenile death penalty has long been controversial. Its supporters believe that it is just punishment for young people who commit savage crimes. If you are old enough to

---

BEFORE *ROPER V. SIMMONS*: FACTS ABOUT THE JUVENILE DEATH PENALTY

- As of September 30, 2004, 72 persons—all males—were on death row for crimes they committed as juveniles. These 72 offenders constituted 2 percent of the total death row population of 3,487.
- The disproportionate representation of people of color under sentences of death was magnified for juvenile offenders. Although 46 percent of adult offenders were white, only 33 percent of juvenile offenders were white. That means that 66 percent of juvenile offenders were African American and Latino.
- Thirty-eight jurisdictions in the United States allowed the death penalty as a punishment. Of these jurisdictions, twenty had chosen eighteen as the minimum age for execution, five had chosen seventeen, and fourteen others had established sixteen as the minimum age.
- Texas had by far the largest death row of juvenile offenders, holding 40 percent of the national total, or twenty-nine of the seventy-two such offenders.

—Victor L. Streib, "The Juvenile Death Penalty Today: Death Sentences and Executions for Juvenile Crime, January 1, 1973–September 30, 2004," p. 11, available at http://www.law.onu.edu/faculty/streib/documents/JuvDeathSept302004.pdf (accessed January 31, 2005)

take someone else's life, they think, you are old enough to suffer the loss of your own. Juries could decide whether the defendant was sufficiently mature to understand what he or she was doing. Furthermore, supporters of the juvenile death penalty argue that the punishment deters criminal gangs and drug-dealing operations from recruiting minors to commit murders for them.

Opponents of the juvenile death penalty point out that juveniles are not trusted to vote, drink alcohol, or make personal medical decisions. Thus, society in this respect already acknowledges the intellectual immaturity and inadequate judgment of its youth. Should they be killed because of bad decisions they make as minors? Moreover, opponents argue that little reliable evidence is available that the death penalty works to prevent young people, who are often impulsive and shortsighted, from committing crimes. These critics have long argued that the United States—until recently the only democratic country with a juvenile death penalty—should join the rest of the world in abolishing the punishment.

Mirroring recent general trends, prosecutors began seeking the death penalty for juveniles less often, and juries imposed it less frequently. In 1994, eighteen juveniles were sentenced to death; in 1999 fourteen were, and by 2000 only two juveniles were. Between 1989 and 2005, six states banned the execution of juveniles.

The Supreme Court and the Juvenile Death Penalty

The death penalty is unlike any other punishment in that it is not only permanent and irreversible but requires an act of state violence against the body of the condemned prisoner. For these reasons, the Supreme Court has long struggled with the issue and faced repeated claims that executions of juveniles are horrific and uncivilized.

In *Thompson v. Oklahoma* (1988), the Court found that executions of people under sixteen violate the Eighth Amendment ban on cruel and unusual punishment and are thus unconstitutional. But in *Stanford v. Kentucky* (1989), the Court upheld executions of sixteen- and seventeen-year old capital defendants. Then the momentum to abolish

Toronto Patterson was executed in August 2002 for the murder of his cousin and her two children. Patterson, seventeen at the time of the crime, was the last juvenile offender to be executed in Texas prior to the 2005 *Roper v. Simmons* decision. The Supreme Court had denied Patterson's appeal for a stay of execution, with Justices Stevens, Ginsburg, and Breyer dissenting on the ground that the Court should consider reviewing the death penalty for persons who commit crimes before the age of eighteen. *Source: J. Gary Hart*

juvenile capital punishment returned when the Court, in *Atkins v. Virginia* (2002), held that executing a mentally retarded adult is cruel and unusual punishment because it exacts retribution against a person who does not fully comprehend what he has done. That decision, which overruled a 1989 case, gave opponents of the juvenile death penalty hope that the Supreme Court would return its attention to the "evolving standards of decency" under the Eighth Amendment. Finally, the Court ended the practice of juvenile executions in *Roper v. Simmons* (2005). The unfolding logic of this sequence of cases has important lessons about how the law develops.

———

THOMPSON V. OKLAHOMA

Supreme Court of the United States
No. 86-6169.
Decided June 29, 1988.

Justice STEVENS announced the judgment of the Court and delivered an opinion in which Justice BRENNAN, Justice MARSHALL, and Justice BLACKMUN join.

Petitioner was convicted of first-degree murder and sentenced to death. The principal question presented is whether the execution of that sentence would violate the constitutional prohibition against the **infliction** of "cruel and unusual punishments" because petitioner was only 15 years old at the time of his offense.

I

. . . In concert with three older persons, petitioner actively participated in the brutal murder of his former brother-in-law in the early morning hours of January 23, 1983. The evidence disclosed that the victim had been shot twice, and that his throat, chest, and abdomen had been cut. He also had multiple bruises and a broken leg. His body had been chained to a concrete block and thrown into a river where it remained for almost four weeks. Each of the four participants was tried separately and each was sentenced to death.

Because petitioner was a "child" as a matter of Oklahoma law, the District Attorney filed a statutory petition, seeking an order finding "that said child is competent and had the mental capacity to know and appreciate the wrongfulness of his [conduct]." After a hearing, the trial court concluded "that there are virtually no *reasonable* prospects for rehabilitation of William Wayne Thompson within the juvenile system and that William Wayne Thompson should be held accountable for his acts as if he were an adult and should be certified to stand trial as an adult." . . .

The jury . . . fixed petitioner's punishment at death. . . .

II

The authors of the Eighth Amendment drafted a categorical prohibition against the infliction of cruel and unusual punishments, but they made no attempt to define the contours of that category.

They delegated that task to future generations of judges who have been guided by the "evolving standards of decency that mark the progress of a maturing society." In performing that task the Court has reviewed the work product of state legislatures and sentencing juries, and has carefully considered the reasons why a civilized society may accept or reject the death penalty in certain types of cases. Thus, in confronting the question whether the youth of the defendant—more specifically, the fact that he was less than 16 years old at the time of his offense—is a sufficient reason for denying the State the power to sentence him to death, we first review relevant legislative enactments, then refer to jury determinations, and finally explain why these indicators of contemporary standards of decency confirm our judgment that such a young person is not capable of acting with the degree of **culpability** that can justify the ultimate penalty. . . .

Our capital punishment jurisprudence has consistently recognized that contemporary standards, as reflected by the actions of legislatures and juries, provide an important measure of whether the death penalty is "cruel and unusual." Part of the rationale for this index of constitutional value lies in the very language of the construed clause: whether an action is "unusual" depends, in common usage, upon the frequency of its occurrence or the magnitude of its acceptance.

III

. . . Justice Powell has repeatedly reminded us of the importance of "the experience of mankind, as well as the long history of our law, recognizing that there *are* differences which must be accommodated in determining the rights and duties of children as compared with those of adults. Examples of this distinction abound in our law: in contracts, in torts, in criminal law and procedure, in criminal sanctions and rehabilitation, and in the right to vote and to hold office." Oklahoma recognizes this basic distinction in a number of its statutes. Thus, a minor is not eligible to vote, to sit on a jury, to marry without parental consent, or to purchase alcohol or cigarettes. Like all other States, Oklahoma has developed a juvenile justice system in which most offenders under the age of 18 are not held criminally responsible. Its statutes do provide, however, that a 16- or 17-year-old charged with murder and other serious felonies shall be considered an adult. . . .

The conclusion that it would offend civilized standards of decency to execute a person who was less than 16 years old at the time of his or her offense is consistent with the views that have been expressed by respected professional organizations, by other nations that share our Anglo-American heritage, and by the leading members of the Western European community. . . . Although the death penalty has not been entirely abolished in the United Kingdom or New Zealand (it has been abolished in Australia, except in the State of New South Wales, where it is available for treason and piracy), in neither of those countries may a juvenile be executed. The death penalty has been abolished in West Germany, France, Portugal, The Netherlands, and all of the Scandinavian countries, and is available only for exceptional crimes such as treason in Canada, Italy, Spain, and Switzerland. Juvenile executions are also prohibited in the Soviet Union.

We have previously recognized the relevance of the views of the international community in determining whether a punishment is cruel and unusual.

IV

The second societal factor the Court has examined in determining the acceptability of capital punishment to the American sensibility is the behavior of juries. In fact, the infrequent and haphazard handing out of death sentences by capital juries was a prime factor underlying our judgment in *Furman v. Georgia* that the death penalty, as then administered in unguided fashion, was unconstitutional. . . .

V

Although the judgments of legislatures, juries, and prosecutors weigh heavily in the balance, it is for us ultimately to judge whether the Eighth Amendment permits imposition of the death penalty on one such as petitioner who committed a heinous murder when he was only 15 years old. In making that judgment, we first ask whether the juvenile's culpability should be measured by the same standard as that of an adult, and then consider whether the application of the death penalty to this class of offenders "measurably contributes" to the social purposes that are served by the death penalty.

It is generally agreed "that punishment should be directly related to the personal culpability of the criminal defendant." There is also broad agreement on the proposition that adolescents as a class are less mature and responsible than adults.

. . . Justice Powell quoted the following passage from the 1978 Report of the Twentieth Century Fund Task Force on Sentencing Policy Toward Young Offenders:

. . . " 'Crimes committed by youths may be just as harmful to victims as those committed by older persons, but they deserve less punishment because adolescents may have less capacity to control their conduct and to think in long-range terms than adults. Moreover, youth crime as such is not exclusively the offender's fault; offenses by the young also represent a failure of family, school, and the social system, which share responsibility for the development of America's youth.' " . . .

"The death penalty is said to serve two principal social purposes: **retribution** and **deterrence** of capital crimes by prospective offenders." . . .

We have invalidated death sentences when this significant justification was absent.

For such a young offender, the deterrence rationale is equally unacceptable. . . . In short, we are not persuaded that the imposition of the death penalty for offenses committed by persons under 16 years of age has made, or can be expected to make, any measurable contribution to the goals that capital punishment is intended to achieve. It is, therefore, "nothing more than the purposeless and needless imposition of pain and suffering," and thus an unconstitutional punishment. . . .

VI

Petitioner's counsel and various *amici curiae* have asked us to "draw a line" that would prohibit the execution of any person who was under the age of 18 at the time of the offense. Our task today, however, is to decide the case before us; we do so by concluding that the Eighth and Fourteenth Amendments prohibit the execution of a person who was under 16 years of age at the time of his or her offense.

Justice SCALIA, with whom THE CHIEF JUSTICE and Justice WHITE join, dissenting.

. . . It is whether there is a national consensus that no criminal so much as one day under 16, after individuated consideration of his circumstances, including the overcoming of a presumption that he should not be tried as an adult, can possibly be deemed mature and responsible enough to be punished with death for any crime. Because there seems to me no plausible basis for answering this last question in the affirmative, I respectfully dissent. . . .

In sum, the statistics of executions demonstrate nothing except the fact that our society has always agreed that executions of 15-year-old criminals should be rare, and in more modern times has agreed that they (like all other executions) should be even rarer still. . . .

Justice KENNEDY took no part in the consideration or decision of this case.

POINTS TO PONDER

- How did the Court use "evolving standards of decency" to reach a decision?
- What do you think about Justice Antonin Scalia's argument that Thompson's age should not matter? Do you agree that some crimes are so heinous and premeditated that the perpetrator's age is irrelevant for the purposes of considering the death penalty?
- Is society doing teen killers a favor by keeping them alive? Isn't everyone—including the killers themselves—better off with them gone?

One year after *Thompson,* the Supreme Court heard a case involving a capital defendant who was seventeen years old when he committed crimes—murder, sodomy, robbery, and receiving stolen property—for which he was sentenced to death. In another case, Missouri certified as an adult a juvenile defendant who was sixteen years old when

In May 2002, the state of Texas executed twenty-five-year-old Napoleon Beazley for the 1994 murder of John Luttig. Beazley, who committed the crime while seventeen, died by lethal injection. *Source: Texas Department of Corrections/Reuters/Landov*

Do you think a big difference in maturity exists between the average fifteen-year-old and the average sixteen-year-old? How about sixteen and seventeen? Between seventeen and eighteen? What does the Supreme Court say about this in *Stanford v. Kentucky*?

he committed a murder. He was convicted of first-degree murder and sentenced to death. The Supreme Court merged the two cases and held in *Stanford v. Kentucky* that imposition of capital punishment on a defendant for a crime committed at sixteen or seventeen years of age did not violate evolving standards of decency and, therefore, did not constitute cruel and unusual punishment under the Eighth Amendment.

KEVIN N. STANFORD, PETITIONER
V.
KENTUCKY

HEATH A. WILKINS, PETITIONER
V.
MISSOURI

Supreme Court of the United States
No. 87-5765.
Decided June 26, 1989.

Justice SCALIA announced the judgment of the Court and delivered the opinion of the Court . . . in which THE CHIEF JUSTICE, Justice WHITE, and Justice KENNEDY join.

These two consolidated cases require us to decide whether the imposition of capital punishment on an individual for a crime committed at 16 or 17 years of age constitutes cruel and unusual punishment under the Eighth Amendment.

I

The first case involves the shooting death of 20-year-old Barbel Poore in Jefferson County, Kentucky. Petitioner Kevin Stanford committed the murder on January 7, 1981, when he was approximately 17 years and 4 months of age. Stanford and his accomplice repeatedly raped and sodomized Poore during and after their commission of a robbery at a gas station where she worked as an attendant. They then drove her to a secluded area near the station, where Stanford shot her pointblank in the face and then in the back of her head. The proceeds from the robbery were roughly 300 cartons of cigarettes, two gallons of fuel, and a small amount of cash. A corrections officer testified that petitioner explained the murder as follows: " '[H]e said, I had to shoot her, [she] lived next door to me and she would recognize me. . . . I guess we could have tied her up or something or beat [her up] . . . and tell her if she tells, we would kill her. . . . Then after he said that he started laughing.' "

. . . Stressing the seriousness of petitioner's offenses and the unsuccessful attempts of the juvenile system to treat him for numerous instances of past delinquency, the juvenile court found certification for trial as an adult to be in the best interest of petitioner and the community.

Stanford was convicted of murder, first-degree sodomy, first-degree robbery, and receiving stolen property, and was sentenced to death and 45 years in prison. The Kentucky Supreme Court affirmed the death sentence, rejecting Stanford's "deman[d] that he has a constitutional right to treatment." Finding that the record clearly demonstrated that "there was no program or treatment appropriate for the appellant in the juvenile justice system," the court held that the juvenile court did not err in certifying petitioner for trial as an adult. The court also stated that petitioner's "age and the possibility that he might be rehabilitated were mitigating factors appropriately left to the consideration of the jury that tried him."

The second case before us today involves the stabbing death of Nancy Allen, a 26-year-old mother of two who was working behind the sales counter of the convenience store she and David Allen owned and operated in Avondale, Missouri. Petitioner Heath Wilkins committed the murder on July 27, 1985, when he was approximately 16 years and 6 months of age. The record reflects that Wilkins' plan was to rob the store and murder "whoever was behind the counter" because "a dead person can't talk." While Wilkins' accomplice, Patrick Stevens, held Allen, Wilkins stabbed her, causing her to fall to the floor. When Stevens had trouble operating the cash register, Allen spoke up to assist him, leading Wilkins to stab her three more times in her chest. . . . After helping themselves to liquor, cigarettes, rolling papers, and approximately $450 in cash and checks, Wilkins and Stevens left Allen to die on the floor.

Because he was roughly six months short of the age of majority for purposes of criminal prosecution, Wilkins could not automatically be tried as an adult under Missouri law. . . . Relying on the "viciousness, force and violence" of the alleged crime, petitioner's maturity, and the failure of the juvenile justice system to rehabilitate him after previous delinquent acts, the juvenile court made the necessary certification.

Wilkins was charged with first-degree murder, armed criminal action, and carrying a concealed weapon. After the court found him competent, petitioner entered guilty pleas to all charges. A punishment hearing was held, at which both the State and petitioner himself urged imposition of the death sentence. Evidence at the hearing revealed that petitioner had been in and out of juvenile facilities since the age of eight for various acts of burglary, theft, and arson, had attempted to kill his mother by putting insecticide into Tylenol capsules, and had killed several animals in his neighborhood. Although psychiatric testimony indicated that Wilkins had "personality disorders," the witnesses agreed that Wilkins was aware of his actions and could distinguish right from wrong. . . .

II

The thrust of both Wilkins' and Stanford's arguments is that imposition of the death penalty on those who were juveniles when they committed their crimes falls within the Eighth Amendment's prohibition against "cruel and unusual punishments." Wilkins would have us define juveniles as individuals 16 years of age and under; Stanford would draw the line at 17.

. . . [P]etitioners . . . argue that their punishment is contrary to the "evolving standards of decency that mark the progress of a maturing society." They are correct in asserting that this Court has "not confined the prohibition embodied in the Eighth Amendment to 'barbarous' methods that were generally outlawed in the 18th century," but instead has interpreted the Amendment "in a flexible and dynamic manner." In determining what standards have "evolved," however, we have looked not to our own conceptions of decency, but to those of modern American society as a whole. As we have said, "Eighth Amendment judgments should not be, or appear to be, merely the subjective views of individual Justices; judgment should be informed by objective factors to the maximum possible extent."

III

"[F]irst" among the " 'objective indicia that reflect the public attitude toward a given sanction' " are statutes passed by society's elected representatives. Of the 37 States whose laws permit capital punishment, 15 decline to impose it upon 16-year-old offenders and 12 decline to impose it on 17-year-old offenders.

. . . It is not the burden of Kentucky and Missouri, however, to establish a national consensus approving what their citizens have voted to do; rather, it is the "heavy burden" of petitioners to establish a national consensus *against* it. As far as the primary and most reliable indication of consensus is concerned—the pattern of enacted laws—petitioners have failed to carry that burden.

IV
A

Wilkins and Stanford argue, however, that even if the laws themselves do not establish a settled consensus, the application of the laws does. That contemporary society views capital punishment of 16- and 17-year-old offenders as inappropriate is demonstrated, they say, by the reluctance of juries to impose, and prosecutors to seek, such sentences. Petitioners are quite correct that a far smaller number of offenders under 18 than over 18 have been sentenced to death in this country. From 1982 through 1988, for example, out of 2,106 total death sentences, only 15 were imposed on individuals who were 16 or under when they committed their crimes, and only 30 on individuals who were 17 at the time of the crime. And it appears that actual executions for crimes committed under age 18 accounted for only about two percent of the total number of executions that occurred between 1642 and 1986. As Wilkins points out, the last execution of a person who committed a crime under 17 years of age occurred in 1959. These statistics, however, carry little significance. Given the undisputed fact that a far smaller percentage of capital crimes are committed by persons under 18 than over 18, the discrepancy in treatment is much less than might seem. . . . To the contrary, it is not only possible, but overwhelmingly probable, that the very considerations which induce petitioners and their supporters to believe that death should *never* be imposed on offenders under 18 cause prosecutors and juries to believe that it should *rarely* be imposed. . . .

V

Having failed to establish a consensus against capital punishment for 16- and 17-year-old offenders through state and federal statutes and the behavior of prosecutors and juries, petitioners seek to demonstrate it through other indicia, including public opinion polls, the views of interest groups, and the positions adopted by various professional associations. We decline the invitation to rest constitutional law upon such uncertain foundations. . . .

We also reject petitioners' argument that we should invalidate capital punishment of 16- and 17-year-old offenders on the ground that it fails to serve the legitimate goals of penology. According to petitioners, it fails to deter because juveniles, possessing less developed cognitive skills than adults, are less likely to fear death; and it fails to exact just retribution because juveniles, being less mature and responsible, are also less morally blameworthy. In support of these claims, petitioners and their supporting *amici* marshal an array of socioscientific evidence concerning the psychological and emotional development of 16- and 17-year-olds. . . .

We discern neither a historical nor a modern societal consensus forbidding the imposition of capital punishment on any person who murders at 16 or 17 years of age. Accordingly, we conclude that such punishment does not offend the Eighth Amendment's prohibition against cruel and unusual punishment.

The judgments of the Supreme Court of Kentucky and the Supreme Court of Missouri are therefore

Affirmed.

Justice BRENNAN, with whom Justice MARSHALL, Justice BLACKMUN, and Justice STEVENS join, dissenting.

I believe that to take the life of a person as punishment for a crime committed when below the age of 18 is cruel and unusual and hence is prohibited by the Eighth Amendment. . . .

I

Our judgment about the constitutionality of a punishment under the Eighth Amendment is informed, though not determined, by an examination of contemporary attitudes toward the punishment, as evidenced in the actions of legislatures and of juries. The views of organizations with expertise in relevant fields and the choices of governments elsewhere in the world also merit our attention as indicators whether a punishment is acceptable in a civilized society.

A

The Court's discussion of state laws concerning capital sentencing gives a distorted view of the evidence of contemporary standards that these legislative determinations provide. Currently, 12 of the States whose statutes permit capital punishment specifically mandate that offenders under age 18 not be sentenced to death. When one adds to these 12 States the 15 (including the District of Columbia) in which capital punishment is not authorized at all, it appears that the governments in fully 27 of the States have concluded that no one under 18 should face the death penalty. A further three States explicitly refuse to authorize sentences of death for those who committed their offense when under 17, making a total of 30 States that would not tolerate the execution of petitioner Wilkins. Congress' most recent enactment of a death penalty statute also excludes those under 18.

In 19 States that have a death penalty, no minimum age for capital sentences is set in the death penalty statute. I would not assume . . . in considering how the States stand on the moral issue that underlies the constitutional question with which we are presented, that a legislature that has never specifically considered the issue has made a conscious moral choice to permit the execution of juveniles. On a matter of such moment that most States have expressed an explicit and contrary judgment, the decisions of legislatures that are only implicit, and that lack the "earmarks of careful consideration that we have required for other kinds of decisions leading to the death penalty," must count for little. I do not suggest, of course, that laws of these States cut *against* the constitutionality of the juvenile death penalty—only that accuracy demands that the baseline for our deliberations should be that 27 States refuse to authorize a sentence of death in the circumstances of petitioner Stanford's case, and 30 would not permit Wilkins' execution; that 19 States have not squarely faced the question; and that only the few remaining jurisdictions have explicitly set an age below 18 at which a person may be sentenced to death.

B

. . . Both in absolute and in relative terms, imposition of the death penalty on adolescents is distinctly unusual. Adolescent offenders make up only a small proportion of the current death-row population: 30 out of a total of 2,186 inmates, or 1.37 percent. . . . And juvenile offenders are significantly less likely to receive the death penalty than adults. . . .

V

. . . There are strong indications that the execution of juvenile offenders violates contemporary standards of decency: a majority of States decline to permit juveniles to be sentenced to death; imposition of the sentence upon minors is very unusual even in those States that permit it; and respected organizations with expertise in relevant areas regard the execution of juveniles as unacceptable, as does international opinion. These indicators serve to confirm in my view my conclusion that the Eighth Amendment prohibits the execution of persons for offenses they committed while below the age of 18, because the death penalty is disproportionate when applied to such young offenders and fails measurably to serve the goals of capital punishment. I dissent.

POINTS TO PONDER

- Do you think Stanford's and Wilkins's death sentences fit the crimes they committed?
- What is the proportionality analysis that the majority and the dissenters describe?
- What determines the "evolving standards of decency"? Is it what the states are doing? What public opinion polls say? The views of lawyers and law professors? The majority in *Stanford v. Kentucky* refused to rest its decision on such "uncertain foundations." Where can we find "certain foundations" upon which to build our understanding of what is cruel and unusual punishment under the Eighth Amendment?

Although the data is still inconclusive, some studies show that the brains of adolescents are not nearly as developed as adults' brains, indicating that teenagers cannot necessarily control their impulses and anticipate consequences. Assuming this is true, does it lessen the culpability of juvenile offenders?

—Paul Davies, "Psychiatrists Question Death Penalty for Teen Killers,"
Wall Street Journal, May 26, 2004, B1

EXERCISE 8.2. You and your classmates divide into three groups: death penalty advocates, death penalty fence-sitters, and death penalty opponents. Review the following case and devise arguments about whether the defendant should be sentenced to death, using what you have learned from the cases discussed in this chapter.

Lee Boyd Malvo, a seventeen-year-old Jamaican youth, was charged with murder by the state of Virginia in connection with the October 2002 sniper shootings in the Washington, D.C., area that left ten people dead. For almost a month, residents of the metropolitan Washington area were afraid to leave their houses, stop for gas, or go grocery shopping, for fear of becoming a victim in this spree of drive-by shootings. Malvo, by media accounts a quiet, respectful young man living illegally in the United States with his mother, was traveling with John Allen Muhammad, a forty-one-year-old army veteran of Operation Desert Storm who took Malvo under his wing and kept him to a strictly regimented diet. Virginia prosecuted Malvo as an adult. In closing arguments, Malvo's attorney passionately argued on behalf of his client:

> Defense attorney Michael Arif said Muhammad indoctrinated Malvo, who was desperate for a father figure in his life, by using rigorous exercise, controlling his diet and personal hygiene, exposing him to violence, playing audiotapes under Malvo's pillow as he slept, and encouraging him to suppress his feelings.
>
> "Right was what John Muhammad said it was. Wrong was what John Muhammad said," Arif said. "Did he [Malvo] know the acts were illegal? Probably. But that was not what was important. Right or wrong is what John Muhammad said it was."
>
> Arif admitted that one psychologist who examined Malvo in jail characterized Malvo as "goofy," saying he smiled inappropriately.
>
> "He's facing potentially the death penalty and he's making lawnmower sounds," Arif said. "Something's wrong."
>
> Arif told jurors, "Lee could no more separate from John Muhammad than you could separate from your shadow on a sunny day."
>
> Arif also said, "the pain inflicted" on victims and families in the sniper shootings "is inexcusable" but "adding another life to that pile of death is not going to solve anything."
>
> "Lee Malvo is gone," Arif said. "What you have now . . . you have John Muhammad junior."
>
> Arif finished his presentation by projecting onto a courtroom screen a photo of a menacing-looking Muhammad and telling the jury that Malvo was "the last victim of John Muhammad."[2]

In January 2004, a jury convicted Malvo of murder and in March 2004 sentenced him to life without parole. In a separate trial, a jury sentenced Muhammad to death. Generally the insanity defense is a plea asserted by a defendant who claims he is not guilty because he lacked the mental capacity to realize he committed a wrong or to appreciate why it was wrong. If you were a juror, would you have believed Malvo's insanity defense?

Execution of People with Mental Retardation

In the 1989 case *Penry v. Lynaugh,* the Supreme Court decided that executing a mentally retarded person did not violate the Eighth Amendment's ban on cruel and unusual punishment. The Court revisited this issue when it agreed to hear *Atkins v. Virginia* in 2002. In the end, it abolished the death penalty for the mentally retarded. Although *Atkins* deals with execution of the retarded, many juvenile death penalty opponents hoped that its logic would be applied to young people, who arguably also have not yet developed the cognitive capacity to tell right from wrong. Does the reasoning of *Atkins* apply to minors as well? Is youthfulness **analogous** to mental retardation? At what age should people be considered mentally capable of distinguishing right from wrong? How does the Court in *Atkins* define mental retardation?

Lionel Tate leaves the Broward County, Florida, courthouse with his mother after a sentencing hearing in January 2004. Tate was serving life in prison for killing a six-year-old, but his conviction was overturned on the grounds that he was never given a mental competency test to determine whether he fully understood the nature of the crime. Tate was twelve years old at the time of the killing in 1999. Under the new agreement, Tate was sentenced to the three years previously served, one year of house arrest, and ten years of probation. *Source: Jon Way/Reuters/Landov*

ATKINS V. VIRGINIA

Supreme Court of the United States
No. 00-8452.
Decided June 20, 2002.

Justice STEVENS delivered the opinion of the Court.

Those mentally retarded persons who meet the law's requirements for criminal responsibility should be tried and punished when they commit crimes. Because of their disabilities in areas of reasoning, judgment, and control of their impulses, however, they do not act with the level of moral culpability that characterizes the most serious adult criminal conduct. Moreover, their impairments can jeopardize the reliability and fairness of capital proceedings against mentally retarded defendants. Presumably for these reasons . . . the American public, legislators, scholars, and judges have deliberated over the question whether the death penalty should ever be imposed on a mentally retarded criminal. The consensus reflected in those deliberations informs our answer to the question presented by this case: whether such executions are "cruel and unusual punishments" prohibited by the Eighth Amendment to the Federal Constitution.

I

Petitioner, Daryl Renard Atkins, was convicted of abduction, armed robbery, and capital murder, and sentenced to death. At approximately midnight on August 16, 1996, Atkins and William Jones, armed with a semiautomatic handgun, abducted Eric Nesbitt, robbed him of the money on his person, drove him to an automated teller machine in his pickup truck where cameras recorded their withdrawal of additional cash, then took him to an isolated location where he was shot eight times and killed.

Jones and Atkins both testified in the guilt phase of Atkins' trial. Each confirmed most of the details in the other's account of the incident, with the important exception that each stated that the other had actually shot and killed Nesbitt. Jones' testimony, which was both more coherent and credible than Atkins', was obviously credited by the jury and was sufficient to establish Atkins' guilt. At the penalty phase of the trial, the State introduced victim impact evidence and proved two aggravating circumstances: future dangerousness and "vileness of the offense." To prove future dangerousness, the State relied on Atkins' prior felony convictions as well as the testimony of four victims of earlier robberies and assaults. To prove the second aggravator, the prosecution relied upon the trial record, including pictures of the deceased's body and the autopsy report.

In the penalty phase, the defense relied on one witness, Dr. Evan Nelson, a forensic psychologist who had evaluated Atkins before trial and concluded that he was "mildly mentally retarded." His conclusion was based on interviews with people who knew Atkins, a review of school and court records, and the administration of a standard intelligence test which indicated that Atkins had a full scale IQ of 59.

The jury sentenced Atkins to death, but the Virginia Supreme Court ordered a second sentencing hearing because the trial court had used a misleading verdict form. At the resentencing, Dr. Nelson again testified. The State presented an expert rebuttal witness, Dr. Stanton Samenow, who expressed the opinion that Atkins was not mentally retarded, but rather was of "average intelligence, at least," and diagnosable as having antisocial personality disorder. The jury again sentenced Atkins to death.

The Supreme Court of Virginia affirmed the imposition of the death penalty. The Court was "not willing to commute Atkins' sentence of death to life imprisonment merely because of his IQ score."

Justice Hassell and Justice Koontz dissented. They rejected Dr. Samenow's opinion that Atkins possesses average intelligence as "incredulous as a matter of law," and concluded that "the imposition of the sentence of death upon a criminal defendant who has the mental age of a child between the ages of 9 and 12 is excessive." In their opinion, "it is indefensible to conclude that individuals who are mentally retarded are not to some degree less culpable for their criminal acts. By definition, such individuals have substantial limitations not shared by the general population. A moral and civilized society diminishes itself if its system of justice does not afford recognition and consideration of those limitations in a meaningful way." . . .

II

The Eighth Amendment **succinctly** prohibits "excessive" sanctions. It provides: "Excessive bail shall not be required, nor excessive fines imposed, nor cruel and unusual punishments inflicted." . . .

"The basic concept underlying the Eighth Amendment is nothing less than the dignity of man. . . . The Amendment must draw its meaning from the evolving standards of decency that mark the progress of a maturing society."

Proportionality review under those evolving standards should be informed by " 'objective factors to the maximum possible extent.' " We have pinpointed that the "clearest and most reliable objective evidence of contemporary values is the legislation enacted by the country's legislatures." . . .

Guided by our approach in these cases, we shall first review the judgment of legislatures that have addressed the suitability of imposing the death penalty on the mentally retarded and then consider reasons for agreeing or disagreeing with their judgment.

III

The parties have not called our attention to any state legislative consideration of the suitability of imposing the death penalty on mentally retarded offenders prior to 1986. In that year, the public reaction to the execution of a mentally retarded murderer in Georgia apparently led to the enactment of the first state statute prohibiting such executions. In 1988, when Congress enacted legislation reinstating the federal death penalty, it expressly provided that a "sentence of death shall not be carried out upon a person who is mentally retarded." In 1989, Maryland enacted a similar prohibition. It was in that year that we decided *Penry,* and concluded that those two state enactments, "even when added to the 14 States that have rejected capital punishment completely, do not provide sufficient evidence at present of a national consensus."

Much has changed since then. . . .

It is not so much the number of these States that is significant, but the consistency of the direction of change. Given the well-known fact that anticrime legislation is far more popular than legislation providing protections for persons guilty of violent crime, the large number of States prohibiting the execution of mentally retarded persons (and the complete absence of States passing legislation reinstating the power to conduct such executions) provides powerful evidence that today our society views mentally retarded offenders as categorically less culpable than the average criminal. . . . Moreover, even in those States that allow the execution of mentally retarded offenders, the practice is uncommon. Some States, for example New Hampshire and New Jersey, continue to authorize executions, but none have been carried out in decades. . . . The practice . . . has become truly unusual, and it is fair to say that a national consensus has developed against it.

To the extent there is serious disagreement about the execution of mentally retarded offenders, it is in determining which offenders are in fact retarded. . . .

IV

This consensus unquestionably reflects widespread judgment about the relative culpability of mentally retarded offenders, and the relationship between mental retardation and the penological purposes served by the death penalty. Additionally, it suggests that some characteristics of mental retardation undermine the strength of the procedural protections that our capital jurisprudence steadfastly guards.

. . . [O]ur death penalty jurisprudence provides two reasons consistent with the legislative consensus that the mentally retarded should be categorically excluded from execution. . . . "Retribution and deterrence of capital crimes by prospective offenders" [are] the social purposes served by the death penalty. Unless the imposition of the death penalty on a mentally retarded person "measurably contributes to one or both of these goals, it 'is nothing more than the purposeless and needless imposition of pain and suffering,' and hence an unconstitutional punishment."

With respect to retribution—the interest in seeing that the offender gets his "just deserts"—the severity of the appropriate punishment necessarily depends on the culpability of the offender.

. . . With respect to deterrence—the interest in preventing capital crimes by prospective offenders—"it seems likely that 'capital punishment can serve as a deterrent only when murder is the result of premeditation and deliberation.' " Exempting the mentally retarded from that punishment will not affect the "cold calculus that precedes the decision" of other potential murderers.

. . . We are not persuaded that the execution of mentally retarded criminals will measurably advance the deterrent or the retributive purpose of the death penalty. Construing and applying the Eighth Amendment in the light of our "evolving standards of decency," we therefore conclude that such punishment is excessive and that the Constitution "places a substantive restriction on the State's power to take the life" of a mentally retarded offender.

Chief Justice REHNQUIST, with whom Justice SCALIA and Justice THOMAS join, dissenting.

The question presented by this case is whether a national consensus deprives Virginia of the constitutional power to impose the death penalty on capital murder defendants like petitioner, *i.e.,* those defendants who indisputably are competent to stand trial, aware of the punishment they are about to suffer and why, and whose mental retardation has been found an insufficiently compelling reason to lessen their individual responsibility for the crime. The Court pronounces the punishment cruel and unusual primarily because 18 States recently have passed laws limiting the death eligibility of certain defendants based on mental retardation alone, despite the fact that the laws of 19 other States besides Virginia continue to leave the question of proper punishment to the individuated consideration of sentencing judges or juries familiar with the particular offender and his or her crime. . . .

In my view, . . . two sources—the work product of legislatures and sentencing jury determinations—ought to be the sole indicators by which courts ascertain the contemporary American conceptions of decency for purposes of the Eighth Amendment. They are the only objective indicia of contemporary values firmly supported by our precedents. More importantly, however, they can be reconciled with the undeniable precepts that the democratic branches of government and individual sentencing juries are, by design, better suited than courts to evaluating and giving effect to the complex societal and moral considerations that inform the selection of publicly acceptable criminal punishments.

. . . [N]either petitioner nor his *amici* have adduced any comprehensive statistics that would conclusively prove (or disprove) whether juries routinely consider death a disproportionate punishment for mentally retarded offenders like petitioner. Instead, it adverts to the fact that other countries have disapproved imposition of the death penalty for crimes committed by mentally retarded offenders. I fail to see, however, how the views of other countries regarding the punishment of their citizens provide any support for the Court's ultimate determination. . . .

Stanford's reasoning makes perfectly good sense, and the Court offers no basis to question it. For if it is evidence of a *national* consensus for which we are looking, then the viewpoints of other countries simply are not relevant. . . .

POINTS TO PONDER

- Do you agree with the dissent's argument that "the viewpoints of other countries simply are not relevant"?
- Many juvenile death penalty abolitionists relied on *Atkins* for support. Do you think the analogy between people with mental retardation and juveniles is an accurate one? Why or why not?
- How did juvenile death penalty advocates use the majority's analysis in this case to bolster their arguments? How about opponents of the juvenile death penalty? Set up a debate in which both sides try to use the reasoning of *Atkins* to support their position.
- Instead of carving out more exceptions to the death penalty, would abolishing it altogether make more sense? Are death penalty opponents trying to dismantle the structure brick by brick?
- According to an ABC News Poll conducted on December 19, 2003, only 21 percent of the public favors the death penalty over life in prison for juvenile murderers. Should "evolving standards of decency" include public opinion polls? Is that a sensible way to decide matters of constitutional law? Should Supreme Court justices refer to public opinion polls?

Schools are supposed to refer to a psychologist those students who demonstrate delays in mental development. If a school is underfunded and a child does not have access to a psychologist, his records may not indicate that he is mentally retarded. Mental retardation must be determined by age eighteen to be admissible as a mitigating circumstance in a convicted murderer's sentencing. What solutions or options exist for mentally challenged criminal defendants who were never properly diagnosed?

Turning Over a New Leaf?

In January 2004, the Supreme Court agreed to examine *Roper v. Simmons,* which raised the issue of whether executing an offender who was seventeen years old at the time of the crime violates the Eighth Amendment's protection against cruel and unusual punishment. The Court heard oral arguments in October 2004 and issued a ruling on March 1, 2005. In a 5-4 decision, a divided Court overruled *Stanford* and held that executing juveniles violates the Eighth Amendment's ban on cruel and unusual punishment. Scott Allen Hain—at the time of the decision the most recent person to have been executed (in April 2003) in Oklahoma for a crime he committed as a juvenile—missed the possibility of his sentence being commuted by less than one year.

Scott Allen Hain, who committed a double murder at age seventeen, had been put to death in April 2003 by the State of Oklahoma, making him the last juvenile offender executed in the United States before the *Simmons* decision. In March 2005, the Supreme Court banned the execution of offenders who commit capital crimes while under the age of eighteen. *Source: Tulsa World*

DONALD P. ROPER, SUPERINTENDENT, POTOSI CORRECTIONAL CENTER, PETITIONER, V. CHRISTOPHER SIMMONS

Supreme Court of the United States
No. 03-633.
Decided March 1, 2005.

Justice KENNEDY delivered the opinion of the Court.

This case requires us to address . . . whether it is permissible under the Eighth and Fourteenth Amendments to the Constitution of the United States to execute a juvenile offender who was older than 15 but younger than 18 when he committed a capital crime. In *Stanford v. Kentucky* (1989), a divided Court rejected the proposition that the Constitution bars capital punishment for juvenile offenders in this age group. We reconsider the question.

I

At the age of 17, when he was still a junior in high school, Christopher Simmons, the respondent here, committed murder. About nine months later, after he had turned 18, he was tried and sentenced to death. . . . Before its commission Simmons said he wanted to murder someone. In chilling, callous terms he talked about his plan, discussing it for the most part with two friends, Charles Benjamin and John Tessmer, then aged 15 and 16 respectively. . . . Simmons assured his friends they could "get away with it" because they were minors.

The three met at about 2 a.m. on the night of the murder, but Tessmer left before the other two set out. . . . Simmons and Benjamin entered the home of the victim, Shirley Crook, after reaching through an open window and unlocking the back door. Simmons turned on a hallway light. Awakened, Mrs. Crook called out, "Who's there?" In response Simmons entered Mrs. Crook's bedroom, where he recognized her from a previous car accident involving them both. . . .

. . . [T]he two perpetrators put Mrs. Crook in her minivan and drove to a state park. They . . . threw her from the bridge, drowning her in the waters below.

By the afternoon of September 9, Steven Crook had returned home from an overnight trip . . . and reported his wife missing. On the same afternoon fishermen recovered the victim's body from the river. Simmons, meanwhile, was bragging about the killing, telling friends he had killed a woman "because the [woman] seen my face."

The next day, after receiving information of Simmons' involvement, police arrested him . . . . After less than two hours of interrogation, Simmons confessed to the murder . . . .

The State charged Simmons with burglary, kidnapping, stealing, and murder in the first degree. . . . He was tried as an adult. At trial the State introduced Simmons' confession and the videotaped reenactment of the crime, along with testimony that Simmons discussed the crime in advance and bragged about it later. The defense called no witnesses in the guilt phase. The jury having returned a verdict of murder, the trial proceeded to the penalty phase.

Missouri death row inmate Christopher Simmons was seventeen when he committed murder. In October 2004, the Supreme Court heard arguments on whether it is constitutional under the Eighth Amendment to execute people whose crimes were committed when they were juveniles. *Source: Missouri Department of Corrections/AP Wide World Photos*

The State sought the death penalty. As aggravating factors, the State submitted that the murder was committed for the purpose of receiving money; was committed for the purpose of avoiding, interfering with, or preventing lawful arrest of the defendant; and involved depravity of mind and was outrageously and wantonly vile, horrible, and inhuman. . . .

In mitigation Simmons' attorneys first called an officer of the Missouri juvenile justice system, who testified that Simmons had no prior convictions and that no previous charges had been filed against him. Simmons' mother, father, two younger half brothers, a neighbor, and a friend took the stand to tell the jurors of the close relationships they had formed with Simmons and to plead for mercy on his behalf. Simmons' mother, in particular, testified to the responsibility Simmons demonstrated in taking care of his two younger half brothers and of his grandmother and to his capacity to show love for them.

During closing arguments, both the prosecutor and defense counsel addressed Simmons' age, which the trial judge had instructed the jurors they could consider as a mitigating factor. Defense counsel reminded the jurors that juveniles of Simmons' age cannot drink, serve on juries, or even see certain movies. . . . Defense counsel argued that Simmons' age should make "a huge difference to [the jurors] in deciding just exactly what sort of punishment to make." In rebuttal, the prosecutor gave the following response: "Age, he says. Think about age. Seventeen years old. Isn't that scary? Doesn't that scare you? Mitigating? Quite the contrary I submit. Quite the contrary."

The jury recommended the death penalty after finding the State had proved each of the three aggravating factors submitted to it. . . .

After [appeals] proceedings in Simmons' case had run their course, this Court held that the Eighth and Fourteenth Amendments prohibit the execution of a mentally retarded person. Simmons filed a new petition for state postconviction relief, arguing that the reasoning of *Atkins* established that the Constitution prohibits the execution of a juvenile who was under 18 when the crime was committed.

The Missouri Supreme Court agreed. . . .

We granted certiorari, and now affirm.

II

The Eighth Amendment provides: "Excessive bail shall not be required, nor excessive fines imposed, nor cruel and unusual punishments inflicted." The provision is applicable to the States through the Fourteenth Amendment. As the Court explained in *Atkins*, the Eighth Amendment guarantees individuals the right not to be subjected to excessive sanctions. The right flows from the basic " 'precept of justice that punishment for crime should be graduated and proportioned to [the] offense.' " By protecting even those convicted of heinous crimes, the Eighth Amendment reaffirms the duty of the government to respect the dignity of all persons.

. . . To implement this framework we have . . . affirmed the necessity of referring to "the evolving standards of decency that mark the progress of a maturing society" to determine which punishments are so disproportionate as to be cruel and unusual.

In *Thompson v. Oklahoma* (1988), a plurality of the Court determined that our standards of decency do not permit the execution of any offender under the age of 16 at the time of the crime. . . . The plurality . . . observed that "[t]he conclusion that it would offend civilized standards of decency to execute a person who was less than 16 years old at the time of his or her offense is consistent with the views that have been expressed by respected professional organizations, by other nations that share our Anglo-American heritage, and by the leading members of the Western European community." The opinion further noted that juries imposed the death penalty on offenders under 16 with exceeding rarity[.]

[T]he *Thompson* plurality stressed that "[juveniles'] irresponsible conduct is not as morally reprehensible as that of an adult." According to the plurality, the lesser culpability of offenders under 16 made the death penalty inappropriate as a form of retribution, while the low likelihood that offenders under 16 engaged in "the kind of cost-benefit analysis that attaches any weight to the possibility of execution" made the death penalty ineffective as a means of deterrence.

The next year, in *Stanford v. Kentucky* (1989), . . . the Court, over a dissenting opinion joined by four Justices, referred to contemporary standards of decency in this country and concluded the Eighth and Fourteenth Amendments did not proscribe the execution of juvenile offenders over 15 but under 18. The Court noted that 22 of the 37 death penalty States permitted the death penalty for 16-year-old offenders, and, among these 37 States, 25 permitted it for 17-year-old offenders. These numbers, in the Court's view, indicated there was no national consensus "sufficient to label a particular punishment cruel and unusual."

The same day the Court decided *Stanford,* it held [in *Penry v. Lynaugh*] that the Eighth Amendment did not mandate a categorical exemption from the death penalty for the mentally retarded. In reaching this conclusion it stressed that only two States had enacted laws banning the imposition of the death penalty on a mentally retarded person convicted of a capital offense . . .

Three terms ago the subject was reconsidered in *Atkins*. We held that standards of decency have evolved since *Penry* and now demonstrate that the execution of the mentally retarded is cruel and unusual punishment. The Court noted . . . legislative enactments and state practice with respect to executions of the mentally retarded. When *Atkins* was decided only a minority of States permitted the practice, and even in those States it was rare. . . .

. . . [W]e now reconsider the issue decided in *Stanford*. The beginning point is a review of objective indicia of consensus, as expressed in particular by the enactments of legislatures that have addressed the question. This data gives us essential instruction. We then must determine, in the exercise of our own independent judgment, whether the death penalty is a disproportionate punishment for juveniles.

III

A

. . . [Thirty] States prohibited the death penalty for the mentally retarded. This number comprised 12 that had abandoned the death penalty altogether, and 18 that maintained it but excluded the mentally retarded from its reach. By a similar calculation in this case, 30 States prohibit the juvenile death penalty, comprising 12 that have rejected the death penalty altogether and 18 that maintain it but, by express provision or judicial interpretation, exclude juveniles from its reach. . . . [E]ven in the 20 States without a formal prohibition on executing juveniles, the practice is infrequent. Since *Stanford*, six States have executed prisoners for crimes committed as juveniles. In the past 10 years, only three have done so: Oklahoma, Texas, and Virginia. . . . In December 2003 the Governor of Kentucky decided to spare the life of Kevin Stanford, and commuted his sentence to one of life imprisonment without parole, with the declaration that " '[w]e ought not be executing people who, legally, were children.' ". . .

As in *Atkins*, the objective indicia of consensus in this case—the rejection of the juvenile death penalty in the majority of States; the infrequency of its use even where it remains on the books; and the consistency in the trend toward abolition of the practice—provide sufficient evidence that today our society views juveniles, . . . as "categorically less culpable than the average criminal."

B

. . . Because the death penalty is the most severe punishment, the Eighth Amendment applies to it with special force. . . . [It] must be limited to those offenders who commit "a narrow category of the most serious crimes" and whose extreme culpability makes them "the most deserving of execution." . . .

Three general differences between juveniles under 18 and adults demonstrate that juvenile offenders cannot with reliability be classified among the worst offenders. First, . . . "[a] lack of maturity and an underdeveloped sense of responsibility are found in youth more often than in adults and are more understandable among the young. These qualities often result in impetuous and ill-considered actions and decisions." . . .

The second area of difference is that juveniles are more vulnerable or susceptible to negative influences and outside pressures, including peer pressure. . . .

The third broad difference is that the character of a juvenile is not as well formed as that of an adult. The personality traits of juveniles are more transitory, less fixed.

These differences render suspect any conclusion that a juvenile falls among the worst offenders.

. . . We have held there are two distinct social purposes served by the death penalty: " 'retribution and deterrence of capital crimes by prospective offenders.' " [T]he case for retribution is not as strong with a minor as with an adult. Retribution is not proportional if the law's most severe penalty is imposed on one whose culpability or blameworthiness is diminished, to a substantial degree, by reason of youth and immaturity.

As for deterrence, it is unclear whether the death penalty has a significant or even measurable deterrent effect on juveniles. . . . Here, . . . the absence of evidence of deterrent effect is of special concern because the same characteristics that render juveniles less culpable than adults suggest as well that juveniles will be less susceptible to deterrence. . . .

In concluding that neither retribution nor deterrence provides adequate justification for imposing the death penalty on juvenile offenders, we cannot deny or overlook the brutal crimes too many juvenile offenders have committed. . . . Certainly it can be argued . . . that a rare case might arise in which a juvenile offender has sufficient psychological maturity, and at the same time demonstrates sufficient depravity, to merit a sentence of death. . . . [P]etitioner and his *amici* . . . assert that even assuming the truth of the observations we have made about juveniles' diminished culpability in general, jurors nonetheless should be allowed to consider mitigating arguments related to youth on a case-by-case basis, and in some cases to impose the death penalty if justified. . . .

We disagree. The differences between juvenile and adult offenders are too marked and well understood to risk allowing a youthful person to receive the death penalty despite insufficient culpability.

. . . As we understand it . . . psychiatrists [are forbidden] from diagnosing any patient under 18 as having antisocial personality disorder, a disorder also referred to as psychopathy or sociopathy, and which is characterized by callousness, cynicism, and contempt for the feelings, rights, and suffering of others. If trained psychiatrists with the advantage of clinical testing and observation refrain, despite diagnostic expertise, from assessing any juvenile under 18 as having antisocial personality disorder, we conclude that States should refrain from asking jurors to issue a far graver condemnation—that a juvenile offender merits the death penalty. . . .

IV

Our determination that the death penalty is disproportionate punishment for offenders under 18 finds confirmation in the stark reality that the United States is the only country in the world that continues to give official sanction to the juvenile death penalty.

. . . As respondent and a number of *amici* emphasize, Article 37 of the United Nations Convention on the Rights of the Child, which every country in the world has ratified save for the United States and Somalia, contains an express prohibition on capital punishment for crimes committed by juveniles under 18.

. . . [O]nly seven countries other than the United States have executed juvenile offenders since 1990: Iran, Pakistan, Saudi Arabia, Yemen, Nigeria, the Democratic Republic of Congo, and China. Since then each of these countries has either abolished capital punishment for juveniles or made public disavowal of the practice. In sum, it is fair to say that the United States now stands alone in a world that has turned its face against the juvenile death penalty. . . .

Justice O'CONNOR, dissenting.

. . . Adolescents *as a class* are undoubtedly less mature, and therefore less culpable for their misconduct, than adults. But the Court has adduced no evidence impeaching the seemingly reasonable conclusion reached by many state legislatures: that at least *some* 17-year-old murderers are sufficiently mature to deserve the death penalty in an appropriate case.

. . . I would demand a clearer showing that our society truly has set its face against this practice before reading the Eighth Amendment categorically to forbid it. . . .

II

A

. . . I take issue with the Court's failure to reprove, or even to acknowledge, the Supreme Court of Missouri's unabashed refusal to follow our controlling decision in *Stanford*. The lower court concluded that, despite *Stanford*'s clear holding and historical recency, our decision was no longer binding authority because it was premised on what the court deemed an obsolete assessment of contemporary values.

. . . Seventeen year olds may, on average, be less mature than adults, but that lesser maturity simply cannot be equated with the major, lifelong impairments suffered by the mentally retarded. . . .

Justice SCALIA, with whom THE CHIEF JUSTICE and Justice THOMAS join, dissenting.

. . . [The Court] . . . finds . . . that a national consensus which could not be perceived in our people's laws barely 15 years ago now solidly exists. Worse still, the Court says in so many words that what our people's laws say about the issue does not, in the last analysis, matter: "[I]n the end our own judgment will be brought to bear on the question of the acceptability of the death penalty under the Eighth Amendment." The Court thus proclaims itself sole arbiter of our Nation's moral standards—and in the course of discharging that awesome responsibility purports to take guidance from the views of foreign courts and legislatures. Because I do not believe that the meaning of our Eighth Amendment, any more than the meaning of other provisions of our Constitution, should be determined by the subjective views of five Members of this Court and like-minded foreigners, I dissent.

I

. . . Consulting States that bar the death penalty concerning the necessity of making an exception to the penalty for offenders under 18 is rather like including old-order Amishmen in a consumer-preference poll on the electric car. Of *course* they don't like it, but that sheds no light whatever on the point at issue. That 12 States favor *no* executions says something about consensus against the death penalty, but nothing—absolutely nothing—about consensus that offenders under 18 deserve special immunity from such a penalty. In repealing the death penalty, those 12 States considered *none* of the factors that the Court puts forth as determinative of the issue before us today—lower culpability of the young, inherent recklessness, lack of capacity for considered judgment, etc. What might be relevant, perhaps, is how many of those States permit 16- and 17-year-old offenders to be treated as adults with respect to noncapital offenses. (They all do; indeed, some even *require* that juveniles as young as 14 be tried as adults if they are charged with murder.) The attempt by the Court to turn its remarkable minority consensus into a faux majority by counting Amishmen is an act of nomological desperation.

. . . I also doubt whether many of the legislators who voted to change the laws in those four States would have done so if they had known their decision would (by the pronouncement of this Court) be rendered irreversible. After all, legislative support for capital punishment, in any form, has surged and ebbed throughout our Nation's history. As JUSTICE O'CONNOR has explained:

"The history of the death penalty instructs that there is danger in inferring a settled societal consensus from statistics like those relied on in this case. In 1846, Michigan became the first State to abolish the death penalty. . . . In succeeding decades, other American States continued the trend towards abolition. . . . Later, and particularly after World War II, there ensued a steady and dramatic decline in executions. . . . In the 1950's and 1960's, more States abolished or radically restricted capital punishment, and executions ceased completely for several years beginning in 1968. . . .

"In 1972, when this Court heard arguments on the constitutionality of the death penalty, such statistics might have suggested that the practice had become a relic, implicitly rejected by a new societal consensus. . . . We now know that any inference of a societal consensus rejecting the death penalty would have been mistaken. But had this Court then declared the existence of such a consensus, and outlawed capital punishment, legislatures would very likely not have been able to revive it. The mistaken premise of the decision would have been frozen into constitutional law, making it difficult to refute and even more difficult to reject."

Relying on such narrow margins is especially inappropriate in light of the fact that a number of legislatures and voters have expressly affirmed their support for capital punishment of 16- and 17-year-old offenders since *Stanford*. Though the Court is correct that no State has lowered its death penalty age, both the Missouri and Virginia Legislatures—which, at the time of *Stanford*, had no minimum age requirement—expressly established 16 as the minimum. The people of Arizona and Florida have done the same by ballot initiative. Thus, even States that have not executed an under-18 offender in recent years unquestionably favor the possibility of capital punishment in some circumstances.

. . . It is, furthermore, unclear that executions of the relevant age group have decreased since we decided *Stanford*. Between 1990 and 2003, 123 of 3,599 death sentences, or 3.4%, were given to individuals who committed crimes before reaching age 18. By contrast, only 2.1% of those sentenced to death between 1982 and 1988 committed the crimes when they were under 18. . . .

II

Of course, the real force driving today's decision is not the actions of four state legislatures, but the Court's " ' "own judgment" ' " that murderers younger than 18 can never be as morally culpable as older counterparts. . . .

Today's opinion provides a perfect example of why judges are ill equipped to make the type of legislative judgments the Court insists on making here. To support its opinion that States should be prohibited from imposing the death penalty on anyone who committed murder before age 18, the Court looks to scientific and sociological studies, picking and choosing those that support its position. It never explains why those particular studies are methodologically sound; none was ever entered into evidence or tested in an adversarial proceeding. . . . [A]ll the Court has done today, to borrow from another context, is to look over the heads of the crowd and pick out its friends.

. . . The Court concludes, however, that juries cannot be trusted with the delicate task of weighing a defendant's youth along with the other mitigating and aggravating factors of his crime. This startling conclusion undermines the very foundations of our capital sentencing system, which entrusts juries with "mak[ing] the difficult and uniquely human judgments that defy codification and that 'buil[d] discretion, equity, and flexibility into a legal system.' " . . .

Nor does the Court suggest a stopping point for its reasoning. If juries cannot make appropriate determinations in cases involving murderers under 18, in what other kinds of cases will the Court find jurors deficient? . . .

III

Though the views of our own citizens are essentially irrelevant to the Court's decision today, the views of other countries and the so-called international community take center stage.

. . . It is interesting that whereas the Court is not content to accept what the States of our Federal Union *say*, but insists on inquiring into what they *do* (specifically, whether they in fact *apply* the juvenile death penalty that their laws allow), the Court is quite willing to believe that every foreign nation—of whatever tyrannical political makeup and with however subservient or incompetent a court system—in fact *adheres* to a rule of no death penalty for offenders under 18.

. . . The Court has been oblivious to the views of other countries when deciding how to interpret our Constitution's requirement that "Congress shall make no law respecting an establishment of religion. . . . " Most other countries—including those committed to religious neutrality—do not insist on the degree of separation between church and state that this Court requires. For example, . . . in France, which is considered "America's only rival in strictness of church-state separation," "[t]he practice of contracting for educational services provided by Catholic schools is very widespread."

And let us not forget the Court's abortion jurisprudence, which makes us one of only six countries that allow abortion on demand until the point of viability.

. . . The Court should either profess its willingness to reconsider all these matters in light of the views of foreigners, or else it should cease putting forth foreigners' views as part of the *reasoned basis* of its decisions. . . .

IV

To add insult to injury, the Court affirms the Missouri Supreme Court without even admonishing that court for its flagrant disregard of our precedent in *Stanford*. Until today, we have always held that "it is this Court's prerogative alone to overrule one of its precedents."

POINTS TO PONDER

- After *Stanford v. Kentucky*, only four states changed their laws to ban the juvenile death penalty. Should that have been enough proof that our standards of decency had changed?
- How did the majority and dissenting opinions consider the relevance of international views on the juvenile death penalty?
- In dissenting opinions, Justices O'Connor and Scalia voice disapproval of the Missouri Supreme Court's overruling of *Stanford*. What do you think of their fear that society will lose respect for the Court, which is seen as the ultimate arbiter of constitutional interpretation, if lower courts overrule its decisions?
- Justice Scalia argues that highlighting the states that ban the death penalty as support for the assertion that state legislatures are moving away from the juvenile death penalty is like asking an Amish man what he thinks of electric cars. What do you think of this comparison?

EXERCISE 8.3. Research different state laws on government executions and decide which ones you would support. Go to http://www.deathpenaltyinfo.org/ for more information.

EXERCISE 8.4. Prepare a presentation about international perspectives on the death penalty. Three primary sources you may wish to consult are the Amnesty International report issued on September 25, 2002, *Indecent and Internationally Illegal: The Death Penalty against Child Offenders*; the International Covenant on Civil and Political Rights, which was signed by the United States and condemns the imposition of the death penalty on juveniles; and the United Nations Convention on the Rights of the Child forbidding countries to kill those who commit crimes as juveniles, which the United States has refused to ratify, despite international pressure.

EXERCISE 8.5. Write down your views on the death penalty, both in general and for youth and then (with your parent's permission) watch the movie *Dead Man Walking*, starring Susan Sarandon and Sean Penn, or read the book of the same title by Sister Helen Prejean and reassess your views.

Notes

1. Kris Axtman, "Death Penalty for Juveniles under Scrutiny," *Christian Science Monitor*, August 27, 2002, available at http://www.csmonitor.com/2002/0827/p02s01-usju.html (accessed November 10, 2004).

2. CNN.com, "Malvo Sniper Shootings Case Goes to Jury," available at http://edition.cnn.com/2003/LAW/12/16/sprj.dcsp.malvo.trial/ (accessed January 31, 2005).

Additional Sources

Amnesty International. *Indecent and Internationally Illegal: The Death Penalty against Child Offenders*. September 25, 2002. Available at http://web.amnesty.org/library/Index/ENGAMR511432002 (accessed November 10, 2004).

Axtman, Kris. "Death Penalty for Juveniles under Scrutiny." *Christian Science Monitor*. August 27, 2002. Available at http://www.csmonitor.com/2002/0827/p02s01-usju.html (accessed November 10, 2004).

Death Penalty Information Center, www.deathpenaltyinfo.org.

Green, Bruce A., and Bernardine Dohrn. "Foreword: Children and the Ethical Practice of Law." *Fordham Law Review* 64 (1996): 1281.

Mauro, Tony. "Court Opens Execution Issue." *Legal Times*. February 2, 2004, 10.

National Criminal Justice Reference Service, http://virlib.ncjrs.org/JuvenileJustice.asp.

Searfoss, Robert E., III. "Waiver of Juvenile Jurisdiction and the Execution of Juvenile Offenders: Why the Eighth Amendment Should Require Proof of Sufficient Mental Capacity before the State Can Exact Either Punishment." *University of Toledo Law Review* 35 (2004): 663.

Streib, Victor L. "Executing Juvenile Offenders: The Ultimate Denial of Juvenile Justice." *Stanford Law and Policy Review* 14 (2003): 121.

———. "The Juvenile Death Penalty Today: Death Sentences and Executions for Juvenile Crimes, January 1, 1973–September 30, 2004." Available at http://www.law.onu.edu/faculty/streib/documents/JuvDeathSept302004.pdf (accessed January 31, 2005).

THE FUTURE OF
YOUTH JUSTICE

9

Adolescence can be the time of life when anything seems possible. For many young people all the pleasures of the world lay before them: going to college, falling in love, finding a job and career, establishing independence, starting a family.

But for others, the turbulent years between childhood and adulthood can become a nightmare filled with alcohol and substance abuse, family dysfunction, delinquency, gang violence, crime, arrest, prosecution, incarceration, loneliness, guilt, shame, and despair. For young people caught up in the criminal justice process, the teenage years become a time not of opportunities found but opportunities lost. One of the incarcerated juveniles participating in Mark Salzman's writing workshop wrote of his daily experience: "Darkness tries to smother my true being day by day. At times the light shines through all the darkness but that's very seldom. Happiness is very scarce, too. It feels as if more loneliness, hate, and anger comes as every minute passes." [1]

Young people go badly astray in their teen years for a variety of reasons. Some suffer psychological, emotional, physical, or sexual abuse and then act wildly out of latent anger and hostility. Some suffer the rupture of losing a beloved parent, sibling, or friend and spiral downward in depression. Some abuse alcohol or illegal drugs and quickly find themselves on a dangerous and antisocial path. Others, searching for a missing structure and sense of belonging in their lives, become part of youth gangs that teach them the habits of violence and crime. Another one of Salzman's students wrote the following from Central Juvenile Hall in Los Angeles.[2]

> They don't know what it's like when you come from a family that didn't have a father there to guide you in the right path. They don't know what it's like when there is nothing to eat when you come home from school. They don't know how it feels when your mother tells you that you need to quit school to get a job, because there ain't enough money for food. They don't know because they come from rich families with parents and money to buy food and pay for their kids' education so they could grow up to go to college to become the judges, lawyers, D.A.'s, prosecutors, politicians, and all them others that are making the laws to put us away for life.

While the causes of young people turning to crime are as varied and complex as the young people's lives themselves, society's collective responses have increasingly focused on a single reaction: to throw the full weight of the criminal justice system against juvenile offenders. Given that Americans aspire to be a self-governing democratic society committed to liberty and equality, they always need to ask how well the criminal justice

Members of the Bloods in Los Angeles show their gang signs and colors. Many such gangs thrive on juvenile delinquency, violence, and crime, but some groups have called for truces among the gangs and for their members to become involved in political organizing and community building. *Source: California Gang Investigators*

policies are working and what kinds of effects they are having on the people, especially the young.

The Goals of Criminal Punishment

Criminal punishment has traditionally served four goals: **incapacitation** (removing the "bad apples" from society so they do not have the chance to strike again), **deterrence** (preventing other people from following offenders on a delinquent path), **retribution** ("paying them back" by matching every offense with a punishment of equal severity and weight), and **rehabilitation** (reform and education of the offender to treat underlying psychological and social problems that influenced the delinquency in the first place).

How well are these goals being served today? While youth are awaiting their prosecution, they oftentimes are held in detention facilities similar to prisons: Their mobility is controlled, they have limited access to the outside world, and they have to follow restrictive rules. When judges find youth guilty (there are no juries in juvenile proceedings), juveniles can be required to perform community service, be put on probation (meaning that they have to check in with a probation officer at regular intervals), or be

---

YOUR THOUGHTS

How well do you think the goals of rehabilitation, incapacitation, deterrence, and retribution are being served in youth detention facilities?

---

placed in a group home, residential setting, or secure detention center similar to a jail. In terms of rehabilitation, the court can order services covering educational, mental health, medical, drug and alcohol rehabilitation, and social needs. Job training, schooling, and drug or alcohol counseling may be required through probation. Often a combination of punishment and treatment is ordered. The stated goal of the juvenile justice system is to provide care and rehabilitation to the youthful offender.

Yet, Americans now seem to have less sympathy for the goal of rehabilitation than they did, say, in the 1960s. How well do the juvenile facilities rehabilitate and educate? How effectively are the offenders' psychological and emotional problems handled? Have their reading, writing, math, and science skills improved? Are they prepared for a tough job market? Are their mental health, their independence, and their life skills enhanced?

How effective is the juvenile justice system at incapacitation? While jail time definitely keeps convicted juveniles off the streets, many of them are still committing crimes behind bars and learning more sophisticated criminal techniques on the inside. A system that fails to rehabilitate offenders and propel them in a positive direction will only increase the chances that, once released, juvenile offenders will be back in prison again down the road.

How about deterrence? When offenders are punished, are the methods used successfully deterring others from joining gangs and committing crimes? Are people being scared straight? It is hard to know, but the evidence does not seem overwhelming that the policy to deter is working. In many neighborhoods, jail itself has become a rite of passage, a routine stop in a hard and bitter life. In some places, jail time is considered a badge of honor. But, most important, considerable medical research indicates that young people have poor judgment and are impulsive and, therefore, do not respond to the kind of abstract deterrence that punishment within the justice system offers.

What about retribution? Given the physical deprivation and negative psychological effects suffered by so many incarcerated juveniles, the goal of retribution is arguably quite well served. The same kind of pain that juvenile criminals have unleashed on their victims is revisited upon them through long sentences, harsh and abusive conditions, indifference to physical and sexual attacks by other inmates, solitary confinement, imposed separation from family and friends, and the absence of the normal pleasures of youth. Do you think it is enough?

The question of whether the balance is right between the different goals of criminal punishment is an important and recurring one. However, a top-to-bottom audit of the juvenile justice process is rarely done. More likely, particular problems and crises that emerge at particular times become the focus.

Record Prison Populations

If you examine incarceration rates all over the world, you will find that the United States locks up more people than any other country. If there were an Olympics event for criminal incarceration of your own population, America would win the gold medal handsdown. Nearly seven million people in the United States are living in prison or in jail or are on probation or parole. This vast population is larger than the number of people

Many of the daytime talk shows, such as those hosted by Maury Povich, Rikki Lake, and Jenny Jones, like to show how bad kids are reformed through private or state boot camps. These institutions are based on theory that bad kids need more discipline, more physical rigor, and more time outdoors. Do you agree with this theory? Would going to boot camp set you straight?

who live in seven states (Delaware, Maine, North Dakota, Rhode Island, South Dakota, Vermont, and Wyoming) and Washington, D.C., combined. If the current rates of incarceration continue, nearly one out of fifteen Americans will serve time in prison during his or her lifetime.[3] The young form an important part of this portrait of a subnation behind bars. More than 100,000 people under age eighteen are incarcerated. Furthermore, the flood of prisoners shows no signs of abating. Between 2002 and 2003, the U.S. prison and jail population increased by 2.9 percent.

Not only is it unclear that detention facilities rehabilitate young people, but the alarming news about abuse of juveniles in detention facilities across the country also has raised significant human rights concerns. The Youth Law Center has litigated or is litigating on behalf of children locked up in fifteen states: Alabama, California, Colorado, Florida, Idaho, Indiana, Kentucky, Louisiana, Maine, New Mexico, North Carolina, Ohio, Oregon, South Carolina, and South Dakota. The children may be subject to inhumane conditions such as long lockdowns and abuses such as use of pepper spray as discipline. The Youth Law Center frequently receives complaints that children are not provided with medical, mental health, and educational services and that learning disabled children receive no special educational services. Many detained youth have undiagnosed mental

The Youth Law Center filed suit against the South Dakota State Training School for the use of excessive force against children and for other abuses. The contested practices included the threat of force with "less-than-lethal" weapon systems, such as this shotgun that fires rubber projectiles. Authorities closed the facility following a settlement between the center and the state. *Source: Mark Soler/Youth Law Center*

disorders, and many are force-fed potent medications to control their behavior. Similarly the Mississippi Center for Justice is spearheading efforts to decarcerate youth in Mississippi who are assigned to training camps for status offenses such as truancy and curfew violations.

First, Do No Harm: State Struggles with Record of Juvenile Injustice
by Brett Potter and Donna Ladd
Jackson Free Press

January 19, 2005

At 17 years old, Tommy Croft has grown up faster than most youth his age in Mississippi. Croft conveys the pain and genuineness in his story about his dark past with his large brown, puppy-dog-sad eyes. Croft wears the same street clothes as many other African-American youth in this state do: an orange bandana and a backward orange-and-white baseball cap with an over-sized baseball jersey. The dark hair on his upper lip is just enough to make him look a few years older.

Croft recalls his first run-in with the law while sitting at a table in Jay's Restaurant in Monticello, where Croft is currently living. He says: "The first time I had to go to youth court, I was charged with receiving stolen goods and joyriding (with someone who did not own the car), and that's why I had to go to Columbia. Later I was charged with the attempted sale of drugs on school premises. I got a year and six months for that in Oakley." He was 13 when he first was locked up.

While at the Oakley Training School in Raymond, Croft got in more trouble for allegedly running through the campus screaming, which added two months to his sentence, and another time for allegedly throwing up gang signs, which added six more months to his sentence. Croft openly admits he used to be a part of a gang, but says he is no longer active. Croft was put in Ironwood—the maximum-security lockup unit at Oakley—for running away with a fellow cadet. He was there for the remainder of his stay, except for the last two weeks.

Croft says his stay in the training school made him more of a criminal. "Oakley actually made me worse. I started smoking weed. Now that's all I was smoking when I got out, but Oakley definitely made me worse. Nine out of 10 of the kids that are up there go back up there for a third or fourth time. [Oakley] is this little prison facility where you get locked up in all day. You have a bathroom in your cell, but sometimes they would cut your water off. That's cruel because if you had to use the bathroom, then you would have to smell that all day while you were in there."

He recalls some of the harsh treatment he observed at Oakley, "One time when I was up there I saw this staff member stomp this boy to the ground for no reason. I also remember this one staff member on duty that told me he would beat the hell out of me a few times."

Worse though, Croft speaks of when he was at Ironwood, the prison within a prison. He remembers a staff member refusing to let a guy use the bathroom, so he decided to defecate in his blanket and throw it outside the cell because he couldn't bear it. "I think he actually got about three more months for that, and he had been holding it all day long," Croft said.

'Cruel and Unusual Punishment'

It would be easy to shrug and say that Croft's stories are merely the tales of a troublemaking kid who doesn't like to be punished—in fact, that's a typical response to descriptions of problems in the state's two training schools. But, in 2003, parents, children and their advocates who had complained for years of severe abuses in the training schools got a credibility boost: the Bush administration's Department of Justice [DOJ] issued a scathing report that backed up their stories, and then some, accusing the state of Mississippi of providing "cruel and unusual punishment in violation of the Eighth Amendment of the U.S. Constitution" to the state's young residents who get in trouble for "crimes" as mild as skipping school.

Following an investigation of Oakley Training School in Raymond and Columbia Training Facilities in Columbia, the U.S. Department of Justice findings showed that the harsh conditions described by Croft are only a taste of what Mississippi's youth offenders have to bear when they are fulfilling their sanctions set by the courts in these "paramilitary" training schools. The investigation, conducted in response to three federal lawsuits filed against these training schools, found that boys and girls—most in for non-violent crimes and most children of color—were being hog-tied, beaten, choked, shackled to poles and even locked into cold, dark cells while naked for hours.

DOJ found that every level of care for these youth was deficient—from safety to education, sanitation to medical care. "Youth at Oakley and Columbia are confined in unsafe living conditions and receive inadequate treatment and care," the DOJ wrote to then-Gov. Ronnie Musgrove. "These conditions exist mainly because of staff shortages, ineffective management and supervision at every organizational level within both facilities, and the facilities' emphasis on control and punishment instead of rehabilitation."

"Oakley and Columbia do not have any system of positive incentives to manage youth," DOJ added, "but instead rely on discipline and force. This leads to unconstitutionally abusive disciplinary practices such as hog-tying, pole-shackling, improper use and overuse of restraints and isolation, staff assaulting youth, and OC (pepper) spray abuse." The DOJ found not only 8th Amendment violations, but infringements of the children's due process rights, as well as their 1st Amendment freedoms, which were violated because they were forced to engage in specific religious activities; if they refused, they would be disciplined.

Equal Opportunity Abuse

Both schools are currently under the auspices of the state's Department of Human Services [DHS]. Children who get in trouble for a variety of offenses—from truancy, to getting into a fight on a playground, to more serious violent offenses—can be sentenced to these two facilities by youth court judges. Indeed, a 10-year-old child who gets in trouble in North Mississippi can end up doing push-ups in the hot sun hundreds of miles from his family.

The Oakley Training School, also called the Mississippi Youth Correctional Complex, rests on 1,068 acres of land contained by fields in Raymond, half an hour south of Jackson. Oakley is designed to operate as a paramilitary program for delinquent boys, ages 10 to 17. DOJ found that the majority of the boys at Oakley were there for property offenses, lower-level drug possession or auto theft.

The Columbia Training School, located in Columbia, two and a half hours northwest of Gulfport, is also on 1,000 acres of land in an unfenced rural setting. Columbia, with many housing and administration buildings surrounding a big field in a lodge setting, has a medical clinic, a school with a cafeteria, a chapel and a gym. Columbia primarily houses girls aged 10 to 18, but is used to incarcerate boys, aged 10 to 15, as well. Most of the girls at Columbia are there for "status offenses"—minor or misdemeanor-level problems such as probation violations or contempt of court. Juvenile justice experts usually recommend that children who commit status offenses be placed in non-secure settings.

However, like Oakley, Columbia uses a paramilitary model for both girls and boys. DOJ is quick to emphasize that paramilitary programs are not, on their face, unconstitutional when used in juvenile facilities. However, it said Mississippi uses paramilitary-style punishment on four segments of the population "particularly unsuitable" for the harsh discipline: younger boys, girls, youth with developmental disabilities and youth who are emotionally or physically fragile.

DOJ outlined instances of school staff using archaic restraints, such as hog-tying and pole-shackling boys and girls, "without penological justification." At least 10 to 15 children of both genders reported being placed face down on the floor with their hands and feet drawn behind their backs and shackled together like, well, hogs. Girls were typically tied in this way for three-hour periods and often left in totally dark rooms.

One girl, who did not follow orders during military exercises at Columbia, was pole-shackled—meaning her arms and legs were handcuffed and shackled around a utility pole for three hours as the rest of the unit performed military exercises around her. Another girl was treated similarly for talking in the cafeteria. Still another because she did not say, "Yes, sir."

Girls at Columbia who "acted out" or showed suicidal tendencies were placed in the "dark room"—a locked, windowless isolation cell, which is often kept pitch-black. The room has nothing in it but a drain in the middle of the floor that the girls can use as a toilet. Most girls are stripped naked when placed in the "dark room." One girl reported being left there without clothes in the dark for three days and forced to eat all her meals there.

The DOJ also found that Columbia girls were often not given access to basic necessities, such as water, personal hygiene items and bathroom facilities, and were not provided adequate mental health services.

Reversing the Abuse

The DOJ report was graphic and chilling in its detail when it went public; more shocking was that this abuse was known by state lawmakers and children's advocates for many years. But nothing had been accomplished to help these children caught in a system where no one wanted to take responsibility. The lawsuits came about because the state—unlike other states that the DOJ had targeted—refused to settle the suits with the government and take responsibility for repairing an antiquated and broken juvenile-justice system that had been in place since Jim Crow days. For one thing, the state didn't want to pay for expensive improvements; for another, many staunch conservatives believed that these troublemakers deserved all the tough love they could get. This was a bipartisan problem with a bipartisan history.

But the lawsuit and the 2003 report got the attention of the state. It was designed to; the federal government was bearing down: "Fix this problem now." Mississippi could no longer ignore its young offenders' rights. Then, during the 2004 legislative session, a coalition of advocates for children, civil libertarians and juvenile-justice experts came together to both demand action and to find ways to make juvenile justice make sense, and be affordable for the state.

Attorney Sheila Bedi is one of those advocates. She is on loan to Jackson from the Southern Poverty Law Center in Montgomery, Ala.; she is working with the Mississippi Center for Justice as an advocate to help lawmakers craft a solution to the training-school dilemma. "With proactive legislation, we can prevent states from dissenting lawsuits over conditions in juvenile facilities," Bedi said.

Bedi is representing a number of the young inmates in lawsuits against the state; she and other attorneys, however, have run into numerous roadblocks in gaining access to their young clients. She represents a 14-year-old, known as K. L. W., who was choked by an adult staff member at the Columbia Training School. The case, *K. L. W. v. James*, was filed in the United States District Court for the Southern District of Mississippi in April

2004. But K. L. W. was initially unable to meet with Mississippi Center for Justice attorneys due to the state's policy restricting visitation to counsel of record in youth court proceedings.

Only last Wednesday, Jan. 12, a settlement was reached. The State of Mississippi has agreed to change its policy on allowing access to counsel at the state's two training schools. Now staff at the training schools will inform each child orally and in writing of their right to access counsel and the courts; they will help facilitate access by providing each child with a list of pro bono counsel; they will help the children contact counsel of their choice; and they will permit attorneys to visit with a child upon notice and with the approval of the child's legal guardian, youth court counsel or youth court judge.

"We're pleased the state will allow the young girls at Columbia access to their attorneys. After all, the DOJ found that these girls were most vulnerable to abuse and lived in the most inhumane conditions," Bedi said.

Fixing the Problem

While other lawmakers and lobbyists spent much of the 2004 legislative session fighting over Medicaid, education funding and tort reform, a coalition of lawmakers and children's advocates spent their time trying to hammer out a solution to the juvenile-justice crisis here. That effort has yielded the Juvenile Justice Reform Act of 2005, authored by Rep. George Flaggs, D-Vicksburg, that will come to the floor this session.

With 18 years of experience as a youth court counselor in Warren County, the loquacious and animated Flaggs is eager to deal with the state's problems with the juvenile justice system. "As I've said from the start, we need to legislate, not litigate. It will be cheaper and more effective that way," Flaggs said.

As part of his research, Flaggs visited both Oakley and Columbia, and he also visited Louisiana, Florida and Missouri to see new community-based programs in the states that have replaced monolithic, prison-type facilities such as Oakley and Columbia. Flaggs has introduced what he believes is a budget-neutral, comprehensive package that will provoke a dialogue that will examine the faults in our current system.

In Mississippi, he argues, court-ordered mandates into an unsatisfactory and poorly run juvenile-justice system ultimately end up costing taxpaying citizens even more money than well-run community-based programs would. The state currently shells out $89.04 per day per youth incarcerated at the training schools. The Mississippi Coalition for the Prevention of Schoolhouse to Jailhouse—a statewide group of educators, community legal and public policy leaders—says that once Mississippi settles pending lawsuits, the cost could rise to $287 per youth, per day. This is much, much more than is spent per pupil for public education in the state ($6,143 per pupil per year).

One way to streamline the costs and the services, Flaggs believes, is to take the juvenile justice system away from the Department of Human Services—which doesn't exactly have a track record of success here—and create a new Department of Juvenile Justice. Historically, the training schools have not always been under the DHS. They used to have their own board that reported to the governor and the Legislature; however, this was changed under Gov. Ray Mabus.

Flaggs also wants to change the names of the Oakley and Columbia facilities to the Juvenile Justice Centers at Hinds and Marion in order to rid the facilities of their old stigma. "If it has a state seal on it," he said, "it ought to represent the best the state has to offer, which is what we plan to offer the youth offenders."

"Right now, the kids are coming out of Oakley worse than they came in because of how they are not getting the proper rehabilitation they deserve," Flaggs added, echoing the belief of Tommy Croft and many other training-school alumni.

Flaggs warns that if the Legislature does not pass comprehensive reform this session, it is going to be more difficult, and more costly, in the longer run. "If we don't legislate, the court will litigate, and this will be less expensive than a court mandate. Just look at the Ayers settlements and the Medicaid settlements," he said.

Meeting Opposition

Still, opposition to the plan is strong. Rep. Virginia Carlton, R-Columbia, a member of the Juvenile Justice Committee, says that Flaggs' bill isn't ready for primetime just yet. "I would not anticipate the bill will pass as is because the youth court judges have just sent us a long list of changes that need to be made," she said. "When it comes time to vote, I'll just do what I believe is the right thing to do with the information I'm provided while using my background and experience."

Carlton has represented juveniles in youth court as a public defender, been a prosecutor for crimes of violence involving women and children, and trained law enforcement and social workers for forensics interviews for child justice cases at the Southwest Mississippi Children's Advocacy Center. She says she has worked years on "making the criminal justice system work more for them to protect them and not further victimize them in child abuse and rape cases."

One of the faults with the Juvenile Justice Act that Carlton points out is Flaggs' projected, rigid caps for the number of children each facility can have. Under the bill, the Center at Hinds (Oakley) could only house a maximum of 365 children by July 1, 2006, going down by 100 kids every year to a total of only 165 by 2008. The Marion center (Columbia) would decrease to 75 youth by 2008. According to Carlton, research needs to be done in order to see what the proper ratio for child-to-staff would be.

Carlton also doesn't trust the financial analysis. "I'm a cautious individual, and I'm waiting for a fiscal note to see the exact figures," she said. "We can't afford a new Department of Juvenile Justice right now. We are in a fiscal crisis with the budget and need to concentrate on getting out of debt first, but I am eager to study this and try and make some changes."

Flaggs and Carlton both agree that Oakley should only be for the worst offenders in the future and that the training centers should concentrate more on educating and teaching a vocation to the youth, while rehabilitating both the youth and their families. DOJ called education at both facilities—especially at Oakley where many students participated in no school work at all—"sorely inadequate" and emphasized that the children are entitled to adequate education and vocational training. Flaggs' bill would create a school district out of Oakley with certified teachers, so the children can stay longer and continue their education.

DOJ also found that youth offenders with mental disorders weren't being treated quickly, thoroughly or individually by mental-health experts—a problem both Flaggs and Carlton agreed should be fixed. The feds also warned that students with mental-health problems shouldn't be subjected to paramilitary-style discipline, which is the bedrock principle that has ruled both facilities, and Mississippi's mindset, for years. Carlton, who is an Army Reserve JAG officer and mother of three, is not opposed to the paramilitary component.

Bringing the Kids Home

One way to alleviate the flood of non-violent offenders into the training facilities is to not send them there in the first place. This may seem like an obvious answer—but it requires a major shift in the thinking of lawmakers and others in the state who believe that "bad" kids should be shipped off to training school (or "reform schools," as they used to be called).

"We would love to see both training schools eliminated," said Ellen Reddy, executive director of the Citizens for Quality Education, a member of the Mississippi Coalition for the Prevention of Schoolhouse to Jailhouse. Reddy said that young people with heavy offenses need a safe environment, just as the public does. She wants a "balancing act" to find out what is happening in the troubled children's lives. "The treatment and rehabilitation comes back to the communities because, ultimately, it comes back to the homes. We need to get away from punishment."

An alternative, which is working wonders in many states including Louisiana (see page 16), is to replace the mega-facility model with community-based programs—especially for children who have committed minor, non-violent offenses. And both Flaggs and Carlton believe this will save the state money—and it will keep "status" offenders from mixing with more violent children.

There are basically three types of community-based alternatives. A Day Treatment Center allows kids to attend school for six hours per day while getting counseling and participating in community-service activities a few days a week before returning home. In an Intensive Mentoring Program, each youth offender is assigned a "tracker" (usually a college student) who monitors the child's school attendance, behavior and performance. In a Home Detention alternative, a child is confined to only school and home with a curfew and is required to call in check-in times. This alternative allows for the child to receive counseling and family monitoring as well.

The coalition argues that community-based sanctions would only cost the state $23.08 per child, per day, and they have released many studies and statistics showing how much more effective these programs are in neighboring states.

But some critics of juvenile justice reform say community-based programs would be merely a slap on the wrist—and thus not very effective. Who's right?

The most compelling argument for these types of programs involves a study released by the National Institutes of Health that revealed that these community-based alternatives involve the families and communities and address the children's mental health needs more effectively than more antiquated models like training schools. NIH reported on Oct. 15, 2004: " 'Scare tactics' don't work, and there is some evidence that they may make the problem worse rather than simply not working," adding that there is "no reason to believe that group detention centers, boot camps and other get tough programs do anything more than provide an opportunity for delinquent youth to amplify negative effects on each other."

Flaggs would like these programs to be in every county or district; his bill calls for at least every congressional district to have a community-based alternative to the training schools by July 1, 2010. Carlton balks at the cost.

Rep. Erik Fleming, D-Clinton, said: "I think Flaggs' bill is very important. It is a budget-neutral plan for now, but we would like to have community-based organizations in all counties. I strongly agree that we need to pull the juvenile justice system out of the DHS. We don't need to treat kids like criminals or train them to be better criminals by letting Oakley stay the way it is."

Even the most conservative lawmakers can see the point of community-based programs. Sen. Charlie Ross, R-Jackson, told the JFP just before Christmas: "In juvenile justice, one size does not fit all. Some juveniles do need to be put away and punished at Oakley; however, I believe that community-based programs are OK for some kids—those with minor offenses, that is."

Of course, not everyone agrees on the definition of the word "minor"—and the truth is that the children, for one reason or another, who end up in the juvenile-justice system have been in trouble of some sort.

Would Tommy Croft—who was charged with a drug offense and riding in a stolen car—be considered a minor offender who deserves the compassion of a community-based program over the military rigor of an Oakley? The answer is not yet clear, but this is a question for the state, and its residents, to ponder.

For his part, Croft doesn't have to worry about uniforms, handcuffs or razor-wire fences anymore, though. Attorney Bedi has helped him maneuver the system and get his home life back on track, he said. "I'm in the clear now, and I was off the papers as of Dec. 7." He's trying to get a fresh start. "I'm drug-free, and I'm trying to get my GED and trying to find a trade. I'm thinking about being an auto mechanic," he said.

Movement toward Decarceration

The use of pretrial detention for youthful offenders has increased substantially over the last decade. Youth detention populations grew by a remarkable 38 percent between 1987 and 1996. Today, over 70 percent of the detention facilities in America are strained and operating at over capacity, meaning that they are holding more youth than they were designed to manage. Despite a decade-long drop in youth crime, the detention population has continued to grow nationally.

Leading a public outcry in many areas about miserable conditions in juvenile detention centers are parents and advocates who say that these centers violate basic human rights—and do not work to serve the purposes of criminal justice. Mainly, they do not work because many young people come out of them knowing more about how to commit crime than they did when they entered. The detention centers operate like secondary schools for crime.

Recently, advocates for youth behind bars have argued strenuously in favor of **decarceration**. Decarceration, or finding alternative rehabilitative community settings instead of institutionalization, is not a new concept. However, it has been revived with some success in several communities.

Throughout the 1990s, public attention was focused on sensational juvenile crime in the Washington, D.C., metropolitan area, which included gang violence and

Protesters in Annapolis, Maryland, demonstrate against abuses and dangerous conditions at the Cheltenham Youth Facility and urge Gov. Robert Ehrlich to close the institution, which was founded in the nineteenth century as the House of Reformation for Colored Boys. *Source: Linda Blount Berry*

Members of the Maryland Juvenile Justice Coalition protest the bad conditions at the Baltimore City Juvenile Detention Center in 2004. *Source: Nonso Umunna*

a soaring homicide rate. Meantime, major litigation took place about the conditions of confinement at the three youth facilities run by the District of Columbia. Reports surfaced that youth were being severely abused and neglected by staff and that no education was taking place inside these facilities. Two centers—Cedar Knoll and the Receiving Home—closed up shop in 1994 and 1995, respectively. Another center, Oak Hill, remains in operation despite similar reports of inadequate and sometimes dreadful conditions.

A natural result of the closure of two detention centers was that the District reduced the number of youth detained. Over the 1990s, as new alternatives to detention programs were put in place, the average daily population of youth detained in D.C. dropped from 411 to 124, a 71 percent reduction in the juvenile population confined.[4]

Meanwhile, in Maryland, the incarcerated juvenile population rose. Although the state, in the late 1980s, closed one facility, the Montrose Juvenile Training School, the average daily population of detained youth grew in the 1990s from 349 to 440—a per capita increase of 3 percent.[5] Many youth advocates attribute this population increase to the lack of readily available alternatives to detention.

Around the nation, long and drawn-out court cases have emerged about the quality of juvenile facilities and the care paid to minors inside them. Many states have entered into

---

YOUR THOUGHTS

If you found yourself in trouble, what is the worst punishment that could be inflicted upon you?

Would staying in a detention center such as Oak Hill or Oakley scare you straight or make you more hardened and ungovernable?

---

consent decrees in which they promise to reform certain aspects of their detention facilities. These agreements often lead to further litigation when they are violated or neglected.

Despite fears that reducing confinement would lead to jumps in criminal activity, the declining use of juvenile detention in D.C. was accompanied by a large drop in juvenile crime. According to Building Blocks for Youth, a nonprofit advocacy group, D.C.'s average daily population of youth in detention fell by 70 percent in the 1990s. Meanwhile, the District experienced three times the drop in the juvenile violent crime rate that Maryland did. Maryland, which saw an increase in the number of youth in detention over the 1990s, experienced a much smaller decrease in violent crime than D.C.[6]

The Racial Dynamics of the Criminal Justice System

The institution of criminal punishment in the United States has been intertwined with the vexed history of slavery and racism. Many of the first police forces were organized to patrol the slave population in the South, and many southern states ran dual justice systems with different criminal laws, different courts, different punishments, and different penal institutions for whites and African Americans. Several recent studies have shown that the death penalty is still much more likely to be handed down against defendants who murder whites than against those who kill African Americans.[7]

Police brutality has been an explosive issue in minority communities. Many African Americans viewed the savage beating of black motorist Rodney King by officers of the Los Angeles Police Department in 1991 not as a freak occurrence but as an accidental glimpse at a systemic problem. The differing reactions to the acquittal of O. J. Simpson in the murder prosecution of his ex-wife, Nicole, and her friend Ron Goldman reflected profound divisions among whites and African Americans in perceptions of racism in the criminal justice process.

Whatever the differences in perception, the criminal justice system clearly continues to have a disproportionate effect on the lives of people in minority communities. The U.S. inmate population is nearly 70 percent African American and Latino today. In 1999, about 800,000 black men were in custody in federal **penitentiaries**, state prisons, and county and city jailhouses. On an average day, one in eight African American males in their twenties wakes up behind bars.[8]

About one in four Americans is a juvenile (or under the age of eighteen)—seventy million Americans.[9] According to the latest demographic statistics, for 1999, 79 percent of juveniles in the United States were white, 16 percent were Latino, 15 percent were African American, 4 percent were Asian, and 1 percent were Native American Indians.[10] Table 9.1 shows the disproportionate representation of racial minorities in the ranks of juvenile offenders. Although whites are still in a majority in most crime categories, African Americans are clearly overrepresented at the arrest phase.

When the process moves from arrest to prosecution, sentencing, and confinement, the racial dynamics intensify further. Much higher proportions of African American and Latino young people are being confined in juvenile institutions than their white counterparts. Consider the dramatic differences as illustrated in Figure 9.1.

People can have different reactions to the data presented in Figure 9.1. Some say that African American and Latino youth are in custody at disproportionately high rates sim-

Table 9.1. Racial Proportions of Incarcerated Youth under Age Eighteen, 1998

| Most serious offense charged | Estimated number of juvenile arrests | Percent of total arrests | | | |
		White	African American	Native American	Asian
Total	**2,603,300**	**71**	**26**	**1**	**2**
Violent Crime Index	112,200	55	42	1	1
Murder	2,100	47	49	3	2
Rape	5,300	59	39	1	1
Robbery	32,500	43	54	1	2
Aggravated assault	72,300	61	37	1	2
Property Crime Index	596,100	**70**	**27**	1	**2**
Burglary	116,000	73	24	1	2
Larceny-theft	417,100	70	26	1	2
Motor vehicle theft	54,100	61	36	1	2
Arson	9,000	80	18	1	1
Non-index	1,895,000	**73**	**25**	1	**1**
Other assaults	237,700	64	33	1	1
Forgery and counterfeiting	7,100	77	21	1	2
Fraud	11,300	64	34	<1	2
Embezzlement	1,600	61	37	1	1
Stolen property, buying, receiving, possessing	33,800	60	38	1	2
Vandalism	126,800	80	17	1	1
Weapons carrying, possessing, and so on	45,200	66	32	1	1
Prostitution	1,400	56	43	1	1
Sex offenses (except forcible rape and prostitution)	15,900	70	28	1	1
Drug abuse violations	205,800	66	32	1	1
Gambling	1,600	15	84	—	1
Offenses against the family and child	10,200	79	19	1	2
Driving under the influence	21,000	91	6	2	1
Liquor laws	157,300	92	5	3	1
Drunkenness	24,600	89	7	3	1
Disorderly conduct	183,700	67	32	1	1
Vagrancy	2,900	71	27	1	<1
All other offenses (except traffic)	453,000	73	25	1	2
Suspicion	1,300	79	20	1	1
Curfew and loitering law violations	187,800	71	27	1	1
Runaways	165,100	78	18	1	3

Source: Adapted from Office of Juvenile Justice and Delinquency, *Juvenile Arrests 1998* (Washington, D.C.: Office of Juvenile Justice and Delinquency Prevention, 1999); Federal Bureau of Investigation, *Crime in the United States, 1998* (Washington, D.C.: Federal Bureau of Investigation, 1999). Population data are from U.S. Census Bureau, *U.S. Population Estimates by Age, Sex, Race, and Hispanic Origin: 1980–1998* (Washington, D.C.: U.S. Census Bureau, 1999).

Notes: Overall percentages of youth population: 79, white; 15, African American; 1, Native American; 2, Asian. Detail may not add to total because of rounding. The data do not disaggregate Latino youth from race. In 1998, 91 percent of Latino youth were identified as white.

Figure 9.1. U.S. Residential Custody Rates by Race, 1997

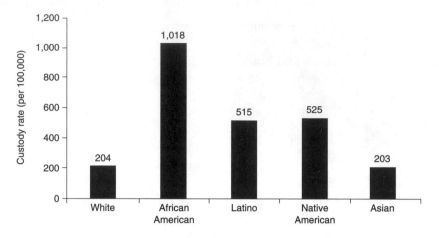

Sources: Juvenile Offenders and Victims: 1999 National Report (Washington, D.C.: Office of Juvenile Justice and Delinquency Prevention, 1999); see also E. Poe-Yamagata and M. Jones, *And Justice for Some: Differential Treatment of Minority Youth in the Juvenile Justice System,* prepared by the National Council on Crime and Delinquency (Washington, D.C.: Building Blocks for Youth, April 2000), available at http://www.buildingblocksforyouth.org/justiceforsome/conclusion.html (accessed November 19, 2004).

Notes: Custody rate is youth in residential placement per 100,000 youth ages 10 through upper age of original juvenile court jurisdiction in each state. Does not include persons of Hispanic ethnicity.

ply because they are more likely to join gangs and commit violent crimes. According to this view, the statistics show nothing disproportionate.

Other people say that the power of the criminal justice system is selectively trained on urban minority populations and that minority kids are treated more harshly for similar offenses. White college kids are rarely arrested for dealing pot, but, when they are, their parents arrange for diversion programs. Meanwhile, poor African American kids face a constant police presence in their communities and will likely be sent to detention facilities for the same offenses that are treated lightly among whites. Some people also reason that wealthier peoples can afford better legal representation than the poor, who are disproportionately racial and ethnic minorities.

In fact, statistically speaking, minority youth are more likely than whites to be arrested and detained for the same charges.[11] When white youth and minority youth are charged with the same offenses, African American youth with no prior admissions are six times more likely to end up incarcerated in public facilities than white youth. Latino youth are three times more likely than white youth to be incarcerated for the same offenses.[12]

Researchers recently studied several of the nation's largest counties and found that minority youth, particularly African Americans, were almost twice as likely to be held in secure pretrial confinement than were white youth. Furthermore, minority youth not only are locked up at a disproportionately high rate for the same crimes as their white peers, but they also are confined for longer periods of time.[13] And, because young people are generally sent to detention facilities close to where they live and because more minority youth live in low-income areas, minority youngsters are more likely to be sent to public instead of private correctional facilities that have the better resources and provide more access to therapy and education.

The Juvenile Justice and Delinquency Prevention Act of 1974 (42 U.S.C. 5601) required states to determine whether the proportion of minorities in confinement exceeded their proportion in the population. If such overrepresentation were found, states must demonstrate serious efforts to reduce it. However, overrepresentation of certain groups remains a pervasive and stubbornly persistent problem.

EXERCISE 9.1. *And Justice for Some: Differential Treatment of Minority Youth in the Juvenile Justice System,* published by Building Blocks for Youth, reported: "Although minority youth are one-third of the adolescent population in the United States, minority youth are two-thirds of the over 100,000 youth confined in local detention and state correctional systems." How can you explain this fact?

Felon and Ex-Felon Disenfranchisement

High rates of incarceration destabilize many minority communities, removing parents from active involvement with their children, destroying in most cases their role as breadwinners, reducing the number of available marriage partners, and generally eroding the bonds of family, friendship, and social life.

High incarceration rates also have dramatic political consequences for the democratic process. Nearly five million Americans in 2005 are disenfranchised—that is, denied the right to vote in federal, state, and local elections—because of felony criminal convictions.[14]

While nearly every state takes voting rights away from felons while they are incarcerated, eight states permanently disenfranchise them. So, even after they complete their sentences, felons can never get their voting rights back—unless they get a pardon from their state governor. More than 1.4 million American citizens served their time and repaid their debt to society but will remain voteless for the rest of their lives.[15]

Many of these people with a political life sentence belong to minority groups. According to the Sentencing Project, in two states that permanently deny the vote to ex-offenders, one out of three African American men is disenfranchised, and, in eight states overall, one out of four African American men is disenfranchised.[16]

The U.S. Supreme Court has recognized the link between race discrimination and at least some felon disenfranchisement policies. In *Hunter v. Underwood,* the Supreme Court in 1985 struck down a state constitutional provision adopted by Alabama in 1901 that disenfranchised persons convicted of any crime of moral turpitude, including vagrancy. The champions of this provision were clear that its express purpose was to disenfranchise black men by catching them up in the criminal justice process and then stripping them of voting rights.

EXERCISE 9.2. Do you think that people who do their time and leave prison should have the right to vote? What about people who are still in prison doing their time?

Should they have a right to vote? Do you consider voting a fundamental right that cannot be taken away or a privilege that can be revoked for criminal behavior such as murder, rape, armed robbery, bribery, and voter fraud?

Many juvenile offenders get prosecuted as adults and then sentenced to prison for life. These offenders will never be able to cast a vote. Does this seem fair and sensible? Have these people lost their right to be citizens? Section 1 of the Thirteenth Amendment says: "Neither slavery nor involuntary servitude, except as a punishment for crime whereof the party shall have been duly convicted, shall exist within the United States." What does this suggest about people in prison? Are prisoners like slaves? Why or why not?

Gendered Offenders

"Boys will be boys," the saying goes. Truth be told, boys, or at least some of them, are expected to be bad as they grow up. But what about girls? Traditionally, they are expected to behave, but they are not sugar and spice and everything nice anymore. The last few decades have shown a steady increase in the number of arrests and detentions of young women, a shock to the justice system that it has not been prepared to absorb.

Gender inequality in the juvenile justice system permeates the various steps of the process—from the courtroom to detention facilities and community-based programs. For example, many judges, probation agents, and attorneys lean toward extreme and unrealistic views of girls. On the one hand, many girls receive minimal punishment for their delinquent conduct. On the other hand, other girls receive much harsher punishment than their male counterparts, seemingly for their protection.

Some courts discriminate more overtly by excluding girls from court programs. Accord-

A steady increase in the number of arrests and detentions of young women has presented new challenges to the juvenile justice system nationwide. In Maricopa County, Arizona, female inmates volunteer to serve thirty days of chain gang duty so that they may leave the "lockdown" punishment cell, in which four prisoners are held in a small room for twenty-three hours a day. The inmates gather trash, weed, or bury bodies. Here, chain gang inmates cry at the gravesite of an indigent infant at a county cemetery. *Source: Shannon Stapleton/Reuters/Landov*

ing to youth justice advocate Stephanie Joseph, in Baltimore, Maryland, the drug court program was boys-only for many years. In some states, many community-based juvenile justice programs including drug treatment, shelters, and job training are only available to boys.

Why do these differences exist? Juvenile justice administrators often complain that they lack sufficient staffing resources to provide adequate programs for the small population of girls in the system.

According to the Office of Juvenile Justice and Delinquency Prevention, girls in 1994 accounted for 25 percent of all juvenile arrests; 18.6 percent of arrests for aggravated assaults; 8–9 percent of arrests for robbery, sex offenses (other than rape and prostitution), and weapons offenses; and 6 percent of arrests for murder and non-negligent manslaughter. Do these statistics surprise you?

Despite the reported increase in violent crimes among girls in many jurisdictions, the charges brought against them are most often status offenses, such as running away, violating curfew, being ungovernable, underage drinking, and truancy. Girls are also often arrested for theft, getting into fights, fraud (passing bad checks), simple assault, and violation of liquor laws. Do boys and girls have fundamentally different natures or are they just socialized differently?

EXERCISE 9.3. According to statistics, a combination of four risk factors significantly increases the likelihood of a female teenager winding up in the juvenile justice system.

1. Having a history of being a victim of violence, sexual abuse, or physical abuse.
2. Associating with peers who engage in delinquent acts, drug abuse, or gangs.
3. Experiencing difficulty in school—with academic subjects, behavioral expectations, pregnancy, or conflicting responsibilities such as care of own young children.
4. Abusing tobacco, alcohol, or drugs.

Do all young women who have these risk factors in their lives end up being involved in the juvenile justice system? Imagine Katrina, a classmate of yours who is quiet and meek at school—when she attends, which is not that often. Another classmate, Kim, is loud and obnoxious and bullies other kids at school. She is constantly getting into trouble and coercing others to do the same. Katrina and Kim together rob a convenience store and are arrested. Assuming both Katrina and Kim displayed all four risk factors, devise a specific treatment and punishment system for each young woman.

Despite the increase of young women being arrested, limited placement options are available specifically for girls. Girls are often inappropriately placed in facilities and programs that were designed for boys or that emphasize security over intervention and treatment. Many facilities serving young people are mixed-sex facilities, where the specific needs and strengths of girls are ignored or shortchanged because they are in such a numerical minority in the facility. When Mark Salzman suggested to the superintendent of Central Juvenile Hall in Los Angeles a one-day writers' workshop for young men and women in the facility, the superintendent had strong reservations about the young women's participation. He admitted, however, that girls "don't get as many activities [as boys], they tend to get overlooked." [17]

Many facilities do not offer programs for pregnant and parenting teens or sexual abuse or substance abuse treatment or educational programs that focus on the strengths and needs of girls. Limited vocational programs often use outdated facilities and push girls toward low-paying, dead-end, stereotypically female occupations. For example boys have access to a computer lab and training in job skills while in detention at Maryland's Cheltenham Youth Center. Detained girls, however, have no computers or career training. Vocational training, if any, is usually cosmetology and hair care.

In addition, youth in the juvenile justice system have transient educational histories. Often, a seventeen-year-old girl may be in the eighth grade with no possibility of graduating from high school. Unfortunately, very few detention centers for girls offer the option of general equivalency diploma (GED) courses and testing.

The problems of poor educational and transitional services that plague the traditionally male system are heightened in the case of young women. The rapidly increasing number of females entering the juvenile justice system tend to arrive there for reasons different from those of boys. They also have different needs in terms of rehabilitation.

Life in Prison without Parole

According to the American Bar Association's Juvenile Justice Center, an increasing number of juvenile offenders, 75 percent of them belonging to minority groups, are sentenced

Mayra Figueroa had her son while serving a life sentence plus twenty-five years for shooting and paralyzing a fellow gang member. Mayra, seen here visiting with her son in 2001 at Valley State Prison in California, had seen him only twice in three years. *Source: Ara Oshagan*

Juvenile prisoners were held in cells such as this one at Cumberland County Jail in Portland, Maine, an adult jail in which a fifteen-year-old boy was sexually molested. In an effort to eliminate the practice of confining juveniles in adult jails, the Youth Law Center brought a lawsuit against the county, and juveniles are no longer held at the facility. *Source: Mark Soler/Youth Law Center*

to adult prisons for the rest of their lives for committing murder.[18] Most people assume that life without parole is automatically preferable to the death penalty, but not everyone agrees with that assumption. Chaos, violence, and sexual abuse run rampant in adult prisons, something that is known from litigation, court opinions, first-hand reports, and the media. According to one study, "Juveniles housed in adult facilities rather than juvenile facilities are more likely to be violently victimized by staff and inmates and five times as likely to be sexually assaulted." [19] Rehabilitation is not likely to occur in such setting, and youth are more likely to become hardened, aggressive, and antisocial simply in response to the harsh realities of prison life.

Moreover, sentencing a fifteen- or sixteen-year-old to spend the next sixty or seventy years in prison without any possibility of parole may constitute a kind of mental torture that is just now beginning to be understood. It is not obvious, in any event, why life in prison for an adolescent should be seen as less of a cruel punishment than the death penalty. Consider the haunting words of one of Salzman's students.

> Here I am
> In this lonely place that has become my life.
> I am all alone.
> My family, my friends, even my dreams are all gone.[20]

EXERCISE 9.4. After claiming he was guided by the devil, a young man commits a heinous crime involving the brutal beating and murder of his twelve-year-old cousin. You are sitting on a jury charged with deciding the appropriate punishment. What punishment would you recommend? Life in prison without the possibility of parole? Life in prison with the possibility of parole after 25 years? Which punishment is more fitting? Which is more cruel? Why?

EXERCISE 9.5. "Our resources are misspent, our punishments too severe, our sentences too long," said Supreme Court justice Anthony M. Kennedy to the American Bar Association.[21] In most states, temporary detention centers are funded primarily through localities, and training camps or more permanent post-adjudication detention centers are primarily funded by the states. A small percentage of funds for both types of facilities also comes from the federal government.

Imagine you are the newly elected governor of your state. Juvenile justice reform is of major concern to your constituents, and you have a budget of $100 million to spend on the system. Devise a set of policies for dealing with juvenile crime, paying special attention to the main goals of the system: rehabilitation, deterrence, retribution, and incapacitation. Address the issues discussed in this chapter, as well as fundamental issues of fairness and creation of a just society. Draw a pie chart allocating different percentages of the budget to different stages of the process—arrest and detention, adjudication, and post-adjudication. What percentage would you spend on what programs? How much would you spend on prevention? How much would you spend on rehabilitation? On detention facilities? On education? What are your creative new proposals?

EXERCISE 9.6. You have decided to run for Congress. In your district, a student has shown up at school at the lunch hour with a gun and shot two people—a cafeteria worker and a fellow student. The community is in an uproar about the incident. You are about to go meet your opponent in a candidate debate. He has just made a big speech attacking the Supreme Court and expressing support for the death penalty for juveniles. What will you say when you take the stage?

Notes

1. Mark Salzman, *True Notebooks: A Writer's Year at Juvenile Hall* (New York: Vintage Books, 2003), p. 97.

2. Salzman, *True Notebooks*, pp. 290–291.

3. U.S. Department of Justice, Office of Justice Programs, Bureau of Justice Statistics, "Criminal Offenders Statistics," available at http://www.ojp.usdoj.gov/bjs/crimoff.htm (accessed November 9, 2004).

4. Building Blocks for Youth, *A Tale of Two Jurisdictions: Youth Crime and Detention Rates in Maryland and the District of Columbia* (Washington, D.C.: Building Blocks for Youth, 2001), 6.

5. Building Blocks for Youth, *A Tale of Two Jurisdictions*, 6.

6. Building Blocks for Youth, *A Tale of Two Jurisdictions*, 6.

7. American Civil Liberties Union, "Race and the Death Penalty," available at http://www.aclu.org/DeathPenalty/DeathPenaltyMain.cfm (accessed March 15, 2005).

8. Statistics are from Eric Lotke, Deborah Stromberg, and Vincent Schiraldi, *Swing States: Crime, Prisons, and the Future of the Nation* (Washington, D.C.: Justice Policy Institute, August 2004).

9. From Juvenile Population Characteristics, available at http://ojjdp.ncjrs.org/ojstatbb/population/qa01101.asp?qaDate=19990930 (accessed January 31, 2005).

10. From Juvenile Population Characteristics, available at http://ojjdp.ncjrs.org/ojstatbb/population/qa01103.asp?qaDate=20020120 (accessed January 31, 2005).

11. "Juvenile Justice in California: Facts and Issues," available at http://ca.lwv.org/jj/groups.htm (accessed August 15, 2004).

12. E. Poe-Yamagata and M. Jones, *And Justice for Some: Differential Treatment of Minority Youth in the Juvenile Justice System,* prepared by the National Council on Crime and Delinquency (Washington, D.C.: Building Blocks for Youth, April 2000).

13. "Juvenile Justice in California."

14. The Sentencing Project, "Felony Disenfranchisement Laws in the United States," available at http://www.sentencingproject.org/pdfs/1046.pdf (accessed on March 14, 2005).

15. The Sentencing Project, "Felony Disenfranchisement Laws in the United States."

16. The Sentencing Project, "Felony Disenfranchisement Laws in the United States."

17. Salzman, *True Notebooks,* p. 117.

18. Jamin B. Raskin conversation with Patty Puritz, November 2004.

19. Jeffrey Fagan, Martin Forst, and T. Scott Vivona, "Youth in Prisons and Training Schools: Perceptions and Consequences of the Treatment-Custody Dichotomy," *Juvenile and Family Court* 2 (1989): 10.

20. Salzman, *True Notebooks,* p. 66.

21. Cited in Lotke, Stromberg, and Schiraldi, *Swing States.*

Additional Sources

Austin, James, Kelley Dedel Johnson, and Maria Gregoriou. *Juveniles in Adult Prisons and Jails: A National Assessment.* Washington, D.C.: Bureau of Justice Assistance, 2000.

Appendix A
THE CASE OF TREVON JONES

The following case is fictional, but its circumstances represent a composite of real cases involving youths in today's justice system.

Trevon Jones, 19, has been convicted of first-degree murder, a capital offense in Florida. One afternoon, he and two young men, Sam, 20, and RJ, 23, who were initiating him into a street gang, broke into a neighbor's house. They robbed the elderly residents, John and Martha Brown, of their money and jewelry. Trevon held the couple at gunpoint while his two friends continued to ransack the house. Trevon became increasingly agitated and repeatedly shouted at his friends, "Are we done here? Can we go?" When Mr. Brown made a sudden move toward the phone in the kitchen, Trevon panicked and fired his gun twice before fleeing. Mr. Brown died immediately of chest wounds. His wife, who was not injured in the attack, died five weeks later of a heart attack.

When one of his associates turned him in as the trigger-man, Trevon was caught, arrested, prosecuted as an adult, and convicted of first-degree murder, a crime punishable by life in prison—with or without parole—or the death penalty. Now Trevon faces a jury that will determine his fate at sentencing. Remember that Trevon's guilt has already been determined by a jury; this jury proceeding is about punishment: Should Trevon be given the death penalty by lethal injection, life in prison without the possibility of parole, or life in prison with the possibility of parole?

Evidence Found by Trevon's Defense Team and the Prosecutors

Trevon had never met his father, and his mother, a prostitute, died of a drug overdose when he was twelve years old. The aunt Trevon loved moved to North Carolina, and he lived with his 23-year-old brother Newton, who was emotionally abusive. Trevon suffered from depression. Since first grade, Trevon's classmates had teased him about his slight lisp, and each year he fell further behind academically. The most positive thing to surface in his academic and social reports was that his aunt had given him a set of drums, which he had learned to play. In fourth grade, Trevon played the drums at a school play and later told one of his teachers, Mrs. Angel, he "felt proud for the first time I can remember." Trevon dropped out of school at age thirteen.

No one came looking for Trevon when he dropped out of school, and he started running with a rough crowd known in his small, racially divided town for causing trouble. Trevon's delinquent friends became his family. When they asked him to do something—often a criminal act—he did it. Prior to the murder, he had been suspended from school five times and had three convictions for shoplifting and one for destruction of public property (a parking meter).

According to Trevon's brother, Trevon was hit in the head with a baseball bat when he was "little" by one of his mother's boyfriends. Although there were no medical records documenting this incident, Newton said that he saw it happen in the backyard of their house. A psychiatrist testified at the hearing that this incident may have resulted in a traumatic brain injury. Traumatic brain injuries (TBIs) can affect judgment, concentration, and planning. People who have suffered from TBI often have difficulty with impulse control, monitoring social cues (that is, understanding what certain behaviors mean to other people), and anger control. They are prone to sudden agitation.

Trevon had been recruited by a youth gang, the Animals, a week before the crime took place. The Animals are known primarily for heroin and cocaine distribution. At trial, there was testimony that Trevon had spent several days dealing cocaine before the robbery but that the crime marked his first involvement with violence or guns. The gang members gave him the gun right before leaving to rob the house but did not show him how to use it.

After he was found guilty, Trevon was depressed and despondent and felt terribly ashamed of what he had done. He told his lawyers, "I want to die because I deserve it. I didn't go in there with any thought about killing anybody but I did, and now I gotta pay too."

For the Class: The Sentencing Hearing

Divide the class into a prosecution team, a defense team, a judge, and a jury. Invite other students to play Trevon; his brother Newton; his fourth-grade school teacher, Mrs. Angel; the young man, William, who recruited Trevon to the gang and later turned him in; and the 30-year-old son and 24-year-old daughter of the elderly victims.

The prosecution and defense teams should decide what sentence they want to seek. Each side should provide an opening statement, call witnesses to testify, and provide a closing statement. The judge should run the deliberations, keep order, and make sure that only one person talks at a time.

Jurors are charged with deciding Trevon's sentence. Their options are to sentence him to life in prison without the possibility of parole, life in prison with the possibility of parole, or the death penalty by lethal injection. Consider the specific facts of the crime, Trevon's life, and the mitigating and aggravating factors in coming to your decision. Mitigating factors are circumstances that tend to lessen a defendant's moral culpability or guilt (for example, abusive past, young age). Aggravating factors are circumstances related to the commission of a crime that increase the level of responsibility (for example, very gruesome details, commission of similar crimes in the past).

Appendix B

CONSTITUTION OF THE UNITED STATES

We the People of the United States, in Order to form a more perfect Union, establish Justice, insure domestic Tranquility, provide for the common defence, promote the general Welfare, and secure the Blessings of Liberty to ourselves and our Posterity, do ordain and establish this Constitution for the United States of America.

Article I

SECTION 1. All legislative Powers herein granted shall be vested in a Congress of the United States, which shall consist of a Senate and House of Representatives.

SECTION 2. The House of Representatives shall be composed of Members chosen every second Year by the People of the several States, and the Electors in each State shall have the Qualifications requisite for Electors of the most numerous Branch of the State Legislature.

No Person shall be a Representative who shall not have attained to the age of twenty five Years, and been seven Years a Citizen of the United States, and who shall not, when elected, be an Inhabitant of that State in which he shall be chosen.

[Representatives and direct Taxes shall be apportioned among the several States which may be included within this Union, according to their respective Numbers, which shall be determined by adding to the whole Number of free Persons, including those bound to Service for a Term of Years, and excluding Indians not taxed, three fifths of all other Persons.][1] The actual Enumeration shall be made within three Years after the first Meeting of the Congress of the United States, and within every subsequent Term of ten Years, in such Manner as they shall by Law direct. The Number of Representatives shall not exceed one for every thirty Thousand, but each State shall have at Least one Representative; and until such enumeration shall be made, the State of New Hampshire shall be entitled to chuse three, Massachusetts eight, Rhode-Island and Providence Plantations one, Connecticut five, New-York six, New Jersey four, Pennsylvania eight, Delaware one, Maryland six, Virginia ten, North Carolina five, South Carolina five, and Georgia three.

When vacancies happen in the Representation from any State, the Executive Authority thereof shall issue Writs of Election to fill such Vacancies.

The House of Representatives shall chuse their Speaker and other Officers; and shall have the sole Power of Impeachment.

SECTION 3. The Senate of the United States shall be composed of two Senators from each State, [chosen by the Legislature thereof,][2] for six Years; and each Senator shall have one Vote.

Immediately after they shall be assembled in Consequence of the first Election, they shall be divided as equally as may be into three Classes. The Seats of the Senators of the first Class shall be vacated at the Expiration of the second Year, of the second Class at the Expiration of the fourth Year, and of the third Class at the Expiration of the sixth Year, so that one third may be chosen every second Year; [and if Vacancies happen by Resignation, or otherwise, during the Recess of the Legislature of any State, the Executive thereof may make temporary Appointments until the next Meeting of the Legislature, which shall then fill such Vacancies.][3]

No Person shall be a Senator who shall not have attained to the Age of thirty Years, and been nine Years a Citizen of the United States, and who shall not, when elected, be an Inhabitant of that State for which he shall be chosen.

The Vice President of the United States shall be President of the Senate, but shall have no Vote, unless they be equally divided.

The Senate shall chuse their other Officers, and also a President pro tempore, in the Absence of the Vice President, or when he shall exercise the Office of President of the United States.

The Senate shall have the sole Power to try all Impeachments. When sitting for that Purpose, they shall be on Oath or Affirmation. When the President of the United States is tried, the Chief Justice shall preside: And no Person shall be convicted without the Concurrence of two thirds of the Members present.

Judgment in Cases of Impeachment shall not extend further than to removal from Office, and disqualification to hold and enjoy any Office of honor, Trust or Profit under the United States: but the Party convicted shall nevertheless be liable and subject to Indictment, Trial, Judgment and Punishment, according to Law.

SECTION 4. The Times, Places and Manner of holding Elections for Senators and Representatives, shall be prescribed in each State by the Legislature thereof; but the Congress may at any time by Law make or alter such Regulations, except as to the Places of chusing Senators.

The Congress shall assemble at least once in every Year, and such Meeting shall [be on the first Monday in December],[4] unless they shall by Law appoint a different Day.

SECTION 5. Each House shall be the Judge of the Elections, Returns and Qualifications of its own Members, and a Majority of each shall constitute a Quorum to do Business; but a smaller Number may adjourn from day to day, and may be authorized to compel the Attendance of absent Members, in such Manner, and under such Penalties as each House may provide.

Each House may determine the Rules of its Proceedings, punish its Members for disorderly Behaviour, and, with the Concurrence of two thirds, expel a Member.

Each House shall keep a Journal of its Proceedings, and from time to time publish the same, excepting such Parts as may in their Judgment require Secrecy; and the Yeas and Nays of the Members of either House on any question shall, at the Desire of one fifth of those Present, be entered on the Journal.

Neither House, during the Session of Congress, shall, without the Consent of the other, adjourn for more than three days, nor to any other Place than that in which the two Houses shall be sitting.

SECTION 6. The Senators and Representatives shall receive a Compensation for their Services, to be ascertained by Law, and paid out of the Treasury of the United States. They shall in all Cases, except Treason, Felony and Breach of the Peace, be privileged from Arrest during their Attendance at the Session of their respective Houses, and in going to and returning from the same; and for any Speech or Debate in either House, they shall not be questioned in any other Place.

No Senator or Representative shall, during the Time for which he was elected, be appointed to any civil Office under the Authority of the United States, which shall have been created, or the Emoluments whereof shall have been encreased during such time; and no Person holding any Office under the United States, shall be a Member of either House during his Continuance in Office.

SECTION 7. All Bills for raising Revenue shall originate in the House of Representatives; but the Senate may propose or concur with Amendments as on other Bills.

Every Bill which shall have passed the House of Representatives and the Senate, shall, before it become a Law, be presented to the President of the United States; If he approve he shall sign it, but if not he shall return it, with his Objections to that House in which it shall have originated, who shall enter the Objections at large on their Journal, and proceed to reconsider it. If after such Reconsideration two thirds of that House shall agree to pass the Bill, it shall be sent, together with the Objections, to the other House, by which it shall likewise be reconsidered, and if approved by two thirds of that House, it shall become a Law. But in all such Cases the Votes of both Houses shall be determined by yeas and Nays, and the Names of the Persons voting for and against the Bill shall be entered on the Journal of each House respectively. If any Bill shall not be returned by the President within ten Days (Sundays excepted) after it shall have been presented to him, the Same shall be a Law, in like Manner as if he had signed it, unless the Congress by their Adjournment prevent its Return, in which Case it shall not be a Law.

Every Order, Resolution, or Vote to which the Concurrence of the Senate and House of Representatives may be necessary (except on a question of Adjournment) shall be presented to the President of the United States; and before the Same shall take Effect, shall be approved by him, or being disapproved by him, shall be repassed by two thirds of the Senate and House of Representatives, according to the Rules and Limitations prescribed in the Case of a Bill.

SECTION 8. The Congress shall have Power To lay and collect Taxes, Duties, Imposts and Excises, to pay the Debts and provide for the common Defence and general Welfare of the United States; but all Duties, Imposts and Excises shall be uniform throughout the United States;

To borrow Money on the credit of the United States;

To regulate Commerce with foreign Nations, and among the several States, and with the Indian Tribes;

To establish an uniform Rule of Naturalization, and uniform Laws on the subject of Bankruptcies throughout the United States;

To coin Money, regulate the Value thereof, and of foreign Coin, and fix the Standard of Weights and Measures;

To provide for the Punishment of counterfeiting the Securities and current Coin of the United States;

To establish Post Offices and post Roads;

To promote the Progress of Science and useful Arts, by securing for limited Times to Authors and Inventors the exclusive Right to their respective Writings and Discoveries;

To constitute Tribunals inferior to the supreme Court;

To define and punish Piracies and Felonies committed on the high Seas, and Offences against the Law of Nations;

To declare War, grant Letters of Marque and Reprisal, and make Rules concerning Captures on Land and Water;

To raise and support Armies, but no Appropriation of Money to that Use shall be for a longer Term than two Years;

To provide and maintain a Navy;

To make Rules for the Government and Regulation of the land and naval Forces;

To provide for calling forth the Militia to execute the Laws of the Union, suppress Insurrections and repel Invasions;

To provide for organizing, arming, and disciplining, the Militia, and for governing such Part of them as may be employed in the Service of the United States, reserving to the States respectively, the Appointment of the Officers, and the Authority of training the Militia according to the discipline prescribed by Congress;

To exercise exclusive Legislation in all Cases whatsoever, over such District (not exceeding ten Miles square) as may, by Cession of particular States, and the Acceptance of Congress, become the Seat of the Government of the United States, and to exercise like Authority over all Places purchased by the Consent of the Legislature of the State in which the Same shall be, for the Erection of Forts, Magazines, Arsenals, dock-Yards, and other needful Buildings;—And

To make all Laws which shall be necessary and proper for carrying into Execution the foregoing Powers, and all other Powers vested by this Constitution in the Government of the United States, or in any Department or Officer thereof.

SECTION 9. The Migration or Importation of such Persons as any of the States now existing shall think proper to admit, shall not be prohibited by the Congress prior to the Year one thousand eight hundred and eight, but a Tax or duty may be imposed on such Importation, not exceeding ten dollars for each Person.

The Privilege of the Writ of Habeas Corpus shall not be suspended, unless when in Cases of Rebellion or Invasion the public Safety may require it.

No Bill of Attainder or ex post facto Law shall be passed.

No Capitation, or other direct, Tax shall be laid, unless in Proportion to the Census or Enumeration herein before directed to be taken.[5]

No Tax or Duty shall be laid on Articles exported from any State.

No Preference shall be given by any Regulation of Commerce or Revenue to the Ports of one State over those of another; nor shall Vessels bound to, or from, one State, be obliged to enter, clear, or pay Duties in another.

No Money shall be drawn from the Treasury, but in Consequence of Appropriations made by Law; and a regular Statement and Account of the Receipts and Expenditures of all public Money shall be published from time to time.

No Title of Nobility shall be granted by the United States: And no Person holding any Office of Profit or Trust under them, shall, without the Consent of the Congress, accept of any present, Emolument, Office, or Title, of any kind whatever, from any King, Prince, or foreign State.

SECTION 10. No State shall enter into any Treaty, Alliance, or Confederation; grant Letters of Marque and Reprisal; coin Money; emit Bills of Credit; make any Thing but gold and silver Coin a Tender in Payment of Debts; pass any Bill of Attainder, ex post facto Law, or Law impairing the Obligation of Contracts, or grant any Title of Nobility.

No State shall, without the Consent of the Congress, lay any Imposts or Duties on Imports or Exports, except what may be absolutely necessary for executing it's inspection Laws: and the net Produce of all Duties and Imposts, laid by any State on Imports or Exports, shall be for the Use of the Treasury of the United States; and all such Laws shall be subject to the Revision and Controul of the Congress.

No State shall, without the Consent of Congress, lay any Duty of Tonnage, keep Troops, or Ships of War in time of Peace, enter into any Agreement or Compact with another State, or with a foreign Power, or engage in War, unless actually invaded, or in such imminent Danger as will not admit of delay.

Article II

SECTION 1. The executive Power shall be vested in a President of the United States of America. He shall hold his Office during the Term of four Years, and, together with the Vice President, chosen for the same Term, be elected, as follows

Each State shall appoint, in such Manner as the Legislature thereof may direct, a Number of Electors, equal to the whole Number of Senators and Representatives to which the State may be entitled in the Congress: but no Senator or Representative, or Person holding an Office of Trust or Profit under the United States, shall be appointed an Elector.

[The Electors shall meet in their respective States, and vote by Ballot for two Persons, of whom one at least shall not be an Inhabitant of the same State with themselves. And they shall make a List of all the Persons voted for, and of the Number of Votes for each; which List they shall sign and certify, and transmit sealed to the Seat of the Government of the United States, directed to the President of the Senate. The President of the Senate shall, in the Presence of the Senate and House of Representatives, open all the Certificates, and the Votes shall then be counted. The Person having the greatest Number of Votes shall be the President, if such Number be a Majority of the whole Number of

Electors appointed; and if there be more than one who have such Majority, and have an equal Number of Votes, then the House of Representatives shall immediately chuse by Ballot one of them for President; and if no Person have a Majority, then from the five highest on the list the said House shall in like Manner chuse the President. But in chusing the President, the Votes shall be taken by States, the Representation from each State having one Vote; A quorum for this Purpose shall consist of a Member or Members from two thirds of the States, and a Majority of all the States shall be necessary to a Choice. In every Case, after the Choice of the President, the Person having the greatest Number of Votes of the Electors shall be the Vice President. But if there should remain two or more who have equal Votes, the Senate shall chuse from them by Ballot the Vice President.][6]

The Congress may determine the Time of chusing the Electors, and the Day on which they shall give their Votes; which Day shall be the same throughout the United States.

No Person except a natural born Citizen, or a Citizen of the United States, at the time of the Adoption of this Constitution, shall be eligible to the Office of President; neither shall any Person be eligible to that Office who shall not have attained to the Age of thirty five Years, and been fourteen Years a Resident within the United States.

In Case of the Removal of the President from Office, or of his Death, Resignation, or Inability to discharge the Powers and Duties of the said Office,[7] the Same shall devolve on the Vice President, and the Congress may by Law provide for the Case of Removal, Death, Resignation or Inability, both of the President and Vice President, declaring what Officer shall then act as President, and such Officer shall act accordingly, until the Disability be removed, or a President shall be elected.

The President shall, at stated Times, receive for his Services, a Compensation, which shall neither be encreased nor diminished during the Period for which he shall have been elected, and he shall not receive within that Period any other Emolument from the United States, or any of them.

Before he enter on the Execution of his Office, he shall take the following Oath or Affirmation:—"I do solemnly swear (or affirm) that I will faithfully execute the Office of President of the United States, and will to the best of my Ability, preserve, protect and defend the Constitution of the United States."

SECTION 2. The President shall be Commander in Chief of the Army and Navy of the United States, and of the Militia of the several States, when called into the actual Service of the United States; he may require the Opinion, in writing, of the principal Officer in each of the executive Departments, upon any Subject relating to the Duties of their respective Offices, and he shall have Power to grant Reprieves and Pardons for Offences against the United States, except in Cases of Impeachment.

He shall have Power, by and with the Advice and Consent of the Senate, to make Treaties, provided two thirds of the Senators present concur; and he shall nominate, and by and with the Advice and Consent of the Senate, shall appoint Ambassadors, other public Ministers and Consuls, Judges of the supreme Court, and all other Officers of the United States, whose Appointments are not herein otherwise provided for, and which shall be established by Law: but the Congress may by Law vest the Appointment of such inferior Officers, as they think proper, in the President alone, in the Courts of Law, or in the Heads of Departments.

The President shall have Power to fill up all Vacancies that may happen during the Recess of the Senate, by granting Commissions which shall expire at the End of their next Session.

SECTION 3. He shall from time to time give to the Congress Information of the State of the Union, and recommend to their Consideration such Measures as he shall judge necessary and expedient; he may, on extraordinary Occasions, convene both Houses, or either of them, and in Case of Disagreement between them, with Respect to the Time of Adjournment, he may adjourn them to such Time as he shall think proper; he shall receive Ambassadors and other public Ministers; he shall take Care that the Laws be faithfully executed, and shall Commission all the Officers of the United States.

SECTION 4. The President, Vice President and all civil Officers of the United States, shall be removed from Office on Impeachment for, and Conviction of, Treason, Bribery, or other high Crimes and Misdemeanors.

Article III

SECTION 1. The judicial Power of the United States, shall be vested in one supreme Court, and in such inferior Courts as the Congress may from time to time ordain and establish. The Judges, both of the supreme and inferior Courts, shall hold their Offices during good Behaviour, and shall, at stated Times, receive for their Services, a Compensation, which shall not be diminished during their Continuance in Office.

SECTION 2. The judicial Power shall extend to all Cases, in Law and Equity, arising under this Constitution, the Laws of the United States, and Treaties made, or which shall be made, under their Authority;—to all Cases affecting Ambassadors, other public Ministers and Consuls;—to all Cases of admiralty and maritime Jurisdiction;—to Controversies to which the United States shall be a Party;—to Controversies between two or more States;—between a State and Citizens of another State;—between Citizens of different States;—between Citizens of the same State claiming Lands under Grants of different States, and between a State, or the Citizens thereof, and foreign States, Citizens or Subjects.[8]

In all Cases affecting Ambassadors, other public Ministers and Consuls, and those in which a State shall be Party, the supreme Court shall have original Jurisdiction. In all the other Cases before mentioned, the supreme Court shall have appellate Jurisdiction, both as to Law and Fact, with such Exceptions, and under such Regulations as the Congress shall make.

The Trial of all Crimes, except in Cases of Impeachment, shall be by Jury; and such Trial shall be held in the State where the said Crimes shall have been committed; but when not committed within any State, the Trial shall be at such Place or Places as the Congress may by Law have directed.

SECTION 3. Treason against the United States, shall consist only in levying War against them, or in adhering to their Enemies, giving them Aid and Comfort. No Person shall be convicted of Treason unless on the Testimony of two Witnesses to the same overt Act, or on Confession in open Court.

The Congress shall have Power to declare the Punishment of Treason, but no Attainder of Treason shall work Corruption of Blood, or Forfeiture except during the Life of the Person attainted.

Article IV

SECTION 1. Full Faith and Credit shall be given in each State to the public Acts, Records, and judicial Proceedings of every other State. And the Congress may by general Laws prescribe the Manner in which such Acts, Records and Proceedings shall be proved, and the Effect thereof.

SECTION 2. The Citizens of each State shall be entitled to all Privileges and Immunities of Citizens in the several States.

A Person charged in any State with Treason, Felony, or other Crime, who shall flee from Justice, and be found in another State, shall on Demand of the executive Authority of the State from which he fled, be delivered up, to be removed to the State having Jurisdiction of the Crime.

[No Person held to Service or Labour in one State, under the Laws thereof, escaping into another, shall, in Consequence of any Law or Regulation therein, be discharged from such Service or Labour, but shall be delivered up on Claim of the Party to whom such Service or Labour may be due.][9]

SECTION 3. New States may be admitted by the Congress into this Union; but no new State shall be formed or erected within the Jurisdiction of any other State; nor any State be formed by the Junction of two or more States, or Parts of States, without the Consent of the Legislatures of the States concerned as well as of the Congress.

The Congress shall have Power to dispose of and make all needful Rules and Regulations respecting the Territory or other Property belonging to the United States; and nothing in this Constitution shall be so construed as to Prejudice any Claims of the United States, or of any particular State.

SECTION 4. The United States shall guarantee to every State in this Union a Republican Form of Government, and shall protect each of them against Invasion; and on Application of the Legislature, or of the Executive (when the Legislature cannot be convened) against domestic Violence.

Article V

The Congress, whenever two thirds of both Houses shall deem it necessary, shall propose Amendments to this Constitution, or, on the Application of the Legislatures of two thirds of the several States, shall call a Convention for proposing Amendments, which, in either Case, shall be valid to all Intents and Purposes, as Part of this Constitution, when ratified by the Legislatures of three fourths of the several States, or by Conventions in three fourths thereof, as the one or the other Mode of Ratification may be proposed by the Congress; Provided [that no Amendment which may be made prior to the Year One thousand eight hundred and eight shall in any Manner affect the first and fourth Clauses in the Ninth Section of the first Article; and][10] that no State, without its Consent, shall be deprived of its equal Suffrage in the Senate.

Article VI

All Debts contracted and Engagements entered into, before the Adoption of this Constitution, shall be as valid against the United States under this Constitution, as under the Confederation.

This Constitution, and the Laws of the United States which shall be made in Pursuance thereof; and all Treaties made, or which shall be made, under the Authority of the United States, shall be the supreme Law of the Land; and the Judges in every State shall be bound thereby, any Thing in the Constitution or Laws of any State to the Contrary notwithstanding.

The Senators and Representatives before mentioned, and the Members of the several State Legislatures, and all executive and judicial Officers, both of the United States and of the several States, shall be bound by Oath or Affirmation, to support this Constitution; but no religious Test shall ever be required as a Qualification to any Office or public Trust under the United States.

Article VII

The Ratification of the Conventions of nine States, shall be sufficient for the Establishment of this Constitution between the States so ratifying the Same.

Done in Convention by the Unanimous Consent of the States present the Seventeenth Day of September in the Year of our Lord one thousand seven hundred and Eighty seven and of the Independence of the United States of America the Twelfth. IN WITNESS whereof We have hereunto subscribed our Names,

George Washington,
President and deputy from Virginia.

NEW HAMPSHIRE: John Langdon,
Nicholas Gilman.

MASSACHUSETTS: Nathaniel Gorham,
Rufus King.

| CONNECTICUT: | William Samuel Johnson, |
| | Roger Sherman. |

| NEW YORK: | Alexander Hamilton. |

NEW JERSEY:	William Livingston,
	David Brearley,
	William Paterson,
	Jonathan Dayton.

PENNSYLVANIA:	Benjamin Franklin,
	Thomas Mifflin,
	Robert Morris,
	George Clymer,
	Thomas FitzSimons,
	Jared Ingersoll,
	James Wilson,
	Gouverneur Morris.

DELAWARE:	George Read,
	Gunning Bedford Jr.,
	John Dickinson,
	Richard Bassett,
	Jacob Broom.

MARYLAND:	James McHenry,
	Daniel of St. Thomas Jenifer,
	Daniel Carroll.

| VIRGINIA: | John Blair, |
| | James Madison Jr. |

NORTH CAROLINA:	William Blount,
	Richard Dobbs Spaight,
	Hugh Williamson.

SOUTH CAROLINA:	John Rutledge,
	Charles Cotesworth Pinckney,
	Charles Pinckney,
	Pierce Butler.

| GEORGIA: | William Few, |
| | Abraham Baldwin. |

[The language of the original Constitution, not including the Amendments, was adopted by a convention of the states on September 17, 1787, and was subsequently ratified by the states on the following dates: Delaware, December 7, 1787; Pennsylvania, December 12, 1787; New Jersey, December 18, 1787; Georgia, January 2, 1788; Connecticut, January 9, 1788; Massachusetts, February 6, 1788; Maryland, April 28, 1788; South Carolina, May 23, 1788; New Hampshire, June 21, 1788.

Ratification was completed on June 21, 1788.

The Constitution subsequently was ratified by Virginia, June 25, 1788; New York, July 26, 1788; North Carolina, November 21, 1789; Rhode Island, May 29, 1790; and Vermont, January 10, 1791.]

Amendments

AMENDMENT I *(First ten amendments ratified December 15, 1791.)*
Congress shall make no law respecting an establishment of religion, or prohibiting the free exercise thereof; or abridging the freedom of speech, or of the press; or the right of the people peaceably to assemble, and to petition the Government for a redress of grievances.

AMENDMENT II
A well regulated Militia, being necessary to the security of a free State, the right of the people to keep and bear Arms, shall not be infringed.

AMENDMENT III
No Soldier shall, in time of peace be quartered in any house, without the consent of the Owner, nor in time of war, but in a manner to be prescribed by law.

AMENDMENT IV
The right of the people to be secure in their persons, houses, papers, and effects, against unreasonable searches and seizures, shall not be violated, and no Warrants shall issue, but upon probable cause, supported by Oath or affirmation, and particularly describing the place to be searched, and the persons or things to be seized.

AMENDMENT V
No person shall be held to answer for a capital, or otherwise infamous crime, unless on a presentment or indictment of a Grand Jury, except in cases arising in the land or naval forces, or in the Militia, when in actual service in time of War or public danger; nor shall any person be subject for the same offence to be twice put in jeopardy of life or limb; nor shall be compelled in any criminal case to be a witness against himself, nor be deprived of life, liberty, or property, without due process of law; nor shall private property be taken for public use, without just compensation.

AMENDMENT VI
In all criminal prosecutions, the accused shall enjoy the right to a speedy and public trial, by an impartial jury of the State and district wherein the crime shall have been committed, which district shall have been previously ascertained by law, and to be informed of

the nature and cause of the accusation; to be confronted with the witnesses against him; to have compulsory process for obtaining witnesses in his favor, and to have the Assistance of Counsel for his defence.

AMENDMENT VII

In Suits at common law, where the value in controversy shall exceed twenty dollars, the right of trial by jury shall be preserved, and no fact tried by a jury, shall be otherwise re-examined in any Court of the United States, than according to the rules of the common law.

AMENDMENT VIII

Excessive bail shall not be required, nor excessive fines imposed, nor cruel and unusual punishments inflicted.

AMENDMENT IX

The enumeration in the Constitution, of certain rights, shall not be construed to deny or disparage others retained by the people.

AMENDMENT X

The powers not delegated to the United States by the Constitution, nor prohibited by it to the States, are reserved to the States respectively, or to the people.

AMENDMENT XI *(Ratified February 7, 1795)*

The Judicial power of the United States shall not be construed to extend to any suit in law or equity, commenced or prosecuted against one of the United States by Citizens of another State, or by Citizens or Subjects of any Foreign State.

AMENDMENT XII *(Ratified June 15, 1804)*

The Electors shall meet in their respective states and vote by ballot for President and Vice-President, one of whom, at least, shall not be an inhabitant of the same state with themselves; they shall name in their ballots the person voted for as President, and in distinct ballots the person voted for as Vice-President, and they shall make distinct lists of all persons voted for as President, and of all persons voted for as Vice-President, and of the number of votes for each, which lists they shall sign and certify, and transmit sealed to the seat of the government of the United States, directed to the President of the Senate;—The President of the Senate shall, in the presence of the Senate and House of Representatives, open all the certificates and the votes shall then be counted;—The person having the greatest number of votes for President, shall be the President, if such number be a majority of the whole number of Electors appointed; and if no person have such majority, then from the persons having the highest numbers not exceeding three on the list of those voted for as President, the House of Representatives shall choose immediately, by ballot, the President. But in choosing the President, the votes shall be taken by states, the representation from each state having one vote; a quorum for this purpose shall consist of a member or members from two-thirds of the states, and a majority of all the states shall be necessary to a choice. [And if the House of Representatives shall not choose a President whenever the right of choice shall devolve upon them, before the fourth day of

March next following, then the Vice-President shall act as President, as in the case of the death or other constitutional disability of the President.—][11] The person having the greatest number of votes as Vice-President, shall be the Vice-President, if such number be a majority of the whole number of Electors appointed, and if no person have a majority, then from the two highest numbers on the list, the Senate shall choose the Vice-President; a quorum for the purpose shall consist of two-thirds of the whole number of Senators, and a majority of the whole number shall be necessary to a choice. But no person constitutionally ineligible to the office of President shall be eligible to that of Vice-President of the United States.

AMENDMENT XIII *(Ratified December 6, 1865)*

➤ *SECTION 1.* Neither slavery nor involuntary servitude, except as a punishment for crime whereof the party shall have been duly convicted, shall exist within the United States, or any place subject to their jurisdiction.

➤ *SECTION 2.* Congress shall have power to enforce this article by appropriate legislation.

AMENDMENT XIV *(Ratified July 9, 1868)*

➤ *SECTION 1.* All persons born or naturalized in the United States, and subject to the jurisdiction thereof, are citizens of the United States and of the State wherein they reside. No State shall make or enforce any law which shall abridge the privileges or immunities of citizens of the United States; nor shall any State deprive any person of life, liberty, or property, without due process of law; nor deny to any person within its jurisdiction the equal protection of the laws.

➤ *SECTION 2.* Representatives shall be apportioned among the several States according to their respective numbers, counting the whole number of persons in each State, excluding Indians not taxed. But when the right to vote at any election for the choice of electors for President and Vice President of the United States, Representatives in Congress, the Executive and Judicial officers of a State, or the members of the Legislature thereof, is denied to any of the male inhabitants of such State, being twenty-one years of age,[12] and citizens of the United States, or in any way abridged, except for participation in rebellion, or other crime, the basis of representation therein shall be reduced in the proportion which the number of such male citizens shall bear to the whole number of male citizens twenty-one years of age in such State.

➤ *SECTION 3.* No person shall be a Senator or Representative in Congress, or elector of President and Vice President, or hold any office, civil or military, under the United States, or under any State, who, having previously taken an oath, as a member of Congress, or as an officer of the United States, or as a member of any State legislature, or as an executive or judicial officer of any State, to support the Constitution of the United States, shall have engaged in insurrection or rebellion against the same, or given aid or comfort to the enemies thereof. But Congress may by a vote of two-thirds of each House, remove such disability.

➤ *SECTION 4.* The validity of the public debt of the United States, authorized by law, including debts incurred for payment of pensions and bounties for services in suppressing insurrection or rebellion, shall not be questioned. But neither the United States nor any State shall assume or pay any debt or obligation incurred in aid of insurrection or rebellion against the United States, or any claim for the loss or emancipation of any slave; but all such debts, obligations and claims shall be held illegal and void.

➤ SECTION 5. The Congress shall have power to enforce, by appropriate legislation, the provisions of this article.

AMENDMENT XV *(Ratified February 3, 1870)*

➤ SECTION 1. The right of citizens of the United States to vote shall not be denied or abridged by the United States or by any State on account of race, color, or previous condition of servitude.

➤ SECTION 2. The Congress shall have power to enforce this article by appropriate legislation.

AMENDMENT XVI *(Ratified February 3, 1913)*

The Congress shall have power to lay and collect taxes on incomes, from whatever source derived, without apportionment among the several States, and without regard to any census or enumeration.

AMENDMENT XVII *(Ratified April 8, 1913)*

The Senate of the United States shall be composed of two Senators from each State, elected by the people thereof, for six years; and each Senator shall have one vote. The electors in each State shall have the qualifications requisite for electors of the most numerous branch of the State legislatures.

When vacancies happen in the representation of any State in the Senate, the executive authority of such State shall issue writs of election to fill such vacancies: *Provided,* That the legislature of any State may empower the executive thereof to make temporary appointments until the people fill the vacancies by election as the legislature may direct.

This amendment shall not be so construed as to affect the election or term of any Senator chosen before it becomes valid as part of the Constitution.

AMENDMENT XVIII *(Ratified January 16, 1919)*[13]

➤ SECTION 1. After one year from the ratification of this article the manufacture, sale, or transportation of intoxicating liquors within, the importation thereof into, or the exportation thereof from the United States and all territory subject to the jurisdiction thereof for beverage purposes is hereby prohibited.

➤ SECTION 2. The Congress and the several States shall have concurrent power to enforce this article by appropriate legislation.

➤ SECTION 3. This article shall be inoperative unless it shall have been ratified as an amendment to the Constitution by the legislatures of the several States, as provided in the Constitution, within seven years from the date of the submission hereof to the States by the Congress.

AMENDMENT XIX *(Ratified August 18, 1920)*

The right of citizens of the United States to vote shall not be denied or abridged by the United States or by any State on account of sex.

Congress shall have power to enforce this article by appropriate legislation.

AMENDMENT XX *(Ratified January 23, 1933)*

➤ *SECTION 1.* The terms of the President and Vice President shall end at noon on the 20th day of January, and the terms of Senators and Representatives at noon on the 3d day of January, of the years in which such terms would have ended if this article had not been ratified; and the terms of their successors shall then begin.

➤ *SECTION 2.* The Congress shall assemble at least once in every year, and such meeting shall begin at noon on the 3d day of January, unless they shall by law appoint a different day.

➤ *SECTION 3.*[14] If, at the time fixed for the beginning of the term of the President, the President elect shall have died, the Vice President elect shall become President. If a President shall not have been chosen before the time fixed for the beginning of his term, or if the President elect shall have failed to qualify, then the Vice President elect shall act as President until a President shall have qualified; and the Congress may by law provide for the case wherein neither a President elect nor a Vice President elect shall have qualified, declaring who shall then act as President, or the manner in which one who is to act shall be selected, and such person shall act accordingly until a President or Vice President shall have qualified.

➤ *SECTION 4.* The Congress may by law provide for the case of the death of any of the persons from whom the House of Representatives may choose a President whenever the right of choice shall have devolved upon them, and for the case of the death of any of the persons from whom the Senate may choose a Vice President whenever the right of choice shall have devolved upon them.

➤ *SECTION 5.* Sections 1 and 2 shall take effect on the 15th day of October following the ratification of this article.

➤ *SECTION 6.* This article shall be inoperative unless it shall have been ratified as an amendment to the Constitution by the legislatures of three-fourths of the several States within seven years from the date of its submission.

AMENDMENT XXI *(Ratified December 5, 1933)*

➤ *SECTION 1.* The eighteenth article of amendment to the Constitution of the United States is hereby repealed.

➤ *SECTION 2.* The transportation or importation into any State, Territory, or possession of the United States for delivery or use therein of intoxicating liquors, in violation of the laws thereof, is hereby prohibited.

➤ *SECTION 3.* This article shall be inoperative unless it shall have been ratified as an amendment to the Constitution by conventions in the several States, as provided in the Constitution, within seven years from the date of the submission hereof to the States by the Congress.

AMENDMENT XXII *(Ratified February 27, 1951)*

➤ *SECTION 1.* No person shall be elected to the office of the President more than twice, and no person who has held the office of President, or acted as President, for more than two years of a term to which some other person was elected President shall be elected to the office of the President more than once. But this Article shall not apply to any person holding the office of President when this Article was proposed by the Congress, and shall not prevent any person who may be holding the office of President, or acting as President, during the term within which this Article become operative from holding the office of President or acting as President during the remainder of such term.

➤ SECTION 2. This article shall be inoperative unless it shall have been ratified as an amendment to the Constitution by the legislatures of three-fourths of the several States within seven years from the date of its submission to the States by the Congress.

AMENDMENT XXIII *(Ratified March 29, 1961)*

➤ SECTION 1. The District constituting the seat of Government of the United States shall appoint in such manner as the Congress may direct:

A number of electors of President and Vice President equal to the whole number of Senators and Representatives in Congress to which the District would be entitled if it were a State, but in no event more than the least populous State; they shall be in addition to those appointed by the States, but they shall be considered, for the purposes of the election of President and Vice President, to be electors appointed by a State; and they shall meet in the District and perform such duties as provided by the twelfth article of amendment.

➤ SECTION 2. The Congress shall have power to enforce this article by appropriate legislation.

AMENDMENT XXIV *(Ratified January 23, 1964)*

➤ SECTION 1. The right of citizens of the United States to vote in any primary or other election for President or Vice President, for electors for President or Vice President, or for Senator or Representative in Congress, shall not be denied or abridged by the United States or any State by reason of failure to pay any poll tax or other tax.

➤ SECTION 2. The Congress shall have power to enforce this article by appropriate legislation.

AMENDMENT XXV *(Ratified February 10, 1967)*

➤ SECTION 1. In case of the removal of the President from office or of his death or resignation, the Vice President shall become President.

➤ SECTION 2. Whenever there is a vacancy in the office of the Vice President, the President shall nominate a Vice President who shall take office upon confirmation by a majority vote of both Houses of Congress.

➤ SECTION 3. Whenever the President transmits to the President pro tempore of the Senate and the Speaker of the House of Representatives his written declaration that he is unable to discharge the powers and duties of his office, and until he transmits to them a written declaration to the contrary, such powers and duties shall be discharged by the Vice President as Acting President.

➤ SECTION 4. Whenever the Vice President and a majority of either the principal officers of the executive departments or of such other body as Congress may by law provide, transmit to the President pro tempore of the Senate and the Speaker of the House of Representatives their written declaration that the President is unable to discharge the powers and duties of his office, the Vice President shall immediately assume the powers and duties of the office as Acting President.

Thereafter, when the President transmits to the President pro tempore of the Senate and the Speaker of the House of Representatives his written declaration that no inability exists, he shall resume the powers and duties of his office unless the Vice President and a majority of either the principal officers of the executive department or of such other body as Congress may by law provide, transmit within four days to the President pro tempore of the Senate and the Speaker of the House of Representatives their written declaration that the President is unable to discharge the powers and duties of his office. Thereupon Congress shall decide the issue, assembling within forty-eight hours for that purpose if not in session. If the Congress, within twenty-one days after receipt of the latter written declaration, or, if Congress is not in session, within twenty-one days after Congress is required to assemble, determines by two-thirds vote of both Houses that the President is unable to discharge the powers and duties of his office, the Vice President shall continue to discharge the same as Acting President; otherwise, the President shall resume the powers and duties of his office.

AMENDMENT XXVI *(Ratified July 1, 1971)*

➤ *SECTION 1.* The right of citizens of the United States, who are eighteen years of age or older, to vote shall not be denied or abridged by the United States or by any State on account of age.

➤ *SECTION 2.* The Congress shall have power to enforce this article by appropriate legislation.

AMENDMENT XXVII *(Ratified May 7, 1992)*

No law varying the compensation for the services of the Senators and Representatives shall take effect, until an election of Representatives shall have intervened.

Notes

1. The part in brackets was changed by section 2 of the Fourteenth Amendment.
2. The part in brackets was changed by the first paragraph of the Seventeenth Amendment.
3. The part in brackets was changed by the second paragraph of the Seventeenth Amendment.
4. The part in brackets was changed by section 2 of the Twentieth Amendment.
5. The Sixteenth Amendment gave Congress the power to tax incomes.
6. The material in brackets has been superseded by the Twelfth Amendment.
7. This provision has been affected by the Twenty-fifth Amendment.
8. These clauses were affected by the Eleventh Amendment.
9. This paragraph has been superseded by the Thirteenth Amendment.
10. Obsolete.
11. The part in brackets has been superseded by section 3 of the Twentieth Amendment.
12. See the Nineteenth and Twenty-sixth Amendments.
13. This Amendment was repealed by section 1 of the Twenty-first Amendment.
14. See the Twenty-fifth Amendment.

Source: U.S. Congress, House, Committee on the Judiciary, *The Constitution of the United States of America, as Amended,* 100th Cong., 1st sess., 1987, H Doc 100-94.

Appendix C
GLOSSARY

ACCESSORY AFTER THE FACT. Role of person helping to conceal or hide a crime after it was committed.

ACCUSATORIAL. Used to describe a legal system in which the prosecution is required to provide proof beyond reasonable doubt against an accused person, with the evidence being assessed by an impartial judge and jury.

ACQUITTED. Discharge completely (as from an obligation or accusation).

ACTUS REUS. Criminal or bad act; a voluntary bad act.

ADHERE. Follow.

ADJUDICATION. Judicial proceeding or decision.

ADMONITION. Warning.

ADVERSARIAL. Of, relating to, or characteristic of an opponent.

AFFIDAVIT. A written statement made under oath before an official.

AIDING AND ABETTING. Helping to commit a crime.

AMICI CURIAE. "Friends of the court" who write petitions in support of or against one side of a pending case.

ANALOGOUS. Similar.

ANTECEDENT. Prior.

APPEAL. Legal proceeding by which a case is brought before a higher court for review of a lower court decision.

ARRAIGNMENT. Legal proceeding when charges are brought against a defendant.

ARSON. Burning of the dwelling of another person.

ARTICULABLE. Describable.

ASSAULT. When someone attempts to commit a battery and fails or someone places another person in fear of imminent (or immediate) injury.

AUTHORITARIAN. Strict, dictatorial.

BATTERY. When someone either causes bodily injury or engages in offensive touching.

BURGLARY. The breaking and entering of the dwelling of another person at night with intent to commit a felony inside.

COERCION. Force or threat of force.

CONFERRED. Implied.

CONSENSUAL. With agreement.

CONSENSUS. Agreement.

CONSENT. Permission.

CONSENT DECREE/CONSENT DECREES. A judgment entered by consent of the parties whereby the defendant agrees to stop alleged illegal activity without admitting guilt or wrongdoing.

CONSPIRACY. An agreement between two or more people to do either an unlawful act or a lawful act by unlawful means and engage in at least one overt act to make it happen.

CONTEMPT. Willful disobedience to or open disrespect of a court, judge, or legislative body.

CONTRABAND. Illegal goods.

CONTRAVENES. Goes against.

CONVICT. Find or prove to be guilty.

CROSS-EXAMINATION. Examination of a witness who has already testified to check or discredit the witness's testimony, knowledge, or credibility.

CRUX. Center; important part.

CULPABILITY. Responsibility.

DECARCERATION. Finding alternative rehabilitative community settings instead of institutionalization.

DECEIT. The act or practice of deceiving.

DELETERIOUS. Harmful.

DELINEATE. Describe, portray, or set forth with accuracy or in detail.

DELINQUENCY. Conduct that is out of accord with accepted behavior or the law.

DELINQUENT. In the juvenile context, a young person who breaks the law.

DETENTION. Stop; hold.

DETERRENCE. Preventing other people from following offenders on a delinquent path.

DETERRENT. Something that discourages or prevents from acting.

DEVIATED. Differed.

DIMINISHED CAPACITY DEFENSE. May be used when a defendant who is not insane argues that he suffers a mental impairment that makes him unable to formulate the required intent for a particular offense.

DISAVOW. Deny.

DISPOSITION. Tendency of something to act in a certain manner under given circumstances.

DOUBLE JEOPARDY. Prosecution of an individual twice for the same criminal offense. This practice is outlawed by the Fifth Amendment.

DUE PROCESS CLAUSE. Declares that no person may be deprived of life, liberty, or property without due process of law. Interpreted to mean that every individual is entitled to a fair trial with significant protections, such as the right to be heard, to call witnesses, to cross-examine witnesses, and so forth.

DURESS. A defendant can claim duress if he commits a criminal act because of the threat of the use of force against him; force or threat of force.

EFFICACY. Effectiveness.

ELICIT/ELICITED. Bring out.

EMBEZZLEMENT. Fraudulent conversion of the property of another by one who is already in lawful possession of it.

ENTRAPMENT/ENTRAPMENT DEFENSE. May be asserted when a law enforcement official or someone cooperating with him has induced the defendant to commit a crime.

EROSION. Decline.

EUPHEMISTICALLY. Indirectly, or the substitution of a word with positive connotations for a word with negative connotations.

EXCEPTION/EXCEPTIONS. Main rule does not apply.

EXCLUSIONARY RULE. Unconstitutionally obtained evidence must be excluded from court.

EXIGENCY. Urgency.

EXONERATION. Clear from accusation or blame.

EXPRESS. Stated.

FALSE PRETENSES. Deliberate false representation that causes a victim to pass ownership of his property to the trickster.

FELONY. A serious crime punishable by a prison sentence of one year or longer (or death).

FICTITIOUS. False or fake.

FORECLOSE. Stop.

FORENSIC. Relating to legal proceedings.

FORMAL INTERVENTION. An action undertaken to change what is happening or might happen in another's affairs, especially to prevent something undesirable.

FRUITS OF A SEARCH. Results of a search.

GRANTED CERTIORARI. When the Supreme Court agrees to hear a case.

HOMICIDE. Any unlawful taking of a human life.

IMPARTIAL. Unbiased.

IMPERATIVE. Necessity.

IMPLICATE. Bring into intimate or incriminating connection to involve in the nature or completion of a bad act.

IMPLIED. Hinted at or suggested.

INADMISSIBLE. Not admissible or allowable, especially in a court of law.

INADVERTENT. Accidental; unintentional.

INCAPACITATION. Removing the bad apples from society so they do not have the chance to strike again.

INCEPTION. Beginning.

INCOMMUNICADO. Without communication with others.

INCULPATORY. Incriminating; something that makes someone look guilty.

INFALLIBLE. Not capable of error.

INFLICTION. Imposition.

INHERENTLY. Deeply part of something; essential or intrinsic.

INSANITY DEFENSE. If a defendant can prove he was suffering from a mental disease or illness such that he could not tell the difference between right and wrong at the time a criminal act was committed, he may be entitled to a verdict of "not guilty by reason of insanity."

INTENT. Desire or purpose to commit a wrongful or criminal act.

INTERROGATE. Question formally and systematically.

INTRUSION. Interruption; imposition.

INVOCATION. Using for support.

INVOLUNTARY MANSLAUGHTER. Unintentional killing committed recklessly, grossly negligently, or during commission of a misdemeanor.

JUDICIAL WAIVER. When a judge decides if a juvenile will be tried as an adult.

JURISDICTION. Power or right to exercise authority.

JURISPRUDENCE. Body of law.

KIDNAPPING. Unlawful confinement of another person, along with either a moving of the victim or an effort to hide him.

LARCENY. Trespassory taking and carrying away of the personal property of another with intent to steal.

LOITERING. Standing around without any apparent purpose.

MANSLAUGHTER. Unintentional killing.

MENS REA. Criminal state of mind; culpable intent.

MILITIA. Part of the organized armed forces of a country that is reserved for emergency situations.

MISDEMEANOR. A crime punishable by less than one year in prison or by a fine.

MODUS OPERANDI. Method of operation; especially a unique pattern that indicates or suggests the work of a single criminal in more than one crime.

MORATORIUM/MORATORIUMS. Delay of an activity, such as enforcing the death penalty.

MOTION. A legal document asking a court to do or not do something.

MUNICIPALITY/MUNICIPALITIES. A political unit, as a city or town, that is incorporated and self-governing.

MURDER. Unlawful taking of a life.

NECESSITY/NECESSITY DEFENSE. Raised by a defendant when he has been forced to commit a criminal act, not by another person but by nonhuman events.

NEXUS. Connection.

PARENS PATRIAE. Latin term referring to the power of the state to act in the best interests of someone who needs protection and is unable to make informed decisions for himself.

PENITENTIARY/PENITENTIARIES. Prison, correctional institution, or other place of confinement for convicted felons.

PERJURY. The voluntary violation of an oath or vow either by swearing to what is untrue or by omission to do or say what has been promised under oath.

PRECEDENT. Previously decided case about similar issues that is binding on the case at hand.

PREREQUISITE. Something that is necessary to an end or to the carrying out of a function; something required beforehand.

PROBABLE CAUSE. Sufficient reason to believe that a person has committed, or is committing, a crime or that a place contains evidence connected with a crime.

PROFFERED. Offered.

PROSECUTION. Pursuing formal charges against an offender to final judgment.

PROSECUTORIAL WAIVER. When a prosecutor decides if a juvenile will be tried as an adult.

PUNITIVE. Relating to punishment.

PURSUANT. In carrying out; in conformity with.

RAPE. Unlawful, forcible sexual intercourse with a female without her consent.

REHABILITATION. Reform and education of the offender to treat underlying psychological and social problems that helped bring about the delinquency in the first place.

RETRIBUTION. Punishment; "paying them back" by matching every offense with a punishment of equal severity and weight.

ROBBERY. Larceny in which the taking of property from someone is accomplished by using force or putting the owner in fear.

SANCTIONS/SANCTIONED. Allows.

SEIZURE. Generally, taking possession or hold of quickly and forcibly; when a person's freedom of movement is restrained by show of authority or physical force (*United States v. Mendenhall* case).

SELF-ACCUSATION. A claim by a person that he or she has done something illegal, wrong, or undesirable.

SELF-DEPRECATORY. Disapproving or disparaging of oneself.

SELF-INCRIMINATION. Incrimination of oneself; specifically, the giving of testimony that will likely subject one to criminal prosecution.

SODOMY. Generally defined as oral or anal copulation.

SOLICITATION. When one person asks or encourages another to perform a criminal act, regardless of whether the other person ultimately agrees.

STATUTORY WAIVER. A statute or law that requires that commission of certain crimes guarantees a juvenile to be tried as an adult.

STRATAGEMS. Tricky strategies for deception.

SUBJECTIVE. Using personal reasons to decide something.

SUBJUGATE. Bring under control and governance as a subject.

SUBPOENA/SUBPOENAED. A writ commanding a person to appear in court or else be penalized for failure to appear.

SUCCINCTLY. Clearly and briefly.

SUFFICE. Meet or satisfy a need; to be enough.

SUPPRESSED. Excluding evidence from trial, usually because it is obtained illegally.

SUPPRESSION. Keeping from being heard or known.

SURROGATES. Substitutes.

SURVEILLANCE. Close observation, especially of a person or group under suspicion.

TAINTED. Spoiled; ruined.

TESTIMONY. A solemn declaration usually made orally by a witness under oath in response to interrogation by a lawyer or authorized public official.

TRIBUNAL. Court of law or forum of justice.

UNCONSTITUTIONAL. Descriptive of actions that are in violation of the commands or guarantees of the U.S. Constitution.

UNHINDERED. Unstopped.

VAGRANCY. Wandering from place to place without a visible means of support.

VOLUNTARY MANSLAUGHTER. Intentional killing committed in the heat of passion, when a person is enraged or emotionally agitated.

WAIVE. Refrain from pressing or enforcing. Give up.

WARRANT. A writ or an order authorizing an officer to conduct a search of a place or to execute an arrest.

Appendix D

BIBLIOGRAPHY

Allen, Ronald, and Richard Kuhns. *Constitutional Criminal Procedure: An Examination of the Fourth, Fifth, and Sixth Amendments and Related Areas.* 2d ed. Boston, Mass.: Little Brown, 1991.

American Bar Association. *America's Children at Risk: A Report of the American Bar Association Presidential Working Group on the Unmet Legal Needs of Children and their Families.* Chicago, Ill.: American Bar Association, July 1993.

American Bar Association, Criminal Justice Section, Standards Committee. *ABA Standards for Criminal Justice.* 3d ed. Chicago, Ill.: American Bar Association, 1993.

American Civil Liberties Union. "ACLU Fact Sheet on the Juvenile Justice System." July 5, 1996. Available at http://www.aclu.org/CriminalJustice/CriminalJustice.cfm?ID=9993&c=46 (accessed December 14, 2004).

American Civil Liberties Union. "Citing Continued Police Denial of Racial Profiling, ACLU Renews Call for Federal Traffic Stops Law." May 16, 2001. Available at http://www.aclu.org/RacialEquality/RacialEquality.cfm?ID=7264&c=133 (accessed November 8, 2004).

Amnesty International. "Indecent and Internationally Illegal: The Death Penalty against Child Offenders." September 25, 2002. Available at http://web.amnesty.org/library/Index/ENGAMR511432002 (accessed November 10, 2004).

Amsterdam, Anthony. "Perspectives on the Fourth Amendment." *Minnesota Law Review* 58 (1974): 349.

Arbetman, Lee, and Edward O'Brien. *Street Law.* St. Paul, Minn.: West Educational Publishing, 1999.

Austin, James, Kelley Dedel Johnson, and Maria Gregoriou. *Juveniles in Adult Prisons and Jails: A National Assessment.* Washington, D.C.: Bureau of Justice Assistance, 2000.

Axtman, Kris. "Death Penalty for Juveniles under Scrutiny." *Christian Science Monitor.* August 27, 2002. Available at http://www.csmonitor.com/2002/0827/p02s01-usju.html (accessed November 10, 2004).

Berkheiser, Mary. "The Fiction of Juvenile Right to Counsel: Waiver in the Juvenile Courts." *Florida Law Review* 54 (2002).

Blumhardt, Lisette. "In the Best Interests of the Child: Juvenile Justice or Adult Retribution?" *University of Hawaii Law Review* 23 (2000): 341.

Braithwaite, John. "A Future Where Punishment Is Marginalized: Realistic or Utopian?" *UCLA Law Review* 46 (1999): 1727, 1738–1739.

Bright, Stephen. "Counsel for the Poor: The Death Sentence Not for the Worst Crime But for the Worst Lawyer." *Yale Law Journal* 103 (1994): 1835.

Bright, Stephen, Stephan Kinnard, and David Webster. "Keeping Gideon from Being Blown Away: Prospective Challenges to Inadequate Representation May Be Our Best Hope." *Criminal Justice*, no. 4 (1990): 410.

Brogan, Pamela. "Report: Juvenile Jails Being Substituted for Mental Hospitals." *USA Today.* July 7, 2004. Available at http://www.usatoday.com/news/nation/2004-07-07-jailed-kids_x.htm.

Building Blocks for Youth. *A Tale of Two Jurisdictions: Youth Crime and Detention Rates in Maryland and the District of Columbia.* Washington, D.C.: Building Blocks for Youth, 2001.

Caeti, Tory, Craig Hemmens, and Velmer Burton. "Juvenile Right to Counsel: A National Comparison of State Legal Codes." *American Journal of Criminal Law* 23 (1996): 611.

Caplan, Gerald M. "Questioning Miranda." *Vanderbilt Law Review* 38 (1985): 1417, 1441–1442.

Chamberlin, Christine. "Not Kids Anymore: A Need for Punishment and Deterrence in the Juvenile Justice System." *Boston College Law Review* 42 (2001): 391.

Cole, David. *No Equal Justice: Race and Class in the American Criminal Justice System.* New York: New Press, 1999.

Connors, Edwards, and others. *Convicted by Juries, Exonerated by Science: Case Studies in the Use of DNA Evidence to Establish Innocence after Trial.* Washington, D.C.: National Institute of Justice, 1996. Available at http://www.ncjrs.org/pdffiles/dnaevid.pdf (accessed January 20, 2005).

Coupet, Sacha M. "What to Do with the Sheep in Wolf's Clothing: The Role of Rhetoric and Reality about Youth Offenders in the Constructive Dismantling of the Juvenile Justice System." *University of Pennsylvania Law Review* 148 (2000): 1303.

Currie, Elliott. *Crime and Punishment in America: Why the Solutions to America's Most Stubborn Social Crisis Have Not Worked—and What Will.* New York: Henry Holt and Company, 1998.

Death Penalty Information Center, www.deathpenaltyinfo.org.

"Defendant's Bill of Exceptions, in *State v. Terry* and *State v. Chilton.*" Nos. 79,491 and 79,432. Reprinted in "*State of Ohio v. Richard D. Chilton* and *State of Ohio v. John W. Terry:* The Suppression Hearing and Trial Transcripts." *St. John's Law Review* 72 (1998): 1387.

Dejong, Christina, and Even Schwitzer Merrill. "Getting 'Tough' on Crime: Juvenile Waiver and the Criminal Court." *Ohio Northern University Law Review* 27 (2001): 175, 175–176, 182–184.

Dressler, Joshua. *Understanding Criminal Procedure.* New York: Matthew Bender, 1991.

Dyer, Joel. *The Perpetual Prisoner Machine: How America Profits from Crime.* Boulder, Colo.: Westview Press, 2000.

Einesman, Floralynn. "Confessions and Culture: The Interaction of Miranda and Diversity." *Journal of Criminal Law and Criminology* 90 (1999): 1, 40.

Emanuel, Steven L. *Criminal Law.* 3d ed. New York: Emanuel Publishing Corp., 1992.

Feinberg, Robert, and Steven Palmer. *Criminal Law.* Los Angeles, Calif.: Multistate Legal Press, 2002.

Feld, Barry. "Bad Kids: Race and the Transformation of the Juvenile Court." *Urban Lawyer* 31 (1999): 1033.

Feld, Barry. "The Transformation of the Juvenile Court." *Minnesota Law Review* 75 (1991): 691.

Fitzgerald, Wendy Anton. "Stories of Child Outlaws: On Child Heroism and Adult Power in Juvenile Justice." *Wisconsin Law Review* (1996): 495.

Grano, Joseph D. "Rethinking the Fourth Amendment Warrant Requirement for Warrantless Searches." *Journal of Criminal Law and Criminology* 74 (1983): 172.

Green, Bruce A., and Bernardine Dohrn. "Foreword: Children and the Ethical Practice of Law." *Fordham Law Review* 64 (1996): 1281.

Gurian-Sherman, Stacy. "Back to the Future: Returning Treatment to Juvenile Justice." *Criminal Justice Spring* 15 (2000): 30, 31–32.

Harris, David A. " 'Driving While Black' and All Other Traffic Offenses: The Supreme Court and Pretextual Traffic Stops." *Journal of Criminal Law and Criminology* 87 (1997): 544.

Herivel, Tara, and Paul Wright. *Prison Nation: The Warehousing of America's Poor.* New York: Routledge, 2003.

"Juvenile Court Procedures." *Harvard Law Review* 81 (1967): 171.

"Juvenile Justice in California: Facts and Issues." Available at http://ca.lwv.org/jj/groups.htm (accessed August 15, 2004).

Kaban, Barbara, and Ann E. Tobey. "When Police Question Children." *Journal of the Center for Children and the Courts* 1 (1999): 151, 165–166.

Kamisar, Yale, Wayne LaFave, and others. *Modern Criminal Procedure: Cases Comments Questions.* 9th ed. New York: West Publishing Company, 1999.

Kaplan, John, Robert Weisberg, and Guyora Binder. *Criminal Law: Cases and Materials.* 3d ed. New York: Aspen Publishers, 1996.

Koontz Jr., Lawrence L. "Reassessment Should Not Lead to Wholesale Rejection of the Juvenile Justice System." *University of Richmond Law Review* 31 (1997): 179.

Krzewinski, Kisa M. "But I Didn't Do It: Protecting the Rights of Juveniles During Interrogation." *Boston College Third World Law Journal* 22 (2002): 355, 360–361.

LaFave, Wayne. *Search and Seizure: A Treatise on the Fourth Amendment.* 3d ed. New York: West Publishing Company, 1996.

Lewis, Anthony. *Gideon's Trumpet.* New York: Vintage Books, 1964.

Lewis, Anthony. "The Silencing of Gideon's Trumpet." *New York Times Magazine.* April 20, 2003.

Lewis, Anthony. "To Realize Gideon: Competent Counsel with Adequate Resources." *Champion* (March 22, 1998).

Linder, Douglas O. "Famous American Trials: 'The Scottsboro Boys' Trials." 1999. Available at http://www.law.umkc.edu/faculty/projects/Ftrials/scottsboro/scottsb.htm (accessed November 8, 2004).

Linder, Douglas O. "Without Fear or Favor: Judge James Edwin Horton and the Trial of the 'Scottsboro Boys.'" *University of Missouri at Kansas City Law Review* 68 (2000): 549.

Lotke, Eric, Deborah Stromberg, and Vincent Schiraldi. *Swing States: Crime, Prisons, and the Future of the Nation.* Washington, D.C.: Justice Policy Institute, August 2004.

Maclin, Tracey. "Race and the Fourth Amendment." *Vanderbilt Law Review* 51 (1998).

Maclin, Tracey. "*Terry v. Ohio's* Fourth Amendment Legacy: Black Men and Police Discretion." *St. John's Law Review* 72 (1998): 1271.

Maher, Deanna M. "Michigan Juveniles Are Denied Equal Defenses Before the Law: The State of Michigan's Reaction to Juvenile Delinquents." *University of Detroit Mercy Law Review* 78 (2001): 259.

Mauro, Tony. "Court Opens Execution Issue." *Legal Times.* February 2, 2004.

McNamara, Joseph D. "Has the Drug War Created an Officer Liars' Club?" *L.A. Times.* February 11, 1996.

Miller, Marc, and Ronald White. *Teachers' Manual Criminal Procedures: Cases, Statutes, and Executive Materials.* 2d ed. New York: Aspen Publishers, 2003.

National Association of Criminal Defense Lawyers. "Lesson Plan: Gideon at 40: Understanding the Right to Counsel." 2003. Available at http://www.nacdl.org/public.nsf/GideonAnniversary/lesson/$FILE/gideon_lesson_plan1-7.pdf (accessed November 9, 2004).

National Criminal Justice Reference Service, http://virlib.ncjrs.org/JuvenileJustice.asp.

Poe-Yamagata, E., and M. Jones. *And Justice for Some: Differential Treatment of Minority Youth in the Juvenile Justice System.* Prepared by the National Council on Crime and Delinquency. Washington, D.C.: Building Blocks for Youth, April 2000.

Raskin, Jamin B. *We the Students: Supreme Court Cases for and about Students.* 2d ed. Washington, D.C.: CQ Press, 2003.

Rosado, Lourdes. "Minors and the Fourth Amendment: How Juvenile Status Should Invoke Different Standards for Searches and Seizures on the Street." *New York University Law Review* 71 (1996): 762.

Salzman, Mark. *True Notebooks: A Writer's Year at Juvenile Hall.* New York: Vintage Books, 2003).

Scheck, Barry, and Sarah Toft. "Gideon's Promise and the Innocent Defendant." *Champion* (February 27, 2003).

Searfoss III, Robert E. "Waiver of Juvenile Jurisdiction and the Execution of Juvenile Offenders: Why the Eighth Amendment Should Require Proof of Sufficient Mental Capacity Before the State Can Exact Either Punishment." *University of Toledo Law Review* 35 (2004): 663.

Shepard Jr., Robert E. "Youth in the Criminal Justice System: An ABA Task Force Report (A Summary of the White Paper)." Available at http://www.abanet.org/crimjust/juvjus/jjpolicies/YCJSReport.pdf (accessed November 9, 2004).

Sherman, Francine T. "Thoughts on a Contextual View of Juvenile Justice Reform Drawn from Narratives of Youth." *Temple Law Review* 68 (1995): 1837.

Smith, Abbe. "Rosie O'Neill Goes to Law School: The Clinical Education of the Sensitive New Age Public Defender." *Harvard Civil Rights—Civil Liberties Law Review* 28 (1993): 48.

Smith, Abbe. "The Calling of Criminal Defense." *Mercer Law Review* 50 (1999): 443.

Snyder, Howard N., and Melissa Sickmund. *Juvenile Offenders and Victims: 1999 National Report.* Washington, D.C.: U.S. Department of Justice, 1999.

Stahl, Marc. "The Impact of Counsel on Juvenile Delinquency Proceedings." *Journal of Criminal Law and Criminology* 84 (1993): 642.

Streib, Victor L. "Executing Juvenile Offenders: The Ultimate Denial of Juvenile Justice." *Stanford Law and Policy Review* 14 (2003): 121.

Streib, Victor L. "The Juvenile Death Penalty Today: Death Sentences and Executions for Juvenile Crimes, January 1, 1973–September 30, 2004." Available at http://www.law.onu.edu/faculty/streib/documents/JuvDeathSept302004.pdf (accessed January 31, 2005).

Thibodeau, Jennifer. "Sugar and Spice and Everything Nice: Female Juvenile Delinquency and Gender Bias in Punishment and Behavior in Juvenile Courts." *William and Mary Journal of Women and the Law* 8 (2002): 489.

Tiffany, Lawrence F., and others. *Detection of Crime.* Chicago, Ill.: American Bar Association, 1967.

Tomkovicz, James J., and Welsh White. *Criminal Procedure: Constitutional Constraints Upon Investigation and Proof.* 3d ed. New York: Matthew Bender, 1998.

U.S. Census Bureau. *Maryland QuickFacts.* July 9, 2004. Available at http://quickfacts.census.gov/qfd/states/24000.html (accessed November 8, 2004).

U.S. Department of Justice, Office of Justice Programs, Bureau of Justice Statistics. *Criminal Offenders Statistics.* Available at http://www.ojp.usdoj.gov/bjs/crimoff.htm (accessed November 9, 2004).

Wake, Paul. "Helping Children through the Juvenile Justice System: A Guide for Utah Defense Attorneys." *Brigham Young University Journal of Public Law* 15 (2000): 31, 32.

Walters, Jennifer J. "Illinois' Weakened Attempt to Prevent False Confessions by Juveniles: The Requirement of Counsel for the Interrogation of Some Juveniles." *Loyola University of Chicago Law Journal* 33 (2002): 487, 506–509.

Ward, Robert. "Consenting to a Search and Seizure in Poor and Minority Neighborhoods: No Place for a 'Reasonable Person.'" *Howard Law Journal* 36 (1993): 239.

"What Are the Possible Consequences of Privacy, Foundations of Democracy: Authority, Privacy, Responsibility, and Justice." Available at http://www.civiced.org/fod_ms_priv06_tg.html).

Appendix E

MARSHALL-BRENNAN FELLOWS 1999–2005

The following lawyers and law students have served as Marshall-Brennan fellows, teaching the "We the Students" constitutional literacy course in public schools in Maryland and Washington, D.C. Their hard work and commitment have been extraordinary.

Accettola, Alison
Aden, Leah
Afzal, Nargis
Ahranjani, Maryam
Alam, Tan
Alvarez, Danny
Amarillas, Fernando
Anderson, Jane
Bacon, Nicole
Barbadoro, Theresa
Barbosa, Maricela
Barrett, Kelly
Bayisa, Ebise
Beall, Jennifer
Bedi, Jonathan
Bedi, Sheila
Begun, Laura
Bernheim, Missy
Beverly, Michael
Blank, Joel
Boal, Alan
Bocanegra, Lauren
Bollinger, Ashley
Bonner, Michael F.
Borho, Ryan
Braithwaite, Aisha
Caleb, Joseph
Cambreleng, Rebecca
Campbell, Jesse
Campos, Chris

Cantillon, Rachel
Caplan, Emily
Caple, Chris
Capobianco, Cassandra
Carlton, Cedar
Carter, Misty
Casper, Jenna
Chang, Jason
Cho, Ed
Chugh, Amit
Clarke, Andrea
Clavijo, Luis
Cohen, Ariele
Cole, La Shon
Coleman, Ilona
Collier, Heather
Conyers, Angela
Cooper, Stephen
Cox, Lisa
Danai, Sam
Daspit, Shannon
Day, Joanna
DeGovia, Kate
de la Gueronniere, Gabrielle
Demetrious, Hani
DiIorio, John
Dimino, Maureen
Duston, William
Eaby, Jeff
Edwards, Lydia

Ellis, Kate
Essed, Salihah
Fabrikant, Erika
Fabrikant, Jason
Fajardo, Laura
Faulkner, Nancy
Fausett, Andrew
Feaster, Riqueza
Ferg-Cadima, Jim
Ferretti, Joe
Fetgatter, Christopher
Fieldsend, John
Fite, Dominique
Flamant, Julie
Ford, Yaida O.
Forrest, Carmen
Fotovat, Kat
Fredlake, Keith
Freedman, Rebecca
Gallegos Kie, Nancie
Garner, Kimberly
Georgi, Dalia
Glover, Michael
Goldfrank, Rebecca
Gonzalez, Oscar
Granderson, Miles
Grant, Andrew
Greenblatt, Andy
Griffith, Sean W.
Haas, Michael
Habeeb, Myriah
Habib, Dan
Halloway Cork, Bruce
Hamlin, Spencer
Hamra, Cynthia
Harrington, Andrea
Harris, Belinda
Hassinger, Karen
Hennessy, Phillip
Hertwig, Edward
Hillman, Alison
Hoffman, Fahryn
Howe, Amanda
Huang, Priscilla
Hudnut, Beverly
Hymowitz, Sarah
Imgrund, Jill
Isa-Odidi, Nabila

Jacob, Michael
Jacobs-Conyers, Zandria
Jamison, Wendy
Jani, Umesh
Jawor, Daniel
Jeyalingam, Jey
Johnson, Alex
Jones, Juria
Jones, Marci
Jones, Raymond
Joseph, Stephanie
Kabir, Sharif
Kamens, Bill
Kasarabada, Ramesh
Kasperson, Kaleb
Kats, Olga
Khumprakob, Malissa
Kraham, Jennifer
Krintzman, Josh
Kudchadkar, Raj
Laquintano, Nicole
Lavacchia, Jill
Leaman, Jenifer
Leavitt, Wilder
Ledford, Laura
Lee, Moira
Lee, Scott
Leiphart, Jane
Leonard, Curtis
Lerum, Eric
Levesque, Christian
Lewis, Christianna
Lockwood, Lisa
Louchheim, Whitney
MacAvoy, Bryan
Maker, Melissa
Maloney, David
Maltz, Sari
Mandor, Melissa
Manning, Jeanette
Margul, Lisa
Marlow, Emily
Marshall, Dena
Masci, Michael
McDonald, James
McGinn, Beth
McKeever, Jennifer
McKenna, Fiona

McLellan, Michael
McManus, Kim
McNamee, Dan
Medrano, Pedro
Mehra, Sasha
Metzer, Danielle
Micheaux, Pamala
Migaleddi, Kathleen
Mikhail, Dave
Milligan, Maureen
Mirabal, Maria
Monaghan, Kathleen
Mooradian, Richard
Mooss, Sujay
Moreira, Sheila
Moutsatsos, Artemis
Murthy, Divya
Nazzaro, Miya
Neufeld, Jennafer
Newell, Sean
Nigam, Anita
Owens, Shaun
Parikh, Swati
Parker, Qiana
Patel, Bela
Peak, Nathan
Perez, Valorie
Perwaiz, Serwat
Pezone, Kristen
Phillips, Roger
Plater, Marja
Prater, Ulani
President, Lori
Prince, James
Rahavi, Jacob
Rajagopal, Runa
Rajakumaran, Sharmalee
Rajan, Claire
Rauert, Tyler
Raymond, Rachel
Reynolds, Delicia
Rich, Seigrid
Richardson, Katie
Rifkin, Melissa
Rinaldi, Laura
Robinson, Ebony
Roddy, Shannon
Rogers, Tracey

Roma, Beth
Rose, Chris
Rose, Trevor
Rosenburg, Zack
Rosenfeld, Aaron
Rouson, Herbert
Ryan, Martin
Sabzevari, Amir
Salsbury, Jessica
Santos, Elna
Sare, Wendy
Saubermann, Jennifer
Scheinkman, Rena
Schumacher, Amy
Scott, Tamara
Segal, Eden
Seymour, David
Shankman, Rebecca
Shenoy, Chai
Sher, Lori
Siegel, Sheila
Sikora, Ashley
Simonian, Nairi
Smith, Shavon
Soni, Lina
Spataro, Rick
Sprovtsoff, Jessica
Stawar, Drew
Steed, Theresa
Strasnick, Jessica
Sussman, Rachel
Swartz, Jessica
Taylor, Hillary
Taylor, Will
Tervalon, Mononique
Thompson, John
Thompson, Shawn
Toof, Jackson
Tsekos, Mary Ellen
Tucker, Whetanah
Upadhyaya, Moxi
Vaccaro, Erin
Vuong, Quoc
Walker, Genese
Walters, Fabian
Washington, Celia R.
Waters, Jessica
Watson, Natalie

Weiler, Jodi

Weintraub, Raanan

Weletz, Carrie

Will, Mike

Williams, Babatunde

Wolf, Debra

Woods, Chenita

Yang, Edna

Yeganeh, Fatema

Yoshimura, Megan

Young, Peter

Index

Principal cases are indicated by italicized page numbers.

Harm, principle of, 42
    constitutional limits on power of government to
        make crime, 37
    due process liberty interests, law violating, 47–50
    Florida anti-vagrancy statute, unconstitutionality
        of, 42–46
Hatch, Orrin C., 18
Health and Human Services Department report on
    student drug use, 163
Heath v. Jones (1991), 243
Hispanics. *See* Racial and ethnic minorities
Hodari D., 86–90
Holmes v. Montgomery (2003), 163, 166
Homicide, 52, 53
Horton v. California (1990), 104
"Hot pursuit" or emergency exception to warrant re-
    quirement, 102–105
Hunter v. Underwood (1985), 293

Identification systems for schools, 177
Illinois v. Gates (1983), 92–93, *93*, 96
Illinois v. Perkins (1990), 208
Illinois v. Wardlow (2000), *129*, 131
Incapacitation as goal of criminal punishment, 279, 280
Incarceration of juveniles, 24–25, 280–281. *See also*
    Abuse of juveniles in detention facilities
    community-based alternatives to, 287, 288–290
    gender inequality and, 294–296
    inmates' views of, 25–27
    life sentences, 296–298
    loss of voting rights and, 1, 293–294
    racial and ethnic minorities, 1, 290–293
    statistics as to, 9, 280–281, 288, 290, 291, 292, 295
Inchoate crimes, 53–54
Ineffective counsel, 241–244
Informants' information as acceptable grounds for
    reasonable suspicion, 132–133
In loco parentis doctrine, 141, 144, 152, 165, 174
Innocent behavior, criminalization of. *See* Harm,
    principle of
Inquisitorial justice systems, 222
In Re. See name of party
Insanity as criminal defense, 56, 57, 261–262
Intent to commit crime, juvenile's ability to form,
    12–13, 27–30
Interrogations of persons in custody. *See* Custodial in-
    terrogation
Intoxication. *See* Drugs and alcohol
Involuntary manslaughter, 52

Janklow, William J., 9
Jay-Z, 9
J. M., In Re (1992), *119*, 121
Johnson, Lyndon B., 233
Johnson v. United States (1948), 97, 99, 101
Johnson v. Zerbst (1938), 215
Joseph, Stephanie, 294
Judicial review
    plea agreements, 21–24
    waiver to adult court, 32–35

Judicial waiver to adult court, 30–31
Juvenile delinquency, concept of, 11, 16, 232
Juvenile detention. *See* Incarceration of juveniles
Juvenile Justice and Delinquency Protection Act of
    1994, 293
Juvenile justice system, 11–21
    funding issues, 298
    goals of criminal punishment and, 279–280
    guardianship and protection duties, 15–16, 34
    historical background, 15–18
    procedures, 18–21, 279–280
    reasons for separate system, 12–15
    self-incrimination, availability of privilege against,
        238
Juveniles
    ability to handle duress or coercion used during
        custodial interrogation, 196–198
    ability to understand *Miranda* rights, 191–198
    death penalty for, 250–251
    mental development of, 261–262, 266
    reasons for turning to crime, 278
    right to counsel, 233–239
    right to *Miranda* rights, 191–196, 238
    waiver of counsel by, 239–241
Juvies (documentary), 8

Kassin, Saul, 210
Katz v. United States (1967), 62–63, *63*, 64
Kelly, R., 9
Kennedy, Anthony M., 298
Kennedy, Robert F., 232
Kent v. United States, 32–33, *33*, 35
Kidnapping, 53
King, Rodney, 290
K. L. W. v. James (2005), 284–285
Kyllo v. United States (2001), 77

Ladd, Donna, 281–288
Lakeview High School, 167–168
Larceny, 50
Latasha W., In Re (1998), *176*
Law as a career, 245
Lawrence v. Texas (2003), *47*
Lawyer, right to. *See* Counsel, right to
Left alone, right to be, 58–59
Lewis, Anthony, 229
Liberty interests and due process (Fourth Amend-
    ment), 47–50
Liebowitz, Samuel, 223, 227, 228
Life sentences for juveniles, 296–298
Linder, Douglas O., 228
Little, Malcolm (Malcolm X), 9–10
Locker searches, 167–175
    drug-sniffing dogs, use of, 167, 168, 169, 171–175
    legitimate expectation of privacy and, 168–171
    limited expectation of privacy and, 171–175
    reasonable suspicion as grounds for, 168–171
Loitering, 37, 38–42
Lowdown, Jimmy, 20
Luggage, searches of, 70–73

Credits

Page 25: Testimonial by Peter M. from *L.A. Youth* (a newspaper by and about teens). Reprinted by permission.

Page 26: "Young and Changing," poem by Sheala, "S.P., formerly incarcerated youth, La.," from *Ya Heard Me,* Special Edition (New Orleans: Juvenile Justice Project of Louisiana, December 2002). Reprinted by permission of the Juvenile Justice Project of Louisiana.

Pages 133–135: From James O. Crane. "Shackled by Mistrust: A Chase, an Arrest and a Cop's Uncomfortable Questions." *Washington Post.* June 21, 1998. Reprinted by permission of the author.

Page 178: "American Skin (41 Shots)" by Bruce Springsteen. Copyright © 2001 Bruce Springsteen (ASCAP). Reprinted by permission. International copyright secured. All rights reserved.

Page 211: Central Park jogger case profile reprinted by permission of The Innocence Project at Benjamin N. Cardozo School of Law.

Page 228: Samuel Liebowitz text excerpted from "The Trials of 'The Scottsboro Boys'" available at www.law.umkc.edu/faculty/projects/Ftrials/scottsboro/SB_bLieb.html by Douglas Linder, University of Missouri–Kansas City School of Law. Reprinted by permission of the author.

Page 244: Excerpted from *No Equal Justice: Race and Class in the American Justice System* (New York: New Press, 1999). Copyright © 1998 *No Equal Justice: Race and Class in the American Criminal Justice System* by David Cole. Reprinted by permission of The New Press. (800) 233-4830.

Page 282: "First, Do No Harm: State Struggles with Record of Juvenile Justice," originally appeared in the *Jackson Free Press* (jacksonfreepress.com), January 19, 2005. Reprinted by permission.